WORLDMAKING

WORLD
Race, Performance, and

MAKING
the Work of Creativity

Dorinne Kondo

Duke University Press   Durham and London   2018

© 2018 Duke University Press
All rights reserved
Designed by Heather Hensley
Typeset in Chaparral Pro by Westchester Publishing Services

Library of Congress Cataloging-in-Publication Data
Names: Kondo, Dorinne K., author. | Container of (work):
Kondo, Dorinne K. Seamless.
Title: Worldmaking : race, performance, and the work of creativity / Dorinne Kondo.
Description: Durham : Duke University Press, 2018. | Includes
bibliographical references and index.
Identifiers: LCCN 2018020447 (print) | LCCN 2018027617 (ebook)
ISBN 9781478002420 (ebook)
ISBN 9781478000730 (hardcover)
ISBN 9781478000945 (pbk.)
Subjects: LCSH: Asian American theater—Social aspects. | Theater and
society—United States. | Racism and the arts—United States. | Creation
(Literary, artistic, etc.)—Social aspects—United States. | American
drama—Asian American authors—History and criticism.
Classification: LCC PN2270.A75 (ebook) | LCC PN2270.A75 K66 2018 (print) |
DDC 792.089/950973—dc23
LC record available at https://lccn.loc.gov/2018020447

Duke University Press gratefully acknowledges the Dorothy
Leonard Endowment for Visual Anthropology from the
Center for Visual Anthropology, University of Southern
California; and the Office of the Dean at the Dornsife College of
Letters, Arts and Sciences, University of Southern California,
that provided funds toward the publication of this book.

ALL PERFORMANCE RIGHTS TO THE PLAY,
SEAMLESS, ARE RETAINED BY THE AUTHOR.

Cover art: Yong Soon Min, American, born South Korea,
Movement, 2008, clear vinyl records, compact discs, mirrors
of varying sizes, painted image. Collection of Smith College
Museum of Art, Northampton, Massachusetts. Purchased
through the initiative of the Korean American Students of
Smith (KASS) and the Korean Arts Foundation (KAF) with gifts
of alumnae and other donors.

FOR

ROY JISUKE KONDO

AND

MIDORI KONDO

contents

Acknowledgments • ix

OVERTURE • 1

ENTR'ACTE 1
Racial Affect and Affective Violence • 17

**ACT I
MISE-EN-SCÈNE**

CHAPTER 1
Theoretical Scaffolding, Formal Architecture • 25

CHAPTER 2
Racialized Economies • 56

ENTR'ACTE 2
Acting and Embodiment • 93

**ACT II
CREATIVE LABOR**

CHAPTER 3
(En)Acting Theory • 97

CHAPTER 4
The Drama behind the Drama • 130

CHAPTER 5
Revising Race • 167

ENTR'ACTE 3
The Structure of the Theater Company • 205

**ACT III
REPARATIVE CREATIVITY**

CHAPTER 6
Playwriting as Reparative Creativity • 209

CHAPTER 7
Seamless, A Full-Length Play • 237

Notes • 311
Works Cited • 325
Index • 349

acknowledgments

Acknowledgments are where authors usually perform gratitude, joy, and pride. In the spirit of the genre-bending this book performs, I fiercely insist on ambivalence, acknowledging joy, gratitude, *and* mourning.

    This book "should have" been done by December 2015, but my life was abruptly interrupted by what doctors told me was the need to have open heart surgery for a leaky valve—a congenital issue that many women share. I was a "good candidate," otherwise healthy, someone who watched her diet, exercised daily since grad school, didn't smoke or drink. The surgery was a partial success; they repaired the valve. (Replacements must be redone every ten years, so the repair was a relief.) The surgeon also cut into my septum, the heart wall; I've received two different stories about why. Two years later I am at best two-thirds of my "presurgery" self. Violent fatigue and flagging energy/spirits are part of everyday life, even as the demands of academe are unrelenting. Most difficult for me: even my passion, theater, exacts a toll. Matinees are staged during my nonnegotiable afternoon downtime, and I cannot stay up for the typical 8–11 p.m. performance. If I muster extra energy to go, the pleasure comes at the cost of a few days of recovery. In the face of trauma and truncated pleasures, I feel valiant in having completed this book at all—particularly since the long-awaited reader comments and subsequent revisions coincided with both the school year and the transitioning of my mother to assisted living. I have dedicated my finite energy and lucidity to daily, short bursts of work. In the midst of an especially hectic semester, trudging through the demands of academe and everyday life, I find that my pride and relief in finishing a book are laced with mourning and exhaustion. The end doesn't seem quite real.

In the contemporary United States, we are supposed to "think positive" and to "fight" our diseases. Emily Martin and Donna Haraway have analyzed the martial masculinity at play in these metaphors of combat in figurations of the immune system. But are those who die those who didn't fight adequately? Are we blaming them for a failure of will? Barbara Ehrenreich's book says it succinctly: *Bright-Sided: How Positive Thinking Ruined America*. If illness and surgery have taught me anything, it is the way we are disciplined into performing "happiness," positivity, in ways that feed productivity for the institution and promote the subject's grandiosity/omnipotence. We are enjoined to split off pain, discouragement, loss. Splitting can take the form of projecting vulnerability onto the other: "poor you" allows "me" to feel all the stronger in the face of your "weakness." (Bullying operates through the same dynamic.) Doctors authorize us too soon to return to work, to drive, thus risking accidents, injury, death. We disavow the possibility that minds and wills cannot always overcome bodily trauma easily—or, perhaps, ever. We sanitize death: the death rattle is real, y'all! We theorize "vulnerability" and "fragility." How much harder it is to embrace those qualities in our everyday lives, for to do so would require us to confront mortality and finitude. Acknowledging pain, limitation, and "negative" emotions is not weakness; rather, it is an attempt to grapple squarely with the unavoidable realities that will, eventually, face us all. Vulnerability is our condition of existence. Perhaps my passion for theater emerges precisely from the ways that theater recognizes—indeed, prizes—emotion and vulnerability.

Flying in the face of manic, oppressive positivity and a capitalist, masculinist imperative to view vulnerability as personal weakness, my acknowledgments refuse to perform the conventional heroics of the Master Subject who has triumphantly completed a master work against great odds. I refuse to perform what Sara Ahmed calls "the duty of happiness" and thus risk dismissal as a (disabled) killjoy. Instead, I insist that we unsettle the Master Subject by recognizing limits, pain, trauma, loss, fear, rage, indeterminacy, and ambivalence as inevitable forces shaping our everyday lives. Just as inevitably, I hope that by the time this book is in readers' hands, I will have recovered more of vibrancy that approximates my presurgery self.

Our primary vulnerability and fragility spotlight our interconnectedness. Over the twenty or more years since I began this "work of creativity," my debts are innumerable and would constitute a list miles long. Apologies in advance for what are sure to be many omissions.

To the artists who feature in act 2—Anna Deavere Smith and David Henry Hwang—thank you for the inspiration of your art and for allowing me to participate in various capacities in your work of creativity.

Granting agencies and institutions enabled research and writing. The Getty Research Institute and the National Endowment for the Humanities supported the year of research that formed the creative nucleus for this work. I also completed one play and the beginnings of *Seamless* that year. A quarter at the UC Irvine Humanities Research Institute further spurred the development of my ideas. Thanks to David Theo Goldberg and organizer Karen Shimakawa and seminar participants, including Rachel Lee and Deborah Wong. USC supported this endeavor through Faculty Research Awards, ASHSS grants, a Zumberge grant, and a Faculty Mentorship grant. The Social Science and Humanities deans, Andrew Lakoff and Sherry Velasco, generously provided subvention funds, and the Center for Visual Anthropology, codirected by Gary Seaman and Nancy Lutkehaus, funded the expenses of color plates and photo permissions. The support is deeply appreciated.

A year at the Stanford Humanities Center allowed me to finish a first draft of the manuscript. Thanks to director Caroline Winterer, Robert Barrick, Roland Hsu, and fellows, especially Regina Kunzel, and colleagues who offered comments/questions, including Matthew Kaiser, Dan Rosenberg, Yi-ping Ong, Tanya Luhrman, Melanie Arndt, Elizabeth Anker, Benjamin Paloff, Keith Baker, and Dylan Penningroth. Warmest thanks for Paulla Ebron's intellectual companionship and Sylvia Yanagisako's mentorship. I benefited immeasurably from stimulating engagements with Stanford TAPS faculty Jennifer DeVere Brody, Harry Elam, Peggy Phelan, and Jisha Menon.

Universities in the United States and abroad provided opportunities for me to share my work: the University of Colorado at Boulder (Center for the Humanities); NYU (Performance Studies); Northwestern University (Performance Studies); Wesleyan University (Center for the Humanities); the Universities of California at Irvine (Anthropology), Los Angeles (Anthropology), Riverside (Humanities Research Institute), and Santa Barbara (Anthropology); Stanford University (Anthropology); the Chinese University of Hong Kong Distinguished Lectureship; and keynotes at the Aarhus University/Copenhagen University MegaSeminar and the "Bodies in Difference" conference at McGill University, Montréal, Canada. And thanks to the graduate students in my introductory seminar in American Studies during the fall of 2017. It was fun to think with you about the book!

My work has benefitted from participation in panels at many conferences over the years, including meetings of the Consortium for Asian American Theatres and Artists, and multiple meetings of the American Anthropological Association, the Association for American Studies, the Association for Asian American Studies, the Association for Theatre in Higher Education, and the Aspen Institute, among many others.

Undergraduate research assistants helped sustain my administrative work and research tasks over the many years this book has been in process. A comprehensive list would constitute half the book, so let me acknowledge those who worked most directly on the current iterations of the book from its 2013–14 draft: Sophia Li, Olivia Cordell (who saw me through the penultimate version), Garrison Hall, Farah Modarres, Sun-Hee Seo, Erica Park, Lorna Xu, Ilani Umel (who animated a scene from *Seamless*), Alyssa Coffey (stalwart support during my heart surgery), YeSeul Im, Jasmine Li, Austin Lam, Camille Langston, Aman Mehra (two years of excellent assistance), Matthew Solomon, and, at Stanford, James Burdick and Julia Starr. Jaemyoung Lee's dedication and intellectual engagement were exemplary; he would work on my citations during designated work sessions and again late at night, after running lights at the theater. Who does that? Jay does! Mara Leong Nichols was a stalwart presence during an especially challenging time, the overlap between a move and my father's death.

Graduate student assistance has provided crucial support over the years: Elizabeth (Biz) Martinez, Imani Johnson, Stephanie Sparling Williams, Anthony Rodriguez, and, at Stanford, Daniel Bush. Jake Peters was my RA for three years, during one of my life's most difficult periods. I couldn't have survived without his help.

Friends and colleagues have offered indispensable institutional support for fellowships: Steven Feld, Don Brenneis, Renato Rosaldo, Julie Taylor, the late Clifford Geertz, Sandro Duranti, and Marcyliena Morgan. Though I do not have a group with whom I share my work (would anyone like to create one with me?), friends and colleagues have read chapters, suggested relevant articles, or offered other intellectual/creative engagement. Thanks to Lisa Rofel, Traise Yamamoto, Amalia Cabezas, Mei Zhan, Shana Redmond, Viet Nguyen. Occasionally, Neetu Khanna and I meet at coffeehouses with our laptops, spurring each other on in our writing. I've done the same with

Sarah Gualtieri. During one of my anxious moments, Judith Butler helped me recenter through her advice, "We do the work we do." Friends provided crucial support in the wake of my father's death and my move, including Shana Redmond, Viet Nguyen and Lan Duong, Beth Meyerowitz, and Anita Ferguson. When I shattered my wrist, Viet and Lan, Monica Majoli, and Richard Kim, among others, offered indispensable assistance.

For my heart surgery, my brother Jeff flew in from the Midwest, and Lisa Rofel traveled from the Bay Area to see me through the trauma of surgery and the even more terrifying transition to recovery at home. Their support was indispensable. Many came forward with food, gift cards, supportive emails, visits, rides. Thanks to Viet and Lan, Mei Zhan, Nayan Shah, Wade Thoren, Anna Deavere Smith, Sylvia Yanagisako, Monica Majoli, Traise Yamamoto, Jih-fei Cheng (many rides to the doctor!), Lee Wochner, Janet Hoskins, Nancy Lutkehaus, Marcos Nájera, Deb Piver, Leslie Ishii, Elaine Kim, Alisa Solomon, Stephen Wadsworth, Marcyliena Morgan, Cecilia Pang, and Monique Girard.

My transition to playwriting has occurred over a good twenty years. *Seamless*, unlike my other plays, has spent an unusually long time in development. I'm grateful to Moving Arts Theatre and to Aaron Henne's playwriting workshops. Readings there, at New York Theatre Workshop and, crucially, at the Lark Play Development Center (thank you, Suzy Fay!) propelled *Seamless* on its journey. Mad props to the directors who worked on this play: Darrell Kunitomi, Liz Diamond, Victor Maog, Eric Ting, and Ralph Peña. Many actors have cycled through various roles in *Seamless*. The process has continued for so long, Emily Kuroda was first Diane and now is Diane's mother! Casts have included Alberto Isaac, Joanne Takahashi (LA Diane), Sab Shimono, Cindy Cheung (NY Diane), Jackie Chung, Jojo Gonzalez, Mia Katigbak, Suzy Nakamura, Matthew Boston, Marcos Nájera, Kipp Shiotani, Jeanne Sakata, Ken Takemoto, Takayo Fisher, Ping Wu, Haruye Ioka, Diane Takahashi, Shaun Shimoda, Samantha Whitaker, Deb Piver, Sarah Wagner, and Terence Anthony. Ellen Lewis, Karen Shimakawa, and Renato Rosaldo offered insightful comments at a reading at the Lark. Karen Shimakawa and Dan Mayeda shared their expertise on constitutional law and the structure of a legal career respectively, informing my portrayal of Diane.

Writing coaches Elena Glasberg (for many years) and Yael Prizant (whose insightful readings, editing, and organizational/dramaturgical skills helped me bring this home) were indispensable interlocutors in this shape-shifting project.

Two anonymous readers offered brilliant comments that sparked my renewed intellectual excitement. David Eng identified himself to me as the third reader. His praise helped me to feel "strong-hearted," as the Japanese say.

Ken Wissoker, thank you for your generous support of my work over the years.

Finally, to my parents—Roy Jisuke Kondo, who died in 2009 at the age of ninety, and Midori Kondo, who passed away this year at ninety-nine, yoku ganbatte kuremashita. Wish you could have seen this book. Sabishiku narimashita.

overture

It's a sunny, hot Los Angeles day. I drive into Silver Lake and park in a mostly Latino neighborhood of wooden houses and small businesses, across from the 7-Eleven at the corner of Virgil and Santa Monica. I cross the street, enter a small, dark building, and step onto the stage of East West Players, the country's oldest Asian American theater company and the longest continuously running theater of color in the United States. At this point, it is still a ninety-nine-seat, Equity Waiver black box.[1] Though I'm a recent transplant from Boston, I've been to East West many times to see plays, hungry for Asian American theater after so many years in a city where such performances were rare.

Today is different. I'm here for the inaugural meeting of the first David Henry Hwang Playwriting Institute. Not, mind you, because I think I possess dormant playwriting talent, but because I can use it as a fieldwork technique: to meet people in Asian American theater, to find out about the pedagogies of playwriting, to learn the elements of the craft. No matter how embarrassing, I tell myself that it will be worthwhile for my ethnographic project. I later think that my attitude is a defense for dealing with the unknown, the scariness of actually trying to write in a different register, when my only connection with the creative had been bad high school poetry and fairy tales I used to write and illustrate in grade school.

We students meet our three mentors: our principal teacher, Ric Shiomi, Japanese Canadian author of *Yellow Fever*, cofounder and artistic director of Theater Mu in Minneapolis for twenty years, and now co-artistic director of Full Circle Theater in Minneapolis; playwright David Henry Hwang; and playwright/screenwriter/director Brian Nelson. The teachers talk to us about what is in store, each in his own distinctive voice: Ric is self-deprecating and witty; David displays his usual sparkling brilliance; Brian talks about his graduate training. Recruiters for film school brought him to see equipment, while in the theater school, he enjoyed direct interactions with live people. I emerge from our first meeting exhilarated and apprehensive in equal measure.

At first a methodological tool and a lark—"just to see"—the playwriting soon takes on a life of its own. Invariably I am tired and grumpy as I drive to playwriting class after a full day of teaching, committees, and office hours at the Claremont Colleges, forty-five minutes away. Yet what I discover at East West—the necessity of hearing, and not merely reading, the scenes; ways that acting can transform words; that I actually can write drama—is revelatory. By the end of class, my whole being feels awakened to the thrill of theater. The drive home flashes by; my mind is racing. I feel so alive and so energized that I can't sleep! I know then that theater and playwriting will have to become a significant part of my life, for this level of passion is something I have never felt before. To see rehearsals and the significant shifts of meaning that a gesture, a change of lighting, an inflection, can evoke; that moment, sitting in the theater, when the curtain rises and I feel alive with anticipation; the magic of an opening night, when the messiness, frustration, and worry of rehearsal are alchemically transformed into a radiant production . . . these moments make theater for me a testament to the life-giving capacities of the arts. This book is a tribute to that life-giving capacity and to the artists who create works of beauty that provoke us, enrapture us, challenge us.

In what psychoanalysis would see as splitting, this romance led me to place my academic work on hold. The academy was for several years a "day job," routine and boring, while creative work was the place of life, excitement, discovery. I see this split as arising from a more fundamental, culturally encoded one: our disciplining into Cartesian dualisms. In the academy, the enshrining of analysis and the intellect, and, in the corporate university, a Taylorist drive toward relentless productivity compel us to repress the body, the emotions, and the powers of fantasy and comedy. Theater is precisely a realm that nurtures—indeed, treasures—these repressed elements. Perhaps because of this exclusion, my plays all rely on fantasy and on comic moments. Certainly, outrageousness and humor are not allowed in conventional academic discourse. For example, scholars can write in discursive registers about comedy, but norms discourage us from writing in comedic ones. And though Clifford Geertz and others have authorized anthropologists to deploy lyrical language, we generally domesticate extremes of emotion—exuberance, pain—into "experience-distant" prose. Theater allows me to mobilize elements the academy would have us repress, in a larger project of integration that should make us think *and* feel.

After some affirmations, I feel I can legitimately call myself a playwright. My first play, *(Dis)graceful(l) Conduct*, won Mixed Blood Theater's "We Don't Need No Stinking Dramas" national comedy playwriting award, an amusing distinction it always gives me great pleasure to mention. In 2003, I received my first production, at the Asian American Repertory Theater in San Diego, of my relationship comedy *But Can He Dance?* That same year New York Theater Workshop, a theatrical venue with an illustrious history—*Rent* and Tony Kushner's *Homebody/Kabul* premiered there—held a reading of my play *Seamless*. A different incarnation of the play, significantly revised, was a finalist in the prestigious Lark Development Center's New Play Festival in 2009, and took second place in 2014 for the Jane Chambers Award for women playwrights. I include *Seamless* in this book to theorize the afterlife of historical trauma, to contest regnant ideologies of the postracial, to reflect on the epistemological implications of becoming a scholar-artist, and to subvert what James Clifford (Clifford, pers. comm., 2013) calls the "law of genre." Throughout my career, I have sought to expand what counts as theory, but this is my boldest attempt thus far.

After the production of *But Can He Dance?* I began to suffer from chronic repetitive stress injuries from years of furious typing, usually at desks that were "made for large men." Bodily limits and the physical toll our profession exacts imposed themselves in ways I could not evade. During the worst periods of pain, I was physically unable to write—and rediscovered my passion for intellectual inquiry. During that year, I was able to reencounter the transformative work of Derrida, Foucault, and Deleuze, the generative contributions of queer theorist Judith Butler, works in critical ethnography such as Saba Mahmood's *Politics of Piety* and Anna Tsing's *Friction*—scholarship that inspires, pushing forward our theoretical paradigms in exciting ways. This book re-members my intellectual passion, integrating it with the passion I felt for theater.

Integrating the Creative and the Critical

This re-membering occurs on multiple levels. First, *Worldmaking* is an ethnography of the theater industry. Ethnographic, *participatory* observation[2] grounds insights into the theater world, through my work as dramaturg, playwright, scholarly critic, character performed onstage, and student in acting class. As in classic ethnography, I delineate the "setting"—mise-en-scène—of racialized economies that marginalize theater, despite its "upper-middle-brow" cultural cachet (Brater et. al 2010), and I challenge assumptions about the merely decorative function of the arts. Here, the mise-en-scène includes theater size and classification, labor (casting, production), and income. It is virtually impossible to make a living from theater alone. Assumptions about the aesthetic sublime—that the arts "transcend" everyday reality—help to keep artists poor.

Second, ethnography's *corporeal epistemologies* enable richly specific, granular insights into *race-making*, a key concept in this book. Participatory observation in theater as both ethnographer and practitioner shapes my distinctive approach to the now foundational concept of race as social construction. *But how*, specifically, do we construct race in our everyday scholarly and artistic practice, and under what structural, historical conditions?[3] Enfleshing "race as social construction" helps us to imagine—thus to make race—otherwise.

Ethnography's corporeal epistemologies compelled me to shift focus from the analysis of representation, the conventional work of drama and cultural studies criticism, to spotlight what I learned as a *participant*: backstage creative processes, the artistic labor that *makes, unmakes, and remakes race*. I ground these insights in my practice as a playwright and my work over the years with Anna Deavere Smith and David Henry Hwang, theater artists of color who are at the pinnacle of their careers. I was a full member of the creative team for three of Smith's productions and a scholar/informal dramaturg with backstage access to the world premiere of Hwang's play *Yellow Face*, which addressed the significance of race in a "postracial" moment—the substantive theme of this book. I shared dramaturgical notes with Hwang and with producer/dramaturg Oskar Eustis, which I reproduce in chapter 5.

Theoretically informed creative processes thus take center stage: acting praxis that performs the radical susceptibility among people, rather than assuming the interiority of the actor's subjectivity; theories of authorship in which interviews and dramaturgical interactions constitute intersubjective modes of writing; dramaturgy as enacting a politics of agonistics and affiliation; writing as revision, where even a single-authored work becomes the site of discursive struggle among racial ideologies; playwriting that crosses scholar-artist divides, dramatizing the afterlives of historical trauma. Subjects cannot be cleaved from culture, power, or history. All these theoretical practices destabilize the disembodied Master Subject.

Ethnography's corporeal epistemologies led me to these theoretical practices, illuminating the power-laden, multifarious ways we make race backstage, within specific historical political economies. These backstage practices are usually invisible to the audience and considered ex-orbitant to theory. Indeed, while many theater scholars are also theater artists, most scholarship in theater and performance studies and the majority of anthropological studies of performance cross-culturally are written from a spectatorial position. Theater studies tends to separate critics from practitioners, theory from practice; indeed, different journals are dedicated to each (*Theatre Journal* vs. *Theatre Topics*). I trouble the theory/practice, theory/method divides—mind/body dualisms that oppose disembodied thought to mindless action—by according theoretical weight to backstage labor, creative process, "methodologies" that count as theory.[4]

Third, re-membering integrates the creative and the critical through bending genre. The book's formal structure evokes a three-act play or musical, tracing a theoretical, psychic, political journey adapting Melanie Klein's concept of the reparative that I elaborate extensively in chapter 1. Klein's positions—not stages—develop from fusion that generates destructive fantasies to provisional integrations that acknowledge "the real" of separation. Similarly, my romance with theater is shattered through affective violence, then moves toward what I call *reparative creativity*: the ways artists make, unmake, remake race in their creative processes, in acts of always partial integration and repair.

Corporeal Epistemologies

The corporeal epistemologies of ethnography inform this book at every turn: forms of experiential knowledge emerging from putting one's embodied "self" on the line. Embodied fieldwork encounters shaped my analytic, highlighting enactment, performance, and process; they inspire my writing practice, traversing multiple genres as ways of conveying the layered complexities of social life. This disciplinary affinity for embodied experience is particularly well suited to the turn toward performance.

Like fieldwork, performance involves a bodily, sensorial, affective, intellectually complex encounter with the world. I argue throughout for the ontoepistemological weight of ethnography and of performance.

In its ethnographic approach to theater, this book delineates the contours of a world that was initially exotic to me. Like the shop floor of a Japanese factory and the showrooms and runways of the high fashion industry, the (back)stage has become a familiar, everyday world. For nontheater readers, I treat the theater world like any other ethnographic field site. For theater practitioners, my analysis of tacit assumptions and theater customs might seem commonsensical, but I hope to provoke estrangement, the defamiliarizing of the familiar characteristic of anthropology as cultural critique (Marcus and Fischer 1986) and of Brechtian political practice. Such an estrangement could allow us to imagine otherwise (Chuh 2003).

Engaged involvement tempered my idealized romance with theater, leading me to see the theater industry as a key cultural site for the reproduction of race, performing visions of possibility alongside reinscriptions of hegemonic ideologies, making and unmaking structural hierarchies. Accordingly, my analytic foregrounds a cluster of power-laden concepts: making, work, creativity, process, production, fluidity, emergence, indeterminacy, movement. These animate multiple (and sometimes incompatible) theoretical perspectives: poststructuralist theory (Derrida's *différance*, Foucault's conception of power as both creative and coercive), production studies (analysis of behind-the-scenes production in film and television) (Caldwell 2008), ethnographies of labor, creativity and work, affect theory, work on "support" in performance studies (S. Jackson 2011), queer phenomenology, performativity, and performance (Austin 1962; Butler 1990; Parker and Sedgwick 1995) being among the most prominent. This general trend in scholarship veers away from fixity, essentialism, and the grid, introducing nonteleological openness and orienting us toward process and enactment.

"Making"—what I called in my first book "crafting"—links structures of power, labor processes, and performances of gendered, national, and racialized subjectivities, in historically and culturally specific settings. Making and labor, including the making of race, become forms of power-laden creativity (Ingold 2013).[5] Far from the auratic product of genius, springing fully formed from the artist's imagination, art is work: sometimes joyous and exciting, sometimes tedious, always requiring craft, prodigious effort, and, especially in theater, collaboration. I claim behind-the-scenes cultural labor as the making of theory, the crafting of politics, and the making and unmaking of structural inequalities such as race. Commonsense binaries between creativity and the arts, on the one hand, and labor, theory, and politics, on the other, split a complex, multilayered process. Creativity is work, practice, method: a site of theory making and political intervention.

I come to these insights through my active participation in theater, which exceeds conventional ethnographic practice. For anthropologists, the immersive, collaborative impulse that informs my fieldwork hews to disciplinary protocols at one level, but the *degree* of my participatory observation remains relatively unusual. Indeed, Oskar Eustis, artistic director of the Public Theater, joked that I had succumbed to Stockholm syndrome! I have joined theater productions as a dramaturg, and as a playwright I collaborated professionally with theater artists during the production of my play *But Can He Dance?* Moving among shifting positionalities, I retain an ethnographic outsider's eye that offers a sometimes skeptical vantage point on taken-for-granted theatrical practices.

In most ethnographies, including the anthropology of media production and performance, anthropologists are positioned as observers, interviewers, who watch processes unfold (Powdermaker 1950; Ortner 2013; Pandian 2015; Ginsburg, Abu-Lughod, and Larkin 2002; Dornfeld 1998). Ethnographies of backstage practice have been relatively few, particularly in the realms of opera, symphony, theater, and other forms of Western "high culture."[6] Even more unusual are accounts based on the anthropologist's actual creative participation, aside from the work of ethnomusicologists and a handful of works in theater and the visual arts (Feld 2012; Wong 2004; Hastrup 2004; Fabian 1990; Ossman 2010).

Participating actively and having a stake in the production as a member of the creative team offers a perspective different from observing or interviewing, from Renato Rosaldo's famous definition of ethnography as "deep hanging out" (quoted in Clifford 1997, 188) or even from working alongside one's informants, but not as a full participant, as I did in my first fieldwork as a part-time laborer in a Japanese factory. Anand Pandian (2015) likens ethnography to wildlife photography, waiting for the exemplary moment. My fieldwork in the high fashion industry assumed this sense of waiting: to garner invitations to sales exhibitions, PR offices, and to Paris and Tokyo collections, then waiting for hours in the Cour Carrée of the Louvre to enter the tents for the fashion shows, amid sour appraisals of status and attire. My active participation in theater offers a vivid contrast. As a dramaturg for Anna Deavere Smith, I was not waiting for something to happen, I was *responsible* for making it happen. The difference between waiting, hanging out, and *full participation* lies in degrees of accountability and the political stakes. The ethnographer as collaborator is a becoming-artist who participates in the work of creativity. Ethnography becomes a way of being in the world and a way to remake worlds through engaged participation.

Collaboration as a member of a creative team more closely resembles a form of activist intervention, where terms like "accountability" acquire crucial significance. Artistic collaboration recalls Kim Fortun's ethnography (2001) of political advocacy or Aimee Cox's account (2015) of women in a homeless shelter where she herself was director, involved in the day-to-day operations of the "field site," in relations characterized by responsibility, partiality of perspective, and shared engagement.[7] The backstage labor of activist involvement in mounting a production fosters heightened appreciation and respect for the artists' labor of crafting, revision, and battling institutions, which shape the final work. Participating in backstage drama, witnessing institutional constraints on creative process while assisting the artist's vision, highlights the contingency of the final production. The result of multiple forces, the production on opening night[8] could have been otherwise, a fortuitous confluence of circumstances that exceed interpretations based on a final, polished performance.

Collaboration as Political Intervention

I build on a collaborative relation of alliance and mutual respect with theater artists Anna Deavere Smith and David Henry Hwang, representing one register of my romance with theater. I analyze their encounters with structures of power, as I attempt to keep an equally critical eye on the ways we are all, inevitably, enmeshed in power, culture, and history. Both artists are celebrated theater institutions in themselves, who have won national and international accolades. Smith is a pioneer of documentary theater, who interviews people and performs verbatim portrayals onstage, blurring lines among journalism, ethnography, and drama. Hwang's *Yellow Face* problematizes the postracial and blurs the lines among (auto)-biography, journalism, documentary, and well-made play. My genre bending finds inspiration in their work. Smith's plays and Hwang's *Yellow Face* feature spectacular cross-racial, cross-gender performances, a focus on urgent social issues, and innovative aesthetic form, unsettling the binary between the real and representation, brute facticity and fiction. They enact the fluidity of identity within historically specific structural constraints, and offer the possibility of political alliance, as they / the actors onstage embody multiple characters of different races, genders, ages, and sexualities. Over the years, I have engaged their work as audience member, critic, informal advisor, and—for Smith's plays—member of the creative team, enacting my alliance with their aesthetic/political interventions. My involvement with Smith and Hwang adds dimension to transformative discoveries that emerged from my participation in theater as a playwright, audience member, and occasional student in acting class.

Smith, Hwang, and I are roughly contemporaries. We have known each other professionally for over twenty-five years. I came to know Smith while we were both on the National Program Committee for the American Studies Association during the year of the Columbian Quincentennial. The scholars of color on that committee caucused and brought to the larger group our objections to the fact that none of the proposed panels offered even a mild critique of the "discovery" of the Americas. That intervention may have led to Smith's impression that I was politically outspoken, even "blunt," and perhaps led to her asking me eventually to join her dramaturgical team. I served as a dramaturg on three of her plays: the world premiere of *Twilight: Los Angeles 1992*, in its world premiere at the Mark Taper Forum in Los Angeles (1993); two workshops for *House Arrest: The Press and the Presidency* (Arena Stage, New York and Washington) and *House Arrest: An Introgression* (Mark Taper Forum, Los Angeles); and the world premiere of *Let Me Down Easy* (2007, Long Wharf Theatre, New Haven).

Smith won national acclaim for her interview-based plays that spotlight urgent social issues and for her virtuoso solo performances of her interviewees. She is the recipient of the MacArthur Award, a Guggenheim, the National Humanities Medal, two Obies and two Drama Desk Awards for her solo performances, an Obie for Best Play, and the Lucille Lortel Award for outstanding lead actress, among other theater and arts-based honors. She was the Ford Foundation's first artist in residence and an artist in residence at MTV. Smith was a regular on *Nurse Jackie*, frequent guest star on *The West Wing* and now on *Black-ish* and is a series regular on *For the People*, produced by Shonda Rhimes; she played supporting roles in films such as *Philadelphia*, *The American President*, *Rent*, and *The Human Stain*. Smith holds an academic appointment in the Tisch School of the Arts and the Law School at NYU and heads the Institute on the Arts and Civic Dialogue, which nurtures artistic work addressing social issues.

I have written about David Henry Hwang's work since 1988, when I saw *M. Butterfly* on Broadway, a moment I described in *About Face*. It was the first time I felt I *must* write about something, as though my life depended on it. "My" racial affect was produced structurally, by the marginalization of artists of color in the theater world and the resulting absence of portrayals that mirror minoritarian audiences. The vision articulated in *M. Butterfly* was unprecedented on the American stage, for its spectacular staging of the imbrications of race, gender, sexuality, and colonialism, articulated through fantasy, desire, and (mis)recognition.

I underline Hwang's position as our most celebrated Asian American dramatist. Hwang was honored as an American master playwright at the William Inge Theater Festival. Three of his plays have been produced on Broadway; three were nominated for the Pulitzer Prize in Drama. *M. Butterfly* won Tony Awards for both Hwang and for principal actor B. D. Wong; as I write, it is in revival on Broadway, in a version directed by Julie Taymor and starring Clive Owen and Jin Ha. Hwang collaborated on the Broadway musicals *Tarzan* and *Elton John and Tim Rice's Aida* and wrote the book for the revival of Rogers and Hammerstein's *Flower Drum Song*. In the 2013–14 season, he was honored at the Signature Theatre Company, which features as part of its season several plays from a major playwright's body of work. Hwang has collaborated extensively on operas, working with composers who include Philip Glass, Osvaldo Golijov, Unsuk Chin, and Howard Shore. He currently writes for the Showtime series *The Affair* and heads the playwriting program at Columbia University. Hwang is the *only* Asian American playwright who has "made it" to this degree. Consequently, he bears on his shoulders the hopes and projections of an entire race and community—a topic about which he writes in *Yellow Face*. Like Smith's plays, Hwang's *Yellow Face* pairs interventions in aesthetic form with challenges to dominant ideologies of race.

This book accords Smith and Hwang a respect for their interventions, while locating them in larger structures of power. I analyze the ways their work disrupts and, inevitably, to some degree reinscribes the racial politics of theater, to the extent that these artists must adhere to certain conventions to be legible in the theater world. They both contest and reinforce foundational assumptions; they reap the benefits of success in their field and, simultaneously, they face challenges related to racialized gender and to their subversion of conventional aesthetic form.

Smith, Hwang, and I are longtime colleagues, in some cases collaborators, linked through mutual respect, shared history, and political affinity.

In this book I trace their evolving concerns and the creative processes animating their work; in so doing, I trace my own trajectory as scholar and playwright. In such an integration, such a reencounter, the writing inevitably serves an archival function. Its temporalities are palimpsestic. Like all books about performance, this one writes against erasure. Despite the impossibility of capturing performance, I hope to convey the immediacy and urgency that animated these past encounters with the artists and their work and to illuminate their historical, theoretical, and political significance.

Theater and Race-Making

Throughout, I connect realms too often considered disparate: the artistic, the political, the theoretical, the personal. What happens onstage, the affects elicited in the audience and embodied by performers, contest and reinscribe power relations, thus making, unmaking, and remaking race. If theater circulates hegemonic visions, then intervening where the mainstream finds itself mirrored is politically significant. Understanding this significance requires theorizing the distinctive features of theater and the political work of high culture. Sites of cultural production like theater circulate hegemonic racial ideologies, securing temporary consent to those ideologies.

I theorize processes of racialization through *racial affect*, which enlivens some and diminishes others, and *affective violence*, especially in sites assumed to be far from racial violence. Race pervades the realms of art, including theater. Power is not confined to police brutality; it occurs as more "refined" reproductions of racial hegemony. When is it okay to laugh at something? How is enjoyment implicated in the reproduction of power relations? High culture, from opera to symphony to dance to theater, is precisely where hegemonic structures and racial ideologies can be reproduced. Laughter and enjoyment—not equally distributed in the audience—can promote consent to those hegemonies, forging racial dominance through barriers of "stickiness" and "viscosity" (Hartman 1997; Ahmed 2004; Saldanha 2007). Alternatively, laughter can be a form of minoritarian critique (J. Brown 2008; Jacobs-Huey 2006). We must attend closely to the politics of pleasure, which interpellates us more securely into normativity or perhaps animates life-giving visions of possibility (Kondo 1997).[9]

Power-laden representations onstage have a material weight. They interpellate us as raced, classed, sexualized, gendered subjects, and they can have life-determining impact. Theater, film, and other domains of the cultural can confer *existence* in the public sphere (Kondo 1997). I theorize this racialized, gendered *reparative mirroring*, necessary for the foundation of both majoritarian and minoritarian subjectivity, through Klein's object relations theory, Lacan's mirror phase, and Freudian accounts of narcissism as foundational for subject formation. Some dismiss desires to "see oneself" as "mere" identity politics, but this dismissal occurs from a site of privilege. We all look to be mirrored; we all desire recognition. Minoritarian subjects remain too often excluded from fully rounded public existence.

The dismissal of "identity politics" arises from a power-evasive notion of identity, occluding the racialized, gendered, colonialist power through which that identity comes into being. The whole subject, a bounded, self-sufficient agent, is presumed to be separate from the world, defined by its consciousness and by an essence of the human. A substance-accident/substance-attribute metaphysics defines this subject. Power, race, gender, sexuality, and other markers of "difference" are considered mere accidents or attributes that are incidental modifiers of consciousness, the presumed defining feature of the human self, which is in turn assumed to be a bounded monad distinct from the forces of culture, power, and history. This definition of the individual is the ideological foundation of the US nation-state and grounds its utopian assumptions of unity and harmony as achievable through democracy. The liberal individual's history is deeply imbricated with colonialism and the rise of industrial capitalism (Lowe 2015; Belsey 1980; Macpherson 1962).

Challenging the individual, the anthropology of the twentieth century critiques the personal as a category that is itself an artifact of language and culture, problematizing the subject/world division. Marcel Mauss (1938), Clifford Geertz (1973), and the anthropologies of selfhood (Rosaldo 1980; Kondo 1990) see the person as a thoroughly social being. The spate of ethnographic work on self and emotion of the 1990s, including my own, joined this quest to problematize the Master Subject's pretensions to universality. Many anthropologists link the political, economic, and historical to what appears initially to be "personal experience." These experiences—experience itself is an abstraction—form dense entanglements of power-laden practices, sensations, and cultural and historical ideologies. The subject is inextricable from the structural.

Feminist, postcolonial, and critical race and ethnic studies, and the work of artists of color, have long challenged the universal Master Subject, revealing his racial, gendered, sexualized, colonial markings. My work shares with Anna Deavere Smith and David Henry Hwang a challenge to the foundational liberal subject that undergirds colorblind ideologies. Power-evasive liberal humanism promotes the pernicious elision of structural inequality under the guise of personal responsibility or individual prejudice. "Hate crime" reduces a structurally predictable phenomenon to individual aberration, while "reverse racism" conflates structural inequality with the hurt feelings of a privileged subject, whose privilege will remain structurally intact. Power-evasive, liberal individualist imaginaries make race by reducing the structural to the individual.

Yet there can be no radical rupture with "the individual," given that the very invocation of the "I," with its ideological baggage of possessive, even (neo)liberal, individualism, renders the whole subject inescapable. Liberal theater is based on individual character and emotion; accordingly, aspects of the artists' and my work inevitably reinscribe that subject to some degree. Both artists and I deploy registers that could be misread as merely "personal," including the seemingly autobiographical "I." Yet the "I" is a linguistic, cultural artifact, a narrative convention (Kondo 1990). Smith and Hwang complicate *both* this subject and the notion of the "merely personal" in their work. I hope this book and my play do the same. At its best, the work of artists such as Smith and Hwang foregrounds the arbitrariness of social classifications, including the "I," while revealing the simultaneously creative *and* coercive power of those ideologies. Subjects are formed through, not transcendent of, racialized power relations.

Another generative perspective on the question of the subject, power, and race requires shifting scale. Foucault's biopolitics opens up the workings of power beyond monarchical/juridical formations to the promotion of life and management of populations (Foucault 2003). Ruth Wilson Gilmore's scholarship and activism provoke us to think about racism as systemic structures with mortal stakes: "Racism is the state-sanctioned and extralegal production and exploitation of group differentiated vulnerability to premature death" (Gilmore 2007, 28).[10] The ways the state manages life can promote this vulnerability. Thinking of race in conjunction with other fields of power resonates with Lauren Berlant's notion of slow death: "The structurally induced attrition of persons keyed to their membership in certain populations" (Berlant 2011, 102). Structural inequality manifests most insidiously not in the dramatic event but in the long-term leaching of life and health from minoritarian populations through bodily conditions such as obesity and diabetes. Slow death indexes class, race, and gender as power-laden social disparities, not simply identitarian markers.¹¹ Thus, racism is an unrelenting, daily affair, not *simply* the spectacular event.

We therefore must attend to structurally overdetermined differences in degrees of vibrant life. One can exist in the flesh, but this is not necessarily "living" in its more expansive sense.¹² Culture matters here. Both in the cultural studies sense of the aesthetic domain of life and the anthropological sense of worldmaking assumptions, culture is a key site where hegemonies are reproduced. Who is allowed to exist in the public sphere? Whose stories are represented on stage and screen? Who counts as the universal? Who is a protagonist, and who is a dispensable supporting player? To what extent do stagings both reflect and shape our understandings of the worth of minoritarian and majoritarian subjects, our right to live and flourish? Whose authority do we accept on stage and off? Whose lives matter?

Smith's play *Let Me Down Easy* provides an example of the ways that theater might intervene into race and class hegemonies, illuminating the imbrications of the "individual" with power structures. Thematizing bodies, inequalities in the health care system, life and death, and, in its world premiere version, genocide, the play stages race as "vulnerability to premature death" (Gilmore 2007, 28). Smith's work offers connection to what that vulnerability might *feel* like (Cvetkovich 2012; Ahmed 2004). Such an intervention can be salutary in the world of mainstream theater, where the typical audience demographic skews toward the white, middle-aged, and upper-middle class. Here, we face the contradictions of any attempt at intervention. On the one hand, our identification with an individual character can allow us to *feel* the effects of structural violence on the everyday lives of minoritarian subjects. On the other, it inevitably reinscribes the humanist subject and courts the dangers of empathy. We may be empathizing only with projections of ourselves (Hartman 1997; Diamond 1992).

In *Let Me Down Easy*, we see the experience of relentless slow death through the eyes of a subject who enjoys race and class privilege. Smith performs Kiersta Kurtz Burke, a young white doctor who worked in New Orleans Charity Hospital during Hurricane Katrina. Burke provides a point of entry for the privileged audience members into the biopolitics of race and class as vulnerabilities to premature death. Idealistic and dedicated, Burke is convinced that FEMA will soon rescue the African American patients and staff. As the days unfold, she realizes otherwise. "The patients at Charity. . . . The nurses at Charity . . . knew we were gonna be the last ones out . . . they knew that the private hospitals were gonna get private helicopters and . . . it wasn't a shock to anybody. But the fact that it wasn't a shock to people was so shocking to me. . . . I'm privileged and this is the first time I've ever been totally fucking abandoned by my government, right? But this wasn't the first time for my patients or the nurses . . . it must feel like that your whole life. . . . That constant feeling of abandonment" (A. D. Smith 2016, 38–39).

Integrating race as vulnerability to premature death, the arts, and questions of the subject and power, I claim affect as a realm where hegemonies are reproduced. I use "affect" provisionally, to indicate a form of public feeling.[13] The uneven distribution of what in English we call enjoyment, rage, depression, envy, and delight can constitute structured inequalities that make race. While I retain an anthropological skepticism about the affect/emotion binary as culturally constructed, I propose that *racial affect* represents a power-laden zone where subjects, feeling, and structural violence intertwine.

Theater helps us theorize racial affect, linking the phenomenological and the structural, in vividly experiential, embodied performances of public feelings. "In performance emotion is a key product, part of the aesthetic excess of drama" (Batiste 2011, xvii). Affect can be mobilized politically (Gould 2009). "Applied theatre" has turned from "effect"—visible, measurable outcomes—to "affect," the joy, beauty, and pleasure that the arts give us (J. Thompson 2009). Still, affect may work differently for minoritarian subjects, whose access to the pleasures of fully dimensional humanity in the arts, as elsewhere, is structurally limited. I have long argued that such pleasures can be life giving, while structural erasure and oppressive stereotypes can flatten liveliness. "The politics of pleasure" (Kondo 1997) animates aesthetic/political/theoretical work.

Questions of the subject, power, and affect are thus central in cultural theory and to this book. Theater—a domain that traffics in embodied subjects and affectual exchange—is a generative point of entry for examining these theoretically and politically urgent questions. Structures and subjects are co-constructed in complex ways, including circuits of feeling and the (re)production of power. Theatrical creativity performs this work. While many accounts of the power of performance and artistic creation highlight affect, few connect it to the reproduction of racial power relations. The same is true for the literatures on public feeling that may gesture toward race but focus primarily on gender and sexuality. *Racial affect* addresses this elision. For minoritarian subjects, a trip to the theater can be a scene of *affective violence* or, too rarely, *reparative mirroring*. Precisely because theater capitalizes on the powers of the sensorium and affect/emotion, it can be life giving for some, life diminishing for others.

entr'acte
1

RACIAL AFFECT AND
AFFECTIVE VIOLENCE

January 2012

An evening at the Mark Taper Forum in Los Angeles, the city's premier regional theater for new work. I have great affection for the Taper, where Anna Deavere Smith's Twilight *premiered in 1993. The audience is another matter. Like most regional theater, it skews middle-aged or older, and overwhelmingly white. I see Bruce Norris's* Clybourne Park *with Shana Redmond, a colleague in African American Studies.*

Clybourne Park *is inspired by Lorraine Hansberry's classic* A Raisin in the Sun, *a tale of the African American Younger family's dreams for a better life.* Raisin *stages the consequences of Langston Hughes's poem "A Dream Deferred": "Does it dry up like a raisin in the sun. . . . Or does it explode?" Matriarch Lena Younger buys a new home in a white neighborhood, prompting the visit of Karl Lindner, representative of the Community Association of Clybourne Park, who tries mightily to discourage the family's move. At the close of* Raisin, *the Youngers leave their home for 406 Clybourne: the setting for Norris's play.*

Clybourne Park *takes up where* A Raisin in the Sun *leaves off. Act 1 takes place on the same day* Raisin *ends, but this time Lindner arrives to dissuade the white family who owns 406 Clybourne from selling their home. Act 2 takes place in 2009, fifty years after act 1. At this point, the formerly* white neighborhood has transitioned, in ways Lindner both predicted and ensured, into a predominantly black, "troubled" area that is undergoing "gentrification." Lena, the grandniece of Raisin's Lena Younger, is a representative of the neighborhood association; they seek to prevent the white, yuppie couple who has moved into 406 Clybourne from remodeling the home in ways that destroy its historic value.

We settle into our seats. As the play unfolds, the largely white audience responds enthusiastically, sometimes laughing uproariously, while my colleague and I are increasingly appalled, both at what is happening onstage and by our fellow spectators. As the evening proceeds, I feel increasingly marginalized, an "affect alien" (Ahmed 2010) who cannot join in the laughter. Yet the affective chasm is more than simple alienation. This is crazy-making. Am I / are we, the only ones who see? Why is the audience laughing? Are they sharing the laughter of discomfort? Recognition? Their laughter feels like Fellini's 8 ½, the screen crammed with faces that taunt: laughing at, not with.

My colleague describes her experiences viewing mainstream theater as an African American woman. The sense of marginalization and invisibility begins with the overwhelmingly white audience and grows. Not only does one not laugh when others laugh, one feels appalled at what is happening onstage. At the end of the play, when the rest of the audience leaps to its feet for the ovation, we race for the exit, escaping our evening of affective violence. As historian Robin Kelley later wrote to me, the play was "an assault."

This affective violence—a form of structural violence—and racial affect are all too common at the theater and in other realms of high and popular culture. One way that theater makes race is through affective violence as the enactment of exclusion. The abyss between our reactions and the play's rapturous mainstream reception intensifies the feelings of anger and wrenching disjuncture between the "killjoy" of color (Ahmed 2010) and the dominant. Predictably, Clybourne Park garnered rave reviews on Broadway, won the Pulitzer in 2011 and the Tony for Best Play in 2012, and enjoyed a long run in London, where it won the Olivier Award for Best Play.

Mainstream theater too often deepens the grooves of problematic racial ideologies, producing discouragement, weariness—what Ann Cvetkovich (2012) calls "political depression," the predictable outcome of histories of inequality, dispossession, colonization. Frankly, one could spend all one's time in ideology critique, so numerous are the plays, operas, and ballets that stage racial affronts or that assume the universality of whiteness. The weary affective response of the killjoy of color is far more than pathological individual weakness. It is a structurally predictable reaction to Amiri Baraka's (1967) "the changing same."

Clybourne Park *is objectionable in multiple ways that I will elaborate in another article, but my surmise is that its "innovative" advance, noted in mainstream reviews, is the staging of white anxiety and guilt. How does the dominant experience dominance? In* Clybourne, *African Americans are yuppie—"we" can meet "them" on the ski slopes and in our offices—but the play also stages white fear. Blacks will jump on "us" if "we" say a wrong word. White anxiety about what to say, how to interact, how to avoid the charge of racism, pervade act 2. The disquiet is connected to guilt for historical privilege, presumed to be a thing of the past. This guilt can act as its own form of self-excitement, preempting concrete efforts to make things better. Apparently, seeing these racialized dilemmas onstage was a source of enormous pleasure—or uncomfortable recognition, which can be its own source of bonding, a "stickiness" (Ahmed 2004) that binds the largely white audience.*

The success of Clybourne Park *lies precisely in its knowledge of its demographic, skillfully tapping that segment's anxieties. Norris baldly states,*

> People ask how come I don't write plays about, say, people in housing projects, and I say, "well, because those are not the people who go to the theatre." You can say, "We should get them to the theatre," but in actual fact, people who buy subscriptions . . . are usually wealthy people. They are almost always wealthy, liberal people. So why not write plays that are about those people, since those are the people who are in the audience? If you actually want to have a conversation with that audience, then you should address them directly. That's what I always think. . . . There is no political value in having sensitive feelings about the world. . . . You go, you watch, you say "That's sad," and then you go for a steak. (Norris 2012)

Norris's response is both predictable and shocking. For him, theater is not a site of the political, unlike the views of the artists of color in this book. Norris rejects the idea that theater can conjure Walter Benjamin's "wish images," what I call "visions of possibility" (Kondo 1997). Perhaps the upper-middle-class white audience is seeking self-confirmation rather than an expansion of consciousness: narcissism, indeed. But that self-confirmation is itself political. It can be life-giving to the dominant. Perhaps this play gives white audiences a moment to discharge their racial anxieties before they go for a steak. Maybe they enjoy the self-recognition of laughing at their own dilemmas and hypocrisies, of having their foibles validated and lightly satirized. I am still at a loss as to how to explain the enjoyment the audience evidenced during the play, since neither my colleague nor I found the play funny, entertaining, or compelling.

One of the ways power functions is to invisibilize the minoritarian subject—to enrage her, to make her feel crazy. No one else sees what s/he is seeing. Surely, then, it is her fault that she is excluded from the laughter and the enjoyment? Perhaps for minoritarian subjects, the creative can provide a register for responding to these power-laden affective assaults. Redressive outrage has served that function for my own playwriting, and I see it in the work of Smith and Hwang.

The artistic director of Baltimore's Center Stage, Kwame Kwei-Armah, created a counterhegemonic response to Clybourne *in his play* Beneatha's Place, *spotlighting a character from* A Raisin in the Sun: *the aspiring medical student Beneatha. In act 1 Beneatha and her Nigerian husband, Joseph Asagai, arrive at their new home in Nigeria. The house's white missionary residents are about to move out. They patronize Beneatha, who is misrecognized as a "provincial" Nigerian woman. Asagai has been excommunicated from a political group for his anticorruption stance and for his support for market women. He leaves the house for a meeting. We hear an explosion. Act 2, repeating the structure of* Clybourne Park, *occurs fifty years later. Beneatha is now an internationally renowned social anthropologist and chair of ethnic studies at the university. The same house, left intact, serves as meeting place for the department, whose mostly white faculty in African American studies propose changing the departmental focus to critical whiteness studies. As in Clybourne Park, act 2 recenters white discomfort in the face of challenges from people of color. This time, however, the outcome dramatically differs. The vote carries, but Beneatha triumphs in a clever plot twist. Center Stage mounted* A Raisin in the Sun, Clybourne Park, *and* Beneatha's Place *in rep: a rotating performance schedule that featured many of the same actors in all three plays. Though some might label this a liberal strategy—hearing all sides—few theaters are this visionary.*

Clybourne Park is only one of many theatergoing experiences that enact racialized affective violence. The work of Tracy Letts—especially the celebrated August: Osage County, *winner of every major theater award, and a film starring Meryl Streep—is exemplary here. The dysfunctional white family saga features a Native American maid who scarcely speaks and who exists to further the journey of the white characters. Letts's* The Man from Nebraska *and* Superior Donuts *circulate equally hoary tropes: white man rediscovers joie de vivre through travel, art, and a woman of color; white man achieves redemptive masculinity through "saving" a young black man.*[1]

Robert Schenkkan's All the Way—*a Tony winner and HBO film—heroicizes LBJ's role in civil rights legislation, marginalizing the pathbreaking work of*

Martin Luther King and the civil rights movement. Indeed, Dr. King appears as an irritant rather than a catalyst for change. The award-winning Avenue Q espouses the liberal "everyone's a little bit racist," conflating individual prejudice with structural inequality, while performing stereotypical portrayals of people of color. The most spectacular, most problematic Broadway spectacle is the winning yet breathtakingly offensive The Book of Mormon. Expert stagecraft, the alluring underdog narrative, the seamless integration of music and movement, and superb singing and acting render the musical irresistible at one level. I saw the talented Ben Platt as the lead; he went on to win a Tony in Dear Evan Hansen. Yet this talent underwrites the "hipster racism" of equal opportunity racial offense. If Avenue Q depends on the presumed equivalence that makes "everyone a little bit racist," occluding the structural inequalities that differentially position people of color and white people, The Book of Mormon comically heightens the gulf between Ugandan villagers and first-world Mormon missionaries. As a regular theatergoer, I find such affective violence to be more norm than exception. Yet to talk about such violence risks being labeled, by progressive and conservative colleagues, as killjoy, hypersensitive, stuck in superannuated civil rights politics inappropriate for our "postracial" age.

Racial affect buttresses structures of constant "microaggression," the (too often unattributed) term coined by my Harvard mentor, Chester Pierce (Pierce and Carew 1977). Microaggression can escalate into full-frontal affective assault, making creative attempts to counter such affective violence even more precious. In mainstream theater, the work of artists of color such as Anna Deavere Smith and David Henry Hwang, among others, thereby becomes even more life-giving. My own attempt at playwriting is one fledgling foray into reparative creativity. Even if nothing escapes the reinscription of power, the difference between affective violence and reparative mirroring matters, even if it is inevitably imperfect and partial. If structural violence can rob us of material well-being and affective violence can relentlessly drain energy, spirit, and the will to live, reparative mirroring can spark racial affects of jubilation at coming into existence, however illusory that subjecthood (Lacan 2002). My mother, a consummate hard worker who survived the Depression and Japanese American incarceration, calls this "giving you a lift"—because "a lift" can be life-giving.

Clybourne Park exemplifies the state of mainstream theater and the circulation of power-evasive discourses in this putatively postracial moment. Problematic plays such as Clybourne and the oeuvre of Tracy Letts circulate internationally to critical and popular applause, marginalizing alternative, minoritarian visions. Still, hope exists. While Clybourne was on Broadway, so were new plays by and about people of color: Lydia Diamond's Stick Fly, Katori

Hall's Mountaintop, *David Henry Hwang's* Chinglish. *The critical and box-office sensation of 2015 was Lin-Manuel Miranda's* Hamilton. *Simultaneously, the problematic Orientalist warhorse* The King and I *won acclaim for its splendid production.*

Though nothing is ever beyond reproach or beyond power, vibrant works by playwrights of color stage acts of reparative creativity. They, and the artists about whom I write, remind us why work by progressive artists of color remains so vital, so urgent, so necessary.

ACT I

MISE-EN-SCÈNE

chapter 1

Theoretical Scaffolding, Formal Architecture

Worldmaking theorizes the production of race—racialized structures of inequality, racialized labor, the racialized aesthetics of genre, racialized subjectivities, racial affect—in theater as an art world. I make the strong argument that, as theater artists are creating their art, they are also making and unmaking race. Theater is an especially rich site for investigating the nexus of race, power, aesthetics, and emotion/affect, for in the interactions between audience and performers, mobilizing the powers of the fleshy sensorium, theatrical performances can stage political and intellectual visions that *move* people. Inspired by the artists whom I analyze and drawing upon my complex relations with theater as ethnographer, dramaturg, and playwright, I enact connections and creative juxtapositions among domains we conventionally label the humanities, the arts, and the social sciences.

Theater and ethnography share their attention to the senses, embodiment, and affect as relationality: affecting and being affected (Deleuze and Guattari 1987). Dialogue performs the dialogic relationality of social life, while the script highlights the ways we constantly script each other into roles. Unlike novels, short stories, or poetry, theater requires performers to live, immediately spotlighting the collaborative intersubjectivity of artistic and scholarly production, as does anthropology's emphasis on collaborative meaning-making and the world beyond the text. This book enacts a relation of mutual susceptibility (Butler 2015) between performance and ethnography.

For readers outside the theater, the differences among theater, film, and television may seem inconsequential—or so I thought before I entered theater worlds. While the domains are related, key differences ground foundational disciplinary claims; they participate in related but distinct political economies and economies of prestige. Theater's definitive difference from film and television (and certainly from written forms like novels and poetry) arises from the mutual impressionability between audience and artist, in which the audience can shape the actors' performances, rather than cinema and television's one-way interaction. Video games allow for increasing interactivity, yet decision trees define pregiven possibilities. Theater gathers bodies, both performers and audience, who share space and time, affecting and being affected by each other. This copresence possesses the potential for forming temporary communities (Román 2005) *and* the potential for exclusionary affective violence.

Performance's multisensory engagements exceed the visual that remains hegemonic in an ocularcentric episteme, and the "multimodality" of performance exceeds invocations of the term that circulate in visual anthropology.[1] The full sensorium in performance cannot be subordinated to the visual or to any other single sensory register. For example, scholars of film, video, and critical race studies theorize hapticity; theatrical performance differs in kind, not merely in degree, from the "skin of the film" (Marks 2000). In small theaters, actors are literally within arm's reach of the audience. The fleshy messiness of theater—its potential for emergence, unpredictability—resonates with ethnography's corporeal epistemologies. Performance engages touch as the haptic and as affect/emotion (Harney and Moten 2013), alongside the kinesthetic, the aural/oral, the olfactory, and the visual.

Debates circulate around ephemerality as the defining feature of performance, its "ontology of disappearance" (Phelan 1993). Others have noted the remains (Schneider 2011), the hauntings (Carlson 2001), the memories and ephemera (Muñoz 2009), the coexistence of memory and disappearance (Moten 2003), the repertoire as embodied performance archive (D. Taylor 2003), and the mediation of "live" performance through cultural technologies such as television and film (Auslander 1999). These revisions are familiar to theater and performance studies scholars, perhaps less so to others. Performance, even within a cultural universe where film, television, and the Internet reign, cannot be captured fully by these technologies (D. Taylor 2016). Performance evokes anthropological analyses of ritual, and like ritual, even though the script is presumably fixed, no two performances are the same.

Finally, theater requires the willful suspension of disbelief, "theater as a domain of metaphor" that differs from the more objectivist, "fly on the wall" quality of cinema (Hwang 1998). From its first premises, theater enlists the powers of imagination and creativity familiar to us from childhood. A shift in lighting can signify the past, a dream, a mood. A stick can be a horse, a weapon, a person. Theater demonstrates that worlds are made, humanly imagined and fashioned, in collaboration with objects and technologies that are themselves replete with possibility. Theatricality shadows the stage, even in naturalistic plays, potentially sparking Brechtian critical reflection on the constitutive role of artistic/social convention and opening possibilities for change. This reflexive estrangement from common sense similarly characterizes theoretical work on performativity and performance.

Making and Performativity

My emphasis on making, production, and process thus takes inspiration from the distinctive features of theater itself, from the corporeal epistemologies shaping my backstage work in theater, and from grounding in the theoretical literatures in gender performativity and performance.[2] I put pressure on this literature and the work on race and performance more generally to theorize more expansively the processes of backstage labor. How do we make art, and in so doing, make race?

I accentuate the productivity of power as both creative and coercive (Foucault 1976), performativity as subversive, unfaithful citation (Butler 1990, 2015), and structure as enabling agential possibility (Gilmore 2007). I spotlight the emergent potential for political contestation animating these frameworks in the face of misreadings of Foucaultian notions of power as totalizing and juridical, and of performativity as always and only restrictive. Some theorists argue that approaches grounded in poststructuralist linguisticism, a hermeneutics of suspicion, or "paranoid reading" can account for only small changes and remain resistant to movement or emergence (Massumi 2002; Sedgwick 2003). Our grammar may fail us here. For example, Derrida's work on citationality (1988) and Butler's formulation of performativity as the citation of norms has been misread in terms of an invariant norm and a (voluntarist) human agent who cites, despite Butler's argument that the doing occurs without a whole subject as doer and that norms are multiple, changing (2015, 2004b).

Sedgwick notes that in the wake of Foucault's critique of the repressive hypothesis, the repression/liberation binary persists in the form of (invariant) hegemony versus subversion, a permutation of "continuity versus change." The theoretical deployment of hegemony reifies the status quo: "One's relation to *what is* risks becoming . . . bifurcated . . . accepting or refusing . . . dramatizing only the extremes of compulsion and voluntary. Yet it is only the middle ranges of agency that offer space for effectual creativity and change" (Sedgwick 2003, 13). I examine these specific, middle ranges of agency, and the everyday ways those hegemonies are made and unmade.[3] Race and structural inequality are not simply inert; they are in flux, fraught with complexity and contradiction.

Theater adds a crucial dimension to readings of performativity and performance as simply reproducing a preexisting, unchanging script, where both script and norm signify rigidity. For theater artists, the script offers multiple, exciting possibilities, transformed and enfleshed by the production: acting, directing (pacing, staging), lighting, set design, music, sound, venue, audience. All shape "the play." The fluid, open relations among script, production, and performance offer ways to think about performativity as openness within historically contingent possibilities and limits.

Taking cues from the script-performer relation in theater, I read the relation between norms and performance/performativity as fluid. Norms (e.g., of gender, race, grammar) are world-making assumptions that delimit intelligibility and meaning, but they can be contradictory, multiple, shifting. They can be rendered unfamiliar, enacted in politically challenging ways, underscoring Foucault's theorizing of power's productivity: potentiality immanent to power. I assume that performances, either onstage or in everyday life, are replete with possibility arising from, not transcending, power.[4] Reading performativity as historically contingent and power-laden, yet offering emergent possibility, re-members my work in theater with my early theorizing of subject formation as "crafting selves" (Kondo 1990).

I introduce the notion of race-making to shift focus from performativity alone. Performativity highlights identity as a doing. Making evokes the worldmaking of contemporary theory and of aesthetic production: world-making cultural assumptions that animate theatrical and social worlds. "Making" and "crafting" connote actions that transform the "material" world; these materials can themselves be "vibrant," as the Japanese artisans in my first book assumed (Kondo 1990). The OED definition of "craft," the more specialized term, designates "an occupation or trade requiring manual dexterity or artistic skill." I expand "manual dexterity" to include bodily techniques and artisanal aesthetics. Ingold (2013) connects art, architecture, archaeology, and (visual) art in his theorizing of making. I turn making toward performance practice, structural inequality, and social justice: making and crafting racial power relations.

I use "making" rather than "creation" to avoid the godlike presumptions of the latter term in "the West." Making is not creation ex nihilo; rather, we make, unmake, remake race within specific cultural and historical political economies. Making can be quotidian; it does not automatically conjure the divine sublime. "Worldmaking" evokes sociopolitical transformation and the impossibility of escaping power, history, and culture. Worlds, like language, are pregiven, and remaking must always work with this givenness. Theater subverts the omnipotence implied in "creation" through the collaborative work upon which "creativity" in theater depends. As director Lisa Peterson says, "It isn't theater if you can do it by yourself" (2002, 104). Acts 2 and 3 illuminate the theoretical implications of my focus on backstage creative processes.

In what follows I analyze racial performativity as denaturalizing estrangement that de-essentializes race, then turn to an analysis of *racemaking* through creative labor in sites from backstage practice to audience engagement.

Performativity, Performance, Race

I have theorized race as performative in multiple senses: theatrical performance; the performative enactment of racialized and minoritarian subjectivities, both on and off stage; the performative call that can bring new political entities into being, for example, Asian American, queer, black British (Kondo 1997). In this book I link performativity and performance to racialization as vulnerability to premature death, slow death, and precarity, moving from the scales of the structural to the subject and back—the divisions themselves undone, reconfigured in that back-and-forth process.

Several points bear repeating. First, racial identities are historically specific, political formations. For example, "black" British identity comprises a coalition encompassing the formerly colonized, including West Indians, Africans, and Asians, performing what Stuart Hall termed "new ethnicities." Second, the definitions of these collectivities are constantly shifting; for example, post-1965 immigration reform challenged the hegemony of Americans of East Asian descent within Asian America.[5] Finally, changing historical and political formations define "races" vis-à-vis one another (Takaki 1979; Omi and Winant 1986; Lowe 2015).

The work of artists Anna Deavere Smith and David Henry Hwang highlights race as performative, an arbitrary collection of conventionally associated traits congealed to establish a presumably fixed normative category. At one level, race, like gender, can constitute a corporeal practice, a citation of archetypes (Butler 1990). Performing race and gender is a process of materialization—citing, extending, contesting conventional racial categories. We see the fluidity of racial identities and the association of a presumably fixed race with verbal, kinesthetic, sartorial, and other conventions (Carbado and Gulati 2013), forged through power-laden histories. We *all* could enact archetypal racial repertoires other than our own. Performing across conventional racial difference both unmoors and cites racial norms, queering conventional identitarian markers. These performances make race.

Cross-racial performance can be read as both an invitation to political alliance and as reenacting minstrelsy. In the context of ethnic/racial nationalism, the move to cross-racial performance among artists of color can create opportunities to forge solidarities across racial borders. Simultaneously, some may misread racial performativity as positing race as a free-floating signifier, equally available to everyone. Yet some performances are appropriative, no matter how well intentioned (Johnson 2003). One cannot escape the histories of white privilege and of minstrelsy in any cross-racial performance, even when people of color perform each other. Racial stereotypes circulate at national and transnational levels, and anyone can support a possessive investment in whiteness (Lipsitz 1998).

I redirect performativity toward processes of making race in multiple registers. Thematics represent one node of race-making. Crucially, Smith and Hwang directly address race as social conflict and structural inequality, historically shifting fields of power that are central to the making of always power-laden identity. My play stages the lingering traces of racialized historical trauma in the lives of seemingly successful "model minorities." Furthermore, making race occurs through enacting commitments to racial justice through creative labor. Smith subverts conventional theater through the unusual move of welcoming dramaturgs who attend to issues of race in the play, and she hires a team of exceptionally diverse creative collaborators, including crew and designers.

Making race occurs in another register for artists of color. We are always considered representatives of the race, so how we perform/make race assumes urgent significance *within* racial groups. Are you a race wo/man? Your work will be judged in part in terms of how audiences of color read its politics of racial representation. Moreover, artists of color can enact political commitments in their work outside the theater. Smith and Hwang participate in progressive community organizations and promote young people's work. While white artists may with impunity reinforce whiteness through hiring choices, casting, thematics, and conservative aesthetic form, artists of color are held responsible for the racialized consequences of their work. We make race in multiple sites, in multiple ways.

Racial Affect, Psychoanalysis, and the Reparative

Racial affect, the hauntings of the stage by intertwinings of structural and affective forces, is one key site where race is made. I construe affect broadly, as a rubric that encompasses public feeling and minoritarian work on psychoanalysis and race, particularly queer theory's productive reappropriations of the psychoanalytic work of Melanie Klein and the reparative. *Worldmaking* stages a journey inflected through psychoanalytic theories of the reparative, extending these ideas from the realm of the individual subject into the realms of artistic creativity. Performance cannot be understood without analyzing affect/emotion; consequently, I follow out the complex interanimations of affect/emotion, performance, and structural inequality.

Among my theoretical inspirations is the florescence of scholarship by minoritarian scholars that productively appropriates psychoanalysis: what I had long dismissed as a universalist, culture-bound discourse.[6] Through critical race studies, performance studies, queer studies, and queer of color critique,[7] innovative refigurations of psychoanalytic concepts illuminate processes of gendered, racialized, sexualized subject formation and politics in "the West." For me, the cross-cultural utility of psychoanalysis remains questionable, but two premises of psychoanalytic theory compel. The first is the openness to history—therefore, to culture, language, power (its universalizing rhetoric notwithstanding), visible in Lacan's famous statement "Desire is desire of the Other" (Lacan 2004). That is, not even our desire is "merely personal"; the state, the family, school, and language (notoriously), among other social institutions, construct "our" desire. This vision of subject formation offers a bracing antidote to US individualist ideologies that promote omnipotence and occlude structural violence by assigning all agency and responsibility to the individual.

Second, psychoanalysis theorizes so-called negative emotions: rage, hate, envy, shame, aggression. Rather than splitting off "undesirable" feelings, psychoanalysis theorizes their inevitable presence. Indeed, Klein argues that love and hate, love and aggression, are inseparable, an affective recto/verso that animates reparation (Klein and Rivière 1964). We never transcend or resolve these contradictions, for reparation presumes ambivalence, guilt, conflict.

Klein's invention of positions, inner worlds, and inner objects (people, or fantasies of people) offers supple ways of thinking through the relations of race, power, subjectivity, and artistic creation. Klein broke from Freud's stage theory and opened the way to thinking subjectivity as shifting positionalities within internal worlds affected by, but not coextensive with, experiences with the external.[8] Her theorizing of the paranoid-schizoid position in infancy, associated with idealization, fusion with the object, splitting of love and hate, the good and bad mother (the one who feeds and the one who is absent and, in fantasy, destructive/destroyed) developmentally enables what Klein calls the depressive position. In everyday parlance, we might refigure the depressive as the realistic, as the infant confronts the real of separation from the (m)other and the entry into a world that resists one's desires and projections. The sober reality of separation ideally becomes the basis for the *reparative*—coming to terms with the shock of the loss of omnipotence, the infant's aggression toward the object (and conversely, through projection, fears of destruction), and the guilt resulting from those impulses. Ideally, the psychic working through restores what, in fantasy, had been destroyed: the relations with the loved (m)other. This working through is reparation.

While building on Klein, I depart from the level of the individual subject to think about the reparative as critical, political, and artistic practice. I unmoor the reparative from its psychoanalytic origins to conceive productive ways to repair the destructiveness of systemic inequality. Drawing inspiration from critically important work on psychic, political, and legal reparation (Eng 2010, 2011; Chambers-Letson 2013), I theorize artistic production as *reparative creativity*.[9] Hanna Segal, one of the Kleinian school, argues that the depressive position, successfully navigated, leads toward creativity, imagination, and play as productive outlets for the brutal confrontation with the real (Segal 1991). I argue that affectively, artistic creativity provides productive articulations of redressive outrage. However, unlike Klein and Segal, who remain primarily at the level of the individual, I link artistic imagination and other attempts at reparative creativity to systematic inequalities. Creativity and imagination never escape culture, power, or history.

Creativity and Imagination

CREATIVITY

Like concepts of culture as both a way of life and a domain associated with aesthetics, or performance as enactments both in everyday life and onstage, creativity opens itself to an expansive reading, roughly coextensive with innovation, and another indicating artistic endeavor. Donald Winnicott (2005, 87) theorized creativity as a capacity for life, an aliveness and genuineness opposing the deadening conformity that compromises the authenticity of the self. In anthropology, creativity assumes both artistic and everyday guises: "Creativity as human activities that transform existing cultural practices in a manner that a community . . . find(s) of value. . . . Invention takes place within a field of culturally available possibilities" (Lavie, Narayan, and Rosaldo 1993, 5). Edward Bruner pinpoints the theoretical assumptions that subtend theories of creativity. If one assumes the relative fixity of the structural, then change becomes difficult and monumental; if one assumes the flux and indeterminacy of everyday life, then theories of radical rupture are less urgent, for change is occurring constantly (Bruner 1993, 321–23).

Hanna Segal theorized creativity by extending the notion of the reparative to the domains of art, imagination, and play. For Segal, artistic creativity is primarily associated with the artist's attempts to repair the destruction of her inner world: "The artistic impulse is specifically related to the depressive position. . . . It is his inner perception of the deepest feeling of the depressive position that his internal world is shattered which leads to the necessity for the artist to recreate something that is felt to be a whole new world" (Segal 1991, 86). This unconscious world, Segal (87) argues—citing Proust—can be a world the artist feels is lost.

Reparative worldmaking necessarily navigates through violence, devastation, shattering, to work toward integration. Segal moves from the artist's inner objects to violence in the outer world when she analyzes Picasso's *Guernica*. The horrors of war are mediated through formal affinities and rhythms, an integration of destruction achieved through aesthetic structure. Segal argues that reparation can never occur without aggression—again, the psychoanalytic refusal to disavow the negative. Similarly, the work of minoritarian artists and scholars can be seen as creative attempts at reparation, to work through both the destructiveness of structural violence and our own desires for destructive vengeance. Integration and reparation are never complete—nor is the work of creativity.

IMAGINATION

While the arts are important sites for imaginative play, the imagination never transcends the social or the political. Further, Lacan's view of the Imaginary (not the imagination as such) links subject formation with misrecognition, in which the infant "imagines," erroneously, that he is a whole subject. Here, the Imaginary and the illusory intertwine.

Crucially, the imagination is always racialized. "To argue that the imagination is . . . somehow free of race . . . is . . . a mistake because our imaginations are creatures as limited as we ourselves are. They are not some special, uninfiltrated realm that transcends the messy realities of our lives and minds" (Loffreda, Rankine, and Cap 2015, 15–16). Most work on the imagination assumes otherwise. The concept of imagination is often related to creativity: "Imagination is an alarmingly creative faculty. Imagination makes things appear . . . impressions of things impossible or yet to be" (Pandian 2015, 152).[10] Imagination undergirds notions of the auratic and artistic genius. Vincent Crapanzano notes that anthropology rarely treats the individual or the imagination, warning of the Enlightenment origins of the term: "The association of imaginative auras and horizons with creativity, however compelling . . . is historically constituted and remains . . . anthropologically hypothetical" (Crapanzano 2004, 19). He further problematizes the historically, culturally specific link between imagination and the visual, excluding other powers of the sensorium (23–24). Imagination is imagined differently within particular cultural and historical horizons.

Klein ([1929] 1975) connected imagination, artistic creativity, and the reparative in a case study of Ruth Kjär, a Swedish painter, who had been prone to depression. A painting sold by her brother-in-law, a famous artist, left a blank space on the wall, provoking Kjär's despair. The emptiness apparently signified an empty space within herself. Eventually, "devoured by ardour," Kjär painted her first painting directly on the wall: a depiction of "a naked Negress" (Michaelis 1929, quoted in Klein 1984, 216–17). She later painted a series of family portraits, including one of an old woman and another of her mother as "magnificent." Klein offers this interpretation: "It is obvious that the desire to make reparation, to make good the injury psychologically done to the mother and also to restore herself was at the bottom of the compelling urge to paint these portraits of her relatives" (Klein [1929] 1975, 218).

Klein offers a detailed analysis of the family portraits, supporting her narrative about mothers, daughters, and reparation, but no such exegesis accompanies the image of the "naked Negress." Surely, the first image Kjär paints deserves explicit attention. Equally surely, the chosen image carries a power-laden valence with respect to histories of imperialism. Why the painter throws herself into artistic creativity through this image remains mysterious; it fails to elicit commentary from Klein or later, Segal, who cites Kjär in her article on artistic creativity. Why a "Negress?" Why is she naked, when Kjär's mother and portrayals of Kjär's family feature fully clothed women? Kjär, Klein, and Segal show us that imagination is inevitably racialized and gendered.

Thus, imagination and creativity never *transcend* the social, given the ways the auratic and disembodied Spirit haunt "transcendence." We can nonetheless challenge, reconfigure, and remix the familiar in innovative ways.

Spectatorship and Racial Affect: Moving through Affective Violence

The racialization of imagination and creativity for the artist extends to the imaginations of the audience through racial affect. Writing against the presumed affective neutrality of scholarly criticism, I underscore the affective consequences of theatrical performances for both dominant and minoritarian spectators. This begs a prior question: how do we theorize the audience?

Rather than inert viewers or passive capitalist consumers, audiences are "co-constructors of meaning" (Duranti and Brenneis 1986). Film, television, and theater elicit ancient prejudices about the putative passivity of the cultural spectator. Mobilizing Bergson, Deleuze, and Gramsci, Kara Keeling (2007) argues for the "affective labor" involved in cinematic spectatorship; audiences are performing this labor, linking image, perception, sensory-motor responses, and "common sense." Rancière (2011) argues that the presumption of spectatorial passivity arises from Platonian prejudices against the theatrical, denigrated because it presumably renders audiences passive, and the celebration of the terpsichorean or choreographic, in which audiences are moved to move. Theater is worthwhile only insofar as it can generate choreographic—visibly active—responses, within and outside the space of theater.[11] "Exterior kinesis" comes to index agency, excluding imaginative forms such as daydreaming (Cervenak 2014, 4).

Whereas the arts are often dismissed in political circles as inefficacious—can art spur us to storm the barricades?—Rancière emphasizes the theoretical/conceptual sophistication of the viewer, puncturing the pretensions of both artist and critic. He foregrounds "the distribution of the sensible": the power-laden schemas that render a work or action legible, possible, within what Foucault calls a regime of truth, and what anthropologists call cultural assumptions or common sense. The binaries that underlie the distance between artist and audience—doing/seeing, activity/passivity—govern our tacit assumptions about the relations of art and politics. Rancière emphasizes instead the active comparison, juxtaposition, and interpretation that a spectator engages while viewing theater.[12]

Rancière meets his limits when he flattens the specificity of the interaction between artists and audience in theater. Revalorizing the sophistication of the spectator's emotional/mental processes, he neglects the impact of audience reaction on theater artists themselves. He "proposes to revoke the privilege of vitality and communitarian power accorded to the stage, so as to restore it to an equal footing with the telling of a story, the reading of a book, or the gaze focused on an image" (Rancière 2011, 22). Perhaps where the mental activity of the spectator is concerned, he is correct. Yet Rancière fails to account for the ways artists themselves are influenced by audiences. Storytelling, too, requires an audience; one can be encouraged/discouraged/interrupted by listeners. In live performance, audiences powerfully affect the artists.

Most conventional drama criticism and performance studies read performance from a generalized spectatorial position that remains undertheorized. In response, I offer concepts of *racial spectatorship* and *racial affect*, in which nonwhite (and progressive white) spectators can be assaulted by psychic violence, rather than enjoying happy interpellation into hegemonic representation. Alternatively, mainstream spectators can be confirmed in their superiority. This presents dilemmas for the *racialized spectator as critic*, to transpose Jill Dolan's phrase (1988). How do we translate differential power relations, especially affective violence and the resulting rage it provokes, into criticism that will be taken seriously, not dismissed as merely personal, lacking objectivity? Like Sara Ahmed's "willful subject" (2014) or "feminist killjoy" (2010) who cannot be interpellated into laughter and amusement, who cannot be inscribed into the "duty of happiness" (2010) by taking pleasure in problematic racial representation, the racialized spectator feels battered, pushed to the margins, outraged. This outrage can be labeled "too emotional," making the racialized spectator "feel crazy" in the moment.[13]

For minoritarian subjects, *affective violence* for the spectator of color can generate desires for alternative subjectivities and a public existence in the face of marginalization and invisibility. In the rehearsal room and in academic discourse, some have dismissed this desire for existence as (mere) "identity politics," a "narcissism" that laments, "It's not about me." The passionate stakes here cannot be reduced to me-ism, a charge mounted from a site of privilege. Only when one has not been granted public existence or when that publicity results in affective violence can one comprehend the depth of desire for that existence. Of course, desiring recognition introduces the paradox of seeking validation from structures generating that marginalization, thereby reinforcing that system of recognition (W. Brown 1995) or reinforcing the problematic assumptions of visibility politics (Phelan 1993). Still, some inscription in public discourse, even if marginalized, can provide a starting point for future contestation, an improvement over the nothingness of erasure (Cox 2015; Nguyen 2016). Most important, though the plush seats of the theater, symphony and ballet may seem far from, for example, the killing fields of the Sonoran desert (De Léon 2015), the bodies and the (racialized) visions that perform the "transcendence of the human spirit" in zones of "high culture" buttress Eurocentricity and white supremacy. They legitimize the desire for more immigrants from countries like Norway and the racist exclusion of immigrants and refugees from s—hole countries.

The work of minoritarian artists can offer minoritized audiences a public, reparative mirroring—the subject of chapter 3. The public performance of minoritarian characters historically excluded from the stages of mainstream theater intervenes into histories of Eurocentricity. Smith and Hwang, among many others, give characters of color this public existence. Who is standing onstage matters. While mirroring celebrities such as Lance Armstrong or President Clinton seems redundant, such reflections could operate differently for minoritized subjects who have never been granted existence on the American stage: Julio Menjívar, a Salvadoran lumber salesman who was mistakenly arrested during the LA "riots"; Hazel Merritt, an African American evangelist who has kidney disease; Jay Yang, Korean American owner of a liquor store in Los Angeles; a young Chinese American college student; Chinese railroad workers; an Asian American playwright; and, in my plays, Asian American women as protagonists, not supporting players. Too rarely have such characters taken center stage in American theater. Minoritarian art can allow minoritized subjects the pleasure of being mirrored, conferring existence in a significant domain in the public sphere, despite the inevitable (mis)-recognition that inaugurates the founding of any subject. This *reparative mirroring* might counter, if only briefly, the raced and gendered epithets that hail us in ways that Frantz Fanon (1967) so eloquently theorized.

Within a historical and political economic matrix, the founding moment of subjecthood—the narcissistic pleasure of seeing the image of oneself in the "Aha!" moment Lacan describes—is inseparable from the politically overdetermined exclusion from this pleasure. Freud argued that we all experience a primary narcissism, "the libidinal complement to the egoism of the instinct of self-preservation, a measure of which may justifiably be attributed to every living creature" (Freud 1989, 546). He proposed two forms of love: the narcissistic, when libido is directed toward the self, and the anaclitic, when attachment to objects becomes primary (Freud 1989, 556). Narcissism is *necessary* for the foundation of the subject; it is problematic only when pathological. When we think of existence in the public sphere, minoritarian subjects are denied even this "primary narcissism" without which subjectivity cannot develop. Seeing "oneself" publicly embodied onstage, on screen, on the page, enables that necessary, primary narcissism.

Ahmed problematizes the distinction between narcissistic and anaclitic love in her analysis of nationalism and racism. The presumably "other-oriented" anaclitic stage is yet another form of narcissism, through which the nation narcissistically idealizes *itself* as tolerant and multicultural through its conditional love for multicultural difference. Immigrants and people of different races are acceptable to the extent that they subordinate their difference to the nation. The state can project "minority" communities as "narcissistic in order to elevate the nation into a multicultural ideal . . . to conceal the investment in the reproduction of the nation" (Ahmed 2004, 138–39). The charge of (pathological) narcissism equally occludes the political structures shaping differently positioned subjects. The elision of primary narcissism with pathology may serve as hegemonic strategies of disavowal and projection. This dynamic operates in ways familiar to us from the mechanisms of classic cinema, which covers over male lack, projecting this constitutive lack onto the female subject. "The 'normal' male subject is constructed through the denial of his lack; he is at all points motivated by a 'not wishing to be.' In short, what he disavows is his own insufficiency, and the mechanism of that disavowal is projection" (K. Silverman 1988, 18). Thus, the normative white subject may deny his own, inevitable, (universally shared) primary narcissism. This denial disavows historically specific structural violence that excludes minoritarian subjects from reparative mirroring, from the jubilation of the promise of existence in the public sphere. Given the power-laden context of affective violence, in which minoritarian subjects repeatedly confront erasure or denigration, reparative creativity becomes a way to give public life to the erased and marginalized.

Thus, I challenge the reduction of historical and social inequality to "me-ism," a charge too often directed at "identity politics," a term that reduces historical relations of inequality to liberal individualism, even navel gazing. The conferral of being in key domains of the public sphere is a substantial intervention, even as the (always illusory) whole subject is called forth in that mirroring. As partial antidote to the traumatic and denigrating interpellations to which minoritarian subjects are subjected and subjectified, the plays of Smith, Hwang, and other minoritarian artists populate the stage with characters who have been historically excluded, fostering reparative narcissism and reparative mirroring. Perhaps the easy epithet of "me-ism" voiced by people in the rehearsal room arises from hegemonic disavowal of the narcissism necessary for existence.

For minoritarian subjects, narcissism can assume forms of self-love and self-fashioning, wresting back the ability to define identities.[14] As Monica Miller (2009, 245) argues, Fanon in *Black Skin, White Masks* opens the possibility for "redemptive black narcissism" that constitutes "a potential mode of refashioning the self." Queer African American artist Lyle Ashton Harris takes inspiration from Fanon's "fierce decolonization of interior spaces . . . a return to the self as a site of interrogation." Harris invents the term "redemptive narcissism" as a reparative act: "Redemptive narcissism or self-love is a form of resistance to the tyranny of mediocrity. I see the mirror not only as a site of trauma and death—Narcissus falling in to drown—but as a space for rigorous meditation" (Harris 1996, 107).

Finally, the so-called narcissism of the subject of color could constitute a critical, political gesture that mobilizes an identificatory coalitional politics: *a politics of affiliation*. Seeing disempowered others who share related historical experiences of exclusion can energize us to make connections, to think through differential historical positionings, and to forge alliances. Far from me-ism, this "narcissism" moves us toward a *politics of affiliation* that presumes hard work and only partial connection, yet potentially offers life-giving possibility.

Thus, moments of affective violence, reparative mirroring, and reparative creativity dramatically make race, "even" in the plush seats of mainstream regional theater and Broadway. In the face of affective violence, the work of Smith and Hwang remakes race through *reparative creativity*. Backstage creative labor, including fraught dramaturgical processes, performs reparative creativity in a different register.

Dramaturgy
Contesting Power-Evasive Pluralism

Dramaturgy allowed me to use a scholar's critical faculties to be part of a creative team. Our common goal was to create the "best" production possible. Of course, opinions inevitably differed pointedly and sometimes painfully about what constitutes the best. The dramaturgical process taught me that conflict can be generative, not merely destructive. The work of creativity involves working through impassioned, power-laden difference.

My most dramatic experience of working through occurred during the dramaturgical process for Anna Deavere Smith's *Twilight: Los Angeles*, the subject of chapter 4. Our fiery backstage conflicts in the wake of the Los Angeles uprisings arguably reenacted the race wars, both reproducing and contesting models of liberal pluralism and multiculturalism. Our difficult yet ultimately reparative process challenged conventional dramaturgical models that assume liberal pluralist values of power-free conversation and unity of interpretation. Instead, our conflictual yet productive dramaturgical process illuminated the incommensurability of interpretations and the repressive gesture in "harmony."

In contrast, the dramaturgical literature circulates tropes of dramaturgy as self-effacing labor. Mary Luckhurst (2008) analyzes dramaturgy's emergence as a professionalized discipline in the United Kingdom, arguing that despite its "secrecy" and "invisibility," dramaturgy is critically significant for the making of plays and to the theater industry. André Lepecki and Cindy Brizzell (2003) characterize the dramaturg as unobtrusive, feminine helpmate whose labor resembles the intricate, domestic craft of weaving. A conventional dramaturg is diplomatic, an idealized mother, who "solves problems, smoothes out the psychosis of the production and, upon request, must always be able to provide the right answer" (Lepecki and Brizell 2003, 15). Shelley Orr (2014) advocates for the dramaturg's "critical proximity" rather than critical distance, urging dramaturgs to respond in the first person, rather than acting as stand-in for the audience. The operative assumption is that standard theatrical protocols discourage a dramaturg from boldly stating her opinions.

Conventional dramaturgy as delicate weaving, a fantasy of the maternal, or ventriloquist for an audience cannot capture our spirited backstage dramas on *Twilight*. Though we shared the common goal of mounting the best play possible, Smith's openness to commentary and the impossibility of providing a single right answer to "soothe" race and class oppression interrupted any fantasy of dramaturgy as healing consolation. We did try to anticipate audience reaction, but as I later elaborate, this proved impossible—vividly illustrating the intentional fallacy. Throughout, we more closely approximated D. J. Hopkins's notions of co-creation and dramaturgy as countertext, aimed at "starting trouble" (2015). We dramaturgs on *Twilight* were often troublemakers in a high-stakes drama in which we were battling theatrical convention and the erasure/oppressive representations of people of color on the American stage.

Magda Romanska's wide-ranging anthology (2014) surveys the place of dramaturgy historically and in the present moment. She defines a dramaturg's key function as knowing "how to fix a play" (more difficult, she implies, than writing the play), for a dramaturg has "comprehensive knowledge of dramatic structure" (2). Both the scope of the anthology and of dramaturgy spans "production process, research, literary office management, audience outreach and public relations" (5), in sites from "opera to musical theatre; from dance and multimedia to filmmaking, video game design, and robotics" (14). Translation between cultures and among disciplines is a key dramaturgical function. Simply put, dramaturgs are charged with "making meaning." Romanska ends with a field-defining claim: if the twentieth century is the century of the auteur, "the twenty-first century will be the century of the dramaturg" (14).

Though I remain skeptical of territorial pronouncements, I am sympathetic to the effort to illuminate the indispensable creative labor that occurs behind the scenes and to claim for it a constitutive role. I highlight dramaturgical critique as more than aesthetic practice tout court. It is an intellectual/political intervention, a step toward the reparative. Dramaturgical critique counters "the deep-rooted suspicion of working models that insist on a dynamic relationship between critical reflection and artistic practice" (Luckhurst 2008, 2).

The interanimation of critical reflection and artistic practice informs my work as dramaturg and this book as a whole. My abilities as a cultural critic are precisely the skills I could offer the creative team. Unlike the position of critic, however, the position of dramaturg meant *full* participation, bearing responsibility for what goes onstage and having a stake in what happens. This political, ethical accountability persists despite the limits theatrical performance presents to authorial intentionality and to issues of control. In a collaborative form like theater, I can present arguments about the politics of representation, but I cannot force artists to take my advice. Nor can any of us fully predict the reception of the play. As the intentional fallacy long ago taught us, authorial (and dramaturgical) intention never guarantees meaning. In chapter 4, I argue that audiences can and will produce multiple, often discrepant interpretations that upend one's intentions.

Knowing that nothing is ever perfect, that any intervention is limited and that as dramaturg, one serves only in an advisory capacity, one must still intervene. The awareness of limitation and accountability resonate throughout this book, shaping an intellectual/political/artistic practice that goes beyond conventional anthropological fieldwork and its "complicity" (Marcus 1998). One cannot create a perfect production, but it can be, in object relations terms, "good enough" (Winnicott 1953)—and the degrees matter. Critique as the mobilization of analysis and theory constitutes a theoretical/political/aesthetic intervention that aims for the "good enough," even as we deploy the ideal as a politically necessary fantasy.[15]

Our dramaturgical process on *Twilight* serves as a political allegory for intervention, a *politics of affiliation* that began from presumptions of difference and partial alliance, rather than an unproblematized "unity." Affiliation evokes membership in social institutions rather than blood ties, in anthropological kinship studies (albeit problematic for its heterosexual presumptions). I see our conflict as ultimately reparative.

Dramaturgical Critique as Reparative Critique

By deploying "critique," I address currently circulating binaries (critique/activism, critique/reparation) in arguments in cultural studies around the notion of negative critique and ideology critique (Cvetkovich 2012).

These accounts are, paradoxically, suspicious of a hermeneutics of suspicion. This argument assumes multiple forms, from surface reading (Best and Marcus 2009) to an emphasis on "care and concern" (Latour 2004) to a turn from "paranoid" to "reparative" reading (Sedgwick 2003) to an argument that Brechtian analytics and pornography share a logic of unveiling (Chow 2012).[16] The turn against critique views critique—implicitly signified as New Historicism, poststructuralism, among other theoretical positions—as by definition destructive, out of touch with everyday commonsense, and/or divorced from affect. On an anecdotal level, I encounter opposition to critique in the form of the admonition that we should forego critiques of theorists/artists who are political allies. We are told to offer alternatives instead. Critique is split off and devalued in favor of activism, care and concern, the reparative. From this perspective, *reparative critique* is an oxymoron.

Sedgwick associates critique with the hermeneutics of suspicion, a vertical spatiality that unmasks underlying truths, and Klein's paranoid position. She proposes the alongside and planar relations as instantiating the reparative. Yet Klein was not a rigid stage theorist; we occupy shifting positions and never excise "paranoia" or the projection of aggressive impulses associated with fantasies of fusion. Paranoia is always possible, even useful; trajectories are not linear or hierarchical. Heather Love (2010) and Ashley Barnwell (2015) note that Sedgwick herself practices critique to "unmask" the assumptions underlying the Foucaultian-inflected positions she outlines. Barnwell argues, "Though Latour and Sedgwick motion toward the utopia of new genres, they re-enlist critique to express their concern. This highlights the ongoing utility of critical interpretation and encourages us to rethink the suggestion that a hermeneutics of suspicion is no longer salient" (Barnwell 2015, 923). Our current political regime makes critique even more urgent, as "alternative facts" and the reconsolidation of race, gender, sexuality, class, and settler colonialist hierarchies reign. Critique "reveals" the ways power relations can pervade realms in which they are thought to be absent.

I argue in spirited response to the turn against critique that reparative critique can create political alternatives. Dramaturgical critique serves as exemplary; it is a crucial phase in the creative process, necessary for effective activist, artistic intervention. Dramaturgical critique serves the collective goal of putting up a progressive, compelling production; it is not separate from or antithetical to activism. Critique is a pivotal step in creating different theatrical/political alternatives, for without a finely grained analysis of what is problematic and why, how can we address those problems, to remake worlds?

That said, I am highly aware that any critique, dramaturgical or otherwise, risks appropriation as sheer negativity. For example, the anthropological autocritique of the 1970s and 1980s was seen by too many, both inside and outside the discipline, as an admission of disciplinary failure, rather than as a salutary intervention. Anthropology's confrontation with its colonialist history at its best fundamentally rethought disciplinary foundations and scholarly inquiry itself: the enmeshment of all disciplines in Eurocentric hegemonies and the reproduction of power/knowledge. Critique, including autocritique, can be salutary.

I deploy critique as a step toward the reparative. My critique of the unbearable whiteness of mainstream theater and theater's racialized economies sets the stage for the work of Smith and Hwang and for my attempts at reparative creativity through playwriting. Sometimes it is necessary to illuminate problematic assumptions that "underlie" our tacit aesthetic and theoretical common sense. As one way of enacting reparative critique, demonstrating the imbrications of the racial, aesthetic, political, and theoretical, I turn to the aesthetics and politics of genre.

Genre as Worldmaking

Aesthetic genres like drama and "nonfiction" genres like ethnography make worlds through form and narrative. In the theater, specific conventions introduce audiences to the "world of the play," and a good playwright must establish that world early on, lest the audience be confused—unless confusion is the playwright's goal, another narrative strategy. Unlike written forms, the worldmaking in theater depends on production: the acting, lighting, space, set design, costumes, pacing, music, and sound that give life to the staged world. Anthropological meditations on form since at least the late 1970s see ethnography as a form of writing that creates a cultural world rather than transparently recording a brute reality. Rhetorical moves such as first-person vignette and vivid description establish the ethnographer's "I was there" authority, while the text as a whole typically deploys an objectivist tone lending an air of scientific/theoretical rigor. These narrative conventions write into existence the world of transnational flows, neoliberalism, the Anthropocene, and the theater industry, just as play and production make theatrical worlds.

The Color and Gender of Drama

Worldmaking advances the bold argument that *race and gender pervade aesthetic form*. When actors step on the stage and writers sit at their laptops, they enter a world defined by assumptions about art in general and about drama in particular. What counts as theater? What counts as a play? What is "good" acting? In short, what is aesthetically proper, pleasing, and above all intelligible? These assumptions can be implicated in processes of racialization. In drama, Aristotelian structures of conflict/catharsis in the "well-made play," the narrative strategies of naturalism/realism, among other formal considerations, are implicated in the reproduction of power, as numerous analysts, from Marxists to poststructuralists, have argued.[17]

Aristotelian structure sends a protagonist on a journey; s/he encounters obstacles along the way, overcoming and/or succumbing to those obstacles in the denouement. The existential dilemmas of the protagonist are foregrounded, while all other characters are by definition ancillary. Supporting characters serve the protagonist's narrative arc, through active assistance or by providing necessary dramatic obstacles. In our historical formation, the race, gender, and sexuality of the protagonist remain predictable, despite increasing emphasis on diversity in the performing arts. The normative straight white male subject still constitutes the Universal, while minoritarian Others exist to support the protagonist's arc (Deggans 2011; McLeod 2015).

For Smith and Hwang, as well as for my own plays, the work is not about a conventional hero journey in which an individual quest ends in triumphant resolution. All of us spotlight characters who are minoritarian subjects, and we eschew happy closure and epistemological certainty. In Smith's case, audiences encounter an array of people who often have never been represented on the mainstream US stage. Smith is most subversive of well-made play structure; her plays are modular assemblages of individual portraits without a central protagonist, evoking circular rather than linear structure. Though she addresses volatile social issues, she does not offer a prescriptive (re)solution. She is interested in the "process of the problems" (A. D. Smith 2002). Hwang's *Yellow Face* features an Asian American male protagonist whose white, male, Pirandellian doppelganger competes for audience attention. The play resolves the doppelganger's identity but ends with an openness that offers no definitive resolution. My play *Seamless* features an Asian American woman as protagonist and ends with epistemological indeterminacy. How do we piece together a history from fragments of conflicting, ebbing memories, from a spotty historical record? All three of us address issues of structural inequality that cannot be resolved in the play. Instead, we turn to the world outside the theater: the political, the communal, the relational.

That said, I am not fetishizing form. *Seamless* reproduces the classic well-made play structure, though it juxtaposes scenes of different style and tone. One intervention would be to proliferate the kinds of protagonists visible onstage and to engage "realist" forms to represent minoritarian subjects "realistically," as I have argued (Kondo 1997). Another would be to disturb aesthetic form itself, creating alternative forms, as Smith and Hwang have done and as the aesthetic avant-garde continues to do—though the avant-garde depends on the conventions against which it rebels and can never remain "avant" for long.

My argument contests conservative, Eurocentric approaches to the arts and to cultural politics. Assumptions about the arts in general tend to reify the aesthetic sublime, positing the autonomy of art and the notion that art transcends what one theater artist called "mere sociology." Though cultural studies has long problematized such notions, decontextualized figurations of the aesthetic sublime remain alive among many artists themselves. Such assumptions are deeply implicated in the reproduction of racial ideologies. From such a perspective, the invocation of issues of social justice or even practices of nontraditional casting can constitute a capitulation to "mere sociology," thus sullying the purity of aesthetic form, an issue I address extensively in chapter 2.

The same unwitting implication in racialization and Eurocentricity undergirds the discourse of universality that too often means transhistorical similarity based on European models—in drama, Shakespeare and the Greeks. Consequently, I argue that the discourse of the universal, as it circulates in the arts and particularly in theater, is racialized and gendered. The normative universal subject is presumed to be free of the markings of race, gender, class, age, or nationality. Let me be clear. I am not suggesting that we abandon attention to the "classics." Rather, I am simply pointing out the racialized consequences of celebrating only Eurocentric models.[18] How "universal" and how racially unmarked is aesthetic form? How "universal" is the even more fundamental binary of fiction/nonfiction?

Remixing Genres: Drama and Nonfiction

Smith and Hwang transgress the borders between truth and fiction, the ethnographic and the literary. These innovations are not merely decorative. They challenge theatrical convention and our most fundamental assumptions about the real, leading us to question accepted notions of genre.

Provoking reflection on both scholarly and dramatic form, Smith mobilizes the powers of the sensorium in what could be called performative ethnography, staging plays that draw upon events and interviews from communities located in place and time, much as an ethnographer or journalist might. Unlike ethnographers, she performs verbatim interview excerpts onstage to create portrayals of characters located in place and time. Hwang's *Yellow Face* crosses the boundaries of memoir, autobiography, comedy, journalism, documentary, and well-made play. Both artists transgress conventional boundaries of identity (race, gender, sexuality, age) and form (documentary, journalism, ethnography, well-made play, comedy, performance art, history), problematizing binaries between art and politics, representation and the real, mind and body. Smith and Hwang expose the arbitrariness of racial classifications while insisting on the ways these classifications remain imbued with creative, coercive power to constitute our reality. Performance allows them to mobilize the powers of the sensorium to move people emotionally as well as intellectually, expanding the rhetorical power of ethnography's textual analysis in ways that can touch lives.

Didier Fassin articulates the divide between the real and the true, the anthropological and the literary, when he asks, "How, then, can social scientists recapture lives? . . . And how different is their enterprise from the creations of fiction?" (Fassin 2014, 42). He cites HBO's *The Wire* as seeming more real than do academic studies (Fassin 2014, 48). Fassin's objective is in part to reclaim the "real" for ethnography, for it establishes "the credibility of the text," though he complicates the nostrum that literature reveals the true, while the social sciences are tethered to the real. Crapanzano (1980) questioned the social scientific fetishizing of the real, contrasting it to the truth of the evocative register. I seek to heighten the literarily true, the affective, in academic discourse and to complicate further the binary between the real and the true.

Smith and Hwang engage documentary and nonfiction in ways that problematize the real as brute facticity. Documentary film relies on its "truth" as a transparent recording of the real. Documentary theater, because of its obvious staging and Smith and Hwang's engagement with cross-race/cross-gender performance, immediately produces a reflexive awareness of our suspension of disbelief; documentary film conventionally does not. In a Brechtian sense, documentary theater introduces an estrangement effect from the outset; at some level we are aware that the actor is not the character/interviewee represented onstage.

Each artist offers slightly different perspectives on this question. Smith uses verbatim excerpts from interviewees; hers is the version of documentary theater most faithful to the canon of verisimilitude. Yet even in her work, originary identity is problematized, for we are compelled to reflect on the disjuncture between Smith and her "real" interviewee. Chapter 3 argues that this rupture is even more disturbing, destabilizing our customary coordinates of identity. Hwang's *Yellow Face* combines documentary material—interviews, excerpts from newspapers, magazines, and trade publications—with personal memoir and fictional characters in a genre-bending narrative. The play's protagonist is DHH, not David Henry Hwang; the relationship between the two is ambiguous, fluid. Through a dispute between DHH and a journalist for the *New York Times* who was responsible for breaking multiple stories that recirculated tropes of Yellow Peril, Hwang explicitly unsettles the permeable border between fiction (drama) and nonfiction (journalism and, by extension, ethnography).

To call the work of these artists ethnographic, journalistic, historical, or documentary is not to reduce art to "mere sociology." Nor is it to construct a new category—ethnographic theater, for example—of which these artists are exemplars (Lucas 2006). Rather, my intent is to call attention to the ways these artists juxtapose, fissure, and expand our categories of genre: ethnography, art, journalism, theater, theory. In doing so, they deconstruct the conceit of art as the transcendent and the aesthetic sublime, of ethnography as an essentialist discourse of culture, and of theory as disembodied citation of canonical European thinkers. They draw attention to the imbrications of genre in making/unmaking racial hierarchy.

As they bring minoritarian concerns to a stage haunted by Eurocentric hegemonies, Smith and Hwang interrupt hegemonic assumptions: of the real, of form, of who belongs onstage, of the relation of art and politics.[19] Their interventions bear family resemblances to the reflexive turn and continuing textual experimentation in anthropology.

Making Theory, Bending Genre

I underline here the political and epistemological imperatives that drove the initial textual experimentations in the anthropology of the 1980s.[20] The questioning of the putative objectivity of ethnography and, by extension, any scholarly form, was one goal (Kondo 1986). Another was to problematize the politics of the colonial anthropological encounter, in effect dramatizing those interactions in order to question them (Crapanzano 1980; Dwyer 1987; Rabinow 1977). This book performs textual innovation as an intervention that disturbs power-laden genre conventions that marginalize the affective and the political.

One genealogy of experimental writing claims montage as model, inspired primarily by Benjamin and Barthes. Anthropologists have productively explored montage as episodic writing.[21] I both draw and depart from the cinematic implications of montage, juxtaposing disparate genres, including first-person narrative, drama, and conventional theoretical discourse. Segment titles reference the well-made play and musical theater ("Overture") as playful attempts at integrating drama with scholarly rhetoric. I write disparate voices in segments of different lengths and genres, rather than seeking a unifying staccato rhythm. In both styles, juxtaposition can jar. It disrupts the unity of the text. It forces the reader to adjust to stylistic shifts, highlighting the differences among different voices. Simultaneously, the sequencing of seemingly unrelated elements invites us to impose similarity upon contiguity, to make connections and find patterns among the disparate pieces.[22]

While recognizing the florescence of genre experimentation in Anthropology and other disciplines, I draw greatest inspiration from feminist work: Marta Savigliano's *Tango and the Political Economy of Passion* (1995) and Carolyn Steedman's *Landscape for a Good Woman* (1987). Savigliano's playful formal experimentation remixes postcolonial theory; first-person narrative; short plays; the fictional memoir of a cancan dancer; comparative analysis of the tango's reception in Argentina, Europe, and Japan; a feminist call; and the innovative theoretical argument that the metropole extracts "affect"—passion—in its consumption of Latin American otherness. Steedman's *Landscape for a Good Woman* interweaves memoir, biography of her working-class mother, working-class history, fairy tale, and psychoanalytic case study. She ends with a magnificent gesture of political refusal. In affect studies/queer theory, Ann Cvetkovich (2012) shares an exploration of multiple genres and a commitment to the reparative and to crafting identities through aesthetic practice. As I was contemplating splitting this book in two, separating the play from the critical essays, Renato Rosaldo (2013) published a volume combining academic essays with a full-length poetic work about the death of Michelle Rosaldo, my undergraduate mentor. At a crucial moment, Renato showed me that integration is possible.

I draw equal inspiration from theater artists: Brecht, Anna Deavere Smith, David Henry Hwang. All have deployed logics of juxtaposition. Brecht's *Verfremdungseffekt*—techniques of estrangement that interrupt the spectator's uncritical identification—aims to provoke the audience to reflect on the artifice of theater and by extension, the malleability and historicity of the social world (Brecht and Willett 1964). Brecht and Benjamin remind us that the aesthetics of illusionism and naturalism can deaden a critical spirit. A Brechtian play breaks the soporific effects of naturalism, interrupting the action with direct audience address, music, placards that announce scene titles, metatheatrical reflection (e.g., deus ex machina), techniques that expose theater's theatricality (e.g., keeping the actors onstage, allowing us to see them change costumes). For Brecht, these estrangement effects can awaken a critical consciousness in the spectator that could be harnessed to intervene in the world.

Daphne Brooks refigures Brechtian alienation, bringing together theater studies with diaspora studies in her concept of Afro-alienation acts: "The condition of alterity converts into cultural expressiveness and characterizes marginal cultural positions as well as a tactic that the marginalized seized on and reordered in the self-making process" (Brooks 2006, 4–6). Afro-alienation registers histories of trauma and captivity, even as it produces subversive, critical performances. Phillip Brian Harper (2015, 1) argues against realist representational strategies in African American art, offering an "abstractionist aesthetics" that takes inspiration from Brechtian alienation effects as a way to challenge "social facts." Reparative critique as the "challenging of social facts" launches the process of worldmaking.

Form as Theory

Worldmaking follows a Kleinian trajectory, from my romance with theater, followed by the shattering of fantasy through the encounter with the "real." Reparative engagements with the artists follow, spotlighting behind-the-scenes labor and process: acting, authorship, dramaturgy, writing, and revision. The book culminates in my own attempt at reparative creativity through playwriting and one of my full-length plays.

The overture and the first entr'acte began in the first person, to specify my affective, intellectual, political positioning and my stakes: my romance with theater is tempered by racialized affective violence as a confrontation with the psychoanalytic "real" that frustrates our fantasies. Racism pervades the theater world as it pervades all others, but *reparative creativity* offers possibilities to work through the effects of affective and structural violence.

Act 1, "Mise-en-Scène" (this chapter and chapter 2) sets the stage. This chapter, "Theoretical Scaffolding, Formal Architecture" establishes the book's theoretical world, as set design builds a theatrical world. Chapter 2, "Racialized Economies," analyzes the racialized, gendered structure of the theater industry, the ethnographic "setting." My anthropological approach leads me to areas too often neglected in theater and performance studies or that are subsumed under a monolithic "neoliberalism." I examine theater as an art industry, including definitions of art as a meaningful category, funding, salaries, structural inequalities in casting and hiring practices, hierarchies in revenue, artistic prestige, and size among theaters, professional associations, and circulating discourses of race and power-evasive liberalism, among other factors. Understanding the work of Smith, Hwang, and my own attempts as playwright—that is, to understand processes of production and performance, both onstage and in everyday life—requires analysis of these powerful, partially determining structures and force fields.

Within such a world, the (too rare) life-giving moments in theater become even more urgently necessary. Act 2, "Creative Labor" (chapters 3, 4, and 5) foregrounds the creative processes of Anna Deavere Smith and David Henry Hwang. My analytics valorize "practice" in theater studies as theoretically significant: acting, playwriting and authorship (interviewing as writing), processes of revision, and dramaturgy. The work of creativity enacts reparative critique, challenging liberal ideology's split of aesthetics from politics: the liberal humanist subject, authorship as the work of the singular imagination, dramaturgy as polite suggestion, power-free conversation, and the audience as unified.

Chapter 3, "(En)Acting Theory," spotlights Anna Deavere Smith's artistic practices of acting and writing as challenges to power-evasive humanisms and the sovereign subject. Her linguistic, processual approach to acting disrupts the dominant mode of actor training in the United

States: derivations of the Method and its presumptions of psychic interiority. Her use of interviews to construct dramatic texts and her openness to dramaturgical input challenge assumptions of authorship to include power-laden intersubjectivity, thematizing the intersubjective nature of all writing and all artistic and academic production. Smith's work destabilizes the whole subject and performs reparative mirroring, when minoritarian subjects can glimpse an existence in the public sphere. Mainstream readings of Smith's work reproduce power-evasive liberal humanism: "the human spirit" and "artistic genius" in Smith's tour de force, one-woman shows. While remaining aware of power's complexity, I offer a progressive reading of her work that contests mainstream reception.

Chapter 4, "The Drama behind the Drama," theorizes our volatile dramaturgical process in *Twilight: Los Angeles 1992*, Smith's play based on the so-called LA riots. Our "fiery battles" over racial representation instantiated a politics of agonistics (Mouffe 2013) and what I call a *politics of affiliation*: respectful yet passionate dissent that can ground a progressive politics. Our process challenged regnant, power-evasive models of dramaturgy. Adjudicating issues of race both then and now requires frankness, an ability to deal with conflict, and a high tolerance for having one's assumptions assailed. Smith opened herself to those possibilities, and my respect for her art is deepened by her ability to work through painful clashes of opinion. The dramaturgs deployed critique in service of a production that remains a historic intervention in American theater: its direct engagement with urgent, timely social issues; the formal innovations Smith's work presents; and its array of characters never before seen on the American stage. The volatile backstage drama ultimately served as reparative critique.

Chapter 5, "Revising Race," written from my positions as critic, spectator, and informal dramaturg, highlights David Henry Hwang's process of revising his play *Yellow Face*. The play vividly deconstructs the contradictions animating the "postracial." I explore Hwang's struggles between opposing points of view: a liberal pluralism that stresses the openness of racial categories and a power-sensitive perspective that recognizes racism's persistence. While I read the play as any drama critic might, I highlight Hwang's process of revision—informed by multiple factors, including audience reaction, dramaturgical input from the creative team, and solicited notes such as mine—that moved the play from a liberal, relatively power-evasive stance on race to a more power-sensitive "final" New York version. Revision is central to a playwright's craft, representing the work of creativity in playwriting; a politics of agonistics can remake race through the clash of multiple, conflicting discourses within the "singular" subject.

Act 3, "Reparative Creativity," focuses on my relation to theater as a playwright. Chapter 6, "Playwriting as Reparative Creativity," analyzes my play *Seamless* as product of ongoing labor: unlearning the rhetorical conventions of academe, learning those of drama, exploring deep registers of painful emotion, and meeting structural challenges (race, gender, age, ethnicity, networks largely outside theater schools) as I seek to produce and market the play. I address questions of genre, the positionality of the ethnographer as scholar-artist, and the thematics of history, memory, and the afterlife of trauma. I engage autodramaturgy, providing historical context that might be in the program notes or lobby display at a production of my play. Above all, I advocate for expanding space in academic discourse for the creative and the affective, as strategies that allow us to move people intellectually, politically, and emotionally.

The book culminates with *Seamless*, a comic drama that stages the afterlife of historical trauma, arguing in a different register against the postracial. Based loosely on interviews with my parents and deploying the form of the well-made play, *Seamless* stages the continuing affective reverberations of Japanese American incarceration in generations born after the camps. How can we know the past? Our parents? How reliable is memory? Is the past ever really past? I juxtapose humor, satire, and the fantastic with more poignant moments, as modes of social critique and as techniques to provoke affective responses. *Seamless* closes the book with an enactment of open-endedness. Hope and the desire to know cannot be extinguished, even in the face of the (im)possibility of knowing.

I intersperse short entr'actes among the chapters. The vignettes serve as bridges from one chapter to the next, introducing themes in the chapter that follows. The first entr'acte is a pivot for the rest of the book, writing the impact of affective violence. The second revisits my experiences in acting class, sparking epiphanies about the differences between theatrical and academic modes of embodiment and the body as emotional archive. The final entr'acte illuminates one of many institutional barriers—the acting company's structure—to producing work by artists of color.

As a title, *Worldmaking* felt compelling on multiple levels. Above all, it calls forth political action animated by political hope. In making our artistic and scholarly work, and in political activism conventionally defined, we try to transform the worlds we inhabit, despite inevitably partial outcomes. "Worlds" invokes the multiple levels at which such interventions occur: the world of the play, our social world, Klein's inner world populated by our inner objects, and the world-making assumptions of theory and culture. Making "the world of the play" can offer opportunities to make/unmake/remake worlds inside and outside the theater.

My emphasis on repair and the reparative throughout the book acknowledges that our worlds are already given, interrupting the Master Subject omnipotence of creation ex nihilo. We are remade as we seek to make. Worldmaking is always collaborative, in relation with other people, abstract forces, objects, and materials that are themselves imbued with potentiality. The reparative highlights the hard work required to make repairs, in service of an integration that is always incomplete and unstable.

The subtitle was an equally deliberate choice, particularly the phrase "the work of creativity." As one theater professional said to me, "those are two words you never hear together!" Creativity is more than the outpouring of divine inspiration channeled through an artistic genius. It is labor. The work of creativity links economics, disciplined interactions with vibrant materials and techniques, and the many elements of performance onstage.[23] Like artisanal craft, the work of creativity is organized, methodical, laborious, absorbing, all-consuming, thrilling. It mobilizes years of training and embodied experience. Further, in theater the work of creativity is never finished. Different versions of "the same" play might exist, as in Smith's many versions of *Twilight*; playwrights may choose to revisit their work in later years, as Hwang has done with *M. Butterfly*. Toward that end, I highlight the differences among various productions of Smith's and Hwang's works. Audiences never see a definitive play; they see a particular production, and that production is in turn different every night—the dramatic work is the result of the ongoing work of creativity.

The politics of performance addresses a career-long mission to unsettle the binary between material and ideal, aesthetics and politics, aesthetics and economics, aesthetics and the social. Creativity, imagination, and the arts are not separate from "the world"; they are zones where power relations—in this book, race in particular—are reproduced and contested.

The work of creativity underscores the training, disciplined labor, and prodigious effort required for artistic production that are inseparable from historical political economies in arts industries and from historically specific cultural ideologies. Creativity takes work; it performs work. It engenders racial affect that can be both life-giving and life-diminishing. It can secure the hegemony of the dominant—the "war machine," the dominance of the straight white middle-class male as Universal subject. It makes race. Simultaneously, the work of creativity can enable the psychic working through of inevitable violence and aggression, enabling provisional, reparative integrations.

I thus come full circle from my first book, *Crafting Selves*, which sought to theorize the aesthetics of factory labor, the cultural assumptions about work that shaped everyday performances of gendered work identities on the shop floor, and the art in artisanal production. In my first and second books I sought to "elevate" factory production and fashion, respectively; our metaphors index the power-laden hierarchical structures that denigrate artisanal work and dismiss fashion as craft at best. In *Worldmaking* I pull aesthetic transcendence back to earth. Creativity and imagination are not free-floating. Whose visions reach the stage? Which artists are produced? Can they make a living from those productions? *The work of creativity*—the creative labor of theater artists—gives us strategies to remake worlds, from the world of the theater to inner worlds shattered by affective violence to political-economic structures. To embark on this journey requires mapping our coordinates: the racialized, gendered economies of the theater industry.

chapter 2

Racialized Economies

> The Public Theater is perhaps the only theater left in the country where diversity is absolutely core to the mission. The theater can't exist without it; it's fundamental to it. . . . George (C. Wolfe, artistic director, 1993–2004) . . . did a remarkable thing in his time here because he really did make this the first major theater in the country that could not be called a white theater. Every other theater is basically a white theater that does outreach. . . . And then you have the ethnic-specific theaters.
>
> —Eustis 2007

Theater as an art world (Becker 2008), art industry (Adorno 2010), and field of cultural production (Bourdieu 1993) is a culturally meaningful domain constituted through the forces of power-laden ideologies, institutional hierarchies, and racialized economies.[1] I sketch key political-economic and institutional structures within which artists of color must work; these structures make race. For those outside theater, this context sets the scene for what is to follow; for theater professionals, I hope to defamiliarize the familiar in ways that could offer fresh insights. For both categories of reader, I argue that the economies and structures of theater are profoundly racialized and gendered.

Oskar Eustis, current artistic director of the Public Theater—the artistic pinnacle for many theater artists—directly comments on the racialization of theater. Eustis contrasts "major theaters" to "ethnic-specific theaters," which apparently occupy a different, lesser echelon. He notes that most theater is not universal but racially marked as white. What discursive, institutional, political-economic, and historical forces overdetermine this appraisal of American theater as racialized and hierarchized?

Racialized, gendered economies are pivotal here. When I began to study the theater industry as an anthropologist, I was shocked—and continue to be startled—by the relative underfunding of theater. Financial precarity is tied both to the relegation of art to the domain of the superfluous and to contemporary articulations of capitalism, generally labeled neoliberalism, that emphasize privatization and the withdrawal of the state from public funding. Neoliberalism—too often a monolithic reification as it circulates in the academic literature—indexes within US art worlds a series of crucial developments: defunding of the arts, moves toward privatization, corporate funding, and entrepreneurial individualism (Harvie 2013; Win 2014). These forces in turn shape the lives of theater artists and remake structural hierarchies, including race, class, and gender.

I begin with a brief sketch of the ideological underpinnings of the arts and their consequences for artists. The penurious existence of most theater artists is justified through the relegation of the arts to the domain of the impractical or, in its auratic guise, the transcendent. This stance reifies the arts as the aesthetic sublime, floating above mundane social and economic structures. The ideological split produces multiple effects; one is the relative impoverishment of artists. I focus primarily on playwrights, given my own creative work and the barriers I have confronted. We need further studies of race/gender/class and how these shape career trajectories of all artists, producers, designers, stage managers, and crew; we need more ethnographic studies of artistic training and education, funding agencies, and decision making in arts organizations, especially about how particular works/artists are chosen for funding and production.

The theater industry organizes theaters according to size, ticket sales, and prestige; the correlation is approximate, as commercial, artistic, and critical success do not necessarily coincide. I analyze both the economic dilemmas all theaters face and the problems particular to theaters of each institutional category (intimate, regional, Broadway/commercial): the controversy over actors' wages in intimate theater, financial incentives for regional theaters to serve as tryout spaces for Broadway, and the move of multinational conglomerates into Broadway.

Financial instability and structural hierarchies in the theater world make racial, gendered disparities. What plays reach the main stage? How do artists' careers unfold? The race/gender/age of the actors, the roles they enact, the theater's vision, the audience, marketing, and the comfort level of artistic directors with multiracial material, among other factors, come into play. Financial considerations can limit cast size, technological requirements, and aesthetic form, genre, and content, encouraging conservatism: naturalism, whiteness as the universal, and noncontroversial subject matter.

Finally, I return to the literatures on neoliberalism and performance. While I acknowledge the political economic, epistemic shifts that "inaugurate" the (neo)liberal, I problematize the theorizing of (neo)liberalism as a monolithic force and as radically new, to argue for the possibility of a progressive cultural politics. Theater and performance, in their imaginative powers of transformation, their ephemerality and intangible product, can challenge capitalist logics. I emphasize theater's *potentialities*, setting the stage for the work of theater artists Anna Deavere Smith and David Henry Hwang and, at the other end of the spectrum, my own fledgling playwriting. All theater artists are subject to the disciplines of the industry. In order to remake racial formations, we need to understand those disciplines.

I begin with our commonsense assumptions about the arts, artists, and aesthetics. Far from innocent, these assumptions inform a political economy that marginalizes the arts and shapes artistic careers.

The Arts as Cultural Work

The assumption that the arts are luxuries that transcend the practicalities of everyday life has dominated Western thought since nineteenth-century Romanticism (Wolff 1993; Watt 1957). Some analysts trace the notion of artist as singular artistic genius to the Renaissance, departing from guild workshops and communalism characteristic of the Middle Ages (Hauser 1968; Wolff 1993). The Romantic notion of the artist in the nineteenth century arose with industrial capitalism and individualism, marked by shifts from systems of patronage to a dealer-critic system that left artists vulnerable to markets. Until that point, artists had been far more thoroughly integrated into social structures, showing in academies, not set apart as maverick creatives (Wolff 1993, 11). The rise of the dealer-critic system further unmoored artists from secure affiliations with patronage or social class. Catherine Belsey makes a similar argument for literature. The theory of expressive realism—"that literature reflects the reality of experience as it is perceived by one (especially gifted) individual who expresses it in a discourse which enables other individuals to recognize it as true"—accompanied the rise of industrial capitalism (Belsey 1980, 7). Expressive realism and the elaboration of the artist's heightened sensibility developed roughly during the mid-nineteenth century in England, integrating Aristotelian notions of mimesis with nineteenth-century Romanticism.

Ideologies of art as the product of ineffable genius are located in particular historical formations, as are artists' locations in economic structures. Far from transcending economic imperatives, artists have always needed economic support. Raymond Williams begins his account of art and institutions with the bard, who was part of court structure as an "instituted artist" (R. Williams 1981, 18). David Hesmondhalgh streamlines Williams's typologies of artisanal institutions and artists' support: patronage, from the Middle Ages to the nineteenth century, when artists were supported by royalty and the wealthy; market professional, from the nineteenth century to the present, when art works are sold on the market; corporate professional, early twentieth century onward, as corporate culture industries hire artists (Hesmondhalgh 2013, 50).

Accordingly, I spotlight the labor of artistic work. The aesthetic/material opposition pits art against commerce, implying that the arts rise above material needs. One result is the stereotype of the starving artist who sacrifices for art; such a view fails to recognize the arts as cultural work. Paltry wages and nonexistent benefits seem justified as a marker of artists' moral superiority, while financial success indexes artistic "sellout." The inability of theater artists to make a living doing theater is a logical outgrowth of this bifurcation of art and work, art and commerce. Thinking of the arts as sublime keeps artists poor (Gutting 2016). This pervasive ideological binary between the aesthetic and the material currently operates within the political-economic episteme called neoliberal capitalism.

Neoliberalism, the Arts, and Race

Neoliberalism in the theoretical literatures is both unstable signifier and reified object, generally signifying an epistemic, historical, and economic shift toward privatization, the retreat of the welfare state, and the financialization of human life (N. Rose 1999; Harvey 2005; W. Brown 2015). Within such an episteme, the arts, like other domains of social life, are cast in economic terms, specifically those of finance capital. Analysts often associate neoliberalism with Pinochet's 1973 coup in Chile and the rise of Chicago-trained economists in restructuring Chile's economy, and with the regimes of Reagan and Thatcher in the 1980s.

But how "neo" is neoliberalism? Lisa Lowe locates neoliberalism within the *longue durée* of capitalism and colonial histories:

> What is currently theorized as the financialization of life as "human capital" in neoliberalism brutally . . . occurred and continues to occur throughout the course of modern empires . . . critical social theory's most astute analyses of neoliberalism . . . continue the elision of the longer history of colonization in ways that reiterate the Eurocentric blindness of liberal political philosophy. The colonial world is mentioned . . . as if their history begins with the International Monetary Fund and the World Bank. . . . Even more importantly, mourning Western liberal democracy as the only form for imagining "the political" universalizes the future of politics . . . subsuming the histories of decolonization in Asia, Africa, Latin America, the Caribbean, and the Middle East to the normative narrative of liberal democracy. (Lowe 2015, 197–98)

Theorists of (neo)liberalism too often repeat the legacies of colonialism, yet again recentering the West. Rather than radical historical rupture, (neo)liberalism represents Amiri Baraka's "the changing same" (1967).

(Neo)liberal shifts within capitalism affect the arts in distinctive ways. The global financial crises of the 1970s and 1980s (Hesmondhalgh 2013; Harvey 2005) spurred moves toward finance capital, privatization, and individual responsibility. Privatization spelled the withdrawal of the state from the public sphere generally and from arts funding in particular. This dismantling of the welfare state is often cited as a key feature of (neo)liberalism, which demanded of artists and artistic organizations an increased reliance on individual, corporate, and foundation funding to compensate for decimated state-sponsored grants.

These developments heighten the financial precarity of the theater industry. The post–New Deal United States has done little to subsidize the arts, in contrast to many countries around the world. For example, though a national theater can be problematic in its reinscription of the nation-state and its reification of national culture (who is represented in the nation?), the existence of such theaters internationally indexes the relative lack of support for theater in the United States. Though no singular definition of national theater exists, these institutions often enjoy some degree of government support and act as symbolic capital for the nation-state. Ghana, Kenya, and Ethiopia have national theaters; Japan maintains dedicated spaces for the traditional performing arts. Korea subsidizes national theaters, both for new Korean/international work and for traditional forms. Argentina and Venezuela have government-subsidized national theaters. The French government partially funds the Comédie-Française, the first national theater. The Royal National Theatre in the United Kingdom receives roughly 17 percent of its funding from the National Arts Council. It remains a premier cultural institution in the British arts scene (National Theatre 2017). For artists, government funds can provide time, subsidized training for young artists, and precious resources for production. Theater artists working in both Europe and the United States often comment on the longer rehearsal periods possible in Europe rather than the usual three or four weeks in the United States. Stephen Wadsworth, who directed Smith in the *Let Me Down Easy* world premiere, commented, "It made me wish that we were living in France . . . where her work would be celebrated with endless support. She would be given a theater where she could go every day . . . performing anytime she wanted" (Wadsworth 2008). Such artistic support is impossible in the United States.

Policies that retreat from public funding render scant support even less available, forcing a turn to other sources: private foundations, corporations, self-funding, crowdsourcing. Even in a British context, where state funding remains relatively robust compared to the United States despite the Conservative budget cuts, Jen Harvie (2013) characterizes the contemporary period as one of defunding, requiring the "artrepreneur" to multitask and to be "flexible." Within the United States, the defunding of the arts—for example, budget cuts to the NEH and the NEA—profoundly affects artists and arts organizations. Even though these institutions were not necessarily at the vanguard for support for edgy work or artists of color, they were among prominent potential funding sources.

The NEA controversies of the 1980s and early 1990s marked a turning point. The Republican Revolution in Congress in 1994 laid the groundwork for neoconservatives to slash appropriations to the arts, based on their objections to work they deemed offensive. The defunding and subsequent legal controversies surrounding the work of visual artists Andres Serrano and Robert Mapplethorpe and the performance art of Holly Hughes, Karen Finley, Tim Miller, and John Fleck characterize this regime. The performance artists (known as the NEA Four) brought a lawsuit against the NEA's rescinding of grants for artists and their sponsoring institutions; the lawsuit went to the Supreme Court. The controversy resulted in devastating cuts to the NEA, including the virtual elimination of grants to individual artists and the reduction of the budget by a third (Ivey 2008, 253).

The (neo)liberal state's abandonment of the arts promotes corporatization and privatization, forcing a reliance on private donations. Dependence on philanthropy can have multiple deleterious effects: the funding of only "pet projects" of the wealthy, the normalization of state withdrawal from the support of cultural production, and the aura of magnanimity and moral virtue that can further consolidate the hegemony of the wealthy, to suggest a few (Harvie 2013, 157).

In the arts industries as elsewhere, this shift often assumes the guise of the entrepreneurial individual and the notion of personal responsibility. (Neo)liberal political economies compel artists to promote their own work. New technologies and social media feed this trend. Now it is common practice for artists to maintain a website, to develop a brand (Banet-Weiser 2012), and to mobilize social media to publicize their art. Frequent Instagramming, Tweeting, and Facebooking become compulsory self-marketing strategies. I have heard artists brainstorming about their Twitter feeds—a tweet a day from rehearsal in order to generate interest in their plays—while they bemoaned the pressure to market. Larger theaters often have dedicated staff for social media marketing in their public relations departments. The subject-citizen as human capital within (neo)liberal rationality means that "homo oeconomicus as human capital is concerned with enhancing its portfolio value in all domains of its life, an activity undertaken through practices of self-investment and attracting investors" (W. Brown 2015, 33–34). Neoliberal rationality fosters the necessity to attract Twitter followers and Kickstarter donors, and to "invest" in one's career.

In order to achieve success, artists are increasingly pushed toward multitasking and flexibility. Emily Martin's analysis of flexibility as a value permeating medicine, business, and academe (E. Martin 1994), and Marxist studies of flexible specialization assume renewed salience (Sabel and Piore 1986; Harvie 2013; Harvey 2005). Martin cautions us to beware of flexibility as a technology of capitalism. In an insecure (gigging) economy, firms increasingly rely on part-time/freelance labor. The pressure on workers to remain flexible makes a virtue of economic necessity.

The requirement to multitask pushes artists to master grant writing, marketing strategy, and social media skills. Certainly, developing multiple skills seems inherently positive. Yet how much time away from the actual making of art do these other tasks demand? The imperative to multitask operates under the guise of individual initiative, reinscribing the (neo)liberal, choosing, psychoanalytically omnipotent individual. Lack of success must be the result of faulty choices and failure to assume sufficient personal responsibility, not structural impediments.

How do these forces make race? Jodi Melamed (2006) argues that multiculturalism becomes a technology of neoliberal capitalism's strategic use of racialization for labor and for opening new markets. Neoliberal multiculturalism produces and polices the need for diversity. Multicultural initiatives provide rationales for increasing the representation of people of color yet simultaneously preempt a thorough critique of racism. For example, theater schools and theater companies are becoming more diverse, but are racial/gender inequalities thereby fully addressed? What plays make it to the main stage? What is legible to audiences? As Bourdieu noted, we can contest some of the rules of the game in any field of cultural production, but as participants, we cannot abandon the game itself (Bourdieu 1993).

(Neo)liberal multiculturalism articulates with colorblind ideology, making race into a multicultural array of power-free difference, while allowing white/Eurocentric visions to exemplify the universal. Yet are (neo)liberal multiculturalism and structural racism always mutually reinforcing? Can we make race otherwise?

Funding: Three Case Studies

My argument here is with theoretical perspectives that split "capitalism" from "intervention," seeing mainstream success as always and only problematic. Do we not want progressive artists of color to "be successful" and to intervene in the "mainstream?" Does success always and only index "sellout," given that artists have always needed financial support? Who among us escapes capitalism?

Both Anna Deavere Smith and David Henry Hwang have had to become artrepreneurs in different ways. Both have received substantial support from private foundations and from paid work in theater and other forms. Individual careers are shaped in and through the enabling constraints of cultural assumptions, political economic forces, and institutional hierarchies.

Smith has navigated the vagaries of artistic support through multiple nongovernment sources. Private foundations have offered robust funding. She was the Ford Foundation's first artist in residence; the foundation financed her Institute on the Arts and Civic Dialogue for three summers at Harvard, for $1.5 million. Other major funders include the MacArthur Foundation (roughly five years of income) and the $300,000 Dorothy and Lillian Gish Prize. Even awards that do not offer monetary compensation can enhance recipients' reputations, increasing their chances for future funding.

Universities are crucial sources of support. Yale and Stanford medical schools commissioned Smith to create performances about medical care that became the creative nuclei for *Let Me Down Easy*. Smith has retained academic appointments throughout her career. Her present position at NYU is split between the Department of Performance Studies (at the Tisch School of the Arts) and the law school. Academe provides a stable, if not necessarily luxurious, income and offers university resources and the imprimatur of the institution. Smith has stated repeatedly that she wishes to avoid exclusive affiliation with theater schools. Her focus on urgent social issues compels her toward nontheatrical forms of engagement with the political.

Smith's Institute for the Arts and Civic Dialogue fosters progressive artistic work. She must therefore court potential donors. She urges young theater artists to become savvy about funding:

> KONDO: *I remember your telling a young, aspiring actor to go to the Business School, not the Theater School, if he wanted support for his work. Can you elaborate on this?*
>
> SMITH: I think theater artists need to know more about money. Successful filmmakers know how to raise money; visual artists know how to make money. We are not very developed in the theater about that reality—we don't even like to acknowledge that Shakespeare was rich. We behave in a vagabond manner. That's not our culture. Theater artistic directors dress in a bohemian way; those who run orchestras and museums are bespoke. And yet some theater artistic directors take home a rather large salary. I don't know why theater still fashions itself in a bohemian way—because Broadway producers are not bohemian and neither are agents. (A. D. Smith 2013a)

Smith has achieved mainstream visibility both within and outside the arts community. She has mobilized with superb skill the flexible, entrepreneurial strategies required to navigate a neoliberal economy. While Smith's career responds to neoliberal imperatives—so must we all—her success simultaneously creates opportunities for her historically significant oeuvre to exist, making crucial connections between art and the political. I argue in subsequent chapters that her interventions far exceed power-evasive multiculturalism or neoliberal individualism, offering paths toward progressive race-making.

David Henry Hwang has won numerous fellowships from sources both public and private, including the NEA and the New York State Council on the Arts in the former case, and Guggenheim, Rockefeller, and Pew Charitable Trusts in the latter. Prestigious playwriting awards add to his support: the $200,000 Sternberg Award for Playwriting and the $275,000 Doris Duke Artist Award, among others. His wide-ranging projects encompass "straight" plays and libretti for opera, including collaborations with musicians such as Philip Glass and Unsuk Chin, screenplays, musicals, and television. These are paid positions; like Smith, Hwang makes a living from his art.

In 2014, Hwang was named head of the playwriting concentration at Columbia University's School of the Arts. Hwang thus adds the stability of an academic appointment to his sources of support. I interviewed Hwang about his academic position and his views of playwriting as a profession:

> KONDO: *Congrats on the Columbia position. What drew you to the post? Does the security of academe have anything to do with your decision? Is it (about) nurturing new talent? . . .*
>
> HWANG: Honestly, I wasn't expecting to end up at Columbia. They had contacted me about the position, and I initially felt I . . . didn't have the time to take on this responsibility. But I went in for a set of interviews, more for the sake of experience, and ended up getting excited about the opportunity. I've always mentored younger writers and felt that doing so is part of what it means to be a playwright. I just never actually thought of teaching as a job. The more I learned about Columbia, however, the more I started to appreciate the resources available there to more effectively help nurture a new generation of writers. So I ended up accepting the position and have been having a great time shaping the program in a way I hope will more effectively serve today's emerging writers.

KONDO: *What advice do you give young playwrights about financial issues? Most won't be able to make a living from theater alone.*

HWANG: Financial advisors often talk about diversifying your portfolio. I feel that the only reason I've been able to maintain a long career is that I succeeded in diversifying my artistic portfolio, i.e., learned to do a lot of things. You can never depend on your plays to earn you a living. Every now and then, if you're lucky, one or two may actually make some money, but you can't rely on that—moreover, I don't believe one can or should "game" one's plays to appeal to the commercial market. Therefore, a playwright needs to have other skills in order to make a living, e.g., screenwriting, TV writing, libretto writing, teaching, etc. It's impossible to remain "hot" in a single genre indefinitely. By diversifying your artistic portfolio, you increase your odds of survival—you may go "cold" in movies, for instance, but hopefully, your star will rise in, say, television, and you can make money over there for a while. (Hwang 2015b)

Hwang's use of financial idioms exemplifies neoliberalism's economistic bias; writers should "diversify their portfolios" as a way of "enhancing (their) portfolio value" (W. Brown 2015, 33). We artists and academics must become entrepreneurial investors in ourselves.

I have a single production to my name, but my position illuminates the beginner's end of the spectrum. Like most playwrights (and unlike those at the highest echelons), I have no agent and rely primarily on submission to a theater's literary manager. Like any profession, but especially in "show business," theater depends on networking—not my strong suit. My position is unusual, in that I am a tenured professor, not necessarily financially dependent on playwriting (though as an underpaid woman of color, I would welcome added income). Playwriting can be expensive, while remuneration is minimal. My plays were written in playwriting workshops, each of which cost several hundred dollars. I sent my comedy *But Can He Dance?* to numerous theaters, and the Asian American Theater Company in San Diego decided to produce it. The honorarium was a few hundred dollars, and I self-funded drives and stays in San Diego for the rehearsal and run of the play. I also donated to the company.

I have sent out *Seamless*, my third full-length play, to at least fifty-five venues for contests, development, or production. Among the barriers I face are age, race, gender, and the fact that I am not a graduate from a major playwriting program. When sending the play to theaters outside major urban areas, I wonder about their ability to cast four excellent Asian American actors of the age of thirty-five and older. Many companies are primarily twentysomethings and overwhelmingly white, often graduates from the same BFA program who start their own company. Their interest in themes facing older adults of color seems unclear. Some applications require a fee, ranging from five to twenty-five dollars. Of those submissions, I won second place for the Jane Chambers Award for women playwrights, given by the Association for Theatre in Higher Education, and honorable mention for the See Change Award from East West Players. The play had three readings at the Lark Play Development Center, a prestigious venue in New York. No money was involved for these honors. At the Lark, actors and directors donate their time, and my trips are self-financed. Some readings have been at least partially supported by university research funds. I have also paid actors out of pocket (twenty-five to fifty dollars, depending on rehearsal time; no remuneration for cold readings) and provided food and drink when artists participate in readings either at my loft or in theater spaces. If I could afford to, I would consider devoting myself full-time to playwriting, but this would mean relinquishing predictable income and benefits for a career in a financially precarious industry.

This precarity can be dire for arts organizations of color, as structural inequalities of race can result in economic disparities that threaten the existence of theaters of color. The DeVos Institute of Arts Management found that arts organizations of color (Latinx and African American) were, with the exception of the Alvin Ailey American Dance Theatre, financially challenged in comparison to white institutions of comparable size.[2] The report recommended that funders concentrate on successful organizations: "Some black or Latino companies might have to be left behind so their stronger peers might grow" (Boehm 2015). Grant makers in the arts opposed this Darwinian approach, citing *structural* inequalities. The DeVos report suggested that financially stable (white) companies collaborate more frequently with smaller organizations of color. Grant makers argued that collaboration rarely results in equal benefits for arts organizations of color (Boehm 2015). Theaters of color observe that grants are more easily won by larger, white organizations seeking to "diversify," reinforcing the greater prestige and cultural capital of the white organizations. In such a scenario, the existence of arts organizations of color is at stake.

Institutional Landscapes

Artists navigate careers within power-laden hierarchies among theaters based primarily on size, income, and prestige. Codified by the League of Resident Theaters (LORT), theaters are classified as for-profit (Broadway/commercial) or nonprofit (tax-exempt), by the number of seats in a venue, and by average weekly box office receipts (Actors' Equity 2008). Different affiliations with labor unions shape working conditions and pay. Race-making occurs in and through this institutional landscape.

Theater size varies widely, from the Broadway theaters that house audiences of one thousand to small spaces that seat fewer than ninety-nine audience members. Small theaters abound. One small theater, where I participated in a playwriting workshop for years, seated thirty. Further, some theater is site-specific—inventively so. For example, after losing their permanent space, Moving Arts Company in Los Angeles produced evenings of "Car Plays," short works staged in parked cars. Audiences proceeded two by two from one car to another, down a row five deep, to watch a ten-minute play unfold in and around the car.

Theater thus varies dramatically in terms of both size and expense. Broadway houses can usually seat over one thousand, and tickets cost well over $100—$140 to $400 for blockbusters like *The Book of Mormon*. *Hamilton* in 2017 ranges from $640 to $2,000 for orchestra on weekends; these are unprecedented prices, even for musicals, which tend to cost more than straight plays due to higher production costs. Regional theater constitutes a middle ground, roughly $30 to $100. In intimate theater, with ninety-nine seats or fewer, tickets may cost less than movie admission or may be as expensive as $30 to $50. A venerable example of free theater is El Teatro Campesino in its early days, when the actors staged political allegory on the back of flatbed trucks for agricultural workers in the fields of California's Central Valley, as a form of labor organizing.

Theater as a signifier conjures for many the vision of the proscenium in a space holding hundreds, even a thousand or more. High production values, spectacular effects, and a large cast complete that vision. The Mark Taper Forum in Los Angeles, where both Smith and Hwang have been produced, holds 739 seats. A visit to the medium-sized (240-seat) East West Players—the oldest Asian American theater and oldest continuously running theater of color in the country—provoked dismissive comments from my undergraduate students about its "small space," a converted church. Students are often aghast when we visit black box performance spaces such as Highways, a nationally known venue famous for its performance art, which accommodates fewer than ninety-nine seats. The minimal props, costumes, and sets apparently flout their expectations.

Theater Classifications

"Off-off Broadway" in New York, "Equity Waiver" in Los Angeles, "or intimate theater" holds up to ninety-nine seats. New York, Chicago, and Los Angeles have slightly different ecologies of labor. In New York, off-off-Broadway theaters can employ actors who are members of the stage actors' union, Actors' Equity. The "Showcase Code" governs labor practices, including rehearsal hours, for Equity actors (e.g., a subway pass for transportation costs), as well as rights to record or extend a production (Holtham 2015). In Chicago, storefront theater defines a lively theater culture; these small, non-Equity houses rent their own spaces. Los Angeles is distinctive because the television and film industries dominate the city; actors often aspire to success in television or film, where both exposure and remuneration far exceed that of theater. Since the 1980s Los Angeles has allowed "Equity Waiver theater" in a special agreement with the union. Small theaters can hire nonunion actors and Equity members without paying Equity wages; the opportunity to be seen by Hollywood creatives becomes the wage.

A recent Equity controversy in Los Angeles demonstrates the conflicts over theater as zone of creative expression versus form of labor. Equity advocated that actors be paid the minimum wage (nine dollars an hour) for the run of the play and for rehearsal time; rehearsal is currently donated labor for Los Angeles actors. Equity Waiver regulations require differences in wages depending on the theater size, ticket price, and length of the run.[3] Actors may not even recoup the cost of gas in Los Angeles, where distances are substantial and gas is expensive.

On the surface, what could be more sensible than offering actors a minimum wage, benefits, and pay for rehearsal? Most theaters in the country abide by these regulations, and state laws consider actors' labor to be subject to the minimum wage. Nonetheless, in April 2015, the actors defeated the Equity proposal by a two-to-one margin. The opposition's arguments centered on the economic consequences for small theater in Los Angeles, rooted in the presumption that paying minimum wage would force small theaters to close.

A second rationale for rejecting the Equity proposal affirmed art as playground. Proponents argued that intimate theater is a space where artists experiment with edgy material unappealing to large audiences. The final argument speaks to the dominance of television and film. Artists may desire to be seen by the powerful in Hollywood, and for this opportunity, some—the majority, apparently—are willing to gamble that theater will be a portal to a paying job. For those who are truly committed to theater as art form rather than waiting room, (artistic) frustration abounds.[4]

The precarious economic state of small theater is both theme and assumption of the debates opposing artistic creativity (theater as site of creative expression) and labor (actors must be properly paid for their work). *Variety* published two views authored by Noah Wylie, from the television show ER and artistic producer at Hollywood's Blank Theater Company, and Charlayne Woodard, an eminent African American playwright/actress. Tellingly, the woman of color/veteran artist advocates a living wage, while Wylie, who achieved financial success in television, promotes apprenticeship and volunteerism (G. Cox 2015a, 2015b).

Is there a correlation between size and racialization? Smaller venues can *potentially* be more receptive to minoritarian concerns. For example, in New York the history of off-off-Broadway is populated with artists of color such as Ellen Stewart at La Mama and Miguel Algarín at Nuyorican Poets Café. Their forward-thinking theater staged minoritarian perspectives rarely seen in larger houses. Smaller theaters can feature experimental work directed toward nonmainstream audiences. Certainly, ethnic-specific theaters tend toward intimate size given the landscape of funding that forces arts organizations of color to live with constant financial precarity. Intimate theater is nonetheless a large category and is not *necessarily* synonymous with the most avant-garde or politically challenging productions.

Regional or LORT theater represents the second level of theater classification. As nonprofits, they are tax-exempt and finance their productions through ticket sales, grants, and patron donations. There are seventy-five LORT B and below theaters across the United States. Most are prestigious institutions such as the Goodman in Chicago, the Guthrie in Minneapolis, and the Mark Taper Forum in Los Angeles. Regional theaters often seat five hundred or more. LORT theaters hire union actors, designers, directors, and stagehands; their mission statement stresses the league's role in negotiating and dealing with labor.

Regional theaters can in theory be more adventurous than Broadway theaters, since they are not dependent exclusively on ticket sales. Nevertheless, critics argue that diminishing funding from both private and government sources compels regional theaters to seek box office revenue. Demand depends on finding plays that "should" appeal to the widest possible audience—often celebrity vehicles, revivals, and plays with proven track records. In most cases, racially marked plays (not musicals) face more barriers to production, unless they feature stars like Denzel Washington or Cicely Tyson.

Broadway producers can substantially fund a LORT production that makes the journey to Broadway, allowing regional theaters to profit from offering space for Broadway tryouts. The regional theater receives a percentage of the royalties if the production transfers. Diminishing funding encourages "artistic directors . . . (to move) in an increasingly commercial direction, adopting a bottom-line mentality that has put publicity and profitability over bold and substantive choices" (McNulty 2012b). Prioritizing profit could back-burner innovative work that treats challenging issues of race and formally unconventional plays (the two are not mutually exclusive).

Historically, LORT theater has relied on its subscription audience: aging, white, and affluent. Though this audience could in theory appreciate challenging work, programming choices suggest otherwise. A recent visit to a regional theater in the Bay Area spotlighted this demographic crisis. My theater companion sardonically commented that the audience was "one step from the morgue." I was the only Asian American in the audience (one usher was Asian American), and I saw one African American in the audience. The theater itself accommodates several hundred people, and the house was close to full. We observed the distinctive markers of regional theater: excellent production values, an aging, white audience, and a relatively conservative play choice. Probably the edgy season selection given its Asian American protagonist, the play remained within familiar formal and thematic conventions. These extreme demographics provoke alarm for the future of regional theater. Without younger, more diverse patrons, theater will literally die out.

The third level of theater classification, Broadway theaters (LORT A), are for-profit (commercial), and generally range from five hundred to fifteen hundred seats. They must hire union artists and stagehands. The Tony Awards are given for plays and musicals produced on Broadway. Forty theaters in New York are designated Broadway houses, most of them located in Midtown Manhattan (Pincus-Roth 2008). Most are owned by the top three producing companies: the Shubert Organization, Jujamcyn, and the Nederlander Organization. The Disney Corporation and now Dreamworks have joined this venerable theater triumvirate as major Broadway producers. Private investors or producing companies put up the capital to fund the production and wait for a return on their investments. Investors may never recoup their initial contributions, for Broadway shows are notorious financial risks. No one has the formula for what will constitute a hit, and costs are now so prohibitively expensive that even a hit may never earn back its initial investment.

The movement of multinational media conglomerates into Broadway is a notable economic development (Brater et al. 2010). Disney and Dreamworks stage versions of their films on Broadway as a way to sustain their film franchises. A Broadway play must draw large audiences to turn a profit and to enjoy a long run; financial success is based on ticket sales relative to costs. This financial constraint has caused some critics to comment on the relatively small number of "straight plays," especially new plays, produced on Broadway. The tendency is to stage musicals—less review-dependent than straight plays—or to mount revivals with film stars who will be a box-office draw. Critics sometimes bemoan the artistic impact of such choices (Katie Holmes in *All My Sons*; Julia Roberts in *Three Days of Rain*).

The move of multinationals into Broadway expands the reach of these conglomerates and, to some extent, homogenizes content. In most Broadway productions, invocations of race or difference cannot alienate the "upper middlebrow" demographic to which Broadway caters. Jessica Brater and Jessica Del Vecchio (2010) analyze the Broadway musical *Shrek* for the postracial ideology that undergirds both *Shrek* and the Obama election: diversity without analysis of systemic inequality. *Shrek* connected racial-ethnic difference to capitalist diversification of income streams, as the musical kept alive the *Shrek* franchise, attracting the upper-middlebrow audience that may have missed the movie. The Obama campaign, too, sold a brand of Americanness premised on a shared humanity, a commonality that presumably transcends race.

How might race play into hierarchies of theater size and prestige? Generally speaking, the larger the theater, the greater the prestige, though considerable variation exists. Those who value aesthetics above all may prefer smaller, more avant-garde theaters. Nonetheless, for a playwright, the entry into regional theater and Broadway is a sign of having achieved national recognition. Consequently, race matters, insofar as work by artists of color often begins at the level of small, ethnic-specific theater, while success is measured by critical and commercial triumph at mainstream venues. For example, a major nonprofit like the Public Theater marks a pinnacle of artistic prestige for playwrights and actors, but Broadway represents the greatest (inter)national visibility. Hwang's *Yellow Face*, which thematized race and featured an Asian American protagonist, played at the Public, but never made it to Broadway; *Chinglish*, featuring a white male protagonist, enjoyed a Broadway run of several months. Hwang's *Kung Fu*, about Bruce Lee, may reach Broadway as a "dance-ical," trading on the fame of its main character and its spectacular dance and martial arts numbers. These observations do not undermine the artistic merit of Hwang's works; my point is that presumed audience appeal can profoundly influence a play's fate.

Nonetheless, the entry of artists of color onto the Broadway stage and major regional theaters is a significant development. We cannot dismiss pathbreaking minoritarian work on Broadway, Hwang's *M. Butterfly* (1988 and 2017) and Smith's *Twilight: Los Angeles* (1994) among them. Lin Manuel Miranda's *In the Heights* (2008) and *Hamilton* (2015) are notable for formal experimentation (hip-hop); *In the Heights* spotlights underrepresented Latino communities, while *Hamilton* subverts whiteness by casting people of color as key historical figures—even if this latter move, as Donatella Gallela (2015) argues, reinforces a conservative vision of liberal multiculturalism and US nationalism. If Broadway audiences are "upper middlebrow," politically progressive visions should be staged there, to interrupt the self-confirming mirroring of this demographic.

Even if multinationals have moved into Broadway, the interrelations between theater *artists* and media conglomerates are complex. For example, Diane Paulus, artistic director of the American Repertory Theater, has worked on musicals and plays for Disney cruise ships (Healy 2012). David Henry Hwang wrote the book for the musical *Tarzan*, an association some consider problematic. I elaborate his rationale for doing so in chapter 5. Precisely because of the cool critical reception of his more pointedly political work, Hwang moved into writing musicals, since musicals are less review-dependent than are straight plays (Hwang 2007b). Further, he found affinities between the character and the positionality of Asian Americans. The involvement of relatively progressive artists of color in cultural works that are viewed by large audiences is not always and only problematic. Hwang is likely to write a far more progressive vision of race than someone without his history of sensitivity to these issues.

Admittedly, many would not expect a family-friendly musical to mount a pointed racial critique, though it would be welcome intervention. Hwang's most sophisticated critiques emerge in his straight plays *M. Butterfly* and *Yellow Face*. Playwrights have long been hired pens in film and television; Brecht himself worked in Hollywood. That does not vitiate the considerable aesthetic and political interventions he made in the theater. As many theater professionals attest, one cannot make a living as a playwright; forays into other media are essential for economic survival.

Political Economies and Their Effects

How do (neo)liberal defunding, corporatization, and individual responsibility affect everyday theater practice? Economics crucially influence the choice of plays that reach the main stage. For example, theaters have for many years preferred plays that require small casts and minimal sets, since these cost less to produce. Accordingly, we have seen a proliferation of solo shows or two-handers (two-person plays), with a single set or a set with a few props (chairs, a table) that can be rearranged to signify different locales. Aesthetic and economic choices can go hand in hand. Playwrights increase chances of production by submitting a ninety-minute two-hander rather than the sprawling plays of a bygone era: large casts, elaborate sets, three acts. Perhaps mainstream audiences derived pleasure from Tracy Letts's three-act *August: Osage County* precisely because of its old-fashioned size and sprawl. For me, these pleasures were vitiated by its stereotypical representation of Native Americans.

Smith's one-person shows may seem especially attractive in such an economy, though her fame in theater circles now means that theaters assume greater costs for supporting her creative staff. Gordon Edelstein, artistic director of the Long Wharf Theater that mounted the world premiere of *Let Me Down Easy*, joked about the expenses of her "one-woman" show. Smith used three theatrical dramaturgs, a movement specialist, and a dialogue coach; I was flown in twice from California. Her play *House Arrest* at the Arena Stage in Washington, DC, and later at the Mark Taper Forum in Los Angeles required a large cast, several dramaturgs, and a small library of tapes and books. The three artistic directors believed in Smith's work and her presumed box office appeal enough to finance her evolving projects.

Overall, cuts in arts funding can mean a preference for safer material. This manifests in regional theater acting as a tryout space for Broadway, and/or through the choice to stay within the fantasized aesthetic/racial comfort zone of the subscription audience. Moreover, economic pressures have defunded workshops, development, and touring.[5] Playwrights of color still bemoan the demise of South Coast Repertory's Hispanic Playwrights' Project, which fostered so many talented writers from 1986 to 2004. The Music Center, home to the largest theater organization in Los Angeles, announced cuts to their education programs (Boehm and Ng 2015). Such choices affect the future of theater. Trying out material is indispensable for performance, for a play must be heard in order to be appraised. Touring brings theater to wider audiences who might not otherwise have exposure to theater, developing audiences and artists.[6] Youth and educational programs cultivate future audiences.[7] All are in jeopardy.

Within this sobering economic landscape, theaters have devised strategies to attract new audiences and to capitalize on their successful productions. Among their marketing innovations are rush tickets or pay-what-you-can nights, designed to appeal to artists, students, and the less affluent. Dynamic pricing is theater's analogue to airline tickets; plays that are in demand are more expensive, and weekends are more expensive than weekdays. Because many younger people do not want to commit to an entire season (season tickets are a source of stable income for a theater), some regional theaters create a "make your own season" approach; consumers can combine plays from its different theaters into a package. Competition for audiences with other platforms—television, streaming services, and the Internet/YouTube—shapes marketing decisions. How, within such structures, do theaters and artists, especially playwrights, survive? How might political-economic forces shape racialization—and vice versa?

Making a Living

Before fieldwork, I assumed theater pay to be equal to that in film and television—but the differences are stark. David Henry Hwang is quoted as saying that he earned $66,000 for his Broadway play *Chinglish*—scarcely a living wage in New York City, and far less than one might expect for such a nationally acclaimed artist (Wetherbe 2012). Moreover, Broadway productions are hardly an everyday occurrence. Diana Son, whose plays were produced at the Public and in major regional theaters, now works primarily in television—as is the case for many playwrights.[8] Son explains, "There's a touching naivete on the part of the theatergoers about the possibility of making a living as a playwright, as though you write for TV as icing on the cake . . . People think it's the difference between making, say, $60,000 and $80,000 a year, when really it's the difference between making, say, $8,000 and $400,000 a year" (Breslauer 2006).

Further, writers are literally the showrunners in television, wielding the greatest power among the creative staff. Son continues, "One way that TV distinguishes itself from film is that the head writer is the boss, which is incomparable to the screenwriter, unless the screenwriter is also the director.... The head writer/showrunner has their hand in casting, scheduling, salaries, everything. The head writer is also executive producer. It's an extremely powerful position" (Breslauer 2006).

Playwright Tony Kushner, arguably the most celebrated living playwright, affirmed the impossibility of making a living in theater. He stated that playwrights could enjoy two or three years of income if they penned a blockbuster like *Angels in America*, but subsequently, they must find other work—often, in film and television. Kushner himself has pursued this route, deeming it necessary in order to have health insurance and to make ends meet (Kushner 2014). In the face of such stunning pay disparities and power differentials, the move of playwrights to television and film is hardly surprising.

For performers, the disparities are still visible, though the astronomical salaries of stars mask the far less dazzling salaries of journeyman actors in film and television.[9] Nonprofit theater does not necessarily pay a living wage. For example, Smith's play *Let Me Down Easy* was produced at Second Stage in New York, a respected off-Broadway venue. Her national reputation as a major theater artist, MacArthur recipient, and advocate for the arts apparently did not translate into lavish remuneration. She explained to me:

> SMITH: We are not paid well in the theater, and I have to use other forms of support to do my work. *Let Me Down Easy* was very challenging. Workshops and performances at all of the theaters I worked in before coming to New York paid me less than my assistant made (because I added my own money on to my assistant's salary so she could survive). In New York I made $719 a week to do 8 shows a week. This is not a fair business model. The nonprofit theater lost its way in terms of fairness. The assumption is artists will work for free and gamble on a more lucrative result from doing this. I feel this cuts a lot of people out of the process and makes diversity even more difficult than it is. Of course movie stars are willing to work off Broadway for nothing. Because it does something else for them. I am sure Broadway salaries are better, however, when a star like Bette Midler goes to Broadway. (A. D. Smith 2013a)

That a major theater artist makes only $719 a week for eight shows was shocking to me. Smith did not mention her playwriting honorarium, but if Hwang's experience is any guide, it cannot have been an impressive sum.

Paltry wages mean that people from working-class backgrounds and, to the extent that these categories overlap, people of color are at a distinct disadvantage. Those who can devote themselves to playwriting may be trust fund babies or have a wealthy partner; otherwise, they must cobble together a living from various teaching appointments, hope to win a writing gig on film or television, or find other modes of employment.[10] As Smith notes, the low theater salaries in nonprofit theater are supposedly offset by the opportunity for actors to be seen by television and film producers.

In this landscape, universities loom large as a relatively stable source of income.[11] The possibility of tenure in at least some departments confers both institutional prestige and predictable support. Universities may provide other sources of employment; for example, a renowned figure in Asian American theater, Mia Katigbak, works at Columbia as an office manager. In her artistic life, Katigbak is a founder of the National Asian American Theater Company, a signal artistic achievement; she is a classically trained actress and a mentor to a generation of Asian American artists (Soloski 2015).

At the other end of the spectrum, performers who are celebrities in other media earn considerably more than Smith's wages for *Let Me Down Easy* (staged at a nonprofit venue), especially on Broadway. In 2010, Julia Roberts earned $150,000 per week for *Three Days of Rain*; Matthew Broderick and Nathan Lane's weekly salary for *The Producers* was $100,000 (Simonson 2010). And Smith was right: Bette Midler earned $150,000 a week in *Hello, Dolly!* However, for the majority of theater artists, work in theater is a labor of love; it cannot guarantee a living wage.

Todd London, Ben Pesner, and Zannie Giraud Voss (2009) conducted a revealing study of "the life and times of the New American Play," focusing on theaters and playwrights who are professional, working artists. The results were sobering: "The average playwright earns between $25,000 and $39,000 annually, with approximately 62 percent of playwrights earning under $40,000 and nearly a third making less than $25,000" (London, Pesner, and Voss 2009, 51). The women surveyed tended to be produced at roughly the same rate as male playwrights and received commensurate remuneration for their career stage, but they tended to occupy lower rungs on the career ladder. Consequently, men earned a higher salary because their careers advanced more quickly and easily (67). Some interviewees commented that women playwrights tended to be grouped with/pitted against each other, which rarely occurred for white male playwrights; another respondent found that female-authored plays tended to be considered smaller, less "universal," and more "emotional," than those written by men.

London, Pesner, and Voss found that playwrights of color were produced at the same rate as other playwrights and enjoyed similar career advancement, which initially seems encouraging. Have we overcome race barriers? Playwrights' responses indicate otherwise. Black playwrights comment wryly that their productions occur only in February, Black History Month, or that they still need a well-known white collaborator to give (his) imprimatur to their work. African American playwrights skewed younger in their survey (are more entering the field, or are more leaving it?), and they receive more of their income through commissions. Is their work being nurtured for eventual production, or is the commission ultimately a *substitute* for production?

The chart in figure 2.1 draws from data gathered by the Dramatists' Guild. Who is produced on the stages of American theater? The disparity is stunning.

This situation may be improving; the twenty most-produced playwrights in the United States in 2017–18 (apart from Shakespeare, number one by far) include Lauren Gunderson, Lisa Kron, Dominique Morisseau, Ayad Akhtar, Quiara Alegría Hudes, August Wilson, Branden Jacobs Jenkins, and Lorraine Hansberry (Tran 2017, 42).

Whether or not this development signifies a structural change remains debatable. The theater world—like other worlds in the contemporary United States—is shaped through unconscious racial, gendered ideologies. Joy Meads, literary manager at the Center Theatre Group in Los Angeles, offers this analysis: "Unconscious bias against an artist can cause us to think less of their work and prime us to look for errors. Multiple studies have demonstrated that people often judge work more harshly when they think the author is a woman or person of color. . . . Fields that value brilliance and genius—fields like theatre, perhaps—tend to hire more white men. . . . In a related dynamic, men tend to be hired on the basis of potential and women on proven performance" (Meads 2015, 49–50).

Racial bias is not synonymous with membership in the Klan, spectacular acts of physical violence, or intentional mendacity. People who occupy

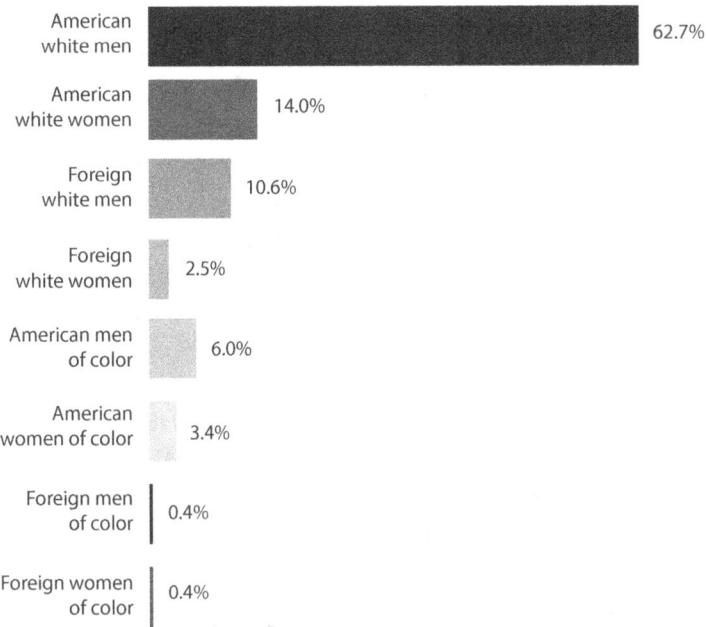

FIGURE 2.1 • "Who Gets Produced?" Based on data from the November/December 2015 issue of *The Dramatist*.

sites of privilege may simply feel more comfortable with those who are like themselves, enacting (un)intentional exclusion. Oskar Eustis shared with me a perceptive self-awareness:

> I spent my life working with artists of color but nonetheless, after my first year here I looked up and I—oh Jesus Christ! Every male, white, lefty, over-articulate, hyper-intelligent playwright *in the world* has now become my best friend and I'm developing all their plays. And—coincidence? I don't think so. . . . All of those people, that's my comfort zone . . . the Tony Kushners of the world. The David Hares. "Hey! Come on in guys!" So . . . it's really hard to figure out how you—and it's not hard to figure out how to produce David Henry Hwang. That's easy. But it is hard to figure out how to really make sure that the Theater doesn't take a big step back. And, fortunately, I think we're doing OK. We've got a lot . . . more to do before . . . we've got it institutionalized; that's for sure. (Eustis 2007)

Though theaters are purportedly attempting to diversify, the upper echelons of power in the theater world remain astonishingly homogeneous.

Lily Janiak (2013) analyzed theater leadership and the dearth of people of color who are artistic directors or managing directors of theater companies. Current artistic directors brainstormed possible ways to address the discrepancy, including a solution modeled on the NFL's "Rooney Rule," which compelled football organizations to interview (not necessarily hire) an applicant of color for its head coach and general manager positions. The rule was initially successful in enabling pro football to diversify its upper managerial staff to 22 percent from 6 percent, though that number has declined to 12.5 percent in 2012. ESPN noted a decline in 2015, from eight in 2011 to six of the league's thirty-two head coaches who are minorities (Fox 2015).

For theater, the numbers are abysmal, though hard data are difficult to find, since LORT and similar organizations do not keep records of interviewing/hiring processes. However, Janiak quotes an artistic director who can name only six LORT leaders of color out of a population of 150 to 170. Why such small numbers?

> The answer is both simple—bias—and complex—the myriad ways that bias manifests. . . . High schools and colleges might not be exposing young people of color to the arts in a way that lets them know they can have a career there. Theatres might not be doing the kind of work that gets young people of color excited enough to sacrifice a more lucrative career elsewhere. In the hiring process, candidates might not have the networks to meet people even if they have the skills. Boards might not know the field from which they're hiring—and if they do, they might know only their own, limited circles, and search firms might not always press them to expand their networks. There's also the tendency . . . to "put people of color in positions where you think they should be"— . . . as community builders rather than decision makers. . . . Even if candidates of color get hired, institutional racism often makes those companies too hostile to sustain the new hire or hire more people of color. Finally, the current numbers prove their own obstacle, says [Oregon Shakespeare Festival executive director emeritus] Nicholson. "If I were a person of color . . . and I looked around the field and I saw that no one who looks like me is in a senior management level. . . . That's a very clear message." (Janiak 2013)

Janiak is particularly insightful about the ways privilege works. She expands Eustis's autocritique into a systemic examination of that privilege:

> Part of the resistance that none of my interviewees mentioned . . . is the fact that, if you're white, it's impossible to talk about the Rooney Rule and not feel that you're part of the problem. . . . Every . . . decision to hire . . . a white person and not a person of color matters—including the decision, however long ago, that got you your . . . job. The very act of writing about the Rooney Rule . . . has heightened my skepticism about how much my own privilege, as a white person . . . has advantaged me in my own professional life . . . which means my successes are not, as I'd prefer to think, born solely of talent and skill. It's hard not to get defensive about that. (Janiak 2013)

Theater is like other domains of society; privilege is difficult to acknowledge. Janiak's frank insights lead the way to possible solutions.

Without being in the room, it is difficult to know how artistic directors shape a season, but economics, marketing (our audiences wouldn't come to that), and aesthetic excellence (what counts as excellence, for whom?) are surely some criteria. In an unscientific survey of several seasons at three prominent Los Angeles theaters of different sizes (none ethnic-specific), the majority of the creative staff—playwright, director, actors—were white and male. The Rogue, the Road, and Boston Court, all known for artistic excellence and critically acclaimed productions, were notable for the lack of playwrights of color, with one recent exception: the 2015 season at Boston Court. Dedicated to nonnaturalistic plays often based on myth, Boston Court staged a South Asian–themed play, a Latino play by MacArthur winner Luis Alfaro, and a play by Martin Zimmerman set in Latin America, directed by Michael John Garcés. Rogue Machine produced a play by Rajiv Joseph but has virtually no actors, directors or playwrights of color. The same is true of the Road. Boston Court, while not in the vanguard of racial representation, has produced Luis Alfaro's *Oedipus El Rey*, a reworking of the Oedipus myth. Nonetheless, that half of their season is devoted to plays by artists of color is a first.

The 2016 seasons at each theater embrace a relatively multiracial set of themes. At Boston Court, one play written by a European playwright occurs in a Thai/Vietnamese/Chinese restaurant, with a multiracial cast that performs across the lines of race and gender. Though I have not seen the play, the description raises doubts. What vision of Asianness is staged there? Another play in their season centers on musicians who are brothers: one is Christian, one Muslim. The Road's current season includes a play about a white man and black woman who ride the bus together each day;

another centers a Haitian woman who moves to the United States. Rogue Machine's 2017–18 season includes Lorraine Hansberry's *Les Blancs* as their diversity entry. In 2016–17 they staged *Honky*, a satire about race written by white playwright Greg Kalleres. Having not seen these plays,[12] I am not optimistic about the artistic visions of race presented in the plays authored by white men, but at least this provides more work for artists of color. The theaters are making an effort, enacting the model of "white theaters that do outreach." Still, even plays that feature actors of color and themes of race often center the visions of white, male playwrights.

Under the directorship of Tim Dang, East West Players, the oldest continuously running theater of color in the country, developed a formula for their seasons: a new Asian American play, in recent years reaching out to younger, non–East Asian audiences (South Asian, Filipino, Cambodian, Vietnamese); a classic Asian American play; the artistic director's choice; and a musical. East West provides training and networking opportunities and casts Asian Americans in roles unavailable to them in white theaters. One of my most memorable theatrical experiences was Sondheim's *Passion* at East West. Jacqueline Kim's Fosca for me surpassed Donna Murphy's performance on Broadway—but Murphy's national recognition has, predictably, eluded Kim. Dang stepped down in July 2016. Part of his legacy is a vision statement urging theaters to institute a 51 percent preparedness plan by 2020: "51% of your organization's artists and production personnel (combined) will be PEOPLE OF COLOR; or 51% . . . will be WOMEN; or 51% . . . will be UNDER 35 years of age" (East West Players 2015, emphasis in original). East West Players' attention to racialized labor is exemplary. Under new artistic director, Snehal Desai, the 2016–17 season celebrated the work of women playwrights, while 2017–18 spotlights collaborations with other theaters, from young Asian American troupes to the African American Robey Theatre Company.

My greatest surprise has been the Mark Taper Forum's 2017–18 fiftieth anniversary season. Most of the productions feature the work of playwrights of color, beginning with a revival of Teatro Campesino's classic *Zoot Suit*, a new play about Serbian nationalism by Rajiv Joseph, MacArthur winner Tarell McCraney's *Head of Passes*, and Quiara Alegría Hudes's Pulitzer Prize–winner *Water by the Spoonful*. David Henry Hwang's world premiere *Soft Power*, originally scheduled for the Taper, moved to the larger Ahmanson for 2018. The acclaimed (all-white) *Heisenberg* took its place. Still, the season begins to mirror the sprawling diversity of Los

Angeles. Whether this hopeful moment links to *structural* change remains to be seen.

Making Race Onstage and Backstage: Crew and Cast

While the mere presence of minoritarian bodies does not guarantee a progressive vision, making race includes the bodies who provide the artistic and creative labor, both onstage and backstage. The presence of artists of color can matter in the arts and in academe; for example, the Academy of Motion Pictures Arts and Sciences' addition of more artists of color prompted predictions that Oscar nominees would be more diverse going forward—and indeed, 2017 was the year *Moonlight* won Best Picture. Both Howard Becker's analysis of art worlds (2008) and Shannon Jackson's investigation of performative/visual art (2011) examine the often unacknowledged labor of support required for artistic production.

A pivotal intervention of Anna Deavere Smith's *Twilight: Los Angeles 1992* was its diverse cast and crew: dramaturgs; hair and makeup artists; costume designers; composers; scenic designers; assistants; stage managers; lighting designers; A/V technicians. Smith performed multiple characters of different races and genders onstage. The hiring of such a diverse production staff and the presentation of such a multiracial array of characters was unprecedented in American theater. The message of *Twilight* extended beyond numerical metrics or a power-evasive display of multicultural difference. The play addressed race and class conflict, subverting a power-evasive liberalism that might efface structural inequality under the sign of the Human—though, inevitably, liberal theater ensures that the Human cannot be avoided.

Labor practices profoundly shape race and class relations, as Smith told me:

> SMITH: Race and gender—well, particularly race—have a lot to do with this. People of color don't tend to go into these careers except as performers—they almost never seek careers backstage or in supportive roles . . . there are very few people of color in leadership positions. I don't know about compensation. I would imagine that all Equity actors make the same and that Will Smith . . . makes as much as a white star in his category. . . . I bet Kerry Washington does too. You can't really look at race in the performing arts in the same way that you look at it in the academy or business. In the arts it is about desire run amok, or

no desire at all. . . . It is not logical, so it's hard to talk about fairness when it comes to performers. That said—we could talk about fairness when it comes to who are the actual workers—real workers—like the hair and makeup people . . . or the people working around the cameras—or in the theater—the people in the offices. These are jobs that are not gone awry by the crazy chemistry that happens . . . between an artist and their public. (A. D. Smith 2012b)

Casting is both an issue of the politics of representation—where most academic critique rests—and a labor issue. In terms of artistic labor, we are still not in a moment when people of color can play themselves. In the summer of 2013, controversies raged in major regional theater circles in California, New York, Philadelphia, and the United Kingdom over Asian American / British Asian casting. La Jolla Playhouse, a major LORT venue, sponsored a workshop of *The Nightingale*, based on a Hans Christian Andersen story. Set in a mythical China, the multicultural cast of twelve included only two Asian Americans. Theater critic Charles McNulty asks,

> Are we really living in a postracial world? It seems like we're back in the 1990s, when all hell broke loose on Broadway after the British star Jonathan Pryce was cast as the Eurasian lead in "Miss Saigon." The "multicultural" casting of "The Nightingale" at La Jolla Playhouse has provoked a similar backlash, with leaders of the Asian American theater community decrying the way a work set in ancient China has been cast with only two Asian American actors out of an ensemble of 12. . . . According to the New York–based Asian American Performers Action Coalition, only 1.5% of all roles were given to Asian American actors in the last five seasons on Broadway. This is inexcusable. (McNulty 2012a)

The article, however, ultimately sides with arguments mounted by Artistic Director Christopher Ashley, the director, Moisés Kaufman, and the composer, Duncan Sheik. Since the play is set in "mythic" China, the director has complete artistic freedom to cast anyone in Chinese roles.

Having written on the problematic politics of representation in *The Mikado*—a "mythical" depiction of Japan—I find this argument insufficient.[13] Lest readers imagine this is an antiquated controversy, recent productions of *The Mikado* in Seattle in 2014, one in New York in 2015, and spirited debate on Twitter testify to the continuing circulation of justifications for racist productions. On September 20, 2015, Melissa Hillman, artistic director of the Impact Theatre, tweeted pungent commentary:

I know exactly what you want, Mikado defenders. You want to be able to perform racism W/O CRITICISM. You want to be able to decide what / is appropriate and what is not, b/c white ppl have always had that cultural power & now that ppl of color are being listened to, yr PISSED. / Mikado defenders: what ever made you believe you'd be able to stage ANYTHING EVER w/o criticism? / You're basically just telling ppl of color to shut up . . . that you get to decide what is racist and what is not. / this is why defenses of The Mikado are racist in and of themselves. White ppl do not get to decide what ppl of color find racist.

Another insidious dynamic may be at work. Defenders of *The Mikado* may attribute the musical form's origins to Gilbert and Sullivan; others see the American musical as originating in African American traditions.[14]

Ultimately, progressive race-making surpasses numerical metrics that presumably index a commitment to diversity. At a Theatre Communications Group conference, Ralph Peña, artistic director of Ma-Yi Theater, challenged the Goodman Theater's self-congratulatory inventory of their inclusion of women and people of color. In a fierce rebuke, Peña stated that diversity is a matter of artistic/political vision (Torres et al. 2012). Yellowface casting controversies perform the disconnect between systematically disenfranchised artists of color and artistic directors of mainstream theaters who trumpet the virtues of artistic freedom. As Daniel Banks states unequivocally, US theater is *segregated* theater (Banks 2013).

For Asian American artists, contemporary yellowface controversies recall the demonstrations over *Miss Saigon* (Kondo 1997). My analysis focused on both labor and the politics of representation, since actors were, paradoxically, lobbying to play prostitutes, pimps, Oriental despots, and asexual cadres. On the positive side, the controversy galvanized Asian American theater artists and gave Broadway experience to a generation of Asian American theater professionals (in stereotypical roles). *The Nightingale* and *The Mikado* are hardly anomalous, even now. Other cases of yellowface/brownface include the Roundabout Theatre's brownface production of *The Mystery of Edwin Drood* (2013), which staged Orientalist visions of "Ceylon" (Gener 2013). The Royal Shakespeare Company cast British East Asian actors as maids and dogs in its production of *The Orphan of Zhao* (2012), a play set in China. Racial insensitivity is hardly a thing of the past (Chen 2012; *Huffington Post* 2015).[15]

The *Nightingale* controversy prompted artists to organize public meetings and to sponsor conferences on diversity. In December 2013, the Stage

Directors and Choreographers Society hosted a forum at the Pasadena Playhouse, "Can Southern California Be a Model Community for a More Diverse Theater?" The *Los Angeles Times* theater critic argued that attention to the bottom line is crippling both racial and aesthetic diversity. Therefore, the lack of diversity is not due to racism. "Holding the American theater back isn't a prejudicial attitude but an economic posture: The worry over keeping these nonprofits in the black is ensuring that they remain predominantly white—and definitely not as vibrant as they could be" (McNulty 2013).

Ralph Peña responded on Facebook, "Prejudice and economic jockeying are not mutually exclusive. Both are at play in the refusal of many theaters to bring new voices to their communities . . . neither one is an acceptable excuse. . . . As an artistic leader, if you can't figure out how to change the orbit of your audiences to include works by women and artists of color—then you are a failed artistic leader. You should resign and hand over the reigns [sic] to someone more capable" (Ralph Peña, Facebook post, December 19, 2013). McNulty makes race by equating prejudice with racism (a term he never uses), ignoring the structural dimensions of race. Economic decisions and the structure of racial hierarchy cannot be neatly disaggregated.

Audiences and Race

Fantasized audience shapes the choice of plays for production. If LORT audiences are considered too conservative for edgy plays, solutions might include diversifying and educating that audience. On Broadway, producers have found a way to draw African Americans: feature classics with an all-African American cast, such as the compelling revival of *A Streetcar Named Desire*, featuring Nicole Ari Parker as Blanche and Blair Underwood as Stanley. I was one of a handful of nonblack people at the show, something I had never experienced on Broadway. Another strategy would target marketing to minoritarian communities. Playwrights of color pointedly argue that theaters generally do not understand how to market to nonwhite audiences and how to keep those audiences coming if they are "found" (London, Pesner, and Voss 2009, 228). This neoliberal imperative for artists to multitask adds yet another job for the artist of color.

Even Anna Deavere Smith must contend with mainstream theater's "zones of sanctioned ignorance" (Spivak 2003). I spent an afternoon on the phone during the summer of 2011 with Smith and her then assistant,

Marcos Nájera—himself an accomplished journalist and performance artist—when Smith was in Los Angeles performing her play *Let Me Down Easy*, at the Broad Stage in Santa Monica. We had to brainstorm about marketing to audiences of color, creating a list of culturally/racially diverse outlets: radio stations, television programs, newspapers, churches. This was the job of the theater's public relations office. Smith should have been on vocal rest, and I should have been writing this book! The public relations staff was evidently not sufficiently familiar with ways to reach audiences of color to perform their job properly. Racism/imperialism as "zones of sanctioned ignorance" seem all too apposite here. Smith generously attributed the lapse to the fact that the Broad Stage was then newly established. She thought her publicist should have been of more help. For me, either excuse is insufficient. Surely the public relations staff could have generated lists of "usual suspects" for the white theater audiences in Santa Monica, and the same is true for Smith's publicist. It was their responsibility to devote the time and effort required to confront their zones of sanctioned ignorance of communities of color. Diversifying who appears onstage implicitly welcomes spectators of color, but audiences first must know about a performance before they can attend.

Smith and the Chicano-Latino male trio Culture Clash strongly advocate for audience diversification and development. Clasher Ric Salinas views audience diversification as a process of education. He observes that LA Latino audiences came in increasing numbers to Culture Clash performances over the years. This involved a learning process, as people become accustomed to the locations of the theaters and chose to shoulder the expense—one, he says, that Latino families might take on for a sporting event or a concert (Salinas 2007). Ideally, this would involve an audience more diverse than, but also including, traditional LORT subscribers. These artists attempt to rethink the role of theater, broadening, diversifying, and activating audiences.

However, we cannot dismiss theatergoers as homogeneous. Diversity to some extent already exists. Smith and Hwang draw a spectatorship that is far more multiracial than standard regional theater audiences, and their work stages aesthetic and political interventions that disturb the seamless reproduction of racialized assumptions—despite the fact that some critics and audiences may read their work in a power-evasive, liberal humanist fashion. Román argues that too often, the left has allowed its "romance with the indigenous"—the presumed authenticity of the "grassroots" or "community"—to discourage serious scrutiny and appreciation of the "engagement of commercial theater with the central questions of contemporary culture" (Román 2005, 48). Convention assumes theater audiences to be monolithic. Román leads us to question our received wisdom and opens other possibilities for cultural critique, arguing that "the language of changing the demographic of Broadway audiences is too caught up in a logic of futurity that fails to see the new audiences already attending these shows" (47). In his view, theatergoers are more diverse than we might assume. We need to continue to work to overcome structural impediments—zones of sanctioned ignorance in marketing, for example—to ensure and expand this diversity.

(Neo)liberalism, Race, and a Politics of Hope

The imbrications of economics and race are complex. Nonetheless, racial zones of sanctioned ignorance cannot be read off economic/capitalist constraints in a deterministic fashion. Race, economics, colonialism, and state power may have intertwined histories, but racially, Baraka's "the changing same" remains all too apposite. (Neo)liberal humanism is implicated in the perpetuation of racial hierarchy. Clearly, neoliberalism in the theoretical literatures cannot be ignored (W. Brown, 2015; Harvey, 2005). "It"—or the congeries of phenomena brought together under its rubric—is said to be a political-economic, generative force in the world; such accounts tend to figure neoliberalism as a monolith (if an unstable signifier) and assume its totalizing reach.

Some analysts offer alternative accounts. Grace Hong (2016) articulates a cultural studies view: that neoliberalism is an epistemological (and, I would add, affective) structure that protects particular lives and disavows the deaths resulting from that choice. Lisa Lowe's genealogy of liberalism (2015) throws the "neo" into doubt; neoliberalism extends liberal principles and histories of colonization/commodification of human lives. Finely grained ethnographic analysis can allow for insights that can interrupt neoliberalism as monolith. Such accounts foreground the *making* of (neo)-liberalism, focusing on process, openness, and inherent friction lacking in much of the literature (Rofel 2007; Ho 2009; Tsing 2005, 2015).

Performance studies has devoted attention to "neoliberalism and global theatres" (Nielsen and Ybarra 2012). One compelling approach shifts the focus to the neoliberal imperatives inhering in the practices of performance itself, as a technology inextricable from "neoliberal systematicity" (Werry 2012). Yet this view tends to deemphasize the "contested . . .

and mutable" qualities of performance, assuming the limitations of minoritarian participation in its analytic object, a museum. The museum's interactivity becomes a neoliberal technology deploying the performative. Margaret Werry notes the rise in participation of Maori peoples in the administration and organization of the museum, but emphasizes the ways that neoliberalism preempts a more radical contestation. While neoliberalism and race may reinforce each other, "neoliberal technologies" might have multiple, discrepant effects. Can minoritarian/decolonial contestations, in this or other contexts, *destabilize* "neoliberal technologies" *as well as* buttress them? The focus on the neoliberal at the expense of the minoritarian may elide the contradictory *potential* effects of the neoliberal. While the author makes a convincing case at one level, we are not given enough information to see if multiple, contradictory forces are at work.

The periodizing of neoliberalism through political regimes (Reagan, Thatcher) can occlude minoritarian intervention. Analyzing commercial theater during the Reagan era, Alan Woods (1993) argues that plays produced on Broadway, including Hwang's *M. Butterfly*, did more to reiterate stereotype and "retreat from the social and political activism of the 1960s and 1970s than they did to advance political critique." I have argued in spirited fashion that *M. Butterfly* reinscribes Orientalist sumptuousness with self-conscious awareness, in service of the deconstruction of race, gender, sexuality, and colonialism (Kondo 1997). Woods finds that Hwang failed to challenge mainstream audience perspectives. My memory of seeing *M. Butterfly* (three times on Broadway, once at the Hangar Theatre in Ithaca, once in the Los Angeles touring production, and once at East West Players) differs considerably. While my evidence is anecdotal, I heard white spectators articulate feelings of disgruntlement, indicating that their comfortable assumptions had been assailed.

Here is my key dispute with the literatures on neoliberalism or views that privilege a monolithic governmental regime/historical period (Reaganism, Thatcherism). I remain unconvinced that neoliberal logics are so thoroughly reinscribed or that, following Lowe, neoliberalism is so new. Rather, "it" extends principles and tendencies, including the occlusion of colonial and racist histories, which undergird liberalism. I remain unconvinced that minoritarian intervention cannot destabilize (neo)liberalism in some respects, even if some radical contestations are preempted. Historical continuity within a presidential regime is an assumption; neoliberalism is not a monolith; minoritarian intervention cannot always be dismissed as simply a technology of capitalism. Neoliberalism and racialization cannot be presumed to be fixed entities in stable relationship, in which minoritarian interventions into political structures *only* buttress capitalism. The abstractions "capitalism" and "racialization"—both a congeries of uneven, power-laden practices—may produce multiple, intertwined, sometimes contradictory effects.

Performance studies scholars and anthropologists see the ephemerality of performance as itself an interruption to Master Subject desires for totalizing schemes of knowledge production and capitalist reproduction (Phelan 1993). Further, if structure represents agential capacity (Gilmore 2007), if neoliberal multiculturalism is a reigning regime of power at this moment, we should be able to locate some of those capacities (Menon 2012). Performance cannot escape neoliberal forces—like anything else, it is formed in/through such forces—but it can constitute an imaginative, unpredictable excess that cannot be fully contained, potentially interrupting capitalist reproductive logics. The imaginative can become a key site for the performance of visions of possibility. In alliance with postcolonial scholars, queer/feminist theorists, and scholars of color (Arzumanova 2013; Dolan 2005; Muñoz 1999; Menon 2012; M. Joseph 2012; Shimakawa 2012), I argue that minoritarian subjects cannot afford the view that all is recuperated in the totalizing logics of neoliberalism. Both the tone and the message of the neoliberal turn in scholarship imply that the belief in futurity and possibility lacks rigor.

Yet even within daunting neoliberal imperatives, subversions of power are possible. I refuse the totalizing qualities of the literatures on neoliberalism, while acknowledging its salutary skepticism toward naïve celebrations of resistance or the contradictions involved in the politics of recognition (W. Brown 1995). Inna Arzumanova argues, "The arts industries . . . are spaces where visibility and legibility of racialized performances are . . . profit-driven and enabled by neoliberal economies, but also unpredictable and potentially unstable because of their dependency on imagination and transformation" (2013, 7).

In solidarity, I argue that performance constitutes a hope, a possibility that fissures any totalizing logic. I join with these theorists in their emphasis on the necessity for hope (Muñoz 2009), for the idea of a better future, for what I have called visions of possibility and the life-giving capacities of the arts (Kondo 1997). On the plane of the everyday, this can involve just getting by in the face of a world where race, gender, class, and sexuality index vulnerability to premature death. In such a present, something that "gives you a lift" can be precious and life affirming. Hope and possibility, even if fraught with contradiction, must animate our intellectual, aesthetic, and political commitments. We cannot afford the life-diminishing trope of relentless recuperation. We need visions of possibility, a suggestion, however fleeting, of a world imagined otherwise, so that we might attempt to remake the world accordingly, even as the world makes us. This is not soft-minded; it is a matter of political survival.

Those glimmers of hope, the complex subversions and reinscriptions of power in the theater, are the subject of act 2. I theorize (my involvement with) the works of Anna Deavere Smith and David Henry Hwang, two artists of color successful in the mainstream. In act 3, I detail my own fledgling attempts to intervene in the theater world as a playwright. Trying to remake theater worlds, to rearrange its power relations, is a political project that can never be pure. Yet interventions still matter. To explore theoretical practices in theater as potentially progressive and reparative, I theorize acting, writing as collaboration, dramaturgy, and processes of writing and revision.

entr'acte
2

ACTING AND EMBODIMENT

Acting class, in the gym of the Hollywood Japanese American Cultural Center. Taped on one wall are instructions on how to write hiragana, the Japanese syllabary; on another, children's drawings, colorful and merry, of flowers and houses and trees. Do they use this space during the day for grade school? Pre-school?

Scene One

As part of our playwriting class with Ric Shiomi, we warm up with acting exercises. Ric asks me to do a monologue, and I stand in front of the class as though I were giving a lecture: centered, in command, making eye contact with everyone, body upright, arms outstretched and open. I finish the monologue, thinking, "Pretty good job." Ric looks quizzical. He gives me direction. "Do the same monologue and pretend you have a stomach ache." I'm stunned. OK. I'm here to learn. So I do the same monologue, but this time my speech is halting and soft, my posture slightly bent over. I finish, feeling skeptical. "Much better!" Ric exclaims. My classmates nod their heads. Really? It felt so . . . vulnerable. I suddenly realize—in acting, you don't have to perform the lecturer's mastery. That bodily habitus is so ingrained, it feels odd, wrong, to stand in front of people and perform "weakness." Academe values the Master Subject, and we strive mightily to embody impermeable strength. Theater's "masterful" embodiment prizes vulnerability.

Scene Two

The same space in Hollywood. Half a dozen of us, mostly Asian American, ranging from our twenties to our forties, sit on metal fold-up chairs. Dom Magwili, veteran actor and our teacher, asks us to do an individual exercise. We never know what it will be. Once I had to sing, and of all things, the only thing I could think of in my limited alto range was "Plaisir d'amour," the Marianne Faithfull version from the . . . sixties? Seventies? Before her voice became smoky, raspy from too much cocaine and cognac. This time—yikes! Who knows?

Dom calls on me and asks me to do the dreaded "counting to ten" exercise. It looks hard. Ten counts of happy, ten counts of angry, ten counts of sad, back to ten counts of happy. The idea is to transition slowly and to use the counting as a way to explore the range of emotion. So . . . here we go. One, two, three . . . the happy part is easy. Slow transition into anger. By sixteen, I rise to a crescendo of deeply felt emotion that is almost frightening, leading to . . . twenty-four, twenty-five . . . heaving sobs. It's an out-of-the-body experience. I no longer feel I have control over what I'm saying or feeling. Dom kneels in front of me and takes my hand. "It's OK. It's OK. Stay with it," he says in a steady voice. I finish with a faint smile: "Thirty-eight, thirty-nine, forty." One of my classmates says afterward, "Boy, there must be something going on with this lady." Later during the break, Dom's wife, Saachiko, herself a veteran actress, puts her arm around me. Dom pats me on the shoulder and murmurs approvingly, "That's good stuff." I stare in amazement. Good stuff?

Coup de foudre! Emotions, whatever their source, are an actor's treasure trove, to cherish and nurture as part of an expansive repertoire. Years later I see Ed Harris on Inside the Actors Studio (2000). One sentence stays with me: "As an actor, your emotions have to be available to you." Emotions are archived in the body, pointed toward the future, as Derrida argued. Even painful personal experiences are priceless. More than a faux pas or an embarrassment to be repressed and overcome, emotion enlivens a craft that can infuse meaning into anything, even a bunch of numbers.

ACT II

CREATIVE LABOR

chapter 3

(En)Acting Theory

I'm sitting in the darkness of the Newman Theater, the largest of the performance spaces in New York's Public Theater. It's the last preview of Twilight: Los Angeles, *a play about the civil unrest of 1992 created through Anna Deavere Smith's portrayals of her interviewees in this distinctive form of documentary theater. I'm here for the official opening tomorrow night and for my interview with Smith. In a few weeks I'll return to New York when the play opens on Broadway. Anticipation mounts. It's an older, largely white crowd, not what I would have expected at the Public Theater for this piece. (Later we find out it was the press opening; these are the critics!) I know this play by heart in its LA version, and I strain with excitement and curiosity to see the changes that Smith, director George C. Wolfe (then artistic director at the Public), and dramaturgs Tony Kushner (author of* Angels in America) *and Kimberly Flynn have made.*

The house lights dim, and the title appears at the top of the stage: "Twilight: Los Angeles 1992," followed by "Prologues." A video projects the horrifyingly familiar images of Rodney King's beating. As the images fade, "Boom!" A pool of white light stage right illuminates Smith. A tall, light-skinned African American woman, she wears a white shirt and black trousers, her basic costume throughout the play. For the first character, she adds a tie. In deep, low tones, she speaks in Korean. Identified in the supertitles is Chung Lee, head of the Korean American Victims' Association, in a vignette entitled "Riot." As he speaks solemnly, then passionately, we see the translation flashing above us. His store is burning down. The "riot" has begun. The second Smith finishes his speech, almost midsentence, we hear another "Boom!" Blackout. White spotlight. Smith moves toward audience right, removing her tie as she talks, performing Chicano-Salvadoreño writer Rubén Martínez. With his characteristic quick, incisive delivery, he denounces police harassment of Latinos: you can be stopped for "just not walking right," the title of his segment. "Boom!" Blackout. Lights up. Smith embodies a defiant Keith Watson, one of the LA Four tried for the beating of white truck driver Reginald Denny. Watson revels in how they "rocked" LA. Blackout. Jaunty music. Now Smith stands stage left: upright, controlled. The slide flashes the supertitle "Dorinne Kondo, Scholar/Anthropologist, 'Sunset Boulevard.'" I gasp and almost hide my head on the shoulder of my theater companion, anthropologist Kamala Visweswaran. Smith utters the words, "And the social geography of Los Angeles," and the audience erupts in laughter. "My" distant academic observations provide stark contrast to Watson, who claims they "ripped the fine fabric" of LA. A few seconds later my character mercifully sounds more sensible as "I" describe driving down Sunset Boulevard, from its Asian and Latino businesses in the east to its trendy restaurants in West Hollywood to the broad avenues of the compound of Beverly Hills. Personal mortification aside, "I" am a bridge to the next section that begins with real estate agent Elaine Young, ex-wife of actor Gig Young. Her "Safe and Sound in Beverly Hills" figures Beverly Hills as a white fortress, as she and her "motion picture business" friends sought refuge at the exclusive Beverly Hills Hotel during the "riots." In this two-act version of Twilight, Smith performs over forty characters, from police chief Daryl Gates to Korean American store owner Mrs. Young-soon Han, and Maria, an African American juror in the federal trial of the officers accused of beating Rodney King.[1] Ironically, this New York production for me captures Los Angeles in its daunting sprawl, its potential for cataclysmic conflict, and its utopian possibility (see Kondo 1996).

My experience of being represented onstage—objectified, if you will—by an artist who is in turn an object of this study, indexes the difference of my research from the classic anthropological project of studying down, representing others in a one-way, neocolonial process. As John Jackson (2013) observes, contemporary anthropologists can be observed, filmed, represented, in roughly coeval relation to our informants.

This chapter claims theoretical significance for practices of acting, writing, and interviewing that are generally relegated to the domains of practice. My experience of estrangement and (mis)recognition propels a discussion of Anna Deavere Smith's overarching project, her approach to character through language, the implications of her performances for theories of subjectivity, race, and acting, and her interventions in aesthetic form that problematize protagonism, Aristotelian structure, the real as brute facticity, and conventional notions of authorship and the auratic. Smith's art speaks to all of us who write about or represent others; our efforts are always power-laden and carry ethical risks. Her work performs a politics of "radical susceptibility" (Butler 2015) and actively engages a *politics of affiliation* requiring arduous work, grounded in partial understandings unevenly positioned in structures of power. My reading of Smith's art assumes that a complex politics imbricates everyday artistic practice, including acting theory and aesthetic form. Throughout, I claim the cultural work of minoritarian subjects as aesthetic, political, and theoretical interventions.

Because any voice outside the celebratory could be misread as admission of failure or cooptation, I reiterate my post-Foucaultian assumption: pristine, noncomplicit interventions are impossible. Attempts to challenge convention, insofar as they are intelligible, reinscribe power; language, for example, is simultaneously coercive and creative. We cannot invent entirely new languages without risking marginalization, unintelligibility— even madness. Yet language also articulates a world. In the realms of cultural production, nothing can be so contestatory that it is completely unrecognizable (Bourdieu and Delsaut 1974, 7–36). Structures constrain, but they also represent agential possibility (Foucault 1976; Gilmore 2007). My theoretical, ethnographically grounded perspective values complexity, paradox, and the messiness of everyday life. Acting in the world—including staging a play—inevitably involves both the reinscription and subversion of power. An intervention is not thereby vitiated; the intertwinings of power/resistance are inescapable. Rather than a binary logic of resistance/cooptation, a more useful approach asks, "What work is X doing?"

I emphasize the deconstructive aspects of Smith's art, complicating liberal humanist readings that evacuate it of political critique. Mainstream interpretations cleave to the power-evasive: Smith is celebrated for her genius, reinscribing the auratic; her solo performances of individual portraits are read through liberal individualism. Mainstream critics see her as showing all sides, or demonstrating "the resilience of the human spirit" (A. D. Smith 2012a). Their readings occlude historical inequality under the sign of the Human. While this recuperation by a power-evasive humanism is inevitable—even part of the appeal of her work—I explore the ways Smith's art *exceeds* these interpretations. My argument strategically spotlights these contestatory moves. Yet no intervention is pure. Productive tensions animate Smith's fundamental challenges to canonical theater, ones I appreciate more fully now that I am a playwright facing the weight of aesthetic convention and institutional power.

Liberal tropes of healing, of cure, of conversation that escapes "systematic distortion" (Habermas 1970), of Smith as stand-in for the nation or the possibility of democracy, miss the ways she stages the *(im)possibility* of knowing the other and of realizing a pastoral, power-free community in the multiracial nation-state. My experiences as a dramaturg for three of Smith's plays showed me her continuing struggles with theater orthodoxy, despite her eminence. Smith's plays, her performances, and her distinctive approach to acting, character, and writing mount significant interventions on multiple levels. They contest regnant acting theories, essentialist concepts of character and identity, conventional aesthetic form, and commonsense assumptions about the relation of art, theory, and politics. They enact a politics of affiliation and openness to others, while recognizing the structural inequalities and incommensurabilities among differently positioned subjects. Reading her work as only a testament to the human spirit misses this attention to history and power.

I highlight Smith's *theoretical* interventions in order to challenge scholarly and popular analyses that label her work "incorporation," "shamanism," "possession," "channeling" (Schechner 1993, 63–64). These views are highly gendered and racialized: "The black woman as the archetype of the maternal" (Modleski 1997, 60). The notion that Smith is merely a vessel possessed by her characters conveniently erases her years of classical training, the painstaking detail of her observations of speech and movement, her highly theorized interventions into acting practice, and her political commitments.

I thus continue my career-long argument for the expansion of what counts as theory and to claim theoretical and political weight for the arts. Academics often assume otherwise; Smith has told me of instances when her work was treated as (mere) entertainment for a conference. Anecdotally, I have encountered scholars who voiced outrage when Smith appeared on television as a commentator on racial issues. The assumption was clearly that they, or at least another scholar, should be the designated expert. Enacting a different perspective, Smith established an institutional space—the Institute for the Arts and Civic Dialogue—where artists, scholars, journalists, and activists can engage art that addresses urgent political issues.

My analysis begins with Smith's innovations in acting theory and practice, its subversions of essentialist, liberal humanist assumptions about character and identity, and ultimately, its vision of a *progressive politics of affiliation*. Her work parallels the challenges of poststructuralism to humanist notions of a transhistorical, bounded, self-identical subject, though there can be no radical rupture with that subject in theory, artistic practice, or everyday life. The very deployment of the "I" partially reinscribes the whole subject. Languages like English explore the anaphoric potential of the "I," reinforcing the impression of the "I" as stable and monadic, while others, such as Japanese, call attention to the relational, contextual construction of the subject (Kondo 1990). While Smith's portraits enact individuals and her virtuosic one-woman performances attract the designation "genius," her work exceeds and complicates these liberal humanist readings. Smith and Hwang enact subjects-in-process, formed through shifting fields of power, language, history, and culture; subjects are affected by and affect others. I share this aim in my own scholarly and creative work. Smith's theory of subjectivity reveals the racial politics underlying conventional theatrical assumptions about character and acting practice.

Acting Theory, Character, and the Performative Production of the Subject

In 1979 Smith inaugurated a series of performances she calls *On the Road: A Search for American Character*. In US actor training informed by psychological realism, the actor's own experiences create the foundation for building character. Smith instead engages a linguistic, externally based approach that involves reaching for the other. For example, acting exercises grounded in psychological realism might explore an actor's sensory memory of drinking a cup of tea, or actors could mine their own traumatic experiences to build empathy with a character. This method, affiliated with early Stanislavski[2]—who in turn was reacting against a stylized, declamatory mode of acting—proves limiting, especially given the youth of many acting students.

A basic tenet of psychological realism is that characters live inside of you and that you create a character through a process of realizing your own similarity to the character. When I . . . became a teacher of acting, I began to become more and more troubled by the self-oriented method. I began to look for ways to engage my students in putting themselves in other people's shoes. This went against the grain of the tradition, which was to get the character to walk in the *actor's shoes* . . . This method left an important bridge out of acting. The spirit of acting is the *travel* from the self to the other. This "self-based" method . . . saw the self as the ultimate home of the character. To me, the search for character is constantly in motion. It is a quest that moves back and forth between the self and the other. (A. D. Smith 1997, xxvi)

Smith thus revised her own classical training in order to develop her own theory. She sought to expand acting repertoire through interviewing other people, observing in painstaking detail a person's language, speech patterns, mannerisms, without necessarily presuming to know their deep emotional conflicts.

Smith's acting theory underscores poststructuralism's emphasis on the linguistic, processual, performative production of subjects and subjectivities. Method acting and other approaches based in psychological realism presuppose an essentialist self that reinscribes a substance-attribute metaphysics: the substance of consciousness, a transhistorical human essence that is merely modified by attributes such as race, gender, sexuality, and age. Similarly, the subject is presumed to exist prior to language. Actors try to make characters their own, through empathizing and projecting from their own experiences. In contrast, Debby Thompson (2003) argues that Smith's theories begin with language and with the linguistic production of the subject, who is always in process. "Identity is a process, and . . . we are every moment making an adjustment" (A. D. Smith 2000, 52).

Smith's theory of acting scrupulously attends to gaps, stuttering, mispronunciations, and laughter as portals into character. During her acting training, Smith discovered that rhythmic changes in Shakespeare indexed moments of emotional revelation. The shift from iambic to trochaic meter (e.g., King Lear's "Never, never, never, never, never!") signals heightened emotional vulnerability and the breakdown of a character's control over her social persona. "If you got a trochee in the second beat, a character was really 'losing it' psychologically . . . this 'loss' made it possible for you to really know something about that character. . . . Losing it is a good thing in that it is a defeat of an imposed rhythmic structure" (A. D. Smith 2000, 36). Smoothly flowing language, such as the speech of politicians and academics, can occlude rather than illuminate character and emotion.

In the rehearsal room, Smith's theories and distinctive acting practice challenge techniques associated with psychological realism. The actor does *not* sit with a text and imagine the character's motivations and objectives by exploring her own psyche. When I worked with Smith on *Twilight* and *House Arrest*, she would bring in a Walkman and repeat the words she was hearing on tape. Years later, *House Arrest* employed a large cast for its world premiere at the Arena Stage in Washington, DC. During our workshop at NYU, it was fascinating to see some actors struggle with the process of repeating what they heard through their headphones. Smith carefully studies the interviews, including work with vocal, movement, and dialect coaches. As technology has developed, her process now includes video recordings of interviewees. To illustrate Smith's reliance on performance rather than on written text in her early work, I emphasize that in *Twilight* we dramaturgs hardly ever saw a script, though it did exist. We reacted to Smith's *performances*, from preliminary excerpts she recited along with her Walkman to the more polished scenes she performed onstage during preview. The script was the artifact of performance, overturning traditional theater practice.

This process evolved in Smith's plays written after *Twilight*, reflecting in part the historical and geographical scope of subsequent work. In *House Arrest*, chief dramaturg Jim Lewis oversaw the voluminous, ever-changing script that included primary historical materials, a "frame play" about a theater troupe performing the interview excerpts for prisoners, and the excerpts themselves. In *Let Me Down Easy*, we who sat "behind the table"—director Stephen Wadsworth, dramaturgs Alisa Solomon and I, stage manager Diane Divita, and dialect coach Amy Stoller—always worked with a script. Thus, after *Twilight*, dramaturgical work shifted into a more conventional dramaturgical practice in which the script was an integral part of rehearsal. Smith described this process: "I used to come in without a script, and lip-synch to tapes. . . . Basically, I present the characters, and Stephen and the others tell me what they see" (Arnott 2008). Wadsworth offered this commentary on the process: "That's such a fascinating conversation that she's . . . having with us which forces her to articulate and to justify her gut feeling as to why something should be in. And she's so brave to. It's more challenging because there are more people who have something real to say" (Wadsworth 2008).

I interviewed Smith the day after the opening of the New York version of *Twilight* at the Public Theatre:

> KONDO: *I wanted to ask you about the genesis of* On the Road . . . *did it not arise in reaction to conventions . . . the notion of "having a part" or the*

convention of the well-made play? . . . I'm wondering whether the interiority of the Method was part of it.

SMITH: No, all of that . . . Certainly the interiority of the Method was disturbing to me. The idea of the centrality of any actor's psyche—I don't understand that. When I get interested in an interview is when I think I can never capture this. (Kondo 1996)

Smith does not aim to master or fully inhabit the other. Instead, she is intrigued by difference and (im)possibility—"when I think I can never capture this." Smith's acting theory begins with the presupposition of *difference* between self and other. It does not project emotional similarity. She emphasizes that she does not *become* the other; for her, the spirit of acting is what she calls the "broad jump" from the self to the other, a metaphor that involves active, propulsive effort that exceeds "travel" or "bridging" (A. D. Smith 2014b). Smith's approach appreciates difference, hard work, and separateness while embracing the possibility of partial connection and partial understanding.

Difference and separation need not mean lack of sympathy. On the contrary, actors generally attempt to love their characters, even the villains. Smith commented on her sense of responsibility to her characters:

SMITH: I want them to know how much I love them. . . . I'm trying to attract your attention with mimicry, so you go, "Oh my god, she's not a cowboy," but once I've got your attention, I want you to really hear what they are saying. . . . That cowboy . . . is saying some pretty incredible things about our health care system, and calling for a flat rate. . . . So the most conservative person has a very progressive call. (A. D. Smith 2012a)

Her work exceeds our power-evasive notions of empathy, a term Smith has invoked for what she does. The demanding work of trying to "walk in someone's words"—what I call "full-body listening"—surpasses the easy empathy presupposed in our commonsense discourse. Smith in practice refuses the colonizing fusion implicit in the empathic collapse of self and other. As Saidiya Hartman argues, empathy can simply involve empathizing with one's own emotions projected onto the other (1997, 17–23); Elin Diamond calls this colonizing identification "the violence of 'we'" (Diamond 1992).[3]

Smith steers a difficult course between extremes, avoiding colonizing empathy and averting its opposite, the positing of ineffable, unbridgeable difference. She explained to me in a letter:

> I resist mushes of identity. I don't believe that when I play someone in my work, that I "am" the character. I want the audience to experience the gap, because I know if they experience the gap, they will appreciate my reach for the other. This reach is what moves them, not a mush of me and the other, not a presumption that I can play everything and everybody, but more a desire to reach for something that is very clearly not me—my deep feeling of my separateness from everything, not my ability to pass for everything. (A. D. Smith 1998)

Smith's work negotiates a tension between this deep sense of difference on the one hand, and a sense of commonality on the other—with all the dangers of appropriation by a power-evasive liberal humanism that this commonality might entail.

Smith destabilizes psychological realism and the self-identical subject, focusing instead on the *work of creativity* required to perform another. This work of creativity draws attention to the racialization that makes the subject.[4] Smith's innovations bear significant implications for conventional acting theory/practice in "the West." Her theories of character, her focus on people of many different races, and her own gendered, raced body spotlight the workings of race and power. These theoretical/political insights elude conventionally avant-garde theater, where race appears as superfluous or merely aesthetic (e.g, the work of Robert Wilson) and cross-cultural approaches that risk exoticism and cultural appropriation.

Smith's theorizing of the breakdown of language offers insight into racial subjectivity. In her HBO master class, Smith asked eighteen-year-old acting students to perform each other, using interview transcripts as scripts. A blonde woman was assigned to perform a black man who had played Trayvon Martin in a performance piece. His interview, hesitant and polite, enacted his fear of offending others. Smith told him, "I think the 'ums' are more about not wanting to say the wrong thing and possibly cause trouble. (Turning to the white woman). . . . The way you fill those is to think about what he *could say* . . . that could be unacceptable." After the young woman's performance, Smith addressed her with passionate intensity:

> You really trusted the dignity, the importance, the beauty of his "ums" . . . when this young African American man is struggling in his life at 18 years to figure out what it all means . . . for you, as a white southern woman, to get a chance to be inside of those ums and to imagine what you would be trying to think through . . . is exactly the gift that is missing in the United States of America. . . . To me this is a

crisis in this country. That we don't know how to *feel* about anybody but the people who not only *look* like us but *think* like us. . . . As a southern beautiful white woman, you get to be inside the fact that your classmate just doesn't know what to think about it or what to do about it. . . . He's giving you a gift. (A. D. Smith 2014b, 14.56)

Smith then addressed the young man: "She's *trying* . . . to take the broad jump to the other . . . across the chasm to get to you." The young woman was given a chance to inhabit, however partially, the young man's existential predicaments, articulated in his speech and movement patterns. Though we cannot *become* another, we can leap *toward* another, through scrupulous attention, effort, hard work, and respect for difference.

This leap to the other is fraught with a complex history of inequality, ethical risk, and urgent political stakes that complicate easy readings of Smith's performances as enactments of democracy. Rather, her work addresses the contradictions of the US nation-state: the (im)possibility of making one from many (Cheng 2001; Nyong'o 2009). Smith practices a radical availability to others, a formulation that in English sounds potentially passive, even though availability is a condition of existence, demonstrating strength and agency. Her art performs openness to others while reminding us of the persistence of structural inequality and the necessity for consciously agentic hard work. What politics animates these performances?

Cross-Racial Representation: Pleasures and Dangers

Smith's travel in her *On the Road* project is both geographic and social. She is perhaps best known for her travel across social boundaries and fixed identities, as she performs people of many different races, ages, cultures, classes, nationalities, and genders. The aesthetic/political effects of these multiple enactments are complex. The Rashōmon-like multiplicity can be well suited to depicting volatile events and bristling tensions, evident in *Twilight* and its immediate predecessor, *Fires in the Mirror*, that focused on the Crown Heights riots in Brooklyn and the conflict between Blacks and Jews. In its best moments Smith's technique presents an array of points of view and gestures toward the historical, political forces that construct these "individual" perspectives. This is my reading of the stage version of *Fires in the Mirror*. Various people speak from complex subject positions, each inviting us into identification with a persuasive point of view, then throwing us out of that identification, as s/he says something slightly problematic at another level, or as we next encounter a character who, espousing an opposing perspective, seems equally persuasive. The play made me understand multiple sides in the conflicts, yet it was deeply disturbing. Forces of history overdetermine individual responses; the cleavages often seem intractable.[5] *Twilight* expands the black-white binary of *Fires in the Mirror* to the inexhaustible racial multiplicity of Los Angeles.

Artists like Smith and Hwang are the agents of a critical vocabulary that reimagines originary identity and its manifestations in race and gender essentialism. Smith's cross-racial performances de-essentialize the subject, throwing into relief the shaping of subjectivity through historically specific bodily disciplines we label race and gender, among other forces. These disciplines and the attributes they ostensibly index are thus exposed as phantasmatic, arbitrary, and performative—forged in and through structures of power. Certainly, there is something astonishing in seeing a person of one race and gender don the characteristics of so many others along so many different axes. Through scrupulous reproduction or hyperbolic exaggeration of gesture, intonation, movement, and accent, Smith casts into relief the ways our essentialist notions of identity are always already citations of cultural ideals and narrative conventions.[6]

Smith's art negotiates a series of tensions, between the fixity and fluidity of identities, the (stereo)typical and the unique. These tensions assume a political valence in performances across conventional racial boundaries. Such boundary transgressions inevitably elicit anxieties about caricature, stereotype, and political allegiance that arise from power-laden histories of continuing racial inequality. No work that engages cross-racial performance in the contemporary United States can escape the historical context of minstrelsy and the complex ambivalence captured in the terms "love and theft" (Lott 1993), the fascination with and appropriation of the other. Smith negotiates tensions between "mimetic rivalry"—hostility and conflict among ethnicities/races—and a "solidarity between ethnicities" (Modleski 1997, 65–66).

Charges of stereotype/caricature carry a political valence, arising from deep, historically specific political anxieties. Is Smith favoring "a side"? Political inequalities amplify the urgency of these queries, for stereotypes can have profound, life-determining impact. In the theater, stereotypes can promote life-diminishing psychic violence. What, then, are the implications of Smith's cross-racial performances? What, if any, political promise could be gleaned from her work within a nation-state whose history includes minstrelsy, the exclusion of artists of color, and continuing systematic inequality?

First, de-essentializing race and gender does not mean disavowal. Smith avers that her own gendered, raced body plays into her cross-racial performances; we never entirely forget the performer's subject position or its political histories. In our interview, Smith's power-sensitive perspective illuminates the thorny issue of cross-racial performance:

> Race is also not arbitrary here. Race, gender, size, beauty . . . are all extremely . . . significant. We live in a society of visual rhetoric. For better or for worse, for most people what you see is what you get. . . . The minute a certain race is put on certain material, it is significant. I believe my work onstage carries with it a racialization which is significant. . . . The model that everyone can play everything, from people to dogs to houses, is one model. . . . But to the extent that it moved into where race and gender as political realities live, I think we are moving into another period of theatre history. My guess is that in the theatre race still has to matter because the theatre hasn't absorbed the degree to which it does matter. (A. D. Smith 1998)

In a deft double movement, Smith de-essentializes race while embracing the awareness that race remains a powerful social force that shapes the creation and reception of her work. Theater, she suggests, is a site that operates through the disavowal of race, reproducing a power-evasive, colorblind stance.

How does Smith's own gendered, raced body matter? Certainly, versions of the mammy trope figure Smith as the vessel for the nation. Given national legacies of slavery, including white guilt and continuing racial inequality, it may be symbolically compelling to see an African American woman perform crossings of race and gender, for she operates from a position of relative historical disempowerment. This tilts the political valence of cross-racial representation toward a "solidarity of ethnicities" rather than simple appropriation, since appropriation becomes more difficult from that political and social location (see J. Y. Kim 2015). Smith herself intends that others perform her plays, and *Twilight* has been produced with multiperson, multiracial casts. Nonetheless, I argue that the audience never forgets completely about the actor's gender or race. Power-laden histories haunt the bodies onstage. For example, Danny Hoch—a white, Jewish male who grew up in what he terms "the projects" and whose work involves dazzling, multilingual performances of characters of color—is celebrated for his solo performances. His gendered, racial positionality makes his performances inescapably appropriative to a degree, though this does not vitiate the progressive politics of his performances. The appropriation is nuanced through his history, his familiarity with characters of different races and ethnicities, and his performative skill, but he cannot completely transcend the relative privilege of whiteness and heterosexual masculinity.[7]

The expansive canvases of *Twilight*, *House Arrest*, and *Let Me Down Easy* extend far beyond the black-white binary, rendering issues of accountability, relative privilege, historical positioning, and potential appropriation even more fraught and intricate. What happens when the story proliferates beyond black and white to people of color performing each other, or travels across the boundaries of nation-states, when an African American performs a Rwandan Hutu prisoner? The historical, political positionings of racial/ethnic subjects, including the histories of nation-states unevenly positioned on a global stage, shape the ethics and politics of those performances.

Attention to political asymmetry challenges the power-evasive, liberal humanist ideology that pervades the mainstream critical reception of Smith's work. For example, several analysts view Smith's staging of conversations that rarely occur in life as a utopian vision of the democratic process (Lahr 1993). These perspectives view conversations as power-free. But as critiques of Habermas have argued, "systematically distorted communication" (Habermas 1970) is the only possible form of conversation in a public sphere where structural inequalities persist (Fraser 1989). Jill Dolan foregrounds these power relations and simultaneously reaches for the utopian potential in Smith's work that "allows you to build new worlds together" (Dolan 2005, 82). She argues that Smith stages conversations instantiating a "politics of coalition" (84). I add a significant caveat: coalition represents a fraught, power-laden process that assumes incommensurability and cannot guarantee a "safe place." In Smith's work, race, gender, and other markers of "identity" index unequal positions in historically shifting fields of power; coalescing is fraught, difficult, always incomplete.

Anne Cheng argues that the true common ground among Smith's interviewees is Smith's gendered, raced body. She finds the question of stereotype and of Smith's ultimate sympathies to be "misdirected, for that line of inquiry disguises the more crucial questions of the ethical and political dimensions . . . of 'stepping into' someone else's shoes. In short . . . we need to ask what it means, ethically, politically, and psychically, to speak as someone else" (Cheng 2001, 186). Instead of raising the usual problematic—parodic or authentic?—Cheng sees Smith's process as premised on immersion: "Ethics comes after identification and complicity—that is, after immersion has already taken place" (188). For anthropologists, this is a compelling argument, given that immersion is the trope by which we conventionally operate in our ethnographic fieldwork. Only through immersion, goes the nostrum, does knowledge emerge. Cheng refuses the liberal humanist utopian gesture—that Smith stages conversations that perform our democratic political ideals, for example—arguing instead for the fraught complexities that Smith negotiates:

> In addition to the conflicted views being presented it is disturbing to witness how those views occupy one stage, indeed, one body. Anyone who has witnessed Smith's performances understands the discomfort of being made to watch the fine lines separating speaking for, speaking as, and speaking against. Critics have read her complicity with various opposing characters as constituting a kind of community, but her complicity with everyone also marks her distance from them. Her work speaks simultaneously to a desire for and a failure of community. It delineates boundaries even as it breaks them. (188–89)

Cheng's acute insights are indispensable. However, we must take this one step further: immersion is never politically innocent. It is always animated by a complex, contradictory politics. Certainly anthropology has confronted the politics of appropriation, colonizing empathy, and imperialism that can animate immersion. In the paradoxical ways Cheng herself describes but does not explicitly thematize, Smith's work enacts the contradictory ethics *and* politics of immersion in the attempt to speak as someone else.

Beyond Stereotype and Authenticity

While I remain aware of the dangers of psychological violence in the stereotype and the ways the histories of minstrelsy haunt any cross-racial performance, I unsettle the (stereo)type/authenticity opposition from another angle. This logic transposes an even more fundamental binary—(authentic) original versus (stereotyped) copy, representation versus the real as brute facticity—that theory and artistic practice of the last century seeks to dislodge. I suggest several ways of disrupting this foundational opposition. My approach insists on seeing interviewees as more than passive victims of representational violence; they, too, are endowed with complex, ambivalent subjectivities. I simultaneously recognize the ethics and politics of representing those who have been historically subjected to life-diminishing representational violence onstage and in everyday life. Politically, it can be strategically necessary to assert "authenticity" in the face of assertions that people of color "cannot represent themselves. They must be represented" (Marx and Engels 1959, 339).

Cherise Smith's critique of Anna Deavere Smith's portrayals demonstrates the critical investment in the real versus representation. She argues that while performances of public figures such as Cornel West may work onstage, "a lesser-known person risks becoming a puppet in Smith's hands . . . the actor's essentialized depiction may usurp an individual's power. In other words, the simultaneous extraction and amplification of the interviewee's 'essence' could result in an uneven differential in which the individual is disempowered and Smith is further empowered" (Cherise Smith 2011, 162). The ethical challenges are urgent for those of us who engage in empirical reportage. At one level, the charge is indisputable, even unexceptionable. All narrative centers the perspective of the narrator, as *Rashōmon* taught us; every narrative does some degree of symbolic violence to the rounded complexity of those who become characters in our narratives, whether in everyday life or on the stage (Kondo 1986). I myself was reluctant to be interviewed and performed for *Fires in the Mirror*, the play preceding *Twilight*, given my experiences with journalists, who had consistently misquoted me. Smith's work shares the problem of accountability to informants with journalists, ethnographers, and academic critics. Certainly, it has been a central issue in anthropology since the 1960s and 1970s.

Simply in terms of requisite institutional protocols, Smith adheres to standard legal and ethical procedures, asking interviewees to sign a release, as they might in a social scientific study. The interviewees are informed in writing of their rights; refusing to participate is of course always a possibility. Furthermore, though some interviewees may not like Smith's portrayals, often they are ambivalent—including those who are accustomed to public recognition. For example, at the opening party for *Twilight* on Broadway, Shelby Coffey, then editor of the *Los Angeles Times*, joked with me that we should hire Charles Lloyd, the prominent African American attorney also portrayed in *Twilight,* to represent us in a class action suit. People who do not ordinarily appear onstage as public figures may feel pleased, even honored, to be included, despite any misgivings. Smith's performance bestows a moment of celebrity. Minimally, her plays write her characters into history, into a significant domain in the public sphere.[8]

Smith's portrayals offer a form of mirroring, reinscribing a pleasurable Lacanian (mis)recognition that is inescapable in the founding of the subject. For many minoritarian interviewees, this represents an otherwise rare conferral of existence in the public sphere. Populations subjected to traumatic, oppressive forms of interpellative violence can be enlivened by mirrorings that are less oppressive—even reparative. Finally, and as the intentional fallacy teaches us, one can never preempt or predict every potential reaction, a point I elaborate in the following chapter.

In her HBO master class, Smith confronted an ethical dilemma with one of her interviewees. A young woman, Jaz, shared emotionally searing stories about her family. Later, when a classmate performed the interview, Jaz reacted angrily. "I felt like the words were no longer mine . . . they were just everybody's to use. . . . I felt like they were just being played with. I felt violated . . . upset . . . exposed . . ." (A. D. Smith 2014b, 17.58). Smith worked with her to cut the offending sections of the interview. Ultimately, Jaz affirmed her trust in Smith, who cautioned her to be aware of the publicity of language. Once released in language, utterances cannot be controlled, whether onstage or in everyday life. Smith reminds Jaz of the intentional fallacy: language is not ours.

Accordingly, I take issue with the stereotype/authenticity binary on two levels: first, in terms of presumptions that underlie the opposition of original to copy, and second, that we are constantly engaged in a dynamic of appropriation on a daily basis. Cherise Smith's objection to Anna Deavere Smith's project arises from an underlying distinction between the real versus representation, in particular the assumption that the representation is a poor copy of the original, that may "usurp the individual." She argues that "Smith's subjects become representations of, and metaphors for, themselves" (Cherise Smith 2011, 187). This is surely true, but the dynamic of usurpation/metaphorization characterizes *both the real and the representation.*

Let me take my own experiences of watching "myself" as exemplifying the politics of caricature/authenticity. Smith's performance unsettled my everyday, existential sense of being in the world, much as any representation might. For example, some of us may be surprised at the way our voice sounds on a recording or at the way we look in photographs. This defamiliarizing shock arises from the splitting of the subject into the subject of the *énoncé* and the subject of the *énonciation*: the difference between the speaking subject and the subject of the utterance (Benveniste 1971). This estrangement was heightened by the embarrassment of realizing that this other, unfamiliar persona may be—indeed, *must* be—how others see one. This gap between the existentially lived and theatrical representation offers insight into Smith's performances and the theories of identity they enact. Smith's portrayals, precisely through their theatricality, call attention to the ways all identities depend on the deployment of conventionally intelligible signifiers. The sense of authentic selfhood thus emerges as illusory, a process of essence fabrication coextensive with the citation of conventions. The original is not as original as we imagine.

Stylized Naturalism, Alienation Effects, Reparative Mirroring

To unpack further the charge of caricature, I situate Smith's work in a political history of theater and a power-sensitive analytic that disrupts our commonsensical notion of the original while attending carefully to the history of inequality that animates the stereotype. This problematic requires close analysis of Smith's acting theory, which I locate within a Brechtian legacy of estrangement and political action.

Smith's acting theory embraces a person's distinctive speech rhythms, especially the gaps, the "uhs" and "ums" where language fails, as insights into character. Thus, to my chagrin, one reviewer called my character a "stuttering sociologist." Her intense focus on her interviewees' mannerisms and speech eccentricities manifests in immersive work with vocal and dialect coaches. What is happening with the soft palate? Where is the tongue placed? A person's signature tics and gestures are theatricalized in what Smith calls her "impressions" of a person, when received rhythms and the smooth surfaces of language break down. These breakdowns reveal character, yet the spectacle of stuttering and other forms of verbal undress disturbs our sense of control, undermining our pretensions to Master Subjecthood. Indeed, my character served as comic relief; the audience's "acoustic mirror" was one of being *laughed at*.

Privileging the margins challenges conventional theatrical language, which smooths over such infelicities. In some playwriting groups, I have been told to delete the "ums" and "uhs" because theater should be the domain of "heightened language." Smith's theatricalizing of "mistakes" and verbal tics disrupts both theatrical convention and the wholeness of the subject. Rather, she makes a deconstructive theoretical move, where seemingly extraneous, even annoying, features become privileged portals into character. Her theory enacts the eruption of the Lacanian unconscious as the discourse of the Other: that which we cannot control. The Other (the structure of language, the Symbolic) inhabits us without our knowing. The fissures in language reveal the workings of this unconscious that rebelliously disrupts our conventional sense of mastery. Smith spotlights the marginal as the site of character; for the young African American man in her class, the "ums" revealed his complex ambivalence about his own gendered, raced place in the world. Privileging the margins problematizes our commonsense version of verisimilitude, our sense of ourselves as Master Subjects, and theatrical conventions that prize flowing, literary language.[9]

Smith, like Hwang, joins with metacritiques of the genres of ethnography, journalism, and documentary, destabilizing any claims these nonfiction genres might make to a transparent inscription of reality. Smith engages what I call *stylized naturalism* that theatricalizes characters' mannerisms, contesting the dominant form of psychological realism we see repeatedly on stage and screen. Her version of heightened language illuminates struggles for meaning and promotes Brechtian alienation.

For example, my surprise at Smith's performance of my character centered on stereotypically feminine speech: tag questions, rising inflections, and trailing off the ends of sentences. All convey the impression of uncertainty, a conventionally feminine softness that I prefer to avoid (consciously, at least). The melodic, jaunty music that accompanied my character heightened the impression of femininity. Sequencing was a third factor. "I" provided jarring contrast to the black masculinity of Keith Watson, the immediately preceding figure, in terms of both gender and the distant voice of academe: "The social geography of Los Angeles" as opposed to "We rocked LA!" Smith often subtly satirizes academics.[10] Caricature or reality? Clearly, personal mannerisms can be accorded heightened significance through elements of performance: sequencing, music, intonation, and gesture. Even now, I cannot say whether my reaction arises from a sense of estrangement from my own representation in any form, Smith's exaggeration of mannerism for theatrical effect, or production factors such as sequencing and music. I suspect all of the above are in play. All problematize representation as a transparent inscription of the real.

Sets and costumes create character in similar fashion. In the film version of *Twilight*, Smith performed on sets and wore costumes that symbolized qualities significant for the narrative. For example, Smith interviewed opera singer Jessye Norman at Norman's home. Reportedly, Norman wore a tracksuit during the interview. For the filming of *Twilight*, the set designer built a tower so that Smith-as-Norman could gaze down on the urban rubble; she wore a long-haired wig, tiara, and makeup that signified "opera diva," not someone at home in casual conversation. Similarly, I was interviewed for the film, in a segment that was cut. My character sat against a vibrantly blue window framing an elegant vase holding tiger lilies. Smith had interviewed me by phone, so the set designer had no idea that I have no such vase nor do I like lilies nor do I have such a beautiful window, but perhaps he felt that this picture looked Asian in its minimalism and serenity. Set and costume, then, reinforce the realization that the people who are performed are characters in service of a narrative.

I was asked not to come onto the set for the shooting of the segment based on my character—Smith was concerned that my reaction might disturb her concentration—but I did accidentally run into her as "me" just before the filming began. Startled, I burst out in shocked laughter. Smith wore a boxy, grey Prada blouse, and though I do not have such a Prada blouse, I did have a nondesigner blouse in a similar shape. She wore bright red lipstick, apparently one of my signature features. I used to wear a single hoop earring, having lost the mate, and I loaned her the earring. It was both startling and amusing to see that I had been portrayed "accurately," in a distillation of my appearance to certain distinctive signifiers: red lipstick, my earring, a blouse that could have been of Japanese design.[11] Smith and I could not be more physically different; she is tall and African American, I am almost a foot shorter than she, and Asian. Yet she found meaningful markers of identity in order to create her "impression" of me. It was a portrayal both familiar and unfamiliar; I was stunned to recognize and to not recognize myself in Smith's theatrical rendition.[12]

Rather than indexing the inauthentic, Smith's work calls attention to the *inevitability* of narrative. Certainly, psychoanalysis posits that we all narrativize in everyday life, scripting others into our own stories, theatricalizing ourselves and our lives. "People become real to us by frustrating us. . . . If they don't frustrate us they are merely figures of fantasy" (Phillips

2013, 29). The mistake would be to think that our encounter with the real occurs without representation or mediation, that it is simply a matter of brute facticity or the revelation of truth. On the contrary, Smith's art enacts the impossibility of an unmediated real.

In a Brechtian sense, Smith's version of stylized naturalism performs a theater of alienation effects: *Verfremdung*, estrangement, when the actor retains a certain distance from the character. For Brecht, this distance possesses a critical, political weight, destabilizing the seductive pull of immersive identification that can be deadening to a critical spirit. The audience remains aware of the actor behind the role and thus of the theatricality of theater. As Carl Weber told Smith, "While I see the person fully, at the same time I still see you as the actress presenting the person and having an opinion about it. Which was exactly what Brecht was writing about" (1995, 57). For Brecht, as for Foucault, identity is forged through history, culture, and power; it does not reflect a transhistorical, universal human nature. Reminding the audience that the theater and the characters are constructions, humanly fashioned, creates a distance that can foster critical awareness and political action, for the human condition is not fixed but historically malleable and therefore open to change. Brecht wanted audiences to think critically and, ideally, to act politically outside the theater—though this goal was never fully attained.

Smith's approach negotiates multiple tensions through alienation effects. Her virtuoso performances de-essentialize identity as she transforms into multiple characters before our eyes. Yet at another level, we never lose sight of Smith's own gendered, raced body or the residual hauntings of her body by the characters she has already performed. Estrangement here appears as (gendered, raced) difference between actor and character. The theatrical quality of her acting heightens this estrangement. Her refusal to allow us to immerse ourselves in identification with her characters constitutes a final Verfremdungseffekt.

The difference between theatrical acting and acting for film or television is crucial here. Most scholars who write about Smith use either the written text or filmed versions of her plays. Attention to theatrical performance is indispensable for the analysis of Smith's art. Theater requires the actor to project and to gesture so that she can reach the audience in the balcony. Given the acoustic and visual demands of theater, film and television actors often come across badly onstage—inaudible for the audience. Playwrights find this extraordinarily annoying, since the dialogue we have so carefully crafted goes unheard. The opposite can hold true in transitioning from theater to film or television. Theatrical actors generally tone down their performances for film; what looks brilliant in the theater can seem exaggerated on screen.

Smith's films of *Fires in the Mirror* and *Twilight* occasionally display this "bigness" of theatrical acting that could contribute to the impression of exaggeration. In the former, overproduction heightened this effect. Whereas Smith performed the stage version of *Fires in the Mirror* on a minimalist set, transforming character with a simple change of gesture, intonation, and clothing, the PBS film utilized elaborate set pieces and costumes. The audience thus lost the pleasure of watching Smith transform before our eyes. When I worked on *Twilight* the film, the creative team was unanimous in our desire to spotlight Smith's transformations, and the film accomplished this goal. Perhaps for some viewers, elements of production and performance contribute to the impression of exaggeration. Theatricalizing speech mannerisms, choosing costumes, and creating sets that may not "accurately" represent the interview, may unsettle literal attempts at verisimilitude. The "exaggerated" mannerism can have a politically salutary effect, fostering *Verfremdung*, reminding us of the performer behind the role, drawing attention to the ways we deploy socially conventional signifiers.

Though Smith seems to inhabit the character, her performance refuses us the comfort of immersive identification. We may identify with a character, but that voice is followed by a different and perhaps conflicting one, in a succession of disparate perspectives placed in often jarring juxtaposition. We cannot be seduced into a single point of view; we are reminded of the characters' different, unequal social locations and histories that inform their perspectives, in an associative montage/collage. Aesthetic form abets the estrangement effect.

Finally, Smith's technique subverts the hubris of individualist ideologies that defines each of us as ineffably unique. Rather, all identities mobilize highly stereotyped, conventional signifiers. In my case, those included red lipstick, boxy blouse, and rising inflections at the ends of sentences. Smith's performance suggests that the combination of signifiers may be distinctive, but to the extent that signifiers are socially legible, they are citations of norms—even archetypes or fetishes. She problematizes our ideology of individualism through the performance of what some might dismiss as exaggeration. Clearly, Smith points out that there is no representation beyond representation, no unmediated access to the real; rather, she *stages* the narrativizing of others that we perform constantly, unwittingly, in our everyday lives.

Indeed, much of the psychoanalytic literature on identification shows the ways the ego as origin of meaning and agency is based on the incorporation and introjection of lost others. One cannot have the Other, so one must *become—or more accurately, take in*—the Other. The uniqueness of the subject paradoxically resides in the reproduction of multiple, lost objects. "Originary" identity, then, is inevitably a product of mimesis, reproduction, citation, appropriation, incorporation, and performance of Others (Freud 1989; Fuss 1995; Butler 1997; Cheng 2001). Smith's work stages this logic of identification through reproducing efforts to become the other, citing multiple, lost objects in an inevitable failure to become those objects. In the failures lies the possibility of agency and of political change, for each repetition is inevitably repetition with a difference. For Smith, "failures"—the gaps in language and rhythm—are *precisely* where character resides and where agency, "authenticity," and distinctiveness can emerge (Cheng 2001; Eng and Kazanjian 2003; Halberstam 2011; Hesmondhalgh 2013).

In sum, Smith's work enacts identity-as-process, offering a critique of the bounded, whole subject of liberal humanism. Smith problematizes the logics of copy versus original, stereotypy versus authenticity, as she stages the ways we inevitably engage narrative conventions and deploy conventional signifiers in everyday life. Theatricalizing attempts to become the other, her performances reproduce the logic of identification itself. By denaturalizing identity, her performances spotlight performativity as a process of continuous citation, one that can go awry, fail, be unfaithful. The failures of seamless reproduction—stuttering, tics, rhythmic shifts—can be the sites of political possibility and individual agency.

Smith thus opens the way, politically, to make/unmake/remake race through her destabilizing moves. Inevitably imperfect, both reinscribing and unsettling the subject, Smith's performances demonstrate "authenticity" arising not from an essential self but from the irruption of the Lacanian Symbolic, in gaps and stutterings that disturb the smooth reproduction of the self-identical subject. Her art both destabilizes identity and reinscribes it in portrayals of individuals of multiple races, some of whom may have never been publicly mirrored. Smith offers us reparative mirroring in a domain, the American stage, where minoritarian subjects have rarely, if ever, enjoyed the jubilation of reparative narcissism: the promise of public existence (Pellegrini 1997).

Genre Bending

Smith's challenges to the theatrical canon are expansive, extending to aesthetic form and to theories of authorship and of writing.

Bending genre (let us remember that gender is *genre* in French), Smith's work contests the form of the well-made play: protagonism, a throughline, and Aristotelian conflict and catharsis. Smith, Hwang, and I share a commitment to an aesthetic of juxtaposition. Smith's aesthetic interventions have a progressive political valence, for her notions of character and her challenges to conventional Aristotelian structure connect with political issues outside the theater. The form of her plays and her creative process refigure authorship and writing as the work of the singular authorial genius who creates purely from her imagination—even as Smith's performative virtuosity reinscribes the auratic idea of genius. Yet, given the disciplines and punishments directed toward her innovations in writing, I argue that she *should* receive credit as author in a conventional sense. I parse the effects of these paradoxes.

The difficulty of classifying Smith's art indexes the ways it subverts conventional categories. Journalism, documentary, shamanism, one-woman show, play, ethnography—her work is all and none of these. Like an ethnographer or a journalist, she gathers perspectives on a place, a gathering (an academic conference, for example), or an incident by interviewing people. Unlike ethnographers and journalists, she constructs her account through performing these people and their words, verbatim, onstage.

In our interview Smith linked protagonism and the well-made play to the political.

> SMITH: Most people really do believe that there is one person in charge or one person who gets all of the attention, and they really invest in that. Even if they say mean things about that person and critique the person, the person is still central.
>
> KONDO: *So the notion of the single, central authority, the law of the Father?*
>
> SMITH: Right. . . . But I missed something in my development that made me—I just feel very bad when I see centrality or I see single heroes or anything like that. It's just not pleasing to me. Now there are many people who see my work, and it's very displeasing, because I do not have a central hero.

KONDO: *So they're searching for it and—*

SMITH: "Who is your favorite?"

KONDO: *So they ask that? Very interesting.*

SMITH: Sure, in LA there were lots of people who . . . said in some way, "Didn't she find anybody who could give us a glimmer of hope? . . . Who of all these people?"

KONDO: *That's right, it was the desire for a voice of authority who would package it and give it narrative closure.* (Kondo 1996, 325)

Smith's acting theory illuminates the *political* significance of assuming the centrality of the protagonist and the actor's psyche. Not only can the actor-focused Method be too self-centered on a personal level but the preoccupation with one's own group and the submission to a voice of totalizing authority can feed nationalism, hostility to difference, and a colonizing of the other.

Smith problematizes standard Aristotelian dramatic structure that follows the journey of a single protagonist through the stages of introduction, conflict, and catharsis. On the level of narrative, the actor-centric method is linked to protagonism, the positing of the singular (always already masculine) hero. The protagonist's emotional dilemmas are central; other characters are inevitably ancillary. If the hero is white and masculine—the case for most mainstream narratives—we are deprived of a similar depth of knowledge about the conflicts and emotions of the subordinate characters. These sidekicks function to further the journey of the central character; this dynamic of protagonist/supporting character is too often gendered and raced. Feminist theory has extensively analyzed the trope of the beautiful dead woman (Clément 1988); others have noted the colored supporting players who die or who serve as the "black best friend" (Deggans 2011).

Smith's method is premised on a different narrative universe. Her plays refuse a single protagonist or a through-line in an Aristotelian sense.[13] Associative thematic connections structure Smith's plays, building a sense of trajectory that is far more elusive than the forward-marching "through-line" and the developmental "arc" and character "journey" of most naturalistic drama. This allusive juxtaposition contests Aristotelian unities of time, in which the unfolding of the plot has a beginning, middle, and end, and even seemingly extraneous elements must contribute to the denouement. Rather, Smith has talked of her fascination with circular rather than linear structure (C. Martin 1993). This differs from Hwang's work, which juxtaposes past and present, and found elements with the fictive, but retains the form of a linear, well-made play, or my own *Seamless*, that juxtaposes different tonalities, temporalities, and styles but unfolds in a linear structure.

In Brechtian terms, Smith plays "each scene for its own sake," making a world for each character. She says, "I have to play every character . . . every scene, as if it's the whole play . . . it's about creating the distinct world these people live in" (C. Weber 1995, 58). Her plays are divided into sections whose titles appear on screens above the stage. These surtitles identify each character, usually by occupation, and project a line from the character's dialogue that serves as a scene title, much like a poem. For example, my character appeared in the Broadway version of *Twilight* in a segment entitled "Sunset Boulevard," a metonym for the race-class divisions in Los Angeles. Smith's "poems" parallel Brechtian practices through their episodic structure designed to provoke the alienation and reflection of the audience: "The individual episodes have to be knotted together in such a way that the knots are easily noticed. The episodes must not succeed each other indistinguishably but must give us a chance to interpose our judgment" (Brecht and Willet 1964, 201). Smith acknowledges other proximate influences, including Ntozake Shange's *For Colored Girls* (A. D. Smith 2013a); Shange's individual (fictionalized) portrayals of black women offered a compelling model for aesthetic structure and political intervention.

The closest analogues to protagonists in Smith's work are the characters who end her plays, who bear the weight of articulating a take-home message. In the world premiere of *Twilight*, political activist Gladys Sibrian left us with the idea that people need to feel that "they can change things." In later versions, the play ended with Twilight Bey, organizer of the gang truce. He involved the leitmotif of Smith's art, that one must make an effort to understand the other: "I can't forever dwell in darkness; I can't forever dwell in the idea of just identifying with people like me, and understanding me and mine." The play ends on a note of indeterminacy: literally, on the word "limbo." No easy solution will quell the violence and level the systemic race/class inequality that provoked it.

Smith's play *Let Me Down Easy* (2007–10) negotiated two different ways of tracing a trajectory within an allusive, associative narrative that ends in death as ultimate closure. As Stephen Wadsworth, director of the world premiere, said in rehearsal, "Now, there's an ending!" In the world premiere version, an emotional and logical arc travels from the body ascendant (world-class athletes, dancers, models) to the body rendered vulnerable through war, natural disaster, illness, and, ultimately, death. This trajectory echoes the rise-and-fall structure of genres such as gangster films. The linear arc of this version of *Let Me Down Easy* plays dissonant counterpoint to its use of juxtaposition, which subverts linearity.

In the first two versions (the world premiere at the Long Wharf Theatre and the second iteration at the American Repertory Theatre) the play ends with Trudy Howell, who works at Chance Orphanage in South Africa, home to children with AIDS. She recounts the death of one of the young girls, ending with an elegiac, insistent exhortation that implicates the audience: "Don't leave them in the dark. Don't leave them in the dark" (A. D. Smith 2011, 135). In contrast, Howell is the penultimate figure in the New York and touring versions of the play. These end with Mathieu Ricard, a Buddhist monk. He tells Smith/us that when a fellow monk dies, the monks turn a teacup upside down, to signify his death. "Finished!" Smith-as-Ricard declares, as she turns her teacup upside down, places it in her outstretched palm, and lets the tea pour through her fingers. "Finished!" physicalizes metatheatrical commentary: the end of a life, the end of the play.

The allusive structure of Smith's plays interrupts our expectations of heroism/protagonism and of closure. Director Stephen Wadsworth commented on the inadequacy of the well-made play model when discussing Smith's work: "That's not what she makes—nor should she. . . . The encouragement should be . . . to not feel that she has to be obedient to some form, because what form could possibly contain her?" (Wadsworth 2008). Structural collage gives roughly equal weight to all characters,[14] performing a Brechtian aesthetic/political attitude, forcing us to confront our own overdetermined desire for a protagonist (W. Worthen 2005, 128–29). Our desire arises from our literary "common sense," based in humanism, empiricism, and idealism (Belsey 1980, 7). Such assumptions foster the pleasure we find in forms of conflict and catharsis, of naturalism, of art as mimesis, of the presumed relation of author to text; they are deeply enmeshed with the growth of industrial capitalism. They reinscribe the auratic and the Master Subject. Conventional naturalistic narrative introduces disorder, reestablishing order by the end of the protagonist's journey, completing the character's arc through the dynamics of conflict and catharsis. Smith's work interrupts our tacit assumptions and desires, illuminating this implication in historically, culturally specific power relations.

What Is an Author? What Is a Play?

Just as Smith's plays intervene in conventional narrative structure by eschewing a heroic protagonist, Smith's writing practice destabilizes discourses of the author as fount of creativity and drama as the product of a singular imagination. It underscores arguments about the death of the author, enacting the dispersal of author-ity and thematizing tensions between this dispersal and a commonsense view of authorship.

Smith's method depends on the verbatim quotation of texts from interviews. Thus, writing becomes a process of arranging and editing found, or rather, co-constructed texts. While found objects are hardly shocking in the arts, at least since Duchamp, the collage of *co-produced* text does not always count as a play in the eyes of theater gatekeepers. Thus, I insist that Smith expands the boundaries of writing in the conventional sense. For her, writing is not simply a matter of composing in solitude; it begins with *interviewing* and *listening*. Questions can elicit desired (or surprising) responses and are thus inseparable from writing. For example, at one point close to the opening of *Let Me Down Easy*, pressures from producers compelled the creative team to make deep cuts—a painful process, since all of us had become attached to certain characters. Director Stephen Wadsworth and dramaturg Alisa Solomon voiced doubts about including Dr. Ashgar Rastegar, a Yale nephrologist, and Dr. Sekagaya Yahaya, an African physician whose segment, "Pot with Holes," spoke to the state of medicine in contemporary Africa. Smith wanted to keep both. Yale Medical School sponsored the performance that became the genesis of the play, and Smith was performing in New Haven. She wanted to include site-specific characters in each version. Rather than eliminate Rastegar, Smith interviewed him again, asking him to comment on the metaphor "pot with holes," thus strengthening her argument that both characters should remain.

The interview-as-writing process emerged clearly in the differences between the world premiere of the play and its second incarnation. At the Long Wharf, act 1 thematized "resilient bodies," including cyclist Lance Armstrong and model Veronica Webb. Act 2 centered the dramatic, searing themes of Rwanda, Hurricane Katrina, the failures of the US health care system, and death. At A.R.T., act 1 articulates refrains of "grace," framed by clerics from various faiths. For this version, Smith had clearly asked her interviewees to comment on the concept of grace, thus eliciting the material she needed for her writing.

Furthermore, for Smith, *listening* becomes part of the writing process. During interviews, Smith can engage an active, intense listening that involves the whole body. Her presupposition is that everyday speech can be a form of poetry, when each person speaks in a way that only s/he can. This, for Smith, is authenticity, when normative language breaks down, and the person performs a distinctive linguistic signature. While serving as a dramaturg for a workshop of *House Arrest*, I watched Smith in action as she "listened for someone's poem." As she interviewed Omar Wasow in front of the actors, she sat in front of him, body leaning forward, gaze fixed on his. It was full-body listening. Attentiveness to the otherness of the other, "listening for someone's poem," requires the interviewer's concentrated physical energy. The questions, the listening, and the responses co-produce meaning, refiguring our notion of writing as the product of singular genius. Rather, Smith enacts writing as an intersubjective, even kinesthetic, process.

The concept of finding someone's poem disperses the author-ity of the writer, implying that the writer's task is to reveal the authorship of the interviewee, to endow her interlocutor with the status of writer/co-writer. The Pulitzer Prize committee cited precisely this issue in the decision to disqualify *Twilight* from consideration "on the grounds that its language was not invented but gleaned from interviews" (Mitchell 1994, 7). Sean Mitchell locates Smith's work in a history of "interpretive nonfiction" and documentary theater, arguing that though these precedents exist, Smith "appears to have established a new genre, and at the moment she is a genre of one. This is a mixed blessing at awards time" (8). Tellingly, he quotes two playwrights, one anonymous and the other the Pulitzer Prize–winner Robert Schenkkan. The anonymous playwright opined, "It's an eloquent performance all right, but there's a lot of concern among Tony voters that it's not a play." Schenkkan concurred. "From a dramaturgical point of view, it's not a work of the imagination. This is not to take anything away from her performance, which is amazing. I think of it as performance art, not as a play." Their model is the well-made play, "a work of the imagination" produced by the singular creative genius of the playwright. Challenging this model, Smith's creative process and dispersal of author-ity perform the intersubjective, collaborative, and dialogic nature of *all* writing.

Furthermore, Smith disturbs theatrical convention through her unconventional use of dramaturgy. Generally, dramaturgs serve the text, conducting research and acting as a third eye between playwright and director. Often, playwrights do not use dramaturgs; rarely is there more than one credited dramaturg per production. By contrast, Smith solicits a variety of viewpoints. In *Twilight,* we *four* dramaturgs were differentiated in terms of race and profession. In the NYU workshop for the Arena Stage production of *House Arrest,* Jim Lewis served as chief dramaturg, who looked after research and the burgeoning text; I came in as dramaturg/consultant for a shorter period. For the version of the play staged at the Mark Taper Forum, Smith used six dramaturgs. One person called this workshop "dramaturgy by committee." For the world premiere of *Let Me Down Easy* at the Long Wharf in New Haven, Smith split functions in her choices: Alisa Solomon, who has a PhD in dramaturgy, served as theatrical dramaturg, offering creative feedback on the text and conducting research for the play; because she lives in New York, she was able to attend most rehearsals. Living on the West Coast, I could come only at the beginning and the end of the process; I gave feedback primarily on the politics of representation of race and offered commentary on general dramaturgical issues. Poet Alice Quinn of the *New Yorker* served as consultant for issues of language, and director Stephen Wadsworth provided creative dramaturgical input throughout. Since Smith's work requires the precise reproduction of language, accent, speech, and movement, dialogue coach Amy Stoller and movement coach Elizabeth Roxas, former dancer with Alvin Ailey, provided crucial input. Though we all served multiple functions as the process unfolded,[15] we were selected for our differing areas of expertise. Smith, unlike most playwrights, welcomes multiple registers of feedback, though she ultimately makes the final decisions that shape her play. Smith described her writing process in our interview:

> SMITH: The first thing . . . is that I've already made a huge choice when I come into the room with the material, because I've decided out of that hour, what I even want to present. So . . . that's a huge, huge choice that's already been made. It's not like everybody is in the editing room looking at raw film. So I've already made that choice, and, in making that choice, I'm . . . beginning to think about structure, and the reason that I invite people in is because, ultimately, I'm trying to make a very public forum, so I can never answer the question of what do you want people to take away, because I know and accept the fact that the audience is bringing so much. So, it seems to me that the first part of the

DNA of that process, of openness, has to be openness in the room. . . . You know that I tend to be more open to dramaturgical people than directors, in terms of the traditional directors. Nothing the matter with that, but I'm also questioning that idea of . . . that authority.

KONDO: . . . That's fascinating. I didn't know that, actually.

SMITH: Well, I am. And that's why I come to blows with them, and now I've figured out ways to not do that and not have that happen, which has to do with making sure that I am prepared for them to arrive and . . . taking more of a stance of "What do you need?" . . . In that way I am not credited for being a producer, but I'm very interested in what the people who are not steeped in a specific theatre tradition have to say to me. So that's why . . . you and Alisa, Hector, because I don't . . . use traditional theatre dramaturgs.

KONDO: Right, exactly.

SMITH: . . . Alisa [Solomon] was [trained], but she was already a journalist and karate person and scholar. . . . She's different . . . she's very available. And . . . you bring a different type of critical eye to the material, which does have to do with race and power, and I don't trust the theatre to inform that, at all. . . . It just doesn't. It still sticks in these other hierarchical forms. . . . I also want to be in a position . . . as painful as it is, even to have my own prejudices assaulted. . . . I'm a much more conservative person than people think, so, as a modern woman I want to have my own . . . thing . . . assaulted by people who are more progressive than I am, and both you and Alisa are, more progressive than me in many ways. (A. D. Smith 2012b)

Thus, Smith wants to work with dramaturgs who are not "traditional theater dramaturgs" trained in the conventions of aesthetic form and obedient/beholden to theater hierarchies. As the next chapter argues, she lays herself open to having "her prejudices assaulted," often dramatically and painfully. Such openness in any arena, including academe, is rare.

Smith intervenes in modern drama in another way: on the page. The visual presentation of text enacts Smith's notion of speech as poetry; it resembles free verse. As William Worthen argues, the arrangement of words on the page echoes the conventions of lyric poetry; its political effects complicate Smith's emphasis on difference in her acting practice. "The design of the page locates the writing relative to the ideology of lyric poetry, asserting a . . . sympathetic, even sentimental likeness among the characters . . . represented in the continuity of their engagement with language" (W. Worthen 2005, 120). Smith makes an equalizing aesthetic and political gesture in the supposition that we all speak poetry. Poetry is not simply effete or elitist; it infuses everyday speech. This democratized poetry becomes the medium for tactical, visual, verbal assertions of our shared aesthetic sensibility.

Smith disrupts the structure of the well-made play and challenges our assumptions about authorship and the singular imagination. Her use of dramaturgs and of interviews in the writing process facilitates the co-production of meaning that echoes the well-known critiques of humanism in Barthes's and Foucault's work on the death of the author. Rather than reifying a transcendent genius who creates ex nihilo from his exalted aesthetic sensibility, poststructuralist approaches call attention to the "author-function" (Foucault 1984). "All writing is itself this special voice, consisting of several indiscernible voices, and . . . literature is precisely the invention of this voice, to which we cannot assign a specific origin . . . it is language which speaks, not the author" (Barthes 1977, 142). Smith's methods echo the poststructuralist problematizing of the original, of the auratic, of the sovereign subject as author. Instead, we see the play of language, the notion of collaboratively produced text as the stuff of poetry and drama, and the dispersal of writing into a continuous process of performance and feedback, through the use of multiple dramaturgs.

Yet in making these claims, I tread delicately in light of the Pulitzer Prize controversy. Precisely because conventional assumptions remain regnant in the theater world, Smith should retain the designation "author" in the conventional sense, and she should be credited for advancing a pathbreaking form of theater. The Pulitzer controversy—is *Twilight* a "real" play, a "work of singular creative imagination?"—demonstrates the persistence of assumptions about the auratic and the exalted sensibilities of singular authorial genius. These hegemonic views dismiss Smith's use of co-produced text and of writing as intersubjective dialogue that requires acute questions, full-body listening, and energetic focus.

Smith's work negotiates and reveals *paradoxes* in conventional assumptions, both challenging and, inevitably, reinscribing those conventions. Worthen sees a contradiction in the controversy about the Pulitzer Prize: "While Smith chose interview subjects, wrote the monologues down, edited them, and gave them dramatic form, activities fully consistent with individual 'writing'... Smith's account of the collaborative nature of this kind of writing also confirms the committee's hesitations.... Like the committee, Smith values drama as principally a form of writing" (W. Worthen 2005, 108).

I argue otherwise, that Smith's work negotiates *tensions* between conventional notions of authorship and collaborative, dispersed author-ity. Smith simultaneously disturbs the binary between drama as a form of writing and theater as the aural/performative, instantiated in the fact that we dramaturgs on *Twilight* so rarely worked with a script. Performance came first. Smith's work highlights precisely these constitutive contradictions, between single authorship and the death of the author/collaborative writing, and between writing and performance.

Indeed, "Anna Deavere Smith" signifies an author-function, as does every proper name. This author-function represents a site for the negotiation of contemporary discursive, aesthetic, and political tensions. What counts as a play? What is writing? Who is an author? How do we think about identity and character? What are the boundaries among genres—in Smith's case, drama, journalism, and ethnography? What counts as the real? "Anna Deavere Smith" delineates a particularly productive site for investigating these central questions of aesthetics, politics, and meaning. Her moves spotlight the ways that race and power pervade the seemingly transcendent domain of the aesthetic and the everyday assumptions/practices of the theater/art worlds. These arenas—troped as both transcendent and mundane—are precisely where race is made.

Smith's innovations are pathbreaking and necessary in a theater world where protagonism and whiteness reign. Aristotelian form continues to characterize the vast majority of plays, films, and television. The avant-garde, devised theater, and posthumanist theater tend toward the elitist, in terms of both content and audience. Smith's interventions in form contest major trends in mainstream American theater, and her performances of underrepresented others onstage intervene in a theater world where such presences remain painfully few. *Fires in the Mirror* and *Twilight* opened American theater to many who had never before taken center stage in a mainstream regional theater or on Broadway.

The following chapter analyzes the creative process as it unfolded backstage during the shaping of *Twilight: Los Angeles 1992*. Written and performed only a year after the Los Angeles uprisings, in the wake of the first Gulf War and the regime of George Bush the First, during the heyday of

1990s multiculturalism, *Twilight* inevitably participated in and exceeded the understandings of race and power extant in the American theater of the 1990s. Our stormy debates illuminate what I call the politics of affiliation, the difficult creative labor of working through incommensurable, power-laden difference as steps toward reparative creativity.

chapter 4

The Drama behind the Drama

In Los Angeles, we have just commemorated the twenty-fifth anniversary of the Los Angeles uprisings. The events of April 1992 remain utterly contemporary: race/class inequality, police violence against people of color, and the spirit of protest. Ferguson erupted in the summer and fall of 2014 in the wake of Michael Brown's death; in 2015, Baltimore exploded after the death of Freddie Gray. It seems particularly fitting—and sobering—that I return now to *Twilight: Los Angeles 1992*, Anna Deavere Smith's play about the uprisings that had its world premiere in Los Angeles in 1993. In April 2015 PBS rereleased the film *Twilight* online, undoubtedly in recognition of the protests of police violence in Baltimore, Smith's hometown. I served as one of the dramaturgs on the theatrical world premiere of *Twilight*; it was my initiation by fire into the dramaturgical process and into the possibilities of and obstacles to (re)making the theater world.

Based on interviews with over two hundred Angelenos, Smith crafted *Twilight*, a portrayal of events, a city, and an ongoing national state of emergency. My program notes commented, "*Twilight* insists on bearing witness to this state of emergency. People of all colors, genders, ages, tell their stories, giving meaning to the violence and bristling tensions of last year's events. . . . Using the particular to illuminate the general, Anna Deavere Smith . . . enacts people who offer us insights into the larger issues of history, language . . . and, especially, race, class and power, that shape their individual experiences. . . . She eloquently demonstrates that difference is not simply a proliferation of exotic flavors and colors, but marks unequally weighted positions in a matrix of power" (Kondo 1993b, 7). My focus on practice and reparative creativity spotlights the dramaturgical process that played an integral role in shaping *Twilight*. My antagonist throughout is power-evasive liberalism in its various incarnations: the humanist multiculturalism that reduces Smith's portrayals to "a proliferation of exotic flavors," the putative universality of the Human, liberal notions of conversation and (implicitly gendered) diplomacy that inform conventional dramaturgical protocols, and the assumption of a unified audience and a unified voice of narrative closure that "transcends" power-laden differences such as race, gender, and class.

This power-evasive liberalism was on full display in 1993, even as critics greeted *Twilight* with celebration: "She is not writing polemical theater but, better, doing theater politically. . . . In its judicious daring, *Twilight* announces that a multicultural America is here and functioning and is capable of noisy but brilliant collaboration. . . . *Twilight* goes some way toward claiming for the stage its crucial role as a leader in defining and acting out that ongoing experiment called the United States" (Lahr 1993, 90–94). *Newsweek* deemed the Taper production of *Twilight* "an American masterpiece" (Kroll 1993). The *New York Times* celebrated the version I saw at the Public Theater: "For its restless intelligence and passionate understanding, it will be welcome. For its appreciation of the singular voice in the howling throng, it should be treasured" (Richards 1994). These critics both recognize the historical advance Smith's work represents and reproduce liberal humanism: "telling all sides," "we're all human beings," the notion of singular, creative genius (contrasted to the "howling" masses), and the reading of Smith's body as a vessel of democracy, e pluribus unum personified.

To problematize the hegemonic reception of Smith's work, I argue for the political significance of our collaborative process.[1] In *Twilight*, we exceeded the representation of marginalized "communities," performing an agonistics that upended the fundamental assumptions of liberal pluralist theater, its "distribution of the sensible" (Rancière 2004; H. Worthen 2014), the tacit common sense that defines what is thinkable, sayable, doable. Power-evasive liberal pluralism valorizes polite consensus, thus excluding exclusion and often justifiable political passions such as rage (Rooney 1989). Conventional dramaturgy institutionalizes this model of polite consensus and the dramaturg as feminized, diplomatic, invisible.

Further, liberal humanism and its cousin, color blindness, disavow the insidious persistence of structural inequality and racialized power relations under the sign of whiteness as coextensive with universality and the human. During the heyday of 1990s multiculturalism, race was often read as a parade of exotic colors. Contesting these multiple forms of power-evasiveness, I begin with an ethnographic analysis of our *politics of affiliation*. Affiliation involves alliance, social relationships, and commitment to a common goal; it is not based on similarity rooted in shared essence. Our creative process enacted these power-laden and sometimes incommensurable differences as we collaborated in mounting *Twilight*'s world premiere. I propose *dramaturgical critique* as a mode of political intervention and a form of *reparative creativity*.

I join dramaturgical literatures by highlighting our creative *process* as we worked on the world premiere (see Shteir and Kalke 2003), including incidents where our creative differences were sharp, even unbridgeable. Unlike liberal versions of dramaturgy that prize harmony, our creative process suggests that incommensurability, conflict, and partial connection offer more politically progressive ways of thinking about dramaturgy and political coalition. The dramaturgical theorizing of *process* interrupts capitalist fetishizing of the final product and promotes theoretical attention to open-endedness, always fraught collaborative labor, and the possibilities of imagining otherwise.[2] This susceptibility, affecting and being affected, characterizes Smith's acting theory. These susceptibilities animated our creative process on *Twilight*.

In the introduction, I detailed the presumptions of the dramaturgical literature, which circulates gendered stereotypes of the feminine helpmate, the diplomatic "fixer," a model based on liberal notions of conversation as power-free. We worked to mount counterhegemonic representations that could offer minoritarian subjects a reparative mirroring in the face of years of erasure and flattened portrayals. This chapter highlights *dramaturgical critique* as indispensable creative labor behind the scenes. Our spirited debates enacted a politics of affiliation, intervening in power-evasive, liberal pluralist theater and liberal multiculturalism as steps toward the reparative.

Allow me to show you. Come with me backstage.

Behind the Curtain

An upstairs dressing room at the Mark Taper Forum in Los Angeles is full of people, our faces bathed in the hot, bright lights of the makeup mirrors: playwright and actress Anna Deavere Smith; producer Gordon Davidson;

artistic director Robert Egan; director Emily Mann; Smith's assistant, Cecilia Pang; Mann's assistant, Eisa Davis; the stage managers; and unusually, tonight, the production designers. In a few days Smith's one-woman show *Twilight: Los Angeles 1992* will open in its world premiere, and we four dramaturgs—Héctor Tobar, a Guatemalan American reporter for the *Los Angeles Times*, now a Pulitzer Prize–winning novelist; the African American poet Elizabeth Alexander, now head of the Mellon Foundation; the Taper's associate artistic director, Oskar Eustis, who is white; and myself—are here to give Smith our reactions to help her shape the play.

It is May 1993, just a little over a year since the Los Angeles rebellion/riots/uprisings/civil unrest,[3] when the acquittal of white police officers, caught on tape brutally beating African American motorist Rodney King in 1991, sparked fiery protest. Los Angeles exploded on April 29, 1992, for three days of violence, burnings, shootings, and "looting," mostly in South Central Los Angeles but extending as far west as La Brea Avenue and to communities such as Long Beach and Pomona.[4] Issues of race and class still bristle with tension, and what feels like a life-and-death urgency animates our dramaturgical discussions as we try to represent the uprisings and race/class inequality through the testimonies of Smith's interviewees. After a lifetime of invisibility or oppressive images of ourselves on the stage, the screen, and the page, finally for us people of color, here is Anna Deavere Smith, an African American artist who strives to represent us in our complexity. Which characters should be cut, and which should stay? On what basis? What are the politics of racial representation being played out onstage? How do we portray histories of race and class oppression? What works theatrically? We hope that she will truly listen, that she will "get it right," that her solo portrayal of an array of characters will do justice to the daunting sprawl, racial complexity, and utopian possibilities of Los Angeles.

Tonight Smith has decided to cut the characters Rudy Salas, a Chicano artist who introduces a long history of police brutality against Latinos, and Dan Kuramoto, the Japanese American leader of the jazz fusion band Hiroshima, who grew up in East Los Angeles always wanting to be a cholo. Kuramoto terms Los Angeles "a whole new racial frontier" (A. D. Smith 1993c, 274). Héctor and I ally in a passionate fight to keep this play true to multiracial Los Angeles, where race has proliferated as far beyond the black/white binary as one can find in the continental United States. Without Rudy and Dan, *Twilight* will remain largely a black-and-white story. Héctor and I argue vehemently that these characters are emblematic of

Los Angeles, and with equal passion I state that he and I owe a responsibility to the people we represent, that "our asses are on the line with our communities," to whom we are ultimately accountable. Smith responds. Her obligation, she says, is to the theatrical community.

I am devastated. I feel excluded, not taken seriously, that my efforts have gone for naught. Héctor and I are near tears. I can scarcely raise my head for fear that my composure might break. As soon as the session ends, I race out of the room, avoiding everyone lest I burst into sobs. Oskar Eustis tries to say something to me, and I brush past him, not wanting him to see me break down. (Later, I discover that he thought I was being "rude.") I go home and sob continuously for two hours. I have poured my heart and mind into the production; the line Smith suddenly has drawn between the "theater community" and the "Asian American community" feels exclusionary and acutely painful. The black-white binary, the invisibility we hoped to challenge, remains intact. Even more alienating: the sea of distant, white faces in that room, looking on in pity or sympathy, as Héctor and I put ourselves on the line. Later, Smith and I talk about how we had inadvertently reenacted the race wars for a silent white audience—people of color fighting each other—precisely what Smith had been seeking to avoid onstage. Right now, though, I feel betrayed, angry, humiliated.

The next day, Smith reinstates both Dan and Rudy, and the tears of the previous night are transformed into radiant smiles. Indeed, my standard line about working on *Twilight* is that I have never cried so much—or been so happy. By opening night, Dan is cut in favor of Salvadoran political activist Gladys Sibrian, but this time I better understand Smith's concern: that we not give comfort to a white audience. A prominent white critic has interpreted Dan's comments about a "new racial frontier," seemingly so appropriate for the ending, to mean simply that people of color should stop fighting one another. In this view, whites remain the unimplicated spectators. Though I still want Dan to end the show, I understand Smith's choice of Sibrian, a leader of the Salvadoran coalition Farabundo Martí para la Liberacíon Nacional, who spoke eloquently of the uprisings as a "social explosion" and of the need for people to feel that "they can change things."

Thus, despite dramatic moments of tension—what Smith called "fiery battles"—Smith and her dramaturgs were able to work through our differences in the process of creating *Twilight*. Our clash of opinions in "that room" mirrored the race wars outside the theater, as we carried out dramatic cross-racial conflict, yet we were still able to work together to mount a production that is considered a landmark in American theater.[5] Because Smith listened carefully to input from the dramaturgs, much of what I take from *Twilight* is an appreciation for her sense of accountability and commitment to other people of color, as she negotiated multiple minefields in a volatile, high-stakes process.[6] Smith's willingness to listen, every night, even in the face of harsh criticism, continues to elicit my fierce loyalty to her work.

Our passionate debates erupted in the context of 1990s multiculturalism, a moment when the culture wars were in full force and when multiculturalism seemed a necessary strategy to challenge monoculturalism.[7] For example, 1993 marked the year of the Whitney's "multicultural" show that earned the mainstream reaction "victim chic." In education and politics, Ward Connerly, a regent of the University of California system, championed the end of affirmative action, which he termed "reverse discrimination." The year 1993 continued Reagan's neoliberal economic policies and imperialist strategies under George H. W. Bush, who led the United States into the Gulf War in 1990–91.

Multiculturalism was and is an unstable signifier, with multiple meanings and political connotations. Avery Gordon and Chris Newfield (1996, 2) articulated four "multicultural dilemmas: 1) antiracist or oblivious to racism; 2) cultural autonomy or common culture revisited; 3) grassroots alliances or diversity management; 4) linking culture and politics or separating them." The answer is all of the above, depending on who was deploying the term and for what ends. "Multiculturalism" during our dramaturgical process signifies essentialized notions of culture and race, or culture as a power-evasive stand-in for race. The problems with essentialism first emerged in the Taper's charge to the dramaturgs to "represent" our racialized "communities." This strategy circulated widely during this period. For example, a PBS program entitled "L.A. Is Burning" (1993) featured (mostly male) commentators/guides from each "community," in equally divided segments: black, Latino, Asian American (Korean American), white. *Twilight* used a more expansive canvas. The focus on the individual is the hallmark of Smith's method, which can produce contradictory effects of both reinscribing the liberal subject and of destabilizing that subject through spotlighting the individual's location in a matrix of racialized, gendered, classed power relations.

Twilight tackled urgent, deeply rooted, historically intractable racial and class inequalities. Smith invited the backstage, cross-racial drama that was itself an intervention in theater hierarchy, one that many playwrights could not tolerate. That drama helped to shape Smith's portrayals onstage, resulting in a production that made an intervention in American theater on multiple levels. Thematically, both then and now, few mainstream plays tackle topically urgent issues of race and class conflict. Performatively, Smith's virtuosity and the all-too-rare sight of an African American actress taking center stage in a major American theater disrupted this Eurocentric, male space. Perhaps even more historically unprecedented were the characters she portrayed, often people of color who had never before been allowed in this bastion of upper-middlebrow culture. The Taper production further addressed the race politics of backstage labor, assembling a multiracial creative team and crew whose diversity is still rare in the arts world. The unbearable whiteness of mainstream theater was, at least for the duration of the production, interrupted.

Furthermore, *Twilight* thwarted desires for comfort and happy resolution, the illusion that we have achieved closure on race. It refused linear progress, a hero, or a single, definitive interpretation. Indeed, the world premiere version ended on a cautionary, activist note, that people need to feel "they can change things." Later iterations of the play end on the word "limbo." For that alone, *Twilight* is a work worth remembering in this "postracial" era. As the deaths of Alton Sterling, Philando Castile, Michael Brown, Freddie Gray, Eric Garner, Renisha McBride, Trayvon Martin, and so many others attest, the themes *Twilight* addresses could not be more salient in our present.

The urgency of structural, racial violence pervaded our backstage process, at times leading to spirited battles. Our politics of affiliation and agonistics flourished through the creative process. Any artist wants to stage the best production possible; Smith approached this goal through the subversion of theatrical hierarchy and the distribution of the sensible in the theater world. She describes her aims in forming her dramaturgical team:

> I developed *Twilight* at the Mark Taper Forum in collaboration with four other people of various races who functioned as dramaturgs. . . . These dramaturgs brought their own real-world experiences with race to bear on the work. They reacted to *Twilight* at every stage of its development. My predominant concern about the creation of *Twilight* was that my own history . . . a history of race as a black and white struggle, would make the work narrower than it should be. For this reason, I sought out dramaturgs who had . . . developed careers and identities, outside the theater profession. I was interested not only in their ethnic

diversity, but in the diversity that they would bring to the project in terms of areas of expertise. I am a strong critic of the insularity of people in theater and of our inability to shake up our traditions particularly with regard to race and representation issues. (A. D. Smith 1994, xxii)

Our dramaturgical assignment, then, was to attend to the politics of racial representation and to "shake up" theatrical tradition. Smith's vision informed our efforts on several fronts. First, we aimed to contest hegemonic racial ideologies, from the racialized bodies of the characters performed onstage to the structural violence shaping those characters' experiences. Second, the sheer presence of multiple dramaturgs and the seriousness with which Smith listened to us contested the power of the single director, advancing Smith's project to destabilize directorial authority and refigure conventional theater hierarchies. Finally, Smith's invitation to the dramaturgs opened her assumptions and her writing to the possibility of being "shaken up," to (sometimes painful) confrontations with otherness. The same radical susceptibility to others that characterizes her theories of acting theory and writing animated the creative process itself: her openness to the unexpected, to what *others* say, not simply what *she* wants to say. She lives an aesthetics and politics of susceptibility and encounter with difference.

The shaking up was far from easy. Now that I am a playwright, I marvel that Smith was able to withstand and to assimilate what must have seemed like a barrage of penetrating criticisms on a nightly basis. She had to adjudicate often incommensurable claims, revise the writing and then perform each night. Reader, if you have received extensive comments in a seminar or from reviewers, multiply that by at least four (the number of dramaturgs) and repeat, six days a week. You might then empathize with the degree of fortitude Smith displayed. Even if the final goal is to make the work better, hearing pointed criticism can be painful, and even helpful criticism can take time to digest.

I read our backstage drama as an enactment of Chantal Mouffe's politics of agonistics (2013)[8] and what I call a *politics of affiliation*. For Mouffe, agonistics—in which adversaries debate incompatible, even irreconcilable positions, attempting to make their own positions hegemonic—arises from the irreducible differences that ground politics. There can be no ideal speech situation in a Habermasian sense, in which rational actors reach consensus through dialogue. Consensus is itself hegemony, masking dissent/difference. Mouffe's position contests rationalist perspectives that privilege the liberal humanist subject and the model of power-free communication (Rawls 1999; Habermas 1970). Such liberal schemes exclude exclusion, the passions (is rage not appropriate to encounters with injustice?), and the constitutive, inescapable workings of power relations. Mouffe envisions instead an agonistic politics of shifting hegemonies, since hegemony cannot be wished away. Agonistic politics—conflict among adversaries—contrasts with *antagonistic* politics: conflict with enemies (Mouffe 2013, 7).

A complex matrix of power was in operation during our work in the rehearsal rooms during *Twilight* that offered no pastoral zone of power-free unity or harmony. Rather, in "that room," all of us found our comfortable, power-laden assumptions destabilized. Smith speaks about leaving our "safe houses of identity" (Smith 2007) to enter a dangerous crossroads that is our only way to a more equitable society. This discomfort, the hard work of adjudicating passionately held, sometimes incommensurable positions, characterizes a *politics of affiliation*. It echoes Bernice Johnson Reagon's classic feminist admonition, "Coalition work . . . is some of the most dangerous work you can do. And you shouldn't look for comfort" (Reagon 1983, 359). A politics that would value justice and equality must be based on a recognition of the inevitability and necessity of conflict, dissent, and the recognition of incommensurable difference, while embracing the possibility of partial connection and progressive change (Davis and Martinez 1998, 306). Our dramaturgical process performed a *politics of affiliation* that requires hard work and the willingness to have one's assumptions assailed.

Our backstage battles debated the meanings of race at that historical moment. We may have reenacted the race wars, but our conflict was ultimately generative, even reparative. Smith has quoted playwright David Henry Hwang, who said that talking frankly about race can be more intimate than sex. We are all afraid of saying the wrong thing. *Twilight* required us to leave our zones of safety to risk a level of honesty that is understandably rare in public discourse, given how brutal our exchanges may have sounded in the rehearsal room. In retrospect, the dramaturgical sessions were a form of sociopolitical "tough love." Cross-racial hostility, misunderstandings, and prejudices are never pretty or easy, and they are to some degree inevitable, yet in *Twilight* the team managed to deal with them productively.

I cannot guess others' motives, but I found myself possessed by what felt like the play's life-and-death significance at that moment, in that city.

We needed to get our hands dirty, to try to make things better in our state of emergency, even if no intervention could be perfect. For me, *Twilight* performs key features of a progressive political practice: its always already processual nature, the need to listen to multiple points of view, the inevitability of conflict, the necessity to take action, even if the action is incomplete or flawed, and the generative impulse to repair. Our politics of affiliation was more than power-evasive consensus; it was agonistic, power-laden, yet dedicated to intervening in theater orthodoxy. Here was a chance to counter oppressive representations and exclusions of people of color. Accordingly, *Twilight* embodies for me a moment of political hope (Dolan 2005; Muñoz 2009), when dramaturgical critique works toward the reparative.

I make these arguments precisely because my analysis is grounded in corporeal epistemologies fostered in the backstage creative process. This perspective differs considerably from a burgeoning critical literature on *Twilight*—a kind of ur-text in cultural studies—and on Smith's work more generally.[9] This critical literature is often based on the film version of *Twilight*, one that does not reproduce any of the three major *stage* versions. Disparities among the versions could lead analysts to significantly different interpretations of the play. Indeed, most of our dramaturgical arguments concerned issues of inclusion/exclusion and sequencing of characters, and each version (world premiere, Broadway, touring version, book, film) was unique. (See plates 3, 4.) Further, the constitutive differences between stage and (small) screen are crucial. My experiences led me to emphasize the *processes* through which race was produced and reproduced backstage, where we both contested and, inevitably—as Foucault reminds us—reinscribed conventional meanings of race.

A focus on the dramaturgical *process* reveals telling insights about the production of race, from institutional enabling constraints to Smith's aims, which were far more power-sensitive and politically progressive than the mainstream reception of her work would have us believe. A focus on process illuminates the creative team's intentions, which may contrast starkly with audience reception, a continuing testament to the intentional fallacy. Smith and her creative team embraced progressive goals, yet no one escapes history and power. We were inevitably enmeshed in the contemporary discourses of multiculturalism and in the political structures of the theater world (see Ferguson 2012). I argue that the disidentifications and excesses we enacted complicated those discourses and structures in productive ways. In *Twilight,* inevitable reinscriptions of power complicate but do not vitiate the intervention in terms of its historical significance in the theater world. We made, unmade, remade race.

Back Story: Enabling Constraints

The challenges that faced Smith and, by extension, the creative team, were daunting at best, even insuperable. We were faced with "representing" the complexities of the uprisings/rebellion and the race/class oppressions that undergirded them. Further, our process mirrored difficulties with regional theater as an institution, as Smith and her team grappled with thorny issues of institutional politics as well as the politics of representation. I strategically recount those challenges in my narrative of the creative process.

After viewing Smith's *Fires in the Mirror*, on the Crown Heights unrest in Brooklyn, producer Gordon Davidson commissioned Smith to create *Twilight* at the Mark Taper Forum in downtown Los Angeles, the city's major regional theater for new work. The Taper is one of three imposing structures on the plaza of the Los Angeles Music Center. It lies between the Dorothy Chandler Pavilion, the erstwhile home of the Academy Awards and now the home of the opera, and the dazzling Ahmanson, host to Broadway touring productions. Regional theater is expensive, and subscribers are overwhelmingly upper-middle-class, older, white, and from the West Side, not downtown.

What I called in the Broadway version of *Twilight* "the social geography of Los Angeles"—race and class segregation—was striking. Though now downtown Los Angeles is ever-gentrifying hipsterland, such was not the case in the 1990s. Westsiders need to drive an hour to downtown; most likely few working-class people of color (Latino, Asian American, African American) who lived near the theater actually attended performances. Downtown was considered dangerous, especially after dark. Mainstream media and scholarly commentators deemed Los Angeles a postmodern city with no center; downtown was supposedly deserted on nights and weekends. This hegemonic common sense erased Latinx consumers, for whom downtown represented a lively commercial district. Apparently, "no center" simply meant that there were not enough whites (Fujii 1993, xii).

Los Angeles is conceptually divided into the East and West sides, where La Brea Avenue marks a rough border; the whiter, more affluent West Side (better air!) and the ethnic, artsy, industrial, poorer East Side mark urban stereotypes that have some basis in reality. The initial events of the uprisings occurred in the largely Latinx/African American South Central Los Angeles, in the southeast. Protests and burnings occurred downtown, in Koreatown (also in the East), Hollywood (well below the Hollywood Hills, where celebrities live), and as far west as La Brea. The racialized disparities between these areas of Los Angeles came into sharp relief during the uprisings; for example, police and fire departments often failed to respond to emergency calls from Koreatown. While Westsiders may have ensconced themselves in the Beverly Hills Hotel or passed rumors that "they burning down the Beverly Center"—a mall in mid-city/Beverly Hills—the brunt of the destruction occurred in the east and the south.

Given these geographic and temporal coordinates, *Twilight* carried a daunting allegorical burden. Nesting synecdoches figured the Taper as metonym for Los Angeles; Los Angeles in turn stood for race relations in the nation.[10] No production could in fact bear that symbolic weight. Seething tensions around race and class were front and center in public discourse as we put together the play less than a year after the uprisings. Burned-out buildings, presidential blue-ribbon commissions, and efforts to "heal" were features of everyday life in Los Angeles. Once the play went into preview, I confronted this hyperconsciousness of race as friends and colleagues voiced their impassioned, often incompatible, opinions about the play.

Race bristled with significance in 1993. Homes and businesses aflame, curfews, the National Guard out in force, tanks rolling through the streets of Los Angeles; those who were born after the events of 1992 would have difficulty imagining the state of siege that was everyday life. Visible racial difference could have dire consequences, as violence throughout the city against people of many colors attested. Mass media trumpeted examples of racial animus, such as "the Black-Korean conflict." A hegemonic liberal multiculturalism premised on essentialized racial "communities" circulated widely.

We dramaturgs were hired in part to give our critical input on the ways our respective racial "communities" were represented and, as Smith stated in the book version of *Twilight*, to shake up theater orthodoxy. However, the task facing us was by definition impossible. No collectivity can be exhaustively represented. Protests and violence revealed the proliferating lines of fracture. As Young-soon Han, a character in *Twilight*, stated, "The fire is still burning. . . . It can burst out anytime."

Narrative Dilemmas

Twilight: Los Angeles 1992 is the fourteenth in Smith's *On the Road* series. The play expands the black-white binary of its immediate precursor, *Fires in the Mirror*, to the striking racial multiplicity of Los Angeles. *Twilight* in its various incarnations mirrors this multiplicity. Its many versions enact the differences between theater and film and among the various *productions*, highlighting the definitive significance of production/performance. I write here of my experiences with the world premiere, while in the preceding chapter, I wrote of my experience as a character in the Broadway version. Throughout, I attempt to specify the particular version under discussion, for the proper name masks striking differences among the productions. This chapter deals primarily with the world premiere of the play at the Mark Taper Forum in Los Angeles and its offshoot, the Princeton version. Markedly different productions were mounted at the Public/on Broadway, as well as in the touring production, the film, and the book.[11] Critical accounts based only on the film miss the dynamic aspects of Smith's transformations onstage and the indispensable role of audience interaction. The world premiere was our attempt to make sense of the daunting complexity of the uprisings and their genesis in the structural violence of race/class inequality.

When Smith received her commission from the Taper, a coalition of Los Angeles–based artists, mostly of color, protested the selection of an "outsider" to portray our city's trauma. Their objections overlooked the fact that Smith had lived and taught in Los Angeles for several years. From the moment the Taper made the announcement, Smith faced controversy.

To further heighten the stakes, Los Angeles presented daunting challenges to anyone who sought to capture the unrest and the city's complexity. Even relating a history of events would be a troubling task. In *Fires in the Mirror*, two acts of violence sparked the conflict: the original killing of the young West Indian boy Gavin Cato by an out-of-control automobile carrying a leader of the Hasidic Jewish community, and the (apparently retaliatory) killing, by black youths, of Yankel Rosenbaum, an Australian rabbinical scholar. Black and white, two incidents, two perspectives: a classic binary.

Where to begin in Los Angeles, the site of multiple acts of violence? Where to begin in a city that hosts the largest Central American and Mexican populations outside their countries of origin (of course, California was once Mexico), the largest Korean population outside Korea, the largest Iranian population outside Iran . . . the list continues. Crown Heights, with its black-and-white tropes of race, formed an elegant piece of point-counterpoint in a binaristic, conventionally satisfying, narrative arc. But in Los Angeles, where race has proliferated far beyond the black-white binary, any tidy narrative was bound to do violence to this complexity. Smith's innovative theatrical form, relying on juxtaposition and thematic resonance, refusing narrative closure, seemed far better suited to capture the epic sweep of a sprawling, racially polyglot Los Angeles than would the conventional well-made play.

Smith faced an equally daunting task of narration. In March of 1991, a group of white police officers were caught on videotape brutally beating Rodney King. The violent spectacle entered living rooms nationwide, setting off police investigations and community protests. The officers' initial trial was moved from Los Angeles proper to virtually all-white Simi Valley, where the jury handed down a "not guilty" verdict on April 29, 1992. That day, white truck driver Reginald Denny was taken from his truck and beaten unconscious; the incident was caught on video and made national news. Mayor Tom Bradley declared a curfew; governor Pete Wilson called in the National Guard; LA was officially declared a federal disaster area. On May 3, 1992, "the *L.A. Times* [reported] 58 deaths, 2,383 injuries, 7,000+ fire responses, 12,111 arrests and 3,100 businesses damaged since the civil unrest began" (Flynn 1994, 32). A second federal trial a year later convicted two of the four police officers (37). How should Smith account for these events and others in a single evening of theater?

To complicate the task of narration, April 29, 1992, was the result of a long history of police brutality and race/class inequality. Should Smith address emblematic events that immediately preceded the uprisings, such as the Latasha Harlins verdict? Almost two weeks after the King beating, Harlins, a young African American woman, allegedly stealing a carton of orange juice, struggled with Soon-ja Du, a Korean American female store owner, who shot Harlins as the girl turned to walk away. The defense lawyer, a prominent African American attorney, argued that the gun had a hair trigger and that the shooting was accidental. In November 1991, judge Joyce Karlin, a white woman, sentenced Du to a $500 fine, four hundred hours of community service, and five years probation, sparking protests throughout the city for the light sentence. Smith included this case in the New York version of *Twilight* and in the film, but it does not appear in the Los Angeles version—a decision decried by Denise Harlins, Latasha's aunt. Thus, the creative team—Smith, above all—faced multiple highly charged decisions in trying to construct a narrative of events. I offer an account of the creative process to illuminate our dilemmas of racial representation.

Dramaturgical Process
Preproduction

To address such challenges required intensive "fieldwork": contacting people, interviewing, and mobilizing networks. Whereas Smith was able to complete interviews for *Fires in the Mirror* in four days, the more than two hundred interviews for *Twilight* began in the fall of 1992, extended through the actual performance in the summer of 1993, and continued almost until opening night of the New York performance in 1994. Appropriately for the city of the freeway, my first contact with the project was from Anna's cell phone as she drove around Los Angeles. Steve Park, the Korean American actor from Spike Lee's *Do the Right Thing*, suggested she contact me for suggestions of Asian Americans to interview.

In the fall of 1992, the Taper organized focus groups for each community of color in order to advance the interview process. In October, I participated in the Asian American gathering. From the outset, the Taper structured the creative process and dramaturgical research along conventional racial lines, echoing the racial essentialism of contemporary media accounts. During the winter, I was asked to come on board as a dramaturg, along with *Los Angeles Times* reporter Héctor Tobar; later, Anna asked African American poet and scholar Elizabeth Alexander and Taper resident director Oskar Eustis to join the dramaturgical team. Emily Mann, artistic director of the McCarter Theater in Princeton and known for her work in docudrama, directed.

The play's development is a drama and political allegory that I tell from my dramaturgical perspective: a partial account that inevitably omits or minimizes parts of the production of which I had little or no knowledge (stage management, set design, costumes, private interactions between actor/playwright and director). As such, it illustrates the partiality of every account—"situated knowledges" (Haraway 1991)—and offers a unique view based on participatory observation.

First Workshop

Four months before our scheduled opening, we hold a two-week workshop to begin shaping the piece. In Rehearsal Room B at the Taper Annex (a boxy, institutional building that is an eloquent statement about funding for the arts), Smith sits in the center of the room, Walkman in hand, headphones in place. A bank of video equipment stands to her left. A cameraman stands poised, ready to record. At a table facing her sit director Emily Mann, Héctor Tobar, and myself; at a table in back of us are Taper staff members in charge of scripts, Smith's assistant, Kishisa Jefferson, and an occasional visitor, such as Lynell George, writer for the *LA Weekly*. Smith turns on her Walkman and begins to repeat sections she thinks are potentially usable for the show, reproducing inflection and, sometimes, body language. When she is through, she stops to ask for comments. Everything—theatricality, content, and the politics of representation—is up for discussion.

Our day-to-day dramaturgy followed this structure. Later, when the play went into preview and moved out of the rehearsal room into the theater, we engaged in feedback sessions I later describe, conducted in a dressing room ("that room"), where Smith listened to comments from the dramaturgs.[12] Though we carried out standard dramaturgical duties (doing research, occasionally suggesting cuts in the text, and acting as the third eye between playwright and director), our job was mainly to respond to Smith's *performance* as she listened to her audiotapes and subsequently performed onstage. We gave our feedback immediately afterward, without the benefit of the hours a traditional dramaturg would spend with the text. It was dramaturgy on the spot. Usually dramaturgs have time to reflect, to think through both the comments themselves and how they might be phrased so that the playwright could hear them. Had we more time for rumination, perhaps our later sessions in "that room" might have been less volatile, less unfiltered—and possibly, less helpful. I tell journalist Lynell George that the dramaturgs are "in-house critics" (a conventional definition of dramaturgy), with the difference that we were to attend to racial representation. My role seems to be developing into that of hypercritical academic, more often than not taking issue with what I see.

Our dramaturgical duties included suggesting interviewees and occasionally conducting interviews ourselves. I interviewed some Samoan American students, seeking to broaden our interviewees beyond Korean

American shop owners to the fraught Asian/Pacific/American collectivity. Héctor conducted interviews in Spanish with a number of people, including some who engaged in so-called looting. Héctor likened "looting" to poverty riots in Mexico and Central America that could be considered critiques of capitalist accumulation and private property. Smith conducted most of the two to three hundred interviews (I have heard/read different numbers) of which twenty-five were used in the world premiere, forty in the Broadway production. Based partially on dramaturgical and directorial reactions and keeping the issue of performance in the foreground, Smith would edit the tapes and arrange the excerpts in her writing process. Assistants did construct a script from her recordings, which changed on a daily basis till the play opened.[13] Smith had final control over the sequencing, characters, and editing of interviews; the vast majority of the interviews for *Twilight* were those she conducted. I believe that all the interviews she used in the final version were hers. In light of the Pulitzer Prize controversy (see chapter 3), I both claim an expansive role for dramaturgy and emphasize that, ultimately, Smith made the decisions that shaped the play. The authorial function should remain definitively hers, given the cultural border patrol that polices aesthetic convention.

Institutional inertia complicated the creative process. During the hiatus between workshop and the beginning of rehearsals proper—a period of several months—apparently the Taper back-burnered the work of tracking down possible interviewees. Smith was performing another play elsewhere, while I continued to fax lists of names and suggestions to the Taper staff. A reencounter with my field notes reveals my frustrations. I will never know the precise reasons, but certainly issues of *time* and the tendency of people to postpone what is not immediately urgent could have been factors. Perhaps they were awaiting Smith's return. Perhaps for them *Twilight* was just another play. For me, the stakes were all consuming.[14]

March 22, 1993

> The thing I'm most upset by is the work with the Mark Taper Forum . . . the Taper has done absolutely nothing. Now that everything is down to the wire, X calls and wants to know the few people to interview, now that they have almost no time. It's ridiculous, outrageous. I have no time, and they have taken no responsibility. I keep faxing names . . . and they don't respond at all. No one has been contacted, as far as I can tell. It's terrible. . . . Do I want my name associated with it? . . . I feel like quitting, to be quite honest. (Kondo 1993a)

After going on to detail several things with which I took issue, some of which I discuss in this chapter, I decry "the problematic, utterly problematic, [representation of] Asian Americans. It's a huge headache, and what was once thrilling is only awful at this point." Obviously, I did not quit, but these misgivings set the stage in part for my comments at a later session, when Smith tries to address the black-white binary.

Let me set these affective reactions in historical and institutional context. Throughout the process of creating *Twilight*, the question of representation is especially thorny for Smith and her dramaturgs. Since one of my chief responsibilities is to give feedback on the portrayals of Asian Americans, I am constantly confronted with the dilemma: How does one "represent" such a historically contingent collectivity?[15] At this point, virtually all the Asian American interviewees are Korean American—understandable given that this community was so disproportionately affected. Nonetheless, most of them turn out to be male shop owners, who are representative neither of Korean Americans nor of Asian Americans. The lack of responsiveness to my faxes is frustrating. Korean American friends express concern, noting how mainstream institutions exploit communities and artists of color. Apparently, the Taper cancelled three appointments with one of the most prominent—and busiest—members of the Korean American community. "No one does that to him," said a friend. At one point, I speak with Smith about my worries of being a "minion of the dominant culture," a phrase that disturbs her, as she clearly wants to save me (and presumably herself) from that fate.

Furthermore, as a Japanese American, I feel uncertain about my reception in the Korean American community or my ability to represent their concerns adequately, since Japan had brutally colonized Korea in the early part of the twentieth century, and memories of that colonization remain understandably vivid. During this time, my grandparents had immigrated to the States, and my grandparents and parents were all incarcerated in concentration camps in the western United States during World War II—but these fine points could easily be lost with some Koreans and Korean Americans. Consequently, I urge Smith to find Korean Americans to do interviews, and she later hires a UCLA student, Nancy Yoo, to help with contacts and interviews.

For me, the dilemmas remained pointed. How does one represent the devastation of Korean American businesses[16] while at least gesturing toward the complexity of the larger Asian Pacific American collectivity, who are connected in multiple ways to the uprisings—such as the Cambodian

American businesses burned in Long Beach, the Vietnamese Americans and Cambodian Americans who felt poignant resonances with their historical experiences of war, violence, and diaspora?[17] Or Chinese Americans and Japanese Americans, from populations with long histories of residence in the United States, who saw the possibilities of multiracial Los Angeles go up in flames? How are Smith and her dramaturgs to represent various racial groups, conventionally defined—Asian Americans, Latinos, African Americans, and whites, with indigenous peoples erased— "accurately?" Is this possible? How do we achieve "accuracy" while keeping in mind the inadequacy and multiplicity of the categories themselves, the mutually interconnected histories among racial groups and the need to construct a compelling evening of theater? How to realize a production that is analytically sound, politically progressive, and dramatically satisfying? At one level, these dilemmas were insuperable. At another, we tried our hardest, and I believe that *Twilight*, though inevitably far from perfect, benefitted from our impassioned involvement.

Rehearsal, April–June 1993: The Politics of Racial Representation

Rehearsals begin with the full production team. We are an impressive advertisement for multiculturalism: set designer Robert Brill, composer Lucia Hwong, movement dramaturg Natsuko Ohama, and I are Asian American; stage manager Ed DeShae, lighting designer Allan Lee Hughes, and dramaturg Elizabeth Alexander are African American; dramaturg Oskar Eustis, stage manager Rich Hollabaugh, sound designer Jon Gottlieb, and director Emily Mann are white; and dramaturg Héctor Tobar is Latino. Though the picture could be dismissed as a multiculti tableau, real political and economic issues are at stake. The theater world tends toward Eurocentrism, and such a diverse cast and crew was virtually unprecedented in mainstream regional theater.

Issues of representation remain fraught, and I find myself out on a limb more than once. I am eager to break up the black-white binary, but this work is more difficult than I anticipated. Mere inclusion does not guarantee a progressive politics of racial representation. In an effort to broaden the black/white racial spectrum, Smith creates a section comprising Chicano artist Rudy Salas, Chicano politician and radio personality Xavier Hermosillo, and a Korean American store owner Chung Lee. In my dramaturgical notes, I argue that simply *including* characters of different ethnicities does not destabilize the black-white binary:

It's certainly true that the last section gives voice to Latinos and Asian Americans . . . that fact in and of itself does some important work in not remaining a strictly black and white thing. What it's about to me, though, is . . . the persistence of the black-white continuum, with Latinos and Asian Americans . . . somewhere in the middle, mediating third terms in what remains primarily a binaristic construction, which is where we always end up, with Asian Americans more toward the white end of the pole, Latinos more toward the black. If I recall correctly, the story goes like this: Rudy vents his anger toward whites (more a stereotypically black point of view); Xavier Hermosillo talks about brown always being left out of the rainbow; Chung Lee compares the Korean American situation to slavery. . . . In other words, in each case, the points of reference are always the black-white continuum. . . . As Elizabeth [Alexander] noted, there are of course good historical reasons why the black-white continuum is a powerful ideological force.

But if your point is in fact to disrupt it, I was wanting to see . . . more unexpected things . . . differences within the category Asian American or Latino . . . or African American identification with Latinos or Asian Americans or Native Americans (that's an absence no one has addressed). . . . I think the last section is about . . . the necessity for all races to fit into the black-white continuum in the dominant conceptual scheme about race. Simply having people from other groups speak doesn't mean that they disrupt black and white on another level. What we need, and what no one has yet, is some other scheme that is not linear, and in which these racial identities are not so monolithic and essentialized. As is, each can be neatly arranged on a linear hierarchy, which belies the incredible differences within. So for me, maybe the last section should be about the power of the black/white continuum in spite of the efforts to disrupt it, or about the inability to find a new language about race. (Kondo 1993a)

However, in the rehearsal room, I am not this diplomatic. Disappointed in the representation of Asian Americans in the play, I say publicly to Smith, "If this is the way Asian Americans are represented (and I were in the audience with Asian American friends), I'd walk out." Smith is understandably taken aback. She looks down, with a serious expression. Is she holding back tears? We four dramaturgs have a spirited dramaturgical session later with Smith, where we try to talk things out. Oskar Eustis tells me that my "emotions" appear to have occluded my "critical faculties," a comment that has a particularly dismissive resonance when its target is a woman. I counter that my comments arose from a principled *and* passionate politics that informs my critical faculties rather than occluding them.

I later find out that Smith cried over our volatile sessions. She has said in a public lecture that after such heated exchanges, she sometimes would receive a fax from me. Rather than the apology she expected, I would say, essentially, "And furthermore . . ." "You were hard on me," Smith once told me, and in a recent public discussion, Smith declared, "She [Kondo] made me cry. She's tough" (Smith 2018). At the time, my presumption was that Smith should encounter this dramaturgical "tough love" in the rehearsal room, before she performed in public and perhaps incurred censure. The process, fraught though it was, exemplifies the difficulty and promise of conflict, the bristling, high-stakes issues of race and class, especially at that moment, in that city. Those issues remain pervasive and have life-determining impact. Working through will never be easy.

Many years later, I interviewed Oskar Eustis about David Henry Hwang's *Yellow Face*, just before its East Coast premiere at the Public, where Eustis is now artistic director. At the end, I asked him about his memories of our dramaturgical experiences on *Twilight*:

> EUSTIS: My memory, which I know isn't strictly accurate, is that everybody in the room threatened to walk out on the project.
>
> KONDO: Well, I know I did.
>
> EUSTIS: I *know* you did! [*laughs*] And I know Héctor did. I actually sort of defined myself as the one guy who never threatened to walk out. . . . But also because you know it just was . . . remarkable that that group of people were able to . . . enter again. And that was to me Anna at her most impressive, her ability to take that degree of . . .
>
> KONDO: *I can't even imagine. I* cannot *even imagine.* (Eustis 2007)

Had I been a conventional dramaturg in a conventional play where race was not the subject, the stakes would have not felt so high, and I would have phrased my concerns more diplomatically. That I didn't indexed the urgency and the sense of responsibility I felt to the play, to Smith, and to the racialized groups to whom I was accountable. Less than a year after the unrest, issues of race felt raw, volatile, bristling with urgency. In my own life, I was in a moment when I was outspoken and blunt, having helped to organize a political protest almost immediately upon taking a new job.

To Smith's credit, we were able to work things out. The day following my threat to walk out, she cut that segment. As difficult as our creative differences were, Smith ultimately took our dramaturgical concerns seriously.

Ultimately, Smith dismantled the section that had prompted our volatile argument. Rudy Salas opens the play, revealing the police brutality that left him deaf in one ear. History repeats itself when his son Steven, a student at Stanford and member of the legendary Chicano band Tierra, is similarly harassed by the police. Other Latinx characters in the Los Angeles version include Julio Menjívar, a lumber salesman who had escaped El Salvador because of the violence. He was arrested during the uprisings for no apparent reason, leaving him humiliated: "Nunca, nunca en mi vida, había estado arrestado" (Never, never in my life had I been arrested). Elvira Evers, a Panamanian American woman, was a random victim of violence. A bullet narrowly missed killing her and the baby in her womb. "Open your eyes," says Evers. "Watch what's going on."

The backstage drama demonstrates the high stakes over which characters are included and who closes the play. Smith performs Dan Kuramoto, leader of the Japanese American band Hiroshima, as the concluding character during previews. However, given critic John Lahr's reaction to Kuramoto, I am satisfied when Smith decides to end with Sibrian instead, who exhorts us to "change things." In terms of Asian American representation overall, the play includes the Park family, about whom I was ambivalent, but it also includes the pivotal character, Young-soon Han. She points out the paradoxical position of Asian Americans as the "middleman minority" (Bonacich 1973)—or from a Marxist perspective, the comprador bourgeoisie—and is thus a powerful figure.

The director characterized our conflicts as, "It's not about me!" Battles of this kind are far more than "me-ism." Given individualist ideology that presumes equally positioned subjects, it is easy to reduce our arguments to versions of pathological narcissism, rather than the primary narcissism required for a subject's existence. Our task was not an individualist one; it was a political struggle to address structural exclusion and to achieve public existence for racialized and classed populations, a public *being* that intervenes in segregated theater and challenges the structural violence of erasure and stereotypical representation. We attempted to address the rage and pain that minoritarian subjects can still experience in sites of upper-middlebrow culture. Smith undertook a mission of unprecedented scope, to represent onstage the perspectives of *multiple* racialized communities, whose concerns and historical experiences are precisely not those of the dominant. Those differences in positioning are overdetermined by structures of power that fueled the eruption of violence on the streets. Onstage, representing points of view that challenge structural inequality can subvert the American theater's assumption of whiteness as the universal. From what standpoint of privilege can one dismiss a concern with the representation of people of color as mere me-ism?

Marking Whiteness

Smith's struggles included pushing for more representation of minoritized and subaltern perspectives and to mark whiteness as a site of privilege. For her, the notion of performing a "parade of color" for a silent white audience was anathema. However, she initially had difficulty in finding appropriate white interviewees, and she had to battle to make *Twilight* more than a spectacle of people of color fighting each other. Whiteness could not remain an unmarked category. I quote from a memo she sent to Oskar Eustis (A. D. Smith 1993b):

> Emily [Mann] and I had another conversation about whites yesterday. You should know what goes through my head each time you all ask me to define the white population.
> 1. When Dorinne and Héctor were asked to track the representation of Latinos and Asian Americans, they gave me strong and clear reactions to what they saw and what was missing. They did some defining. They did not put the full responsibility of definition back on me.
> 2. Who are the whites that you . . . would like to see represented? You have a white population that frequents the theatre. How should they be mirrored? I don't know them. I have not been introduced to them. Whenever I have done *On the Road*, the first step is "What would you like to know about your community?" "How can I give voice to the unheard in your community?" Although the Taper aspires to broaden its base, as do many theatres, its community is still a white community. I need *you* to lead me to those people in *your* community who should be mirrored. It is *false* to pretend that many people of color we have met in our pursuit mirror *you*. I am committed to broadening your mirror. . . . I am dependent on you for that; I can't answer that.
> 3. That's why I feel so pushed up against the wall every time you ask me these questions. The Taper has not yet answered the big question

in their own words, which is who are you from your point of view. Not mine.
4. It is crucial that whites in the audience find points of identification. Points of empathy *with themselves*. To create a situation where they merely empathize with those less fortunate than themselves is another kind of theatre.
5. These points of empathy may be points of empathy with white fear, white guilt, white righteousness, white rage, but they *even* could be points of empathy with white love.
6. If these points of connection are not found, I will be playing for 90 minutes in front of a very disturbing silence. Alone. I'm not sure that's healthy. Certainly not for me. And likely not for them.
7. My political problem is this. Privilege is often masked, hidden, guarded. This guarded, fortressed privilege is exactly what has led us to the catastrophe of non-dialogue in which we find ourselves. I'm not talking about economic privilege. I'm talking about the basic privilege of white skin which is the foundation of our race vocabulary.
8. California was not always white. How did it become white? This historical moment is yet unmarked in the play. I need you to help me mark it.
9. A parade of color is what multi-cultural theatre has been about. Much of what I have been telling you is that I don't want to march in the parade for whites standing on the sidewalk with drooping flags. I'd like a Mardi Gras in the first part of the show. Won't you invite some of your friends?
10. This is an amazing historical moment. I'm not going to do an eye for an eye and leave whites out of this part of United States history. I need you to help answer the question of WHO? WHICH WHITES? Just as Dorinne and Héctor answered their WHO.

Love,
Anna

Ultimately, the Taper version of *Twilight* incorporated eloquent commentary from many white people in Los Angeles, including police chief Daryl Gates, who claimed it was "awfully hard to break away" from his fundraiser to attend to the "blossoming" riot. Reporter Judy Tur enacts white anger: "People are people . . . but what's happening in South Central now . . . they're really taking advantage. Now I'm mad, and you know what? I'm sick of it." Tur locates the people "taking advantage" in South

Central (the poorer, black, and Latino areas of LA) rather than acknowledging race and class privilege that creates segregation. An anonymous talent agent at a prestigious Hollywood agency articulates the paradox of privilege: "the *system* / plays unequally / . . . I started to / absorb a little guilt and say . . . / I deserve it. / . . . I don't mean I deserve to get my house *burned down* / but the *us* / did / . . . it's so / . . . *heartbreaking* / seeing . . . people reduced to *burning down their own neighborhoods* / burning down *our* neighborhoods / I could see. / But burning down their *own* / that was more dramatic / to me" (A. D. Smith 2002, 93).

The later Broadway version included more such perspectives, including real estate agent Elaine Young, who cocooned in the Beverly Hills Hotel during the "riots," and Diane Van Iden, who worried about the safety of her teenagers: "What if somebody brings the gun to the prom?" Sometimes, the characters were used to convey information and to add irony and humor. *Los Angeles Times* editor Shelby Coffey said that their stringer from Beirut called to see whether everyone in LA was "all right." "You know you've got some trouble in your city when your stringer from Beirut calls to say are you . . . alright." Most of *Twilight*'s depictions of white people combined some aspect of white privilege with a feeling of nostalgia, a longing for a simpler time, when privilege remained unassailed. These characters gesture toward racial hierarchies in Los Angeles and the nation at large. No play about race could allow whiteness to remain the unmarked, so that people of color are the only ones who "have" race. I underline the critical importance of Smith's repeated battles with institutional inertia so that she might represent these perspectives. The Taper, despite its location in downtown Los Angeles and its relative proximity to South Central and other communities of color, was/is symbolically aligned with the white West Side. Every gain required a fight.

A segment popular with the largely white audience performed power-evasive, liberal humanist sentiment. Smith sought to problematize such a stance. Truck driver Reginald Denny, who suffered the notorious beating captured on videotape, proclaimed, "Someday when I . . . get a house / I'm gonna have one of the *rooms*, / . . . of all the riot stuff . . . it's gonna be a happy room . . . there won't be / a color problem / . . . It's not a color / it's a person! So this room . . . it's just gonna be a blast. One day, Lord / willing, it'll happen" (A. D. Smith 2002, 114–15). Denny's liberal humanism is both laudable—the reach for the human that we must embrace—and naïve, for as our experiences working on *Twilight* taught us, as poststructuralist and Marxism argue, there can be no room, no pastoral utopia, free of race and power. In performance, Denny comes across as spacey—perhaps the influence of painkillers—and as repressing the terrible violence he had suffered. Smith reported in an interview with me that George C. Wolfe, who directed the Broadway version, said, "I wouldn't like to see that man when his anger comes out" (A. D. Smith 2012b).

In versions from the Princeton performances onward, Smith includes as counterpoint African American activist Paul Parker, the brother of one of the LA Four defendants who allegedly beat Denny. Parker's perspective starkly opposes Denny's liberal humanism: "Because Denny is white, that's the bottom line. If Denny was Latino, Indian, or Black, they wouldn't give a damn. . . . When I finally get my house I'm gonna have just one room set aside. It's gonna be my 'No Justice, No Peace' room . . . and have all my articles and clippings . . . so my children can know what Daddy did . . . what it takes to be a strong black man. . . . You either stand or you fall. You either be black or you die" (A. D. Smith 2002, 116–18).

I argued fiercely in rehearsal that Parker was a necessary antidote to Denny's feel-good, power-evasive version of race relations. Parker is simultaneously problematic, as he embraces a logic of revenge: "Basically, you puttin' a race of people of notice. We didn't get to Beverly Hills but that doesn't mean we won't get there." Parker is compelling in his narration of history and problematic in his masculinity: "We supposed to have some empathy or some sympathy toward this one white man? . . . how 'bout the empathy . . . toward blacks? . . . you kidnapped us, you raped our women, you pull us over daily, have us get out of our cars, . . . take all our papers out, go through our trunk . . . and drive off" (A. D. Smith 2002, 117–19).

Parker's life experiences of driving while black and his telling assessment of slavery and rape are eloquent, but he simultaneously embraces a problematic masculinism ("our women"). Nonetheless, his point of view is crucial, so audiences understand the political, historical context of the Denny beating and the outraged reactions to the acquittals that condoned police violence against African Americans.[18]

In my interview with Eustis, I revisited the issue of how our racialized positionalities shaped our perspectives on the Reginald Denny character:

> EUSTIS: You were great. I mean seriously. The story I tell about that occasion . . . Remember when . . . we finally got that interview with the truck driver . . . Reginald Denny, and Anna came in that day, and she—that afternoon—was still wearing the headphones, and she just

ran through it and all of us just . . . euphoric. Fantastic. And I just said, "That's it! That's the end of the show!" [laughter] And she says, "You would think that, wouldn't you?" And . . . I knew . . . she was absolutely right. That was my . . . white hippie's end of the show. And we . . . all hold hands and sing "Kumbaya." And the black people drive me to the hospital. . . . That's exactly an example of how the truths we perceive are always through the lens of our own. It doesn't matter how many weeks, months I spent with the material, inside of it—you know for me, at that moment, when we reach an emotional climax, I'm the white hippie. And . . . you should know that. And therefore try and stay out of the way because it's not your show. (Eustis 2007)

Many years later, when I interview Smith, we agree that ending with Denny would not have worked.

Incommensurability

Smith and we dramaturgs found ourselves facing unexpectedly intractable dilemmas as the play took shape. Different spectators from different cultural communities could view the identical performance and come to opposing conclusions. I had consented to my role as dramaturg assuming that I could predict, at least partially, problematic audience reactions if the play reinforced racial stereotypes. But when *Twilight* went into previews in front of an audience, the feedback from friends and colleagues shattered my assumptions. One example serves to illustrate. In the Taper version, the characters all stood alone, save for one triptych: the Park family, comprising Walter Park, his wife June, and their stepson, Chris Oh. Park had been "lobotomized" by an African American man who shot him, "execution style," during the uprisings. From my dramaturgical notes to Smith: "My companions and I had the same reaction to the Park family this time . . . although what they say is moving, because the triptych effect is the only one in the entire piece, it has as one of its readings, '3 Asians make 1 other person,' or a reinscription of the notion of strong family values and/or of the subordination of the individual to the group, both of which are problematic" (Kondo 1993a).

The triptych structure elicited contradictory reactions. An African American feminist critic told me that, because the play spent so much time with the Park family, she was afraid that they would become "the locus of unassailable pathos." In her view, the sympathy accorded Asian

Americans would detract from the sympathy accorded African Americans, in a zero-sum game for people of color. An Asian American friend of mine and I looked at each other as we heard this, repeating, "You're kidding. You're kidding." To us, far from attracting audience sympathy, the Park family perpetuated Asian American stereotypes: the affluent model minority (the family was depicted seated on Louis XVI chairs), the Korean merchant, and the selfless Asian woman, the mediating third term in a black-and white-binary. Even though Korean Americans were killed in the uprisings, the Parks did not represent them. Indeed, a Chicana scholar was singularly unimpressed: "A gunshot wound? That isn't so bad. Those privileged Asians. Chicanos are getting killed every day of the week." To complicate interpretation even further, the depiction of Asian Americans as victimized property owners can serve as a stand-in for whiteness, allowing whites to identify "sympathetically" with Korean Americans and to condemn the "riots" in a politically correct way (Palumbo-Liu 1994).

Equally disturbing was the representation of Mrs. Park. I asked Smith, "Why does the only woman who is the picture of selfless devotion to her husband have to be Asian American?" To my mind, this reinforced the stereotypes of servile, passive Asian women that I must fight on a daily basis. However, Smith's dialect coach, a Korean American woman, thought that Smith's performance of Mrs. Park wasn't demure *enough*. Two Asian American women expressed diametrically opposed opinions on how the Asian American women should be represented.

Such were the complexities of just one segment of a play that included over twenty characters in its Taper version, over forty in its Broadway version. Arguably, all the objections raised are understandable, valid points of view given different positions within racialized histories. This incommensurability supports Smith's decision to hire multiple dramaturgs who might articulate points of view from these positions. How to adjudicate each choice of character, when people's lives and histories and passions were all focused directly upon Smith, and to a lesser extent, the dramaturgs? Such were the highly charged decisions Smith and her team had to negotiate. And choices had to be made, despite the impossibility of pleasing the entire audience.

PREVIEWS AND OPENING

The play's opening is delayed for ten days, as Smith continues to incorporate new material, including the interviews with Reginald Denny and with Maria, a juror from the federal (second) trial. At one point during previews,

Smith is "on book"—script in hand—and *Twilight* has a running time of close to three hours. The list of characters and the sequencing changes nightly until opening, a headache both for Smith, who must memorize her lines, and for the technical staff and stagehands, who must make appropriate adjustments. Ultimately, she pares down the list to the final version with twenty-six characters.[19]

On June 13, 1993, *Twilight* opens in its official world premiere at the Mark Taper Forum. Ever critical, I still have some misgivings about its politics of representation, but the festive atmosphere of opening night and the warm audience reception highlight the historic nature of this production: an African American woman taking center stage, addressing politically urgent issues in a virtuoso performance in a major regional theater. Through giving voice to so many new characters in US theater—a Salvadorean lumber salesman, a Korean American store owner, Rodney King's aunt—*Twilight* authorizes all of us to take center stage, to tell our stories in infinite evenings of stories that illuminate the complexity of our historical moment. Smith's expansive embrace of ordinary people, including people of color, stages a Los Angeles that feels like the world I live in. Her notion that all of us speak in "organic poems" implies that all of our stories are worth telling. In a mainstream theater world where blockbuster spectacle, revivals, linear narrative, safe topics, and sure commercial bets are the norm—and where people of color continue to be conspicuous by their absence or being confined to stereotypical roles—*Twilight* makes a significant intervention in the politics of racial representation, aesthetic form, and its thematic focus on urgent social issues. The presence of an African American woman performing people of different races and genders enacts a potentially utopian gesture of political solidarity—the politics of affiliation—and of fraught (humanist) possibility, enacting our potential for multiple ways of being in the world.

In *Twilight*, the multiracial tableau both onstage and off was especially striking in comparison to the more Eurocentric fare that populates conventional mainstream theater. Though such a spectacle of multiculturalism cannot guarantee a progressive politics, it can model the preconditions for such a politics, and it remains rare enough in US theater to attract comment. This struck Smith one day when another engagement compelled her to leave our postplay discussion with Los Angeles high school students. Six of us who worked on the production were onstage: two Asian American women, a white woman, a white man, a Latino man, and an African American woman. Smith caught sight of us on the television monitor backstage, and she stopped for a moment to watch her "many-hued dramaturgs" (Lahr 1993, 90). She wrote us this thank you note (A. D. Smith 1993a):

> Dear Dorinne, Héctor, Emily, Elizabeth, Oskar and Natsuko,
>
> Yesterday as I was leaving the student show, I caught a glimpse of all of you sitting up there on the stage, talking to the audience. I was so dazzled by you, and so happy. I really wished that I could be in the audience. It didn't seem right to leave. . . . I would have loved to watch you perform.
>
> I thought about it all the way home, and this morning, I felt that
>
>> Diversity,
>> Un named
>> Is alive.
>> The name is a waiting
>> For something that is.
>> Makes it into a possibility
>> . . .
>> It's real.
>> . . .
>> You are real.
>> Your brilliance is real.
>> Your generosity is real.
>> In my life, in this moment,
>> You are the proof
>> That
>> "a change's gotta come"
>> has come
>> I am so proud.
>> And glad
>> And clapping.
>> And so fully grateful that you have been willing to work with me.
>
>> Love,
>> Anna

The danger of this multiplicity, for both Smith and her dramaturgs, is that the mere presence of bodies of "many hues" might be seen as sufficient, a multicultural smorgasbord in which issues of power and inequality no longer exist. The multiracial spectacle might be too easily read as a power-evasive form of liberal pluralism, a vision of happy multiplicity in which color is evacuated of its positioning in a matrix of power and becomes merely another consumer choice. In such a scenario, an audience might concur with mainstream critics, seeing *Twilight*'s message as "everyone has a right to his point of view," and the artist is simply "presenting all sides."

Yet the claim that Smith's work is reducible to a flabby form of liberal pluralism misses the degree to which there is a point of view expressed through the questions asked in the interviews, the selection and arrangement of the material, the performance, and the elements of production, including lighting, sets, music, costumes, and movement. Through my participatory observation backstage, I know that Smith sets out to frustrate audience desire for neat narrative closure, for a central unifying voice, and for a liberal humanist reading that "we're all human beings," a reading that fails to analyze the workings of historically specific power relations rendering some human beings more human than others.

A commonsense view of narrative might collapse authorial intention with the meaning of the play. Indeed, that is partially what I am attempting in this chapter, to recuperate Smith's intentions from the critical reception of *Twilight*. Yet serving as a dramaturg on *Twilight* helped me to appreciate the complexity of the creative process and the multiplicity of factors that can affect meaning in ways that escape the control of the author or the director. Never has the intentional fallacy—that authorial intention never guarantees meaning—seemed so apparent. Despite our best efforts to preempt stereotypical readings of characters, the audience brought its own preconceptions to the production. Hence, the *New Yorker* writer thought Dan Kuramoto, who spoke of Los Angeles as a "new racial frontier," meant merely that people of color should stop fighting each other. Hence, audience members produced a startling array of conflicting interpretations of the Park family. Everyone interprets through a positioned perspective; one can try to guide those understandings, but ultimately it is impossible to anticipate them fully or to control them. Smith was precisely in this position. She gathered a diverse team of dramaturgs because she understood the partiality of every perspective, including her own. While the intentional fallacy is well known in philosophy and literary criticism, I could not understand the degree of its fallaciousness until I *participated* in the creative process, coming to my understanding experientially, through a corporeal mode of knowing.

Twilight leads us beyond power-evasive notions of liberal consensus to the unpredictable, incommensurable differences in audience reception. I realize now that we had imagined that we would be able to preempt most, if not all, problematic racial representations. Such a view depends in part on the assumption that the audience, even if internally differentiated, can be known and is predictable. Liberal pluralist assumptions about audience reception presume an ultimately harmonious and generic universal audience. Differences of race, gender, class, sexuality, and age, among other factors, are assumed to be "accidents," in a substance/accident metaphysics of the subject. Accordingly, different interpretations can theoretically be overcome through an interpretive unity. In contrast, *Twilight* recognizes the *incommensurability* of interpretations in its very form, juxtaposing irreducibly contradictory perspectives. Similarly, David Henry Hwang employs juxtaposition to raise questions about a singular "real," and my own play juxtaposes characters' conflicting memories to problematize a singular truth. Aesthetic form enacts a power-sensitive politics.

Normative desire for the One animated the recurrent question journalists posed to Smith: "Is there a central unifying voice that gives us hope?" For Smith, no such voice exists. In all versions of *Twilight* except for the Taper production, Twilight Bey, the architect of the gang truce, talked about his reach for the other: "I cannot forever dwell in the idea . . . of identifying with only me and mine." For Bey, twilight is "limbo." The play ends on "limbo," leaving us with indeterminacy: the perilous uncertainty of the future, the lack of any clear solution. How do we transform society to end race and class oppression?

The lack of closure is a key aesthetic/political move, familiar from Brecht, who argued that art should make audiences think, disrupting our comfortable commonsense assumptions (Belsey 1980; Brecht and Willett 1964). Further, the notion of "limbo" and the penultimate segment, which ends with "the fire . . . can burst out, anytime," interrupts an Aristotelian unity of time, where events (and plays) have a beginning, middle, and end. There is no easy solution to race and class inequality. *Twilight*'s open-ended, ambiguous ending challenges audience desire for a Master Subject voice that offers neat resolution to a phenomenon as complex as the LA uprisings. Smith herself resists the notion that her work is designed to find solutions to social problems; instead, she says that she is interested in the "process of the problem" (A. D. Smith 1994, xxiv).

The play revealed the limits of the liberal pluralist assumption of a singular message conveyed to a universal audience who is amenable to general persuasion, what literary critic Ellen Rooney calls "seductive reasoning" (1989). *Twilight* brought forward the problematic assumptions underlying dramaturgical practice: that we can know/predict audience reaction and that a politics of representation satisfactory for the academic critic/dramaturg will be sufficient. *Twilight*, in both its form and its thematics, interrupted those assumptions.

Rather than a univocal message or even a message that could be predicted on the basis of assumptions about various communities, *Twilight* demonstrated the *incommensurability* of audience interpretations and the *impossibility* of imparting/receiving a singular message or even compatible messages. This irreducible incommensurability, the fundamentally irreconcilable differences among interpretations, points to a politics that recognizes historical specificity and political positioning. There is no universal audience unmarked by race, gender, sexuality, or class. As the interpretations of the Park family dramatically demonstrated, historical experiences and uneven locations in a matrix of power shape different understandings of "the same" object. Reginald Denny's desire for the pastoral "happy room," free of race and power, starkly contrasts with Paul Parker's power-sensitive "No Justice, No Peace" room. The assumption of a universal audience, common to pluralist rhetoric, is itself a power-evasive move that masks the always already marked character of diverse and incommensurable audiences-in-the-plural, who are unevenly positioned in multiple matrices of power.

As an anthropologist and academic critic of theater/performance, I learned through corporeal epistemologies the *impossibility* of controlling representation. My experiences now give me far greater sympathy for the (im)possible task of putting a production onstage, particularly when issues of race, power, and representation are at stake. We could not preempt every criticism. My dramaturgical notes to Smith reveal the contradictions of both her position and that of the dramaturgs, arguing for the critical role of participation rather than a purely spectatorial reading:

> There's something else I find weird with some people (other Asian American academics in particular) . . . a certain implication that I've let down the race (and of course the implication that they could have done better). Frankly, at times I've felt like saying, "You try it, then!" In that sense, it's been good for me as a critic (David Hwang also mentioned this), to be part of *creating* something . . . it's impossible to avoid problematic images or stereotypes altogether, and then with . . .

other constraints . . . multiple constituencies . . . how on the edge we were with schedule, and your . . . openness to changing things until the last minute . . . it's truly a tribute to your . . . willingness to take risks. (Kondo 1993b)

Participating in the making of *Twilight* foregrounds the intersections of critical reflection, creative practice, and political intervention. The corporeal epistemologies informing dramaturgical critique illuminate the animating assumptions of liberal theater, its distribution of the sensible—that politics are ex-orbitant, even antithetical, to aesthetics. On the contrary, race, gender, and power in their multifarious forms are ever present in the aesthetic domain.

Our creative process on *Twilight* modeled a vision of aesthetics inseparable from politics. Institutional constraints from our designation as representatives of our communities, inertia in contacting interviewees, and the limits of time and deadlines shaped our creative process. In the wake of violence and destruction, *Twilight* became a play/production of enduring significance, despite—or rather because of—our fiery battles backstage. Liberal consensus was insufficient. A vibrant politics of affiliation risks agonistic conflict and the possibility of destructive hostility, while opening possibilities for the reparative. The dramaturgical process in *Twilight* enacted a theory of the political that took difference, zones of incommensurability, and conflict as inevitable, even generative. Our challenges to liberal civility undermine our comfortable, power-evasive assumptions, clearing the way for transformative change.

Smith's vision disrupts fixed schemes of race, disturbs notions of genre and the well-made play, provokes us to think about difficult social issues, and performs a politics of paradox and shifting identities. The reinscription of liberal humanism is inevitable, if only because her work characterizes particular people in a one-woman show. Her performative virtuosity inevitably attracts labels of auratic genius. In chapter 4, I argued that Smith opens out the individual to history and power. Any political intervention both subverts and reinscribes power. What work is it doing? For whom? To what effect? Smith challenges us to dwell in the discomfort of uncertainty, destabilizing our safe, pleasurable common sense to negotiate unknown, politically risky terrain. Resolution, fixity, are left behind for the challenges of complication and destabilization. Exploring the pleasures and dangers of this instability could occasion new and different conflicts, and it can offer unexpected possibilities.

As participants in her work, the creative team cannot occupy a space of purity—nor can any academics or political activists. Complicitous critique (Hutcheon 1992; Kondo 1997) is the only kind possible, though degrees of enmeshment with power can differ significantly. We must remain as aware as possible of contradictions, contestations, and reinscriptions of power at work in any attempt at intervention, even in political movements tout court. Complicitous critique is not confined to the theater world or the domains of culture. It is the condition of our being-in-the-world. Structures both enable and hamper agency. That constitutive paradox should not stop us from deploying reparative critique in a lifelong struggle to remake worlds.

Twilight Coda, Twenty Years Later

May 2012, just after the twentieth anniversary of the Los Angeles uprisings. In Los Angeles, media outlets are taking stock, both on television and in print journalism—notably, in a series in the *Los Angeles Times* "twenty years after." Many stories follow people affected by the unrest, such as Fidel López, whose name few remember. He was brutally beaten at the intersection of Florence and Normandie, along with the well-known Reginald Denny and many who were forgotten. Op-ed pieces trumpet the fact that we *do* all get along or that organizing has transformed the landscape of inequality to the extent that no "riot" could ever happen again. A few stories analyze continuing, indeed worsening, economic inequality. In his characteristic grooving on the apocalyptic—with which I agree in this case—Mike Davis lists disturbing new ways labor and progressives have become comfortable playing with big business.

Among the front page articles is one about *Twilight: Los Angeles 1992*. Despite the fact that some dismissed the play in 1993 as having a short shelf life, the persistence of racial and class inequality has meant that the play's influence has endured.

Twenty years after the fact, the commemoration of the "riots" highlights the pivotal issue of framing. Because Smith's play refuses easy answers and because liberal theater inevitably foregrounds individuals and emotion, the mainstream sees Smith and *Twilight* as instantiating power-evasive multiculturalism. In this view, we can prevent another riot if "we all get along," presumably at the level of one-on-one interaction. Yet, *Twilight* can be read in precisely the opposite fashion: a warning that, unless we dismantle systemic inequality, the "riots" could "burst out, any time" (A. D. Smith 2002, 169).

I attend a commemorative event for *Twilight* at a state-of-the-art performing arts high school in Los Angeles, sponsored by an organization called Facing History and Ourselves. Their mission: "By studying the historical development of the Holocaust and other examples of genocide, students make the essential connection between history and the moral choices they confront in their own lives" (Facing History and Ourselves 2016). In practice this means reinforcing liberal humanist notions of racism as individual prejudice. The locus of change remains individual "choice," a problematic concept that enshrines the voluntarist subject. For example, one speaker stated that the message of *Twilight* should be "get to know someone different than yourself." Certainly, getting to know someone different than yourself is better than killing someone or harming a person physically. But leaving the onus on the individual disavows structural violence and hence perpetrates the violence of color blindness. Structural inequality engendered by capitalist accumulation, racism and legacies of colonialism, and the police as the repressive state apparatus will not disappear through a lifetime of organizing—as important as that is. Structural violence certainly will not disappear when reduced to the level of individual attitude. We need to act, but we need to think collectively and to address the structural.

The following Sunday, Smith performs excerpts from *Twilight* at a conference for people of color who work in philanthropic foundations. Her performance is sponsored by AAPIP, Asian Americans/Pacific Islanders in Philanthropy, in association with other groups in the Council on Foundations—notably, the Association for Black Foundation Executives. I weave my way through the labyrinthine Marriott Hotel at L.A. Live. Both affinity groups reference structural inequality in their mission statements: "AAPIP leverages, builds and accesses philanthropic capital for our communities to develop their capacity to meet community needs and *solve systemic inequities*" (AAPIP 2015).

Similarly, the mission statement of the Association of Black Foundation Executives (ABFE) celebrates the achievements of their affinity group, recognizing that "Black communities and the philanthropic leaders who serve those communities still face institutional and structural barriers that often hinder efforts to leverage philanthropy's powerful tools for positive, enduring social change" (ABFE 2013). Susan Batten, the president of ABFE, introduces Smith by analyzing structural racism, giving Smith's work a meaningful historical, political frame. Her remarks enable the performance of *Twilight* to be read through the analysis of structural violence.

This event destabilized my own stereotypes about funding agencies. I was encouraged to learn that officers in philanthropic foundations are acutely attentive to the level of the structural and the historical, attuned to the insidious persistence of inequality even within our power-evasive, postracial present. Their incisive analysis countered, at least partially, my sobering encounter with the performance for high school students. The latter ethos remains hegemonic, for liberal humanism continues to reduce structural and physical violence to individual choice. But there is hope. Framing matters.

chapter 5

Revising Race

THEATERWEEK. Take a look at the face on the cover of this magazine. Is he Chinese American, Asian American, plain American? Or someone in yellowface? Does any of this matter? These are some of the questions raised in David Henry Hwang's new farce *Face Value*.

DHH. Is race a construct which is still useful or is it mythological?

—Hwang 2009, 17

David Henry Hwang develops his career-long exploration of the meanings of race in *Yellow Face*. What is race in a postracial era? Are the political formations forged in the 1960s adequate to the complexities of our lives now? Is race an identity? A role? A biological fact? A political collective? A culture? A field of historically specific power relations? How do we deal with the increasing population of mixed-race, adoptive children of different races and the ideological, gender, sexuality, and class diversity within supposedly monolithic racial groups? Ours is a moment when "barriers" of race and ethnicity are becoming increasingly porous, and "society is evolving another relation to race and identity" (Hwang 2007a). Theater is an especially compelling site to explore such questions, for it intervenes in hegemonic discourses of race, in ways that mobilize the powers of the sensorium, compelling us to think *and* feel.

In this chapter, I take a prismatic approach, viewing *Yellow Face* from multiple perspectives of critic, ethnographer, dramaturg, and playwright, following out its provocations on these timely issues. Thematically and formally, *Yellow Face* is a rich, multilayered work that captures the zeitgeist: from academic discussions about race, genre, and truth to media culture, where reality television and video game avatars blur the lines between truth and fiction, to the complexities of contemporary racial formations and subjective experiences of race. Hwang's work performs the *tensions* between the deconstruction of conventional ideas about race and identity and the reinscription of our commonsense assumptions, in a work innovative in both form and content. On the levels of theory, epistemology, politics, and aesthetic form, *Yellow Face* addresses issues of race, identity, nation, and geopolitical power. Part 1 of this chapter highlights the compelling questions the play poses.

Part 2 shifts to a participatory, dramaturgical register of reparative creativity. I follow Hwang's *creative process* to analyze theoretical/political contradictions in racial discourses, marking key shifts in three versions of the play as it evolved from a liberal humanist, power-evasive perspective to a power-sensitive take on race. I include the notes I sent David and producer/dramaturg Oskar Eustis, writing my concern that early drafts closed with a romance with the primitive and a power-evasive desire to efface racial/cultural inequalities under the sign of the Human. I was not hired as a dramaturg, but I had strong reactions to the play and wanted to put pressure on what I believed to be problematic authorial and production choices, given my commitment to Hwang's work. Whether or not my note was an influence—the *post hoc ergo propter hoc* logical fallacy—the ending became less romantic and more progressive in its subsequent New York iteration. I asserted dramaturgical critique as reparative critique to sharpen the play's progressive treatment of race and subject formation.

This section highlights three key iterations of the play: the first draft (Hwang 2005); the world premiere version (Hwang 2007d) staged at the Mark Taper Forum (hereafter Taper/EWP), co-produced with East West Players and the Public Theater; and the "final" version at the Public Theater (December 2007), eventually published by Theatre Communications Group (Hwang 2009). Through the revisions, Hwang grapples with character, structure, and questions of race/racism. He writes the *struggles* in an ideological field, between a liberal humanism that wishes to throw off racial markings and a recognition of structures of inequality that continue to shape our lived experiences of race. In chapter 4, I analyzed the politics of agonistics enacted in our spirited dramaturgical debates. Here, the politics of agonistics animate struggles within a "single" consciousness as *discursive* debates that exceed the "individual." The revisions of *Yellow Face* illuminate the process of rewriting as remaking race into more power-sensitive forms. The chapter coda gestures toward Hwang's newer work and its performance of the complications of Asian American racial formation: diaspora, transnationalism, and intra–Asian American tensions. The plays stage the unwieldy yet necessary collective "Asian American" as a process refigured through historical developments, critical scholarship, and artistic intervention.

I elaborate and perform *dramaturgical critique* as dialogical exchange between artist and audience, artist and academic critic. Critique serves the process of reparative creativity. Dramaturgical focus on race may be unusual in theater practice, given the assumed universality of whiteness and the relative rarity of race as an explicit thematic: the majority of plays are white but rarely marked as such. The plays Smith and Hwang write demand close attention to the intertwinings of text, aesthetic form, and histories/politics/epistemologies of race. My dramaturgical, processual emphasis enacts the theoretical perspectives of this book. Instead of asking what race *is*, I ask what work it is doing, when, for whom? A focus on process complicates the ontological, spotlighting shifting structures that are phenomenologically resonant.

The Stakes and the Politics of Location

Reparative critique assumes heightened resonance given Hwang's unique position in Asian America (see "Overture"). Hwang is *the only* Asian American dramatist who has achieved his degree of national and international prominence. Until recently, he was *the only* Asian American whose plays have been produced on Broadway[1] and *the only* Asian American playwright to win a Tony. His collaborations cut across the upper tier of popular and high culture, from opera libretti to the books for Broadway blockbusters such as *Tarzan* and Elton John's *Aida,* and lyrics to a song by Prince. Hwang is the most produced living opera librettist (Columbia University School of the Arts 2016) and *the only* Asian American to achieve this level of prominence. In short, Hwang is in the peculiar position, both exalted and vexed, of having been *the only one*. He stages the existential fallout from this sometimes-burdensome responsibility in *Yellow Face*. From the inception of his career, Hwang found himself called upon to represent the Asian American community (assumed to be monolithic) and even to be a China expert. This pressure to be the exemplary Asian American, an awkward dilemma that Hwang attempted to fulfill with aplomb and grace, faces Marcus, the white actor mistaken for Asian in *Yellow Face*.

Hwang's unique status persists despite the plethora of talented Asian American playwrights, from generations senior to Hwang (e.g., Wakako Yamauchi, Hisaye Yamamoto, Genny Lim, Frank Chin), his contemporaries (e.g., Ric Shiomi, Philip Kan Gotanda, Velina Hasu Houston, Ralph Peña) and younger generations that include numerous Asian American playwrights trained at NYU, Yale, Brown, and Juilliard (e.g., Ayad Akhtar, Christopher Chen, Julia Cho, Prince Gomolvilas, Naomi Iizuka, Rajiv Joseph, Young Jean Lee, Qui Nguyen, Rey Pamatmat, Lloyd Suh, and Lauren Yee, among many others). Hwang is a gifted playwright, but is that the only reason for his preeminence? Perhaps the disparity arises from the notion that minoritarian groups need only one representative, and to the multicultural moment when Hwang began his career. Whatever its cause, to date no Asian American dramatist has yet achieved Hwang's visibility.

Precisely because of his mainstream acceptance, including writing for Disney musicals, some critics view Hwang as problematic. For them, success signifies sellout, a notion already problematized in the introduction and in chapter 2. Art and commerce are not *necessarily* opposed; their complex relationship must be analyzed in specific contexts. Hwang wrote the book for the Disney musicals Elton John's *Aida* and *Tarzan*, but its politics are more nuanced than detractors might allow. When I interviewed Hwang, he humorously called *Tarzan* "an Asian American story. . . . Because it's about a guy; he's from one people; he grows up as an immigrant in another culture; he thinks he belongs to that other people, then he meets his original people and has an identity crisis . . . that was . . . my access into the story" (Hwang 2007b).

Furthermore, films/cultural products made by Disney, Pixar, and other Hollywood powerhouse studios cannot be automatically dismissed. Such films may constitute archives "that have opened up new narrative doors . . . and unexpected encounters between the childish and the transformative and the queer" (Halberstam 2011, 186).

In our interview, Hwang told me something he had never before shared publicly: his venture into musical theater was partially a response to the powerful role of the New York critics. A bad review from the *New York Times* spells death for the financial success of a straight play, whereas musicals are far less review dependent:

HWANG: I don't feel that Ben Brantley [principal theater critic of the *New York Times*] likes me. . . . After *Golden Child* I started to feel that, "Okay, I've gone through a period in my life where the *Times* was really behind me, and now I'm going through a period in life where the *Times* is not behind me." . . . I think it's why I've done so many musicals in the past ten years. Because I feel like I needed to shift to a form which was less . . . review dependent . . . so now to venture out again and write a play, I . . . feel like it's great that they liked it here (LA) . . . we're going to New York and I feel a bit like . . . we're going to be crushed by Loki. (Hwang 2007b)

Loki did not crush the play, though Brantley's review, while generally positive, was grudging and odd in tone (Brantley 2007).[2] *Yellow Face* was extended at the Public and nominated for a Pulitzer Prize, losing to the formally traditional blockbuster—and racially problematic—*August: Osage County*.

Hwang's involvement with Disney attempted to negotiate a path through the structural barriers that confront minoritarian theater. The power of the *New York Times*, the paper of record, to determine box office, endures. Might Brantley's cool reception of Hwang's work (unconsciously) be in part a reaction to racial critique from an Asian American? Since Asian Americans are stereotyped as the model minority that has presumably achieved full equality, some bristle when we challenge racial hegemonies—as though an ungrateful house pet has bitten them. Sexuality may be another issue; the complex bending of gender and sexuality in *M. Butterfly* is muted in Hwang's subsequent work.

The cool reception of Hwang's plays by the *Times* exemplifies a structural dilemma that faces minoritarian artists. How far can we go? What is both contestatory and acceptable enough to be produced? Plays must "be on their feet" to exist in the world, and access to mainstream venues means that more people will see the work. Before I was a playwright, I was more critical of artists who sought production/acceptance by regional theater or Broadway, but I now more viscerally understand that plays need to be seen in order to live. For those dependent on writing to make a living rather than enjoying the privileges of tenure, the dilemma is even more acute.

As a working playwright, Hwang chose (and was given opportunities) to collaborate on Broadway musicals and operas; he himself is a trained violinist. The entry of Disney-financed musicals on Broadway indexes the entry of multimedia conglomerates, a sobering political-economic development. Yet the global circulation of Disney products gives their racial representations undeniable power. Since multimedia conglomerates are a Broadway reality, surely an artist of color with an intelligent take on racial issues might pen a more progressive libretto than would a mainstream artist. Disney representations matter, for good or ill. Should artists remain on the fringes, or should we try to shift hegemonic representations, even those circulated by multinational conglomerates? After all, the two alternatives are not mutually exclusive.[3] Participation in the mainstream can offer opportunities to disturb hegemonies, however partially, especially if the work achieves wide distribution. Still, *Yellow Face*, a straight play financed by nonprofit theaters, is a different animal than a Disney musical. Here, Hwang is able to articulate his own vision rather than adapting an already existing work or listening to corporate input. *Yellow Face* is remarkable for its challenges to postracial ideologies, genre conventions, and conventional assumptions about truth.

However, the path to the final version, like the journey of any world premiere play, required a process of hard work over a period of years, with the input of multiple collaborators. The notion of singular artistic genius occludes the collaborative labor and intersubjective exchange that undergird any artistic or scholarly endeavor. In Hwang's case, the writing and various productions of *Yellow Face* are a tribute to the common political project that engages Hwang and other intellectuals and artists: to intervene in the theater world, to produce progressive, layered views on urgent social issues, to move audiences and to make them think. *Yellow Face* instantiates the contradictions and tensions of our contemporary ideologies about race, truth, and genre that animate everyday common sense and academic discourse alike. The play's various iterations enact those discursive struggles. I deploy *dramaturgical critique* as reparative critique, aimed at creating more progressive cultural work.

An engaged history informs this critique. In *About Face* I wrote that seeing Hwang's *M. Butterfly* on Broadway (1988) was life changing, the first time I had seen a play that so searingly addressed the existential dilemmas of Asian American women / gay men / all Asian Americans, the first time I *had* to write about something as though my life depended on it. Never before had I seen such a theatrically splendid, theoretically savvy deconstruction of Orientalism, colonialism, race, gender, and sexuality. That pivotal moment acted as reparative mirroring, bringing Asian Americans into existence in the public sphere. Nothing could be more opposed to the affective assault of *August: Osage County* or *The Book of Mormon*. For Asian Americans, *M. Butterfly* was a historical watershed that spawned both celebration and controversy (Kondo 1997). I acknowledge that legacy precisely through reparative critique: pushing artists' work toward its most progressive potential.

I have followed Hwang's work since 1988; our relationship is collegial. A full interview with Hwang and my article on *M. Butterfly* are in my book *About Face*. When Hwang was named winner of William Inge Award for Distinguished Achievement in American Theatre, he asked me to be an academic commentator for one of the scholarly panels on his work (I agreed but had to pull out at the last minute because of illness), and I was part of their video tribute to Hwang's career. Hwang is a generous public artist, as is Smith, fostering even more incentive to write about their work. For example, when NYU's Asian/Pacific/American studies hosted a performance of *Yellow Face*, I interviewed Hwang onstage at the Public. Hwang has donated his time to students; when Asian American faculty invited him to speak at the Claremont Colleges, he did so without accepting an honorarium. He guest-taught at East West Players' David Henry Hwang Playwriting Institute, where I first studied playwriting. Building on this collegiality, my fieldwork with *Yellow Face* included observations at several Taper rehearsals, a special Q and A for Stanford alumni at the Taper, opening/closing performances and an opening party (Taper), and several previews and performances at both the Taper and the Public. I interviewed the director Leigh Silverman, actor Hoon Lee (who played DHH), Eustis, and Hwang.

My collegial relations with Hwang have unfolded over more than twenty-five years. My ethnographic fieldwork, long-standing support of Hwang's plays, and acquaintance with Eustis through our work as dramaturgs on Smith's *Twilight* set the stage for the dramaturgical notes I sent Eustis and Hwang. In my memory, the notes were solicited by Tim Dang, artistic director of East West Players, which co-produced *Yellow Face*. At one point during previews, Hwang found puzzling the audience's reaction to the ending, so Dang asked a playwright friend and myself (and many others, no doubt!) for our thoughts, which Dang transmitted to Hwang. My companion composed a short letter; my email was a five-page, single-spaced analysis that included suggestions on how to address the problematic issues of romanticism and primitivism. I had run into Oskar Eustis at the opening night party and shared the notes with him soon after. Even if these artists did not agree with my suggestions, they seemed to listen.

Eustis expressed surprise that I would write in such detail (gratis!). This unrecompensed labor indexes the significance of Hwang's work for my own formation as racialized subject and my passion for theater.

Theater is a site where urgent intellectual and political debates can be staged in ways that are theoretically sophisticated, emotionally engaging, and aimed at an audience that extends beyond, yet still includes, the intelligentsia. Smith and Hwang demonstrate that the theater need not dilute its message for a general audience; their work is "good to think with" (Lévi-Strauss 1962), offering smart takes on social issues and anticipating academic theory in ways that move people. Inspired by their example, it is what I hope to achieve with my own work as a playwright.

Play, Production, and the Politics of Representation

To appreciate *Yellow Face* and its aesthetic, political, and theoretical moves, I begin with the convention of the synopsis: plot, characters, themes. *Yellow Face* is a comedy of mistaken racial identity. The protagonist, a playwright known as DHH (is he David Henry Hwang? To what extent?) inadvertently casts white actor Marcus Dahlman as an Asian American in his play *Face Value*. Key incidents in Hwang's own life appear onstage. Like Hwang, DHH takes an active role in the *Miss Saigon* controversy, actively supporting Asian Americans protesting the choice of white actor Jonathan Pryce to play a Eurasian character.[4] Thus, DHH's mistake of casting Marcus as Asian American assumes heightened irony.

Act 1's lively farce of racial crossings and mistaken identities transitions to a more somber act 2, with the racial harassment of the central characters. During the 1990s, prominent Asian Americans, including DHH's father, HYH, and "fake" Asian American Marcus, are charged with funneling illegal contributions from China to the Democratic National Committee. Both Marcus and HYH are scarred by anti-Asian ideology. A second anti-Asian scandal of the 1990s features in the play: the Wen Ho Lee case, in which the government accused the Chinese American nuclear physicist with spying for China, placing Lee in solitary confinement for nine months on charges that were never proven.[5]

Marcus is DHH's doppelganger/nemesis. DHH fires Marcus upon discovering Marcus is white—though legally, DHH cannot reveal the reasons for the decision. Marcus continues to pose successfully as an Asian American actor and even becomes a role model for the Asian American community. The campaign finance scandals eventually compel Marcus and DHH to confess the racial masquerade. Punctuating the play are interludes from Marcus's travels to China, where he finds acceptance among the Dong, a minority "tribe." In the last scene we learn that Marcus is a Pirandellian character, the playwright's creation.

DHH's father, the larger-than-life HYH, hyperbolically embraces the American Dream. He trumpets the fantasy of cross-racial identification and colorblindness, where he could be Jimmy Stewart and Marcus could be Chinese. HYH's antics turn darker in act 2, when he succumbs to cancer, as the campaign finance scandals and his harassment by the government escalate. Did that persecution hasten his death?

Performance and production are central to the appreciation of the play.[6] The two productions of *Yellow Face* I saw used nonnaturalistic staging: minimal sets and props; quick transitions from scene to scene; lively comedic pacing; lighting cues indicating shifts in time/space; cross-racial, cross-gender casting for the many roles except for DHH and Marcus; and Brechtian direct audience address, in which the character breaks the fourth wall. The Taper/EWP version featured a framed screen/mirror on which images and patterns were projected; at the end, HYH and Marcus appear as the screen parts to reveal a stunning blue sky. The Public version, on a proscenium stage, eliminated this fixed set element, becoming yet more minimalist. The red brick background at the Public imbued the stage with an unfinished, industrial feel, accentuating the play's vivid theatricality. (See plates 5,6).

The themes, characters, and production choices all spotlight the blurring of the real and the fictive, combining real people and historical events with fictive creations through its boldly theatrical aesthetic. This in turn promotes a metatheoretical engagement with the process of remaking race, illuminating critical race theory.

Thematics: Race as Mobile Fiction

Act 1 of *Yellow Face* throws open our notions of race as essentialist identity, leading to more nuanced concepts of a changing racial matrix and to the intertwinings of identification, desire, and power in cross-racial performance. *Yellow Face* suggests that race is a mobile fiction.

Yet race as mobile fiction is forged in the currents of history and politics, and it has life-determining, power-laden consequences. Race is phenomenologically resonant, pulling us toward the ontological, assuming qualities of being through its "stickiness" (Ahmed 2004) and "viscosity"

(Saldanha 2007). In act 2, Hwang opens race to shifting historical forces, suggesting that all-too-familiar forms of racism endure, shaping our lives. The principal characters find themselves embroiled in anti-Asian paranoia fueled by the fear of China's entry onto the global stage. If in act 1 Hwang suggests that racial categories in the United States are now more fluid than ever, act 2 stages the persistence of familiar racisms—Yellow Peril, sneaky Asian—as they resurface in a historically specific guise.

Yellow Face anticipates and performs developments in critical race theory, addressing contradictions and multiplicities in how we think about race in a presumably postracial era. Theoretical moves open the individual to the scale of the geopolitical. Race is not merely skin color; it is "vulnerability to premature death" forged through power-laden structural inequalities (Gilmore 2007). *Yellow Face* thematizes the *contradictions* of our postracial moment: the struggles between a liberal humanist notion of race as accidental attribute, merely modifying the human, and a power-sensitive view of race as structural inequality.

Yellow Face destabilizes our notions of truth on multiple levels. First, it unsettles the presumptive fixity of racial identities, in a nuanced portrayal of cross-racial identification, desire, and appropriation, spotlighting controversies around real/fake racial identities, real/fake lives. Second, *Yellow Face* crosses genres: (auto)biography, well-made play, memoir, documentary. Is it mockumentary? Comic memoir? Fictive autobiography? Hwang explicitly thematizes the blurred boundaries between fiction and non-fiction. Like anthropology's reflexive turn that unsettled ethnography as the transparent inscription of the real, Hwang shows that the real is inflected through authorial perspective and generic conventions. Any nonfiction genre mobilizes narrative conventions to establish its authority, for narratives must be intelligible *as* truth. Through the conflict between DHH and a journalist for the *New York Times,* Hwang casts into relief the selectivity of the "truths" both drama and journalism present. *Yellow Face* thus offers a lively metatheatrical meditation on genre and the shifting line between fiction and nonfiction.

The tensions between destabilizing our conventional notions of race on the one hand and reinforcing power-evasive, conventional forms of identity and liberal humanism on the other are dilemmas that haunt all work on race. *Yellow Face* performs the complexities of race as both historically fluid and as subject to power-laden limits to that fluidity. As Hwang told me, "You have to deal with the disadvantages of . . . assuming any identity, whether racial or not. . . . Second . . . I think anyone has to acknowledge, as much as we can theorize that we should be or even that we are in a postracial period, the reality of life on the ground is that we aren't. A complete examination of this means that you have to represent and explore both of those sides" (Hwang 2007b). *Yellow Face*, then, represents a level of sophistication about race that is virtually unprecedented onstage.

Act 1 is a smart, hilarious deconstruction of race, a self-mocking memoir, and a provocative meditation on the notion of true identity and the permeability of stable racial categories. Hwang points to multiple ambiguities of contemporary racial formation when he writes about the difficulties of ascertaining a person's race nowadays. In the opening scenes, DHH dismisses the possibility that a white actor could be cast in a Eurasian role:

> DHH: You're sure the actor's white? Maybe he's mixed-race. Nowadays, it's so hard to tell. He could have a Caucasian father, so his last name wouldn't sound Asian or maybe he's one of those Korean adoptees, or—
>
> BD: David, it's Jonathan Pryce. (Hwang 2009, 9)

Hwang further complicates racial categories, echoing scholarship on whiteness and Jewishness: that Jews "became" white, though the status of that whiteness is still ambiguous (Brodkin 1998). DHH argues, "Judaism is a religion, not a race"; therefore, "Jews are both waves and particles" (Hwang 2009, 26), both white and not-quite-white, an expedient justification of his attempt to pass Marcus off as a Siberian Jew. Siberia functions as a comic bridge between East and West; DHH shows the audience a photo of Siberian model Irina Pantaeva, who looks East Asian (Hwang 2009, 31). Hwang draws on the Orientalist histories of "Jewishness" and "Siberia" in these passages.

Characteristic of his body of work, Hwang plays with the fluidity of identity, in terms of both race and one's sense of true selfhood. Are feelings of belonging determined by race, nationality? Marcus finds belonging among the Chinese minority "tribe," the Dong, when villagers allow him to participate in their communal celebration, the "Big Song." Initially, Marcus invokes problematic notions of tradition: traveling to the village is like going "back in time," locating "the primitive" in an earlier temporal dimension (see Fabian 1983). Hwang complicates tradition, showing the villagers' connections with a transnational world of tourists, cell phones, and satellite dishes. Marcus discovers histories of interconnection; Dong music most likely originated in Eastern Europe, entering China through the Silk Road trade. For Hwang, the Dong symbolize the "mongrel" nature of humanity and culture. In the first two versions of the play, the Dong figure as a romantic space of power-free belonging, while the New York version undercuts this romanticism, more clearly highlighting multiplicity/impurity.

The character HYH opens questions of identification and desire across racial and national lines. Is one's "real self" defined through race or nation? Not for HYH.

> HYH: Even when I didn't know anything more about America than I saw in Shanghai at the movies . . . I knew my real life wasn't the one I was living in China. . . . I knew that was a fake life, and my real life was here. All those movie stars—Humphrey Bogart and Clark Gable and John Wayne—they were the real me . . . after I started the bank and it became a success, I looked around . . . and I thought, now, I am finally living my real life—here in America. (Hwang 2009, 16)

HYH makes us see the seductive power of a color-blind, power-evasive view of race.

Similarly, HYH argues that Marcus could find a "truer" self in an Asian American community: "When I first saw him in your show, I thought, 'He's not Chinese.' But now that I read his words, who cares? . . . in my heart, if I can be Gary Cooper . . . then maybe—in his?—he can be Marcus Gee" (Hwang 2009, 40). Speaking as a role model for the Asian American community, Marcus protests the limitations of being defined by appearance: "Never let anyone tell you that what you look like is who you are. Those are the limitations we have to fight. Even people who look like me. Especially people who look like me" (Hwang 2007d, 49). Of course, Marcus's sense of belonging is premised on racial masquerade. In turn, the notion of masquerade implies an underlying originary identity. Just as drag can both destabilize and consolidate essentialist identity, Marcus's passing both destabilizes and consolidates essentialized racial identity.

Eustis noted that both HYH and Marcus articulate a utopian, color-blind vision of race. "Henry Hwang, David's father, had . . . a colorblind vision of America . . . where race didn't matter. As did Marcus. . . . The question is . . . how true does that turn out to be? And what's the truth value and what's the use value of that vision" (Eustis 2007)?

Beyond Free Play

In act 2, Hwang directly addresses this question. The deconstruction of race can too easily be read as a free play of identity, where race is reduced to mere skin color and evacuated of power relations. If historically specific racisms constitute race, then Hwang convincingly stages the continuing significance of anti-Asian racism through documentary materials, including the Wen Ho Lee case and the legal harassment of his father during the campaign finance investigations of the 1990s. Tonally contrasting with the staccato farcical style of act 1, act 2 finds the character of Marcus confronting the downside of adopting Asian America: the inevitable encounter with racism. Through his newfound fame as an Asian American actor and community activist, Marcus attracts accusations of illegal campaign contributions. To disarm the investigation, DHH and Marcus come clean about Marcus's cross-racial impersonation. Act 2 clearly demonstrates that, however we may want the postracial, racism limits racial fluidity. Racism makes racial categories, defining and circumscribing lives, indexing vulnerability to premature death. Eustis comments:

> The idea of a colorblind society . . . (where race) is . . . essentially a biological fiction is a desirable but not real place. . . . We can simultaneously see the attraction of the vision . . . without being able to act as if that vision is real. . . . Ultimately the Asian finance scandals of the late nineties . . . serve as a . . . grounding reminder to us and to David in the play that race still matters. . . . To . . . prematurely declare a colorblind society is actually a reactionary move. It's . . . a concession to . . . the powers that would like to believe that we have a level playing field now. (Eustis 2007)

In writing that complexity, Hwang engaged play structure: act 1 stages the allure of cross-racial performance as a free play of identity; act 2 reveals the disciplines and punishments for such crossings. Hwang commented on the writing challenges in showing this complexity:

> I always thought that it [*Yellow Face*] would begin with the *Miss Saigon* protest and drive through to the story of my father being accused of laundering money for China by *The New York Times*. . . . To me, there was always a relationship between these two things, and . . . we're still . . . [before the New York production] struggling textually as well as production-wise . . . how to integrate those two plots. But to me, they were always very similar because if you're going to . . .

> take on another identity, . . . it's not legitimate until you also begin to deal with some of . . . the disadvantages of taking on that identity, which . . . comes down to experiencing and dealing with racism. So I felt you had to show both sides of that.
>
> In any typical . . . rise and fall narrative . . . a gangster movie for instance, the first half is the rise, and the second half is the fall, so I think that Marcus has to have this amazing experience being Asian and then . . . begins to see the dark side of what that means. So that . . . got into the whole . . . anti-Chinese paranoia in the late nineties, which happened to . . . engulf my father . . . and provided a certain unity as to what the DHH character is doing there throughout the . . . length of the play. (Hwang 2007b)

The inevitable intrusion of racism appears in the guise of objective reportage. DHH discovers that the same *New York Times* journalist who broke the campaign finance scandal story also broke the Wen Ho Lee spy investigation. Closer to home, the same journalist instigates investigations of David's father's bank and charges of money laundering for China.

In perhaps the play's most telling scene, DHH consents to an interview with the journalist, who evinces interest only in details that would link HYH to China. DHH realizes the reporter's true agenda: to recirculate familiar tropes of Yellow Peril.

> DHH: You look at folks like my Dad—like Wen Ho Lee—and suddenly their eyes might as well be taped-up and covered in piss-colored makeup. Cuz all you see are all those bad guys in the movies who . . . put on yellow face.
>
> NAME WITHHELD ON ADVICE OF OFFICIAL COUNSEL: I search for a story to fit the facts, not the other way around.
>
> DHH: But you arrange the facts, decide what's important and what's not—until you find a story that makes sense to your mind.
>
> NWOAOC: You don't like my stories, fine, I present them as theories.
>
> DHH: And I present mine as fiction. (Hwang 2009, 61–62)

Hwang underscores scholarly critiques of objectivity and the ways supposedly objective genres—journalism, scientific writing, ethnography, social science—abide by narrative conventions in order to sound plausible. Every work of nonfiction selects and arranges "facts," for "facts" are themselves theoretical constructs. Hwang's staging of the conflict between journalism and playwriting underlines academic theorizing of the production of narrative authority in our writing practices. He further taps the zeitgeist by inviting reflection on the nature of truth in an era of reality television and video game avatars. Such genres blur lines between the fictive and the real. Now more than ever a deconstruction of these categories seems timely; Hwang's play advances that important work.

Actor Hoon Lee, who played DHH from early workshops through the New York production, offered similar observations about the play. Lee, a trained visual artist/designer, compared reality television to *Yellow Face*: "It's a narrative that's cobbled together from documentary elements. . . . He's put purely fictional elements in there as well, but the . . . form mirrors the quick cut editing style [of the] modern television show or modern film . . . so there is a visual quality to it that is interestingly not visual. It's a visual narrative that's been grafted onto a more traditional form. . . . It still . . . plays strongly as drama; the play is clearly defined, clearly delivered. . . . The clarity . . . is . . . the unsung hero of the piece, given how much is going on" (Lee 2007).

Perhaps because the play blurred the boundary between fiction and nonfiction, the audience, including some cast members, remained highly attached to the real. One of the actors was:

KONDO: . . . *trying to figure out what's true, what isn't . . . to me it's . . . not the question . . .*

HWANG: I don't think it's the question either, but it says something about us and our culture . . . that . . . it's one of the first things that people want to know. . . .

KONDO: . . . *It's* [Yellow Face] *a very smart commentary on writing . . . of any sort, but certainly creative writing, which . . . always draws on your own . . . experience . . . and maybe some's fictionalized, maybe some's verbatim, but . . . once it becomes narrative or once it's staged, it's a different sort of entity.*

HWANG: . . . I also hope it dovetails with a . . . critique of journalism . . . to some extent what I'm doing in the play is doing a faux-journalism type of thing, which is to take a bunch of found material and construct them into my own narrative. (Hwang 2007b)

The question of truth is further linked to the assumption of stable identity and to race as a fixed category. Hwang returns to the question he articulated in earlier work: what counts as racial authenticity?[7] For example, in act 2, Hwang directly takes on the question of who is really Asian American, and who is fake. Are the questions themselves premised on faulty assumptions? DHH runs into Marcus unexpectedly at a community function, when they both win awards from an Asian American organization. Reporters and organization representatives fawn over Marcus and ignore DHH. Galled, trying desperately to "out" Marcus, DHH confronts him:

> DHH: You're running around. Pretending to be Asian. You're lying! To everyone!
>
> . . .
>
> MARCUS: I am trying really hard not to lie. . . . I am doing my best to speak only the truth.
>
> DHH: Your whole life is a lie! . . .
>
> MARCUS: You said yourself. . . . It doesn't matter what someone looks like on the outside.
>
> DHH: I didn't mean that literally!
>
> MARCUS: . . . Do you have a problem with anything I'm saying?
>
> DHH: No, it's not *what* you're saying—
>
> MARCUS: It's that *I'm* the one who's saying it? Doesn't that make your position kind of racist?
>
> DHH: . . . In order to be Asian, you have to have at least some Asian blood!
>
> MARCUS: I'm just saying some things that need to be said. . . . I mean, *someone's* gotta step up . . . I've been attending a lot of community functions lately. And I don't see you at any of them.
>
> DHH: *You're* lecturing me? On how to be Asian? . . . I was an Asian American role model back when you were still a Caucasian! . . . You don't have to live as an Asian—every day of your life. No, you can just skim the cream . . . you . . . ethnic tourist!
>
> MARCUS: You're right. I don't *have* to live Asian every day of my life. I am *choosing* to do so.
>
> DHH: Funny thing about race. You don't get to choose. If you'd been born a minority, you'd know that. (Hwang 2009, 42–43)

Here, Hwang articulates commonsense and political/scholarly takes on race. At one level, racial authenticity lies in one's contributions to the community: race as felicitous performance. Thus, Marcus elicits DHH's guilt through community involvement.

Tellingly, Marcus utters a commonplace about race—that taking into account *who* says something, rather than the statement's lexical meaning, is racist. Such a view presumes that people are equally positioned and that referential meaning exhausts the significance of an utterance. However, if one takes into account historical and political context—what is at stake, who is speaking, who is being addressed, with what intentions, then the significance of an utterance can change markedly. This is Acting 101; context and subtext determine meaning. It *does* matter who is saying something, to whom, and what stakes are in play.

Marcus's condescending attitude resonates with histories of Western imperialism: I know you better than you know yourself. DHH rightly calls attention to the issue of *choice*. Marcus can choose whether or not to be Asian, while race for a minoritarian subject is precisely about the inability to choose one's definitive markings, regardless of one's desires. More than Asian blood, the distinctive feature of race at the level of subjectivity arises from markings that one cannot choose or refuse completely.

Yellow Face thus complicates easy notions of the postracial, anticipating and underlining arguments in critical race studies. Arriving at such a nuanced stance is a process; it does not emerge full-blown via the artist's or scholar's auratic genius. Play making, theory making, are collaborative, processual forms of labor. The following section traces the development of Hwang's point of view from a liberal, power-evasive vision to a more progressive, power-sensitive stance: a move from race as mask to race as vulnerability to premature death and to the (im)possibility of a postracial society.

Revision and Reparative Critique

Like any world premiere play, *Yellow Face* underwent numerous iterations before its final version published by Theater Communications Group and produced at the Public Theater. The play was workshopped at the Lark Play Development Center and the Stanford Center for Creativity in the Arts before its world premiere. I analyze three of the many versions of the play, tracing the evolution and clarification of Hwang's argument about race in *Yellow Face* through a focus on key characters and relationships: HYH and the relationship of his death to racism, and the relationship of Marcus and DHH. In all versions, we learn that Marcus is an autobiographical character

DHH created. This raises provocative issues of desire, identity, and the politics of racial crossing. What does it mean when a white male character is the alter ego of an Asian American man?

I close with an analysis of the endings of the play in its different versions. Endings are critically significant; they articulate the take-home message for the audience. The multiple endings ofABnin Yellow Face embody the central tensions in the play between the desire for fusion with the undifferentiated Human in order to remove power-laden markings of race, and the encounter with racism as the psychoanalytic real: the frustrating, complex, yet necessary confrontation with racism as structural inequality. These tensions in the play repeat our own ideological struggles in the academy and in everyday life in the contemporary United States. Some scholars desire to excise the category of race by melting into the unmarked Human collectivity (Gilroy 2000). In both scholarly writing and drama, the dream of a utopian future beyond race is a noble ideal, but it can prevent us from grappling with the real as the ongoing struggle to combat enduring racism.

The play's key battle, between power-evasive and power-sensitive versions of race, emerges most clearly through HYH, DHH's father. HYH claims that in America, you can be anyone you want to be, but his dream disintegrates in the face of racial persecution. A notable shift through the versions is the amplification and clarification of HYH's role as the play moves toward the power-sensitive. Eustis observed, "Every time his dad was on stage there just seemed to be an enormous amount of theatrical life in the exchanges" (Eustis 2007). The HYH role expanded accordingly. The "theatrical life" Eustis references benefited from the veteran actors who played HYH. In the Taper version, Tzi Ma, who has worked with Hwang from early plays such as *The Dance and the Railroad*, brought hilarious, outsized verve to HYH; Francis Jue imbued the character with wit and elegance in the New York production.

I noted the prominent role HYH plays, particularly in the world premiere and New York versions of the play.

KONDO: I . . . see the play, Act Two, as a tribute to your father . . .

HWANG: It is somewhat, yeah.

KONDO: . . . It's a different . . . father than in Rich Relations, for example.[8]

HWANG: . . . Yeah . . . all the . . . things that I've been lambasting through the early plays have . . . become more humanized as I get older. . . .

> When DHH says to the reporter.... "Thank you for giving me something to write about again," I think there's some truth to that, because ... I am offended and angered by the way that my father got caught up in ... these ... race persecutions ... and ... that happened towards the end of his life ... made his life less ... pleasant than it otherwise would have been ... and that, "Wow, this sort of stuff still happens, and it can touch me." It's very visceral.... Therefore, ... issues of racism ... are humanized and personalized through the experiences of my father.... Also, it's an outlet for my anger. And I think anger generally tends to be a good thing in my plays. (Hwang 2007b)

Yellow Face is notable for staging race as slow death/vulnerability to premature death. No matter how wealthy or successful he became, HYH could not insulate himself from the forces of racism arising from power-laden, geopolitical histories of war, manifesting in stereotypes of ineffable foreignness (sneaky Asian, despotic Asian). *Yellow Face* develops increasingly complex, crisply articulated connections between HYH's death and the "race persecutions" that rob him of the will to live. Hwang's work underlines key developments in critical race theory that refigure our assumptions about race by addressing racism at the level of the biopolitical (Foucault 2003) and the necropolitical (Mbembe 2003). If race is not merely skin color but also "vulnerability to premature death" (Gilmore 2007), an artifact of how life is managed in biopolitical terms, and a matter of "slow death" (Berlant 2011) rather than singular dramatic event, we discover the life-diminishing effects of racism. Was there a link between HYH's death and the accusations of espionage that haunted him in his final days?

The first draft asks baldly whether HYH's death was hastened by the campaign finance scandals that engulfed him.[9]

> DHH: Was there a connection? Between the collapse of my father's career and his cancer? Who can ever know? (Hwang 2005, 102)

In later versions, this passage disappears, but the connection is elaborated. After submitting to investigations by Senate committees, we see that HYH loses his dream of America as a utopian society. That loss represents a spiritual death that promoted physical death.

In the Taper/EWP version, Hwang further sharpens the connections between racial persecution and the loss of HYH's American dream:

> HYH: ... Son, I used to believe in America, but ... I don't any more. I don't even put my money into Chinese banks anymore. I put it into

mainstream banks, where I know it's going to be safe. (*Pause.*) Son, if it's my time, I'm ready to go. (Hwang 2007d, 83)

Racial harassment weakens HYH's life force and leads to premature death.

This iteration gives HYH a utopian end he could not achieve in real life. HYH and Marcus appear in ghostly white (the color of mourning in China) and exchange words in English and in Dong, alternating lines, sometimes speaking in unison. They melt into each other, into an undifferentiated Human. The ending clarifies Hwang's intention (and echoes my dramaturgical notes to Hwang and Eustis, whether or not they had an impact):

> DHH: Characters in plays, in books and movies, can find their true selves and join the chorus as the lights fade. Marcus can be accepted, without having to lie about his face. And my father can arrive in a new land, one that will never break his heart. (Hwang 2007d, 89)

DHH ends the play: "They're smiling now. Their journey has just begun. And I go back to my world—to keep looking for my face" (Hwang 2007d, 90).

The Public/final version eliminates the interchange between HYH and Marcus that I explicitly labeled problematic in my dramaturgical notes to Hwang and Eustis. It states clearly the relation between the loss of HYH's dream of a color-blind America and his death.

> DHH: But here's the part that gets me. In the end, he even lost his dream. . . . Maybe that's what really killed him. Sick as I got of hearing his shtick, it had been Dad's whole life: His faith that in America, you can imagine who you want to be—and, through sheer will and determination, become that person. (*Pause.*) If only it were true. (Hwang 2009, 67)

This shift, clearly linking racism and premature death, is pivotal. Racism is more than dramatic event and extremist ideology—lynchings and the Ku Klux Klan. It works on the level of everyday "microaggressions," the relentless wearing away of one's life energies, health, and will to live (Pierce 1977). Consequently, even seemingly privileged model minority subjects can experience racism as vulnerability to premature death. The evolution in HYH's character sharpens Hwang's stance on the life-determining impact of racism.

The three versions of the play similarly clarify Marcus's role. This evolution is pivotal, for we discover that he is in fact DHH's creation; Marcus, not DHH, is the autobiographical character. In successive versions, Marcus becomes more rebelliously Pirandellian. In the first draft, Marcus's status as DHH's invention is mentioned in a throwaway line; by the final version, Marcus forces DHH to confess that he is but the playwright's creation, a revision that heightens the self-deprecatory portrayal of DHH.

Play structure offers a point of entry into Marcus's evolution. *Yellow Face* subverts genre, using presentational elements, found text, supporting players performing multiple roles, yet at the level of structure it remains a "well-made play" with a protagonist, a journey, an arc. A key shift from the first draft to the last is that DHH emerges ever more strongly as the central character. In the first draft (2005), Marcus is essentially the protagonist of act 2; he occupies such a substantial part of act 2 that both DHH and HYH take a back seat to Marcus's journey. Marcus finds acceptance among the Dong, then disappears. DHH closes the first draft saying, "And I never heard from him again" (Hwang 2005, 103). Thus, the last line references Marcus, not DHH. Hwang says that in early iterations:

> HWANG: Essentially the play becomes Marcus's story for awhile.... And while ... in theory, [it] seemed like a perfectly good structure, the more that I hear the play and the more I hear ... audiences respond to it ... the more I had to face that fact ... at the risk of sounding even more megalomaniacal, the DHH stuff is the stuff that's really interesting.... Going into the Marcus story was ... maybe a way to duck that.... It's fun to write DHH, but it's less charged or less weighted to do the other characters.... Ultimately ... the big movement of the rewrites is, wherever possible, to make everything happen through DHH's eyes and see how it affects him.[10] (Hwang 2007b)

In the world premiere version, DHH retains control in his final scenes with Marcus by breaking the news that Marcus is "an autobiographical character" (Hwang 2007d). In the New York final version, the tables are turned. Marcus forces a confession from DHH, who reluctantly avows to the audience that he created Marcus, "because ... I'm a writer. And, in the end, everything's always all about me" (Hwang 2009, 68). This development heightens the tension between the two characters and amplifies the reflexive, self-deprecating humor of the play. This version makes an equivalence between Marcus and DHH; both wear yellow face.

> DHH: Years ago, I discovered a face—one I could live better and more fully than anything I'd ever tried. But as the years went by, my face

became my mask. And I became just another actor—running around in yellow face. *(Pause.)* That's where you came in. To take words like "Asian" and "American," like "race" and "nation" and mess them up so bad no one has any idea what they even mean anymore. Cuz that was Dad's dream: a world where he could be Jimmy Stewart. And a white guy—can even be an Asian. *(Pause.)* That's what you do after your father dies. You start making his dream your own. (Hwang 2009, 68–69)

Making a parent's dream one's own can represent the introjection of the lost object; here, melancholic subject formation occurs around the dream of racial equivalence. In this ending, race becomes a mask that hides a more genuine self—a trope Hwang explored in *Bondage* and *M. Butterfly*. The play in its final version indulges the utopian desire to efface difference, but it also recognizes the impossibility of this dream in the contemporary moment.

Nonetheless, the notion of Marcus as autobiographical character presents a conundrum. Why does the playwright identify as a white man? Isn't it politically problematic? My interview with director Leigh Silverman broached these issues:

> KONDO: *Is there anything about the thematic that you'd want to elaborate on a little more? What it says about race or identity?*
>
> SILVERMAN: . . . My big question . . . to David early in the process was, "Why does the white guy get to be Chinese?" . . . I think because it used to be a very different kind of play. . . . I felt particularly offended by it. . . . Y'know, the white guys get to do everything all the time anyway!
>
> KONDO: *(Laughter.)*
>
> SILVERMAN: . . . Why does he get to be Chinese, and why is that okay, and why does David let him? It used to be posited in a much different way.
>
> KONDO: *That's right.*
>
> SILVERMAN: . . . David was like, "Yeah, I guess you're right," and, "I dunno." And so . . . he set about to . . . create a play and a character . . . of Marcus but really of DHH, who by saying, "I'm willing to let go of some of my preconceived notions, because . . . what it's really about is being the bigger human being on the planet, and I've been limited in what I've . . . been thinking." . . . That's really radical; . . . it's a very progressive way to look at race. . . . I worked on a play . . . about ten years

ago, about someone who's trans-gender and . . . I . . . got into this discussion with people, because they would say, ". . . just because you feel like you are a different sex than you were born, doesn't mean that you are." . . . My feeling about it is . . . if you feel like you're really someone else, you're allowed to go around being that other person. . . . If you feel like if you do the work. . . . Certainly there are parameters, not if you're a psychopath or killing people . . . but what harm is it doing? If I believe I'm this other thing, and I wanna be this other thing. . . . It relates to gender politics but also . . . race politics. . . . It takes a . . . big mind and a big heart to put yourself at the center of that struggle and just say, as David does, ". . . Maybe we should mess all these words up," because . . . he related it to this idea of purity and impurity. . . . That's really fantastic, because then it wasn't about . . . a white guy who got to be Chinese. It was about that none of us are pure. . . . That's a very beautiful sentiment . . . that part of the play was very late in coming, and I think will . . . continue to be elaborated upon. But . . . that's very progressive. Very exciting. (L. Silverman 2007)

I too was puzzled by why Marcus gets to be Chinese and is so easily accepted in China, and I was uncertain about the meaning Hwang meant to give the ending, when DHH acknowledges Marcus as an autobiographical character. Why is DHH—or Hwang, for that matter—best represented by a white man? Hwang responded that he himself had felt out of his depth when, in his twenties and a national success, he was constantly asked to be a spokesperson for Asian America and even for China—a role he attempted to fulfill as best he could. In that sense, he identifies with Marcus's position:

KONDO: *Can you talk a little bit more about having Marcus as an alter ego? Like having a white guy as an alter . . . (Laughs.)?*

HWANG: Well, because . . . when DHH says, "The autobiographical character is you" . . . what I mean by that is there's a part of me that doesn't quite understand how it is I got here. . . . People [in media] . . . were asking me . . . to be . . . a representative and make statements about Tiananmen Square, about . . . things that are Chinese, but . . . I have no real knowledge or authority to speak on them. But . . . because of the way that media culture operates and people's laziness, I all of a sudden became all these things. . . . I tried to fulfill these roles as best I could—as I think Marcus does. . . . In some ways it was very satisfying. I mean, I actually am more interested in China now. While I don't feel

> I'm an authority, I feel like I am at least a little closer if someone starts to ask me some of those questions. . . . Throughout a lot of the 80s . . . so my early twenties, being asked questions about . . . what it means to be an Asian American, Asian identity, I felt a little out of my depth. And then after *Butterfly*, when I achieved another level of visibility, to be asked questions about China, I felt out of my depth. But . . . I think I managed to pull it off as best as I could, which . . . is what happens to Marcus. In a way, I felt like a white guy in that position. (Hwang 2007b)

Hwang accents race as felicitous performance for "the community." In this notion of authenticity, one must prove allegiance by disavowing anything that might be considered too white. Yet performing authenticity may not feel genuine. Race becomes an exterior imposition enforced by the dominant or by other minoritarian subjects. Thus figured, we better understand the allure of casting off that "mask" imposed from outside the self (J. Lee 2003). However, if we think of race as constitutive of identity in all its contradictions, this casting off becomes impossible, as long as structures of racism persist. Here is the problem with early versions of the play. They paid perhaps too reverent an homage to the dream of color-blindness without sufficiently highlighting the ways structural inequalities such as racism still endure, with life-determining impact.

The endings of the play—often an issue with world premieres—write these ideological tensions: the conflicts between liberal humanist, power-evasive tropes of race that subsume difference into the category of the human, and a power-sensitive, "impure" vision of race and identity that realizes its (im)possibility. The first draft ends with the melting of individual identities into the multitude.

> DHH: In the end, I prefer to imagine Marcus . . . amidst faces so different from his own, who, for this one moment . . . appear to have accepted him—as one of their own. (*Pause.*)
>
> . . . I begin to lose his features in the multitude. For a few moments, I still catch glimpses of the man I knew. . . . In the last moments, I think I recognize his features in the face of a young girl. Or an old man. Or a bored youth, drunk on barley wine. He's smiling now. His journey has just begun. And then, Marcus G. Dahlman disappears. And I never hear from him again.
>
> *Full cast joins in "Ten thousand people sing together."* (Hwang 2005, 103)

At work in this passage is a powerful urge for acceptance and for absorption into a collective humanity. Identity morphs, softens, blurs. In this alluring vision, difference disappears. The desire to efface difference repeats the equality/difference conundrum that animates US and Enlightenment ideology. When differences among people are so apparent, how can we say they are equal? One solution is for differences to melt away, for only then can true equality be achieved—or so goes this version of hegemonic ideology. We can be stymied by the difference-equality conundrum in liberalism: the assumption that the two are incompatible (see Scott 1988).

I analyze the ending of the Taper/EWP production below; this version propels DHH into the world to do the hard work of making a life within the existing structures of power, not escaping into the undifferentiated Human. Still, I was dismayed by aspects of this version, as were my various companions who accompanied me on different nights at the theater. After viewing several preview performances, I sent Eustis the notes I had promised. Whether or not they actually had an impact, later versions did change toward a more progressive end. (This could be the *post hoc ergo propter hoc* logical fallacy.) Both Hwang and Eustis acknowledged my remarks in their interactions with me, but I cannot know whether they were simply being polite. My hope is that the notes exemplify dramaturgical critique as reparative. My aim is to serve the work and to advocate more progressive, or at least less problematic, moves. This aesthetic/political intervention assumes urgent importance given Hwang's stature in American theater and his prominence in the community.

Dramaturgical Critique

Hi Oskar and David,

I promised Oskar I would send notes . . . though it is late for the workshop, hopefully better late than never. . . . What I'm sending is in part my assessment, in part the distillation of comments from various others with whom I've discussed the play, including colleagues/friends in Asian American and Latina/o Studies, theater/acting, and visual art. I offer these comments in the spirit of collegiality and the complementary roles intellectuals and artists can play for each other. The analytic/critical comments are intended as (I hope, helpful) dramaturgical notes.

First, it's such a smart, funny important play that taps the zeitgeist: What counts as "real" in contemporary media culture? How do we define race and identity at this moment in history, when clearly the categories of the 1970s are straining at the seams? Anything I have to say is designed to sharpen and clarify what is already brilliantly insightful and theatrically arresting.

. . .

The big issue I mentioned to David has to do with the function of the Dong as a site, not only of the mongrel and the impure, but of nostalgia, longing, and belonging. . . . The play ends with the trope of face as HYH and Marcus exchange words in Dong and in English, alternating lines, sometimes speaking in unison. . . . "They're smiling now. Their journey has just begun. Then I go back to my world—to keep looking for my own face" (Hwang 2007d, 90).

. . . The last words of the play signify a choice for the complexity of everyday life over the seductions of perfect narrative closure and happy endings. Marcus can have a place of perfect belonging in a play. . . . Hwang can rewrite his father's fate, giving him the . . . pleasant end-of-life untainted by scandal and unjust accusations, an America that "won't break his heart." . . . But DHH must, at the end of the play, look for his own face . . . —how to live his life—beyond the seductive closure of the happy ending and of fantasy. I'd advocate for the play to amplify the contrast between the real and the fantasy and to strengthen DHH's choice for the frustrations and complications of "real life" and to . . . render the fantasy of acceptance/fluid identities in a more ironic voice . . . that shows us that the playwright is aware of its impossibility and potential sentimentality.

The fantasy seems to be a longing for perfect acceptance, which from a psychoanalytic standpoint could be thought of as the longing for fusion with the pre-Oedipal mother, the bliss of complete belonging. That fantasy of fusion is something we all share at a basic, even primitive level, a longing that most of us are loath to acknowledge and fiercely defend against. Yet who among us would not long for perfect acceptance and perfect recognition? The desire for fusion is a powerful force that . . . can animate many utopian ideals: religion, the dream of racial equality, romantic love. Politically, the unspoken fantasy is that the "intragroup" conflicts over authenticity, represented in Frank Chin's feisty, over-the-top vituperation,[11] and the external persecution by government authorities and by racism more generally will melt into the acceptance of fusion with the (maternal) body, represented by the Dong. A powerful wish that . . . fluid identities, here in the form of morphing, will efface difference, plays in opposition to the choice for a different, more troublesome and complicated "face" in the "real world." This tension permeates the play.

This fusion/belonging/acceptance is impossible yet seductive, and—what the play does not yet recognize—the fantasy is not just alluring. From a psychoanalytic and political standpoint, it is aggressive and can pose a danger to identity, for fusion into the collective body . . . is also the death of distinctiveness, the annihilation of difference by the Same (presumably, the Human or Man). The desire for power-free spaces of belonging, identity, and the erasure of race is also the effacing of difference, of the frustration that constitutes the real (the encounter with the other, that which fails to succumb to our own projections). What desires for fusion do not acknowledge is our own implication in power relations, in an aggressive wish to subsume the Other, or a drive toward stasis, to be subsumed into a greater whole . . .

I hope David will consider rendering the contradiction in this ending more explicit. I . . . advocate that he undercut the Dong sections with more irony and . . . attention to the impossibility of the fantasy of unconditional acceptance. . . . Real life in its . . . contradictions is in fact more interesting, more challenging, and ultimately, more rewarding. A statement from DHH that is more metatheatrical, . . . ironic, would help. He could say that happy endings may seem satisfying in the movies or in plays, that we can allow for sentimentality in those realms, but we should also recognize the dangers of the happy closure and perfect belonging. . . . He could amplify the excitement of facing the challenges of real life in all its complications . . .

The second major argument has to do with the Dong and the way they function as both a trope of the impure and . . . of the primitive. First, they call themselves the Kam. The Dong not only reproduces an unfortunate pun (my grad student assistant thought those sections were a sly joke on the audience!), but it is the name given by the Chinese state. More important, they seem to play a standard minoritarian function . . . [serving] the protagonist as a vehicle of enlightenment. (Did you see the Simpson's movie, where there is an Inuit figure who plays exactly this role—fostering epiphany?) Most of all, Oskar, please do not have a National Geographic–style display and program notes in the Public version! I did an analysis of the program notes . . .

The romanticizing of the Dong is undercut to some degree in the play, as they stand for the "mongrelizing" of culture rather than for an unproblematized Chinese essence or an unproblematized "tradition." However, . . . the Taper program and a poster display in the upper lobby fell into the conventions of a modernist anthropology that essentializes the Other. An article that is part of the program . . . argues that the remoteness and isolation of the Dong "has had its advantages; the Dong have, for the most part, been neglected by the Chinese government and thus allowed to preserve much of their traditional culture" (Breyer 2007, 10). The presumption of a timeless, ahistorical tradition . . . has long since been challenged in the anthropological literature. . . . The very term "the Dong" . . . reinforces the impression of "the tribe" as an undifferentiated, bounded whole, much as modernist anthropology used to describe "culture." . . .

Furthermore, . . . the Dong become the trope of unconditional acceptance, the minority "tribe" that serves the white male protagonist as a vehicle for enlightenment. This echoes the traditional role people of color fill in mainstream cultural representation. "The Dong" are essentialized . . . presented as . . . internally undifferentiated. The article continues in the voice of modernist anthropology, calling the Dong a "sociable and garrulous people." Their architecture features mortise and tenon techniques, wood fitting into wood, without nails or other "manufactured" materials. Their religion (pantheistic, animistic) . . . is described and . . . they "do not, for the most part, take the world for granted or consider it theirs to exploit." They therefore presumably stand closer to nature than do . . . Westerners or the Han Chinese. . . ." Most central to Dong life, identity and expression is music. . . . Their songs . . . can be choral or solo . . . and, remarkably for China, polyphonic." Breyer points to the ritual Hwang describes . . . : "The Big Song." Picturesque cultural difference, proximity to nature, a more rustic aesthetic, and communalism are the themes . . .

Imperialist nostalgia (Rosaldo 1989) and the wistful voice of salvage ethnography emerge at the end of the piece . . . an implicit mourning for the imminent passing of "tradition" and "culture": "the central government has become proud of its more picturesque minorities and is even allowing the Dong to receive primary education in their own language—but one cannot but wonder what will happen to the Dong as they merge with mainstream China" (Breyer 2007, 10). CDs and a DVD documentary are available from the Western China Cultural Ecology Research Workshop. The Dong are on display, National Geographic–style, with all the attendant problems of essentializing, exoticism, and the . . . tropes of cultural holism, tradition and the primitive. And their exoticism and cultural difference are commodified and available for sale.

Why should a minority "tribe" in China be the vehicle for Marcus's enlightenment, or for ours? That they represent the impurity of culture and of the human is important here. Hwang astutely problematizes Marcus's romanticizing assumptions that are undermined when the character confronts the ways Dong people are thoroughly connected to the larger world through technology and . . . the tourist economy. This move could possess an even more powerful effect if the play further gestured toward the political and economic differences between "the Dong" and the Han Chinese/PRC government, and the Dong as figuring the primitive . . . for the Chinese state, for Marcus and for us, no matter what our race, given that we are . . . residents of the First World US.

So the representation of the Dong . . . of perfect acceptance are the major issues I'd have with the play, and . . . they are the single most repeated comments I have heard from my academic friends. I don't think it would take much to address the issues. Rendering the ending more ironic would go a long way . . . finding parallels between the ways the Chinese state and Marcus romanticize the Dong/Kam and undermining that romanticism. Maybe rendering the gesture of inclusion/fusion . . . more ironic would be useful; . . . perhaps "the Dong" let all tourists climb to the top of the pagoda, Marcus knows that, but he still feels good about it, even though he's a first-world tourist . . . that can be ok, for a moment—but he realizes that it isn't unconditional acceptance. A few sentences here and there could really help. (email from author to Oskar Eustis, 2007)

The postpreview versions of the world premiere did undercut to some degree this fantasy of fusion and the erasure of difference. In the last words of the play, DHH chooses the complexity of everyday life over the seductions of perfect narrative closure and happy endings. Marcus can have a place of perfect belonging in a play or other work of fiction; Hwang can rewrite his father's fate, giving him the more pleasant end of life untainted by scandal and unjust accusations, an America that "won't break his heart." But DHH must, at the end of the play, look for his own face, how to live his life beyond the seductive closure of the happy ending and of fantasy. In DHH's final words, Hwang leaves us with moves toward complexity, maturity, and the real over the ideal.

The New York final version went even further. Marcus becomes more obviously DHH's creation, an embodiment of Hwang's position as community role model. In a generative sense, the ending performs classic melancholic subject formation. The subject introjects the lost object, forming identity through incorporating traces of the other. In this case, DHH introjects the dreams espoused by the lost object: his father's fantasy of racial equality, in which a level playing field would enable his father to become Jimmy Stewart and Marcus to become Chinese. This is a noble goal, but since we remain far from postracial, such an ideology can be "reactionary." Eustis encapsulates the script changes, referencing my correspondence:

> I think you've ended up with an increasing distillation of the production . . . and honestly . . . you and I have had exchanges about this—there was a sentimentality in David's initial attempt to wrap up both his father's death and the Dong into the climax, which had to do with . . . viewing the Dong as a kind of stand-in for the afterlife or a utopian future where the dead live again and where all contradictions are resolved. . . . I think he realized . . . again with a lot of our discussion, that that actually isn't the function. . . . That's not real. That's not a right way to use them. So . . . he instead . . . has come up with both a much more ironic and nuanced picture of the Dong . . . going beyond the simple ironies of . . . deconstructing it. Because . . . the fundamental understanding is that that which appears to be pure . . . is actually just as much of a construct as anything else. . . . The other side of the play's dialogue about race . . . is on one hand understanding that race as a political category, we are still trapped within it . . . we still have to function within race as a category because race still matters. . . . But as a cultural category . . . there is no such thing as ethnic purity or a pure cultural identity. . . . Culture, by its nature, is cross-pollinated and bastardized. . . . We are still bound within the politics of our time. And I think that that's . . . a pretty sophisticated response to our current state of identity politics. . . .

... The way I think of it as an artist is art.... Within the Dong ... music is not some kind of ethnically pure music. Balkan Slavs ... came across the Silk Road from Yugoslavia a thousand years ago, and it formed that singing ...

One of the last lines that ... David wrote ... is ... imagining ... a future where his father could be Jimmy Stewart and where Jonathan Pryce can play an Asian. But that's not now.... We were trying to parse this very exactly; it had to be conditional. We can't have a future where it's OK for Jonathan Pryce to play an Asian unless you have a reality where his dad can be Jimmy Stewart *(Laughs.)*. (Eustis 2007)

I view it as my collegial duty to push Hwang further, precisely because I consider myself a partner in an urgent intellectual/aesthetic/political project. Acknowledging the complementary roles intellectuals and artists can play—and the ways scholarly criticism can be mobilized for dramaturgical purposes—I want to think of creative ways to foster a better play and production, not simply to critique an object as an intellectual exercise. *Reparative critique* serves the revision of the play; above all, it enacts a notion of politics, theory, and art as collaborative endeavors. My work as analyst and as dramaturg performs political affiliation with artists like Hwang and Smith. No work is perfect and beyond power; my own experience as a playwright has taught me that. Within the parameters of the theater world, what progressive interventions can we make? How can we remake those worlds to be more progressive? Dramaturgical critique deploys research, theory, and scholarship for reparative ends.

Hwang continues to offer theoretically resonant insights into contemporary political issues in more recent work. I sketch ways these plays stage current theoretical/political moves in (Asian) American studies and critical race studies. *Yellow Face* addressed the racial multiplicities, contradictions, and indeterminacies of our "postracial" moment in the United States, while gesturing toward larger geopolitical relations between the United States and Asia. First, historically located Orientalisms and geopolitical rivalries affect domestic politics (the campaign finance scandals, the Wen Ho Lee case). Second, transnational travel to China offers a space of both cultural impurity and a "homeland" that represents unconditional belonging.

After *Yellow Face*, Hwang directly addresses China's economic and political ascendancy at this historical moment (*Chinglish*). He engages a related node of Asian American theory by re-thinking Asian/American masculinities through the transnational figure of Bruce Lee (*Kung Fu*). *Kung Fu* speaks to both the promise and the conflicts within collective racial formations, as did *Yellow Face*, leading us toward both (trans)-nationalism and the histories of conflict among Asian nations that may endure in the diaspora. *Yellow Face* set the stage for Hwang's explicit embrace of theoretical moves toward transnationalism, geopolitics, and the fraught differences within racial formations.

Coda: Transnationalism, Critical Race Studies, and Differences Within

Chinglish and *Kung Fu* underscore the challenges to the nation-based foundations of Asian American studies. We could tell many origin stories, but the dominant narrative spotlights US anti–Vietnam War student strikes and political coalitions across the lines of national origin and race. Activists fought for an Asian American (as opposed to Oriental) racial formation, asserting Third World solidarity among peoples of color and "claiming America" (E. Kim 1982) for Asian Americans in order to combat oppressive discourses of Asian Americans as ineffably foreign. Claiming America was a crucial move at a particular historical moment, given the life-determining impact of hegemonic ideologies. Politically, it remains a necessary assertion.

Yet any intervention both contests and reinscribes power. A later generation of scholars argues that a nation-based formation implicitly buttresses the nation-state form. Instead, they advocate an emphasis on the transnational and the diasporic (Kondo, 1997; Hoskins and Nguyen, 2014; Chuh, 2003; Manalansan, 2003; Mankekar, 2015). This shift participates in a general trend in American studies (Rowe 2000), African American studies (Gilroy 2000; Edwards 2003), anthropology (visible in journals such as *Public Culture*), cultural studies and feminist/queer theory (Gopinath 2005; Eng 2010), and the scholarly journal *Diaspora*, among other academic formations. The shift has been institutionalized; for example, Berkeley's Asian American studies is now Asian American and Asian Diasporic studies. Similarly, many African American studies departments chose the appellation Africana studies, expanding beyond the nation-state.

Hwang's *Yellow Face* engages with the transnational when Marcus journeys to China, while transnationally circulating Orientalisms arising from interimperial rivalries profoundly affect Asian Americans in act 2.

KONDO: ... China is almost a character.... You've said you're increasingly interested in China, and you've visited quite a bit.

HWANG: Yeah, I've been going back and forth more.... I'm wanting to do more work there.... After a whole career ... which is largely about "I'm Chinese-American, I'm not Chinese," all of a sudden I'm sort of interested in being Chinese! ... I think it's motivated by a number of things.... What's happening in China ... as it ... becomes more powerful is fascinating. The nature of its relationship with United States ... will have real impact on ... those of us who live here.... There's amazing artistic stuff happening; you have a whole generation now that has been exposed to Western forms enough to digest them.... The ... East-West work that they're doing there ... that's where everything is happening. So, I ... want to be ... part of that. (Hwang 2007b)

Hwang—like activists and scholars in Asian American studies—insisted initially that he was Chinese *American*, in response to the stereotypes of Asian Americans' primordial foreignness. Yet, as I have argued (Kondo 1997), why should Asian immigrants and US-born children of those immigrants be compelled to deny their ties to Asia? Americans of European descent are not disciplined into doing so. The mobility of capital, post-1965 immigration, and technological innovations problematize any radical rupture between Asian and Asian/American.

Nonetheless, we cannot assume that the nation disappears in the putative "global flows" of people, information, and capital. First, flows are never smooth; "friction" complicates global encounters (Tsing 2005). Second, while the boundary of the US nation-state is problematized, the "return" to China presumes a point of origin reinscribing the centrality of the "homeland." Purnima Mankekar productively complicates the association of homeland/diaspora with territoriality, refiguring this binary as "archives of affect and temporality." Homeland and diaspora both "unsettle" and produce the nation, sometimes taking the form of hypernationalism (Mankekar 2015, 23). Hwang grapples with transnationalism's pleasures and dangers in *Chinglish*.

Chinglish was mounted on Broadway in 2011 and toured regional and ethnic-specific theaters in the United States and in Asia. The play unfolds in China, extending transnationalism a step further than does *Yellow Face*, staging humorous cross-cultural misunderstandings when Daniel Kavanaugh, owner of a signage company in Cleveland, tries to enter the Chinese market. Peter, an Englishman living in China, poses as a consultant, advising Daniel to cultivate *guanxi*, connections. Daniel's subsequent pursuit of local government support incites a comedy of errors and mistranslations. We see the intractability of deeply felt cultural assumptions that fail to translate, including notions of love and marriage. Incommensurability *and* possibility coexist in this lively comedy of off-kilter transnational capitalist, personal, and governmental exchange.

The running joke in *Chinglish* is mistranslation; the audience views surtitles that hilariously miss the mark. Conflicting cultural assumptions throw personal interactions equally off balance. When Daniel has an affair with self-possessed Chinese official Yan Xi, he falls in love and wants to leave his wife to marry Xi—but Xi will have none of it. Marriage for her does not require romantic love—a situation common across the world—throwing into relief the historical and cultural specificity of US assumptions about love and marriage. As Xi says: "'Love,' it is your American religion" (Hwang 2012, 110). She also discovers that Peter's business is at present a front. Paradoxically, his confession of a secret—that he was almost jailed for his part in the Enron scandal—inspires Xi to promote Daniel as a "high-roller" to the government. Ultimately, through the intervention of Xi's husband—a judge who becomes mayor—Daniel successfully establishes his business in China. Xi is appointed vice minister of culture; she and her husband make a picture-perfect political couple.

Chinglish ends on a note of epistemological uncertainty. The play is framed by Daniel's lecture on how to enter the Chinese market. His take-home message: "I've sorta come to love the mistakes. . . . In black and white, you can see that we really don't understand each other too well. So . . . we'll all have to keep struggling—with Chinglish" (Hwang 2012, 123). A later version (2015) at East West Players in Los Angeles intercuts the scenes of the perfect Chinese political couple with Daniel's lecture, closing with the continuing need to cultivate guanxi.

In the Broadway version, Hwang flirts with the dangers of reinscribing inscrutability and a view of China, personified by Xi, as emotionally pragmatic and obligation-bound, even as she clearly feels deeply for Daniel. The upside of seeming inscrutability is Hwang's recognition of, even affection for, epistemological indeterminacy. Incommensurability and unknowability interrupt the US white male subject's historical omniscience, now threatened by China's economic power. Cultural assumptions matter; power at various scales (interpersonal, the state, capitalism) is ever-present. We cannot necessarily know another person, another nation, even ourselves, fully. This epistemological vertigo also runs through Smith's work and is the message of my own *Seamless*.

The East West Players version emphasizes the importance of guanxi for Daniel's business, implying that the United States must continue to cultivate "connections" if we expect interpersonal, economic success in China. This revision highlights the continuing labor required for transnational capitalist/interpersonal relations to exist; we cannot simply "be successful" in China. We must engage in the ongoing work of social exchange that enables capitalist exchange. The "merely" personal shapes and is shaped by economic ties. Yet this ending avoids a critique of capitalism as such.

Hwang's second theoretical/political intervention thematizes the instability, hierarchies, and exclusions within any identity. Since inception, Asian American racial formation has been fraught with tension and contradiction. Many scholars have theorized these complications (Lowe 1996; Palumbo-Liu 1999). Kandice Chuh (2003) argues that Asian American studies has no stable referent; it is a "subjectless" discourse. Viet Thanh Nguyen (2002) questions the leftist political project that gave rise to Asian American studies by problematizing the political as a foundation for the field. Rachel Lee (2014) problematizes the dismissal, in critical race studies and Asian American studies, of a serious theoretical consideration of bios/bodies, which become stand-ins for fixity. She notes the ways the literature in the field has turned from resistance to affect, through the work of Anne Cheng (2001), David Eng (2010), and Sianne Ngai (2005), who theorize racial melancholia and irritation/boredom as failures to reproduce hegemonic epistemic regimes.

These contradictions and exclusions manifest dramatically in Asian America's uneasy yet utopian coalition of nationalities and ethnicities. Differing immigration histories promoted the dominance of Asian Americans of East Asian descent (particularly Chinese Americans and Japanese Americans, who immigrated toward the beginning of the twentieth century) at the inception of Asian American studies. The Hart-Celler Act of 1965 loosened immigration restrictions on non-Europeans, enabling South and Southeast Asians and Koreans to immigrate to the United States in larger numbers, transforming "Asian American" racial formations. Further, the "Pacific Rim"—embracing political solidarities as it reinscribes both US foreign policy interests and census categories—circulates as a trope imbued with geopolitical power. Institutional formations enact these historical developments; for example, NYU's Asian/Pacific/American studies expands Asian/America, addressing some key multiplicities and exclusions (Davé et al. 2000). Both Berkeley's and NYU's departments address in different ways the complexities of Asian American racial formation, a loose collectivity that shares little except for origins in regions that border the Pacific, experiences with US imperialism both in the "home country" and in the United States, and a history of racism in the United States.

Hwang's *Kung Fu* (2014) addresses the complexities of transnationalism and of differences/exclusions within Asian American racial formations. The play premiered at the Signature Theater in New York, during a season devoted to Hwang's work. *Kung Fu* stages the life of Bruce Lee during his early days of chasing Hollywood success and ends as he returns to Hong Kong, where he will become a global icon. Hwang calls the play a "dance-ical," where dance and martial arts moves carry narrative significance. A dazzling spectacle, starring the multitalented Cole Horibe as Bruce Lee, the play entertains as it comments on the discrimination Lee and other actors of color experienced in the 1960s and 1970s. The cruelest blow was the casting of white actor David Carradine as the lead in the television series Lee pitched to Warner Brothers: *Kung Fu*.

The Signature production's cross-racial casting heightened its vivid theatricality. Aside from the actress playing Lee's wife, there were no white actors. Men of color play various roles, including racist white studio executives. An African American actor plays James Coburn, a white actor famous in the 1960s and 1970s. Like Lin-Manuel Miranda's *Hamilton*, *Kung Fu*'s spectacle of actors of color playing white roles can be subversive, for they thereby both claim the power of whiteness and offer a critique of whiteness as the universal.

What of these cross-racial performances and their intersections with the *tensions* within political/racial formations such as Asian American or people of color? Chuh (2003) analyzes the exclusions in Asian American racial formation through the crisis precipitated by the book prize awarded to Lois-Ann Yamanaka's novel *Blu's Hanging* at the Association for Asian American Studies meetings in 1998. A dark portrayal of life in paradisical Hawaii, the poverty, neglect, and physical and sexual abuse that pervade Yamanaka's novel spares no person or group. Nevertheless, the family at the center of the narrative is Japanese American, while the rapist/molester is Filipino American—hardly innocent choices. The controversy spotlighted the marginalization of Filipino Americans and galvanized activism around intra-Asian/American racisms. Hierarchies among Asian American groups with different immigration histories, from nations with sometimes contentious, colonial, relations with each other, can produce a normative Asian American subject that is by definition exclusionary.

In this light, two moments of cross-racial casting in *Kung Fu* gave me pause; had I been a dramaturg, I would have sent Hwang notes. The first was a Korean American actor playing a Japanese American man emasculated by the internment experience; the character is timid, fearful. Japanese American masculinity is staged as (irreparably?) damaged by the internment, while Bruce Lee embodies masculine energy, strength, and sexuality. Even if Lee is temporarily undone through his confrontation with the impenetrable barriers of Hollywood, we know that when he lands in Hong Kong, he will become a global superstar. This Chinese/Chinese American ascendancy is nuanced by the racialized body of Cole Horibe, a Hawaiian-born Asian American at least partially of Japanese descent, judging by his Japanese surname. Yet any invocation of China *and* Japan inevitably evokes histories of interimperial rivalry and colonialism, particularly the brutal colonization of Manchuria by the Japanese, as well as China's imperial history. The addition of a Korean American man—an immigrant from another nation ruthlessly colonized by Japan—multiplies the ironies. Perhaps one could read these representations of masculinity as tensions between a recuperation of Chinese/American nationalism in the face of interimperial rivalries (vis-à-vis both Japan and the United States) and a pan–Asian American solidarity. The issue of heteronormativity is elided here, and both nationalities are East Asian.

The second moment occurs when Bruce Lee and James Coburn, played by an African American actor, are touring India. Lee tries to persuade the bankable star to join his project, to heighten its appeal to Hollywood moguls. Another African American actor plays their Indian driver, complete with accent, in a parodic portrayal of subservience. When the driver spoke, a young South Asian American couple sitting next to me exclaimed in unison, "Oh, no!" Here are the dangers of cross-racial performance. Is an African American actor performing "the accent" any more acceptable than Ashton Kutcher or Fisher Stevens, white actors who played South Asians, whom Aziz Ansari so acutely satirizes in *Master of None*? In some ways, people of color enacting "cross-racial hostility" (Anzaldúa 1990) are even more disappointing. Reclaiming Asian American masculinity may sometimes reify a nationalist vision in which Chinese diaspora is celebrated, while both interned Japanese Americans and South Asians figure masculine abjection.

In his plays, David Henry Hwang brings issues of contemporary geopolitical, theoretical, and aesthetic significance into the public sphere. His interventions into racial formation put him into productive conversation with scholarship in critical race theory, demonstrating the ways Asian American racial formation—indeed, any identity—is fraught with multiplicity and contradiction. *Yellow Face* stages a vivid, sophisticated, self-reflexive discussion of the postracial and its limits that affects us emotionally, politically, intellectually.

Yellow Face traces journeys between the United States and China, centering the persistence of Orientalist tropes across national divides. Both *Chinglish* and *Kung Fu* extend this transnational push, inviting reflection on urgent theoretical and political issues: in *Chinglish*, geopolitical rivalry/cooperation and cultural, epistemological incommensurability; in *Kung Fu*, Asian American masculinities, differential histories of immigration and racial exclusion, the shadow of the "homeland," and tensions within Asian American racial formation. The works I discuss could all be considered "in process"; Hwang tried something new in the East West production of *Chinglish* and rewriting for a film version, and *Kung Fu* may be going to Broadway, which would necessitate adjustments for a larger stage and broader audience. Most tellingly, a revival of Hwang's classic *M. Butterfly*, in a newly revised version, opened on Broadway in 2017. The cultural work of remaking race, remaking theater, remaking worlds, is never done.

Inspired by both Smith and Hwang, I move to my own struggles toward reparative creativity.

entr'acte
3

THE STRUCTURE OF THE
THEATER COMPANY

I am talking to a member of a theater company where I've taken playwriting workshops. A funny, talented writer dedicated to the company, he's encouraged my work.

The man praises my play Seamless. I am delighted. He continues, "Too bad we won't be able to produce it. We don't have any Asian American members." My joy evaporates. I look at him, speechless. I think, "This is Los Angeles! The largest pool of Asian American actors in the country!"

What are the politics of his statement? At one level he is right, given the structure of the theater company, particularly if it is primarily an acting company. Actors pay monthly dues and donate a certain number of hours of service in exchange for casting preferences in readings and company productions. Thus, the company will likely select plays that provide roles for its members. Those members are in this case overwhelmingly white (with one Asian American and two African Americans). They don't have enough Asian American actors for my play.

Nonetheless, company structure aside, what about a coproduction with an Asian American theater? Better yet, the company could actively recruit Asian American actors. Racial inertia works to keep the status quo in place. As Tavia Nyong'o writes, "White Americans . . . would be more committed to racial justice if only it were easier" (Nyong'o 2009, 2).

Honestly, it is not just a problem facing white Americans. To change power structures requires work. If I want my play produced at that company, I would have to make these suggestions and help the company find other members and/or do the work of seeing whether East West Players, the Asian American theater company in Los Angeles, or the younger Artists at Play would offer cosponsorship. Of course, I am "sending out the play," starting with the handful of Asian American theater companies across the country. But must my work be seen only by Asian American audiences?

Now I understand the dilemmas facing artists of color. When I was writing on Japanese fashion, I secretly looked askance at the dislike, common among designers, of the appellation "Japanese designer." "Why not embrace who you are? Why can't you just be proud of your identity?" I used to think. I get it now. Viscerally. You have spent years of labor, resources, and creativity on a piece of work. You want—need—it to be seen in order to be appreciated. Plays need other people to live. Playwrights must first hear the play in order to figure out whether it works, and plays must be "on their feet" in order to come alive. And of course one needs an audience. One option would be to self-produce, but on my academic salary, that isn't an option.

The likelihood of racial marginalization looms large, given that Japanese American incarceration is part (but only part!) of the play's thematics. Seamless addresses issues about history, memory, and the aftermath of injustice that could in theory reach broad audiences. What is the meaning of history? How can we know the past? How can we know our parents? How can we know? Don't these themes crosscut the conventional lines of race, sexuality, ethnicity, gender? The play goes on to ask: What is the price of identifying with the dominant when you are a minoritarian subject? Must people be (hetero)sexually paired and have children in order to be full-fledged adults? How should women negotiate the conflicts between career and family? How far does one go, ethically, when one knows one's clients are in the wrong? But because of the "camp play" aspect, which my dramaturg/director calls "almost a red herring," I see that mounting a production, then attracting an audience, will be a challenge. People rarely think across conventional lines. Perhaps the white audience will think the play will make them feel bad about themselves. If only it were easier.

ACT III

REPARATIVE CREATIVITY

chapter 6

Playwriting as Reparative Creativity

Seamless presents a theatrical view of contemporary Japanese American identities and history, refracted through gender, generation, work, and family. Shifting from comedic to poignant in a beat, the play centers on Diane Kubota, a successful corporate attorney, who has a seamlessly perfect life—on the surface. When Kathleen Goto, a Japanese American Harvard psychologist, interviews Diane about her parents' incarceration in camps during World War II, the questions launch Diane's quest to discover the most profound aspects of herself, her family, her culture. A play about history and memory, the afterlife of trauma, and the (im)possibility of knowing the people you love most, *Seamless* leaves the audience asking their own questions about themselves, their families, and their past.

—*Seamless* synopsis included with theater submission package

The judges commended this play's moving, complex meditation on Japanese American identities. . . . The shards of scattered memory, history and self that your protagonist comes to journey, the play's shift of styles, and sophisticated work with language made it stand out as a distinctive, excellent feminist play.

—Maya Roth, email message to author, June 20, 2014

Translating between worlds, I address the work of creativity in my own playwriting: the creative labor that is a through-line for the book. Playwriting allowed me new ways of being, new tools for working through affective violence toward what I call reparative creativity, new forms of activist intervention in circulating racial discourses that shape our worlds, including the theater industry. My reflections are equivalent to the talk-back or interview; were I a full-time playwright, my work would stand alone, without explicit discussion of process or thematics. Artists' commentary on their own work generally follows the work temporally and is of a different genre.

I position the play as culmination of the book. Though in theory it should speak for itself, framing matters. Translating among discourses allows me to set out more explicitly the stakes of putting a play—more precisely, *this* play—in *this* text. In so doing, I set out the theoretical, political, and affective stakes, revisit Kleinian reparation, and offer an account of the creative process that interweaves theory and historical context. I end with the labor of sending out the play for production and with ideas for further creative work.

Reparative Creativity as Theory and Politics

Seamless stages the gendered, racialized effects of historical trauma in the aftermath of global conflict. It asks: How can we know history? Ourselves? Our parents? What are the emotional and existential consequences of this (im)possibility of knowing? Drawing together the affective, the epistemological, and the political, *Seamless* writes the incarceration of Japanese Americans during World War II as a story that cannot be told. It refuses totalization. It is not over. Nor can any historical violence or dislocation ever be over. There is no "getting over" race. For Japanese Americans from the continental United States, internment remains the "mournful reference point" that defines our histories (CWRIC 1997, 261). I examine our specific case to think about theoretical figurations of historical memory and trauma, epistemological certitude as a ground for political claims, and the nature of political resistance.[1]

In exploring questions of traumatic memory, psychoanalytic theories of melancholia (Freud 1989) illuminate racial trauma and subject formation (Butler 1997; Cheng 2001; Eng 2010; Fuss 1995). Psychoanalysis opens processes of subject formation to history, destabilizing boundaries between the psychic and the social. Psychoanalytic theory, particularly notions of racial melancholia, show us that the past can never be over in any simple sense; losses are introjected, becoming constitutive elements of the subjectivities of the living. Indeed, analysts have argued that our subjectivities are the graveyards of our losses, which never disappear. If (racial) trauma has an afterlife—if structural racism persists in the very constitution of the subject, whether majoritarian or minoritarian—the postracial becomes an impossibility. On the planes of theory, politics, and affect, *Seamless* challenges the postracial.

Seamless stages fissures in history and memory, their inevitable narrativization from particular points of view, producing often irresolvable conflicts of interpretation. The audience confronts the corporeality of history and the epistemological (im)possibility of knowing oneself, another, the past—what is lost when someone dies? We can never fully recover a singular "truth" of internment and family history. What happens, then, to the epistemological solidity of history and memory, and political/theoretical projects based on the recovery of an objectivist truth? What does grief do to grievance (Cheng 2001)? What is the relation of psychic reparation to political reparation (Eng 2011)?

Furthermore, *Seamless* implicitly challenges popular and scholarly notions of resistance, a theme of my work throughout my career. In the Japanese American case, tales of resistance tend to assume either a martial masculinity or the (always already masculine) heroics of political protest conventionally defined. Compelling scholarship elucidates the relation between psychic and political reparation—a relationship that is especially resonant in the Japanese American case, in which the movement for political reparation inspired activism that won an apology from the US government and a $20,000 payment to formerly incarcerated individuals.[2] But political reparation cannot eliminate the haunting of the present by the past, and the emphasis on legible political action can occlude the everyday heroics of coping and surviving. Here, *racial affect* as a theoretical concept helps us understand attempts to survive the outrageous injustice of the camps. Drama allows me to deploy affect as a theoretical/political tool.

In a Kleinian sense, my active participation in playwriting allows me to essay a repair of my love for theater and to engage the social world in a dramatic register. Reparative creativity becomes a way to remake worlds. Unlike the infant in classic Kleinian theory, who is racially unmarked and therefore read as white, the minoritarian subject is from the outset in a position of relative disadvantage in the external world. Minoritarian subjects may experience violence and destruction of inner worlds as *both* projection and the encounter with structural violence. Klein's discussion of reparation and artistic creativity ([1929] 1975) centered on the reparative in cases in which the artist worked through destructive impulses vis-à-vis her inner object world. Hanna Segal (1991) extended Klein's theories, acknowledging the artist's early memories of a harmonious inner world and subsequent aggression toward that world. She links the depressive position to the creative impulse as a way of repairing the loved object/inner world, through the process of making new worlds. "The artist's need is to recreate what he feels in the depth of his internal world. It is his inner perception of the deepest feeling of the depressive position that his internal world is shattered which leads to the necessity for the artist to recreate something that is felt to be a whole new world" (Segal 1991, 86).

Segal further explores "how the creative impulse rises out of depressive anxieties," naming three key factors shaping that process: "the capacity to symbolize, perception of inner and outer reality, and ability to bear eventual separation and separateness" (1991, 97). For her, "All reparative activity has a symbolic element. What is unique about artistic creativity is that the whole reparative act is in the creation of the symbol" (95). Segal counters stereotypes of artists as disconnected from reality, arguing that artistic imagination and creativity are grounded in the depressive position: the confrontation with the real as the capacity to distinguish inner from outer objects, acknowledging the separateness of the loved object/the world. Unlike Klein, whose analysis of art foregrounds the artist's reparation of infantile conflicts, Segal connects the journey from the paranoid to the depressive positions (harmonious inner world to destruction/aggression to reparation) to the "outer" world (war, conflicts in classic tragedy, the ugliness of misshapen forms). Reparation—what I call reparative creativity—reconfigures the shattered world into a mobile, always incomplete, integration.

For me, playwriting offers a way to remake worlds to counter the affective violence of minoritarian life. David Henry Hwang once joked that all playwrights are megalomaniacal because we create worlds according to our own desires. Perhaps we could say this of all artists. Still, the difference between megalomania and the reparative is critical. The former is a kind of omnipotence. In contrast, the reparative recognizes the separateness of the (m)other, of the world, and the role of aggression/violence—both in terms of one's own projections and in the external world. Revisiting histories of affective violence in acts of reparative creativity (re)makes that violence while refusing to romanticize a prelapsarian, pastoral anterior.

Seamless enacts reparative creativity through staging multiple existential dilemmas that unravel seamlessly perfect images of the model minority's integration into the body politic: the afterlife of racial trauma; gendered conflicts between work and family; the ethical choices we make in our work; and the question of how well we know ourselves, our parents, the past.

Creative Process

The mixing of genres in this book performs an argument for creative work to count as serious scholarship and as theory, mobilizing the powers of theater/performance to move people intellectually, politically, and affectively. Readers will judge whether these efforts have worked for them when they read the play—or better, if they are able to see a successful staging of the play. A script is a flexible scaffolding, a skeleton to be enfleshed in particular, unrepeatable embodiments.

I begin with an account of the play's genesis. In keeping with the book's theoretical concerns, I center the writing process and dramaturgical autocritique: responses to comments received from others and to my own ongoing assessments. My dramaturgical sensibilities are always present, but as a playwright one must both keep these critical faculties in mind and attempt to access unconscious, painful, wacky impulses before the critical voice silences the creative. At another level, the premise of dramaturgy is that someone else may see something the playwright and director do not. In that sense, autodramaturgy is an impossibility.

I began writing *Seamless* in 2000. Based loosely on my own and my family's histories and on interviews with my parents, the play foregrounds the afterlife of Japanese American incarceration during World War II among my generation: the Sansei, or third generation, the grandchildren of immigrants. Most of us were born after the camps. My first inspiration was the desire to know more about the life histories of my aging parents, for the Nisei generation is largely in their eighties and nineties now, and recording their stories feels ever more urgent. One of my high school classmates, who volunteered at the church where we held my father's funeral, told me, "I'm way too busy" every weekend with funerals. "The Nisei are dying." Both in our lives and in the play, we share a sense that histories are dying with them.[3]

A second inspiration arose from an incident in my own life. Donna Nagata, a Sansei scholar then in the Psychology Department at Smith, asked me to participate in her study on the "legacy of internment" among Sansei. I agreed with alacrity. After all, I was down with the Asian American program; I had taught Asian American studies on course overload at Harvard, in the face of heartbreakingly insistent requests from students. I was ready to talk—or so I thought. Donna began by asking me a simple question. Interestingly, I don't remember the question exactly; in my memory it was a general query, such as "Do you think internment affected you and your family?" I started to answer, but I couldn't speak—as though, if I did, I might choke and break down, sobbing. My reaction utterly shocked me. Where did it come from? The sensation of choking felt like a knot at the core of my being, an obstruction as physical as a furball. Indeed, despite the fact that I have been director of Asian American studies and had to speak about internment publicly on occasion, I still cannot speak about the incarceration for long without this same sensation of choking/choking up.

Lest readers assume this is mere personal idiosyncrasy or character weakness, judge Lance Ito, who presided over the O. J. Simpson trial in Los Angeles, did the same on television when he was talking about a relative whose life was shattered by the camps. When I have publicly lost composure, some in the audience respond with pitying sympathy—"poor little Asian woman" is my reading—but the emotion that chokes is not merely sorrow or pain. It is rage: that this could happen in a nation presumably dedicated to equality and that it happened to my parents, who hardly deserved such a fate. I wanted to explore that legacy of sorrow and pain and rage in my generation, who are still marked in some way by the incarceration, though we were never in the camps and though it was barely discussed in our homes (Kondo 1997, 9–10). What does it mean to choke on history?

Psychoanalytic accounts of race offer insight into metaphors of ingestion and the afterlife of trauma. Cheng's theory of racial melancholia—the incorporation and keeping alive of the lost other within the self—is central here. Freud posits melancholia as the introjection of a loss that he calls "devouring" in the oral or cannibalistic stage of libidinal development, associated with narcissistic identification (Freud 1989, 587). Cheng elaborates: "The swallowing does not go down easily.... Thus the melancholic is stuck in more ways than just temporally: he or she is stuck—almost choking on—the hateful and loved thing he or she just devoured" (Cheng 2001, 13–14).

Japanese Americans had to consume—choke down—the pain of incarceration, the racial humiliation, the loss of dignity, property, humanity. Choking down humiliation may have been especially difficult, given the persistence of harassment after the camps. Japanese Americans returned to a mainstream population that had at least tacitly supported their incarceration, and discrimination continued. When my mother's family returned to their home in Hood River, Oregon, they found the possessions they had stored had been looted. White families would sic their dogs on the smaller children as they walked to school. Some businesses refused to serve Japanese Americans even after the war. In the face of ongoing hostility and racial humiliation, the choking enacts the dramatic push-pull between choking *down* the pain that threatens to suffocate, enforced by punishments that seek to keep trauma encrypted within the body, and (involuntary) choking *up* as the impulse to expel and release.

Nicolas Abraham and Maria Torok call the afterlife of trauma the phantom, "the gaps left in us by the secrets of others.... The presence of the phantom indicates the effects, on the descendants, of something that had inflicted narcissistic injury or even catastrophe on the parents" (Abraham and Torok 1994, 171–74). The move toward expelling what they call a "foreign body" within the subject—as in the choking that prevented speech—may be an "attempt at exorcism ... by relieving the unconscious by placing the effects of the phantom in the social realm" (Abraham and Torok 1994, 176). In a related register, Neetu Khanna analyzes figures of expulsion/explosion in Fanon's *Black Skin, White Masks*: laughter, nausea, vomiting, ejaculation (forthcoming). Multiple temporalities and muscular tension point to the explosion of a revolutionary consciousness and the desire for freedom, to expunge the burden of colonialism. When Japanese Americans choke on history, perhaps we desire to expose publicly what had seemed to be individualized pain, to forcibly bring to light a historically overdetermined "structure of feeling." Certainly, the hearings conducted by the redress movement served as the scene for expulsions of, and chokings on, racial affect.

But how, exactly, does a playwright bring the history that chokes into the light?

Anna Deavere Smith sits in the Beverly Hills condominium she is renting while she works on the television show "Presidio Med." She bears an early version of my play in her hands. Smith observes that I have yet to face the pain entirely. She says, pointing to her head, "It's here." She draws her hand down to her solar plexus, palm parallel to the floor. "Maybe here." She lowers her hand, still parallel to the floor, to her abdomen. "But it has to be here." I gulp.

My first and most daunting challenge: how to access, then how to dwell in, the pain? After all, who wants to? For an intellectual, the dilemma is especially acute, given our professional disavowal of the body and emotion. Like Marcel in *Remembrances of Things Past*, I consciously try to recover the memory of painful experiences, but frankly, that doesn't work. Rage and pain are linked, but initially, it is easier to connect with the rage over political injustice, for both the incarceration itself and for the wide support for the internment from even "liberal" politicians such as Earl Warren, who, as chief justice of the Supreme Court, supported *Brown v. Board of Education*, the key case in school desegregation. The incarceration was erased from history books; people emerge periodically to justify internment or refuse to believe it actually happened. I (and anecdotally, other Japanese Americans) continue to experience fear on December 7, Pearl Harbor Day, for the racist behavior it can elicit. Rage arises from injustices perpetrated and disavowed, even now.

The puzzle of choking pain and rage forced me to explore emotional depths I had not yet reached in my first two full-length plays. Both comedies staged laughter and painful emotions, but neither was directly connected to the camps or to my parents. Both were relatively easy to write, in comparison to the (seemingly endless) work I have done on *Seamless*. The first, *(Dis)-graceful(l) Conduct*, my exorcism of Harvard, revisited experiences of sexual and racial harassment (mine and others') in the academy in a "high disco revenge fantasy" that enacts women of color solidarity. The second, *But Can He Dance?*, staged and problematized gender, sexual and racial stereotyping, as an Asian American woman dances through relationships with men and women of different races. Both plays were developed in playwriting workshops, and both went through several readings. In 2003 the San Diego Asian American Repertory Theatre gave *But Can He Dance?* a lively production, with clever staging and exuberant choreography. I started *Seamless* in 2000, while writing *But Can He Dance?* and commencing research for this book. Since 2014 I have been sending the play to theaters (fifty-four as of this writing) and to contests in hope of a production. I anticipate further revision in the rehearsal room, should it be produced.

What strikes me on rereading *Seamless* is its presentational style, enacting the Brechtian influence in my work from the first play I wrote in the early 1990s: direct audience address, metatheatrical commentary, theatrical fantasy, dream interludes, and (ideally) lively pacing. These elements characterize all three of my plays.[4] The evolution of *Seamless* traces my attempts to make the play speak in my own comic, stylized theatrical voice that diverges from "kitchen sink realism," while exploring depths of emotion new to me. Though I hope the play has accessed pain in ways that move people, I could not write dialogue that was unrelievedly somber for any length of time, even—or perhaps especially—in a play with such a serious theme.

Humor and the fantastic can enliven a work that might otherwise be off-putting for an audience. Who wants to go to the theater to feel guilty and depressed? Humor can relieve tension and allow the audience a point of entry into sensitive issues, injecting joyful, sometimes ironic sentiment into the darkest situation. Both Smith and Hwang are masters at deploying humor at crucial moments. The shift from the comedic to the politically urgent and deeply moving is all the more effective given the emotional distance the audience travels. To deploy humor is thus not necessarily to make light of difficult questions but to approach pain, injustice, life, and death in ways that allow the audience to experience their feelings more deeply. The political valence of deploying humor depends on how the moves are executed, by whom, to what effect.[5] That is, I hope my comedic writing is not as racially problematic as what we encounter in *Clybourne Park* or *The Book of Mormon*.

The drive to know more about my parents, to explore the choking sorrow and rage, resulted in two phases and genres of writing. My first creative impulse was to write an elegiac tone poem to my parents. I quickly discovered that a tone poem—at least *my* tone poem—was not *theatrically* compelling. Though perhaps my first forays could have been effective as poetry of a sort, the results were boring onstage. This was my first confrontation with the rules of genre, sparking the realization that rules can exist for a reason. For the well-made play and Aristotelian structure, drama is conflict. Given my playwriting milieu and the choice of the well-made play form, I had to explore conflict among and within the characters.

Choking on political rage and sorrow was a powerful inspiration, but remaining on the plane of political rage could take me only so far as a playwright. Anger was a necessary motivator, but stylistically, it led me to agitprop—particularly tempting at the nascent stage of learning the playwright's craft. Perhaps if my writing chops were more highly developed, I could have created more compelling versions of the play from a place of rage. Certainly, agitprop has a venerable history as a tool in political organizing, but it does not necessarily lead us to complex, contradictory, and nuanced accounts of the psychic effects of political inequality. It was this complexity I ultimately sought to illuminate.

Consequently, the evolution from tone poem to agitprop to well-made play involved hewing to certain generic conventions by making the characters more than allegorical figures. Corporeal epistemologies, via my experiences as a playwright, taught me the utility of at least some aesthetic conventions. Forms and genres are designed to produce specific effects, and that is one reason I seek to deploy multiple genres rather than trying to find a unified "lyrical" voice. Agitprop failed to serve my aims. The characters had to be multifaceted, in conflict with themselves and each other, lest the play fall into caricature, and the play had to build conflict, lest audiences find it boring. In my head, I heard the voice of Chay Yew, now artistic director of Victory Gardens Theatre in Chicago, commenting on a play (not mine, thank goodness): "Interest waning! Audience leaving!"

In the development process, plays go through readings, for often it is only when playwrights *hear* a play that we can make decisions about what works. For academics, this reliance on hearing contrasts starkly with the academic fetishizing of text alone. A good reading demonstrates what good actors could bring to a script. A bad reading is less helpful, since it can be difficult to parse out the cause(s) of the difficulty: acting, direction, writing? Sometimes, we try to preempt problems. For example, Diane, the protagonist, could seem unsympathetic, elitist, uptight. Actresses could play her as always and only hard-edged. Anna Deavere Smith advised me to "actor-proof" the script. Now, in newer iterations of the play, character description and stage directions reveal Diane's vulnerabilities, pushing the actor to embrace vulnerability as well as hyperprofessional competence.

In its early iterations (New York Theatre Workshop reading), Diane's white husband was a patrician WASP: blue-blooded, Harvard Porcellian Club alum. I wanted to parodize the sentimental *Love Story* narrative so that the ethnic woman doesn't conveniently die, releasing the WASP-y protagonist from confronting the socially negative consequences of his choice of spouse. However, my acquaintance with finals club members is limited, except for a few former Harvard students, and consequently, the husband (then called Blair Winthrop) seemed flat. I wrote an early agitprop incarnation of the play immediately post-9/11, drawing parallels between the internment and the racial profiling of anyone who looks Muslim/Arab. While my gesture to make alliance with demonized others felt urgent in the moment, the agitprop tone didn't work theatrically.

The various readings of *Seamless* at the Lark and in-house—the latest, just as I was finishing this book—helped me to hone what has been the most problematic aspect of the play: what to do with the relationship between Diane, the protagonist, and Kathleen, the professor at Harvard who is conducting the study. Should Diane adopt the position that knowing your history is better? If she does, is that "self-serving," since I was then a director of Asian American studies? And what is Kathleen's ontological status in the play? Is she real, in which scenes, in what sense? Readers will have to judge whether my solution—that Kathleen is "real" in act 1, scene 2, and phantasmatic in the rest of the play—works for them.

When I have lectured about *Seamless*, some ask why I chose the well-made play structure that I problematize in other chapters. What about an avant-garde approach that deploys a more "distant" perspective? First, we need context specificity and flexibility when thinking about issues of aesthetic form. We cannot legislate once and for all a single best political/aesthetic strategy; in practice, I advocate for a range of strategies, depending on context. We must remain aware of the enabling constraints of each. For some minoritarian subjects, realism and naturalism may yield much needed "realistic" portrayals in the face of flattening stereotypes (Kondo 1997). Form is but one level of intervention. Given the preference of regional, commercial, and even most intimate theater for conventional Aristotelian form, we need an abundance of progressive, well-made plays that confront issues of race, inequality, and power.

Second, in *Seamless* I seek to push beyond kitchen-sink realism to metatheatricality. *Seamless* switches tone and genre, from dream and fantasy sequences to characters playing multiple roles, including a database and a CD. Ghosts and fantastic figures pop in and out. Characters address the audience. Both in writing this book and in the play, I juxtapose style and tone, revealing the seams. I hope *Seamless* is a well-made play with a difference, that pushes against conventional naturalism and the hero journey toward resolution.

If production is a goal, then adding nonlinear, unconventional structure to a largely Asian American cast creates yet another barrier to production. Young Jean Lee remains one of the rare Asian Americans who has successfully crossed into the downtown avant-garde. Furthermore, I wanted to embrace a form that my parents would understand and appreciate; while nonlinear forms can be engaging to an elite, they may exclude a wider audience.

What about the avant-garde's presumably more distant stance? The questioner pronounced that "distance is good," reacting to the "highly personal" nature of the play. I take issue with both the presumption that the personal is "merely" private and that distance is necessarily "good." The personal is always simultaneously structural; the "personal" and the public/private binary are culturally, historically specific tropes (Mauss 1938; Geertz 1973; Kondo 1990). When the demands of theatrical narrative and "my life" have come into conflict, I have chosen dramatic narrative. Even verbatim excerpts such as Smith's performances are not transparent reproductions of "real life," as chapter 4 argues. Finally, my body of work argues precisely against the view that objectivist distance is always "good." Every stance carries ethical/affective valences. "All too often, standards of scientific objectivity in ethnography have masked points of view that are merely distant and unsympathetic" (Kondo 1986, 84). Because I began as an academic, adopting a distant stance would reinforce this spurious objectivity. This book is an argument for the personal that is always structural.

Audiences often ask about the relationship between the "personal" and the dramatic. Many treat the play as a lightly fictionalized version of my own life: "Are you Diane?" A handful assume that I am Kathleen, since I have taught Asian American studies, and because Kathleen's point of view prevails to some degree. Playwrights often see ourselves in all our characters. Clearly, I have borrowed elements of "my" life, but the demands of narrative have generally trumped literal transpositions of "real life" into drama. For example, Kathleen was inspired by my experience as Donna Nagata's interviewee, but for the sake of narrative I deleted my choking inability to speak. While I draw on family history, *Seamless* is certainly a "work of the imagination." That is, "I" am in all the characters to some degree, but am not reducible to any character in particular.

The well-made play's dramatic imperative to foreground conflict emerged as a key writing strategy. In life, Diane and Kathleen could be elements of the same person (one can be a Francophile and a Japanophile simultaneously). The primary conflict in *Seamless* is internal, between protagonist Diane and the imaginary Kathleen, the hyperbolic, parodic voice of political correctness in Diane's psyche. The real Kathleen appears only in the second scene and acts as a catalyst, not as the antagonist. Subsequently, Diane argues with Kathleen as devil on her shoulder; this allowed me to have fun with staging, including the fight where Diane and Kathleen spout legal arguments as they thrust and parry with samurai swords. *Seamless* splits two parts of a self in order to heighten dramatic conflict.

A second animating conflict in the play pits work against family. Diane's actions foreground her ambivalence about children, in the face of her husband's growing impatience. Will she prioritize husband and family or will she dedicate herself to the case that will secure her promotion? A third dilemma is ethical. To what extent will Diane compromise her ethics to support a corporation charged with gender and racial discrimination?

The central conflict arises from Diane's reluctance and subsequent desire to learn more about her history. Her parents mount seemingly insurmountable obstacles to her new curiosity. They don't want to talk about internment, perhaps unwilling to relive the trauma. They'd rather eat their dinner. Diane encounters frustrations at every turn. Knowledge is unstable. Resolution remains elusive.[6]

This epistemological uncertainty has upset some audience members, even actors, at readings. "It's the end of the play, and I still don't know anything about the camps!" That, of course, is the point. The play thwarts desires for omniscience and a politics based on the recovery of historical truths. *Seamless* offers a perspective different from camp plays so central to Asian American theater, refusing an objectivist portrayal of the camp experience, even as I make alliance with this foundational work of an earlier generation. Most Sansei were not there; representing a "truth" of camp life would be a phantasmatic projection. Instead, I chose to stage the narrative entirely from Diane's skewed point of view. *Seamless* does not assume that excavating our history leads to answers, although one early iteration ended with Diane and her mother opening boxes of mementoes from camp ("Sitting with her history," said the director). That certitude is, I think, far more satisfying to many, but it is inadequate for this play. Indeterminacy—the power-laden, sometimes random, aspects of writing history—induces epistemological vertigo, not happy certitude.

As director Ralph Peña stated, *Seamless* "is not a camp play." Aaron Henne, director and dramaturg for several readings, concurred. "Internment is almost a red herring." The danger is that critics, audiences, and even I will focus too much on the camps themselves. While Diane faces the specific challenges related to the afterlife of Japanese American incarceration in generations born after camp, her dilemmas carry a wider resonance. How do we know our parents? The past? The ways the past haunts the present?

Yet *Seamless* is undeniably about the camps as the residue of the past that lives on across generations. Why should we deny this legacy to achieve a spurious universality? Though at one level I want *Seamless* to address themes with which anyone could identify, I want simultaneously to explore the specificity of Japanese American incarceration and the resonance of its afterlife for epistemology (how can we know the past?), affect (what are its emotional residues?), and politics (are we truly postracial? How can we work for social justice?).

The Necessary (Alas) Historical Context

The position of minoritarian subject entails having to educate on the one hand, and to risk boredom among the cognoscenti on the other. While internment may still be erased or marginalized in mainstream histories, incarceration is one of the touchstones for early Asian American studies scholarship. Like a dramaturg who supplies historical background that might help audiences understand a play, I offer this context as an act of autodramaturgy.

The general outlines are these.[7] After the bombing of Pearl Harbor, president Franklin Delano Roosevelt issued Executive Order 9066, mandating the removal from their homes and subsequent incarceration of over 120,000 Japanese Americans, two-thirds of whom were US citizens born in this country, in ten concentration camps. The Issei (first-generation) immigrants were at that time legally barred from becoming citizens or owning land, making their suspiciously foreign status an ironic tautology. It was not until the Taft-Hartley Act of 1954 that naturalization became possible, while the Alien Land Law was officially invalidated in 1952 by the California Supreme Court. A perverse logic of wartime necessity informed the decision to imprison an entire racial population. General John DeWitt of the War Relocation Authority stated, "The very fact that no sabotage has taken place to date is a disturbing and confirming indication that such action will be taken" (CWRIC 1997, 6). Neither German Americans nor Italian Americans were systematically singled out for mass incarceration, nor were foreign-born German Americans or Italian Americans barred from citizenship or land ownership, highlighting the racial unconscious at work in the Japanese American case.

Japanese Americans were ordered to abandon their homes with "only what they could carry," selling their possessions at a loss, storing what they could. Lives and livelihoods were disrupted. Their total property loss is estimated at $1.3 billion, and net income loss at $2.7 billion (CWRIC 1997). Japanese Americans were carted to temporary assembly centers, often stockyards or horse stables (my parents were in the Portland, Oregon, stockyards). Subsequently, the government shipped them out on outdated trains, the windows darkened so that no one could see out or see in, to ten camps scattered from Arkansas to inland California. Desolate landscapes, severe weather, makeshift barracks, lack of privacy in the public latrines and showers, barbed wire, guard towers, and armed sentries became normalized features of everyday life.

In 1944 FDR officially declared the closure of the camps. The last was Rohwer, Arkansas, in November 1945; the detention center in Crystal City, Texas, closed in 1946. Internees sometimes returned home to find their belongings gone. My mother's family discovered that their possessions, stored in the attic, had been stolen. In *Seamless*, I drew upon an incident my mother related to me: "When we got back from camp, I went to use the neighbor's phone—and I saw *our* linoleum on *their* floor. Boy, that really got to me!" In the documentary *History and Memory*, Rea Tajiri narrates her family's shocking story: their entire house had been uprooted and carried away. Who did this, how they managed to remove an entire house from its foundations with impunity, remain a mystery. The theft of a home becomes a devastating metaphor for mass dispossession.

After the camps, collective amnesia reigned in mainstream American culture. Anecdotally, I still meet people who have never heard of the camps and stare at me in disbelief when I mention them. The Civil Liberties Education Fund reported in 1997, "Ignorance persists. Many are not aware of the terrible story; others deny that the incarceration ever happened" (CWRIC 1997, xxi). What are the affective consequences when the trauma of removal and the effects of racism are disavowed?

Layered emotional complexities animate the legacy of internment. Many Nisei buried their feelings, and while Japanese Americans as a whole undoubtedly reacted in multiple, differing ways, silence was common. Indeed, a major work on the redress and reparation is titled *Breaking the Silence* (Takezawa 1995). Donna Nagata (1993) notes various strategies of coping, including silence, avoidance of anything "Japanese" and identification with whiteness (protagonist Diane's strategy), and internalized shame/racism (Nagata 1993). In a different theoretical register, Joshua Takano Chambers-Letson (2013) analyzes the subject positions hegemonic discourses allowed Japanese Americans in the camps, that drove many to performances of (hyper)patriotism in order to avoid the only other available subject position: enemy alien. The position of hyperpatriotic model citizen promotes silence through preempting a critical scrutiny of the conditions of structural racism that underlay the incarceration.

The redress movement of the 1970s and 1980s, generally credited to a coalition of activist Nisei (second-generation, the US-born children of immigrants—my parents' generation) and Sansei (third-generation, children of the Nisei), set out to rectify the injustice and challenge the presumption that incarceration was a wartime necessity. The multipronged effort to secure redress cannot be adequately encapsulated here; I selectively gesture toward a few key historical moments. In the early and mideighties, a series of legal challenges brought to court pivotal cases that cleared three internees arrested for curfew violations related to the incarceration: Korematsu, Hirabayashi, and Yasui. Arguing the government had knowingly falsified charges of espionage and disloyalty, the volunteer legal teams won their cases on a legal technicality. Coram nobis corrects errors of fact after the convicted person has served his/her sentence; that is, the convictions were vacated, but the legality of the orders themselves still stands: a point of contention in the swordfight between Diane and Kathleen as they debate legal doctrine.[8]

Further activism on the part of many—a nonexhaustive list includes the Japanese American Citizens' League, the National Coalition for Redress and Reparations, the National Council for Japanese American Redress, and (Japanese American) members of Congress—led to the congressional creation of the Commission on Wartime Relocation and Internment of Civilians. The CWRIC held extensive hearings with former internees in ten locations, mostly on the West Coast. The testimonies at the hearings were often painful and wrenching, the bursting forth of long-hidden memories. The commission's *Personal Justice Denied* documented and historicized the incarceration, and ultimately attributed internment to racial discrimination, wartime hysteria, and lack of political leadership—not military necessity.

The report gestured toward the intertwined histories of Japanese Americans and First Nations peoples. The Aleuts were removed from their islands presumably to protect them from Japanese invasion. They faced appalling living conditions, economic hardship, and damage/destruction of their property by US troops, heightening settler colonial legacies of dispossession and state violence. In another such resonance, the internment camp at Gila River, Arizona, was built on the Pima Indian reservation, home to Pima and Maricopa indigenous peoples, while the Poston camp was constructed on the "Colorado River Indian Reservation": palimpsests of forced removals and enclosures.[9]

Congress passed the Civil Liberties Act in 1988, actualizing the CWRIC recommendations. Japanese Americans received an official apology and monetary reparations ($20,000 for each camp survivor), and the act created the Civil Liberties Public Education Fund, designed to educate a wide audience about the commission's findings. Surely then, for Japanese Americans and for all Americans, internment is over and reparation is complete? Such is our collective common sense in our colorblind, post-Obama, postracial era. Yet, as David Eng (2011) observes, political reparation rarely occasions psychic reparation; indeed, the relation between these two registers may be one of radical disjuncture. *Seamless* performs this disjuncture.

Seamless contests dominant narratives that romanticize the triumph of democracy and elide the continuing effects of racism. The work at the heart of this play and this book suggests the contrary. Perhaps the effects of the incarceration are even more insidious and persistent when we attempt to forget—and that this is true, *even for generations who were never in the camps* (Nagata 1993). Such findings bear profound implications for understanding all forms of exclusion. From this perspective, the postracial is an impossibility—or at best, a goal that will be (infinitely) deferred.

Japanese Americans appear to be unlikely candidates for arguments against the postracial. Perhaps the most assimilated of minority populations, Japanese Americans appear to be the very image of the model minority. With the highest out-marriage rate of any Asian American ethnic group (37.3 percent for men, 56.5 percent for women, including marriages with other Asian ethnic groups) and with median incomes that, while lower than that of Asian Americans as a whole, surpass the general American population ($65,390 median annual income of Japanese American household, as compared to $66,000 for all Asian Americans and $49,000 for the general American population) (Pew Research Center 2013), Japanese Americans often serve discursively as exemplars of patriotism, model citizenship, and the American Dream. William Petersen's (in)famous *New York Times* article "Success Story: Japanese-American Style" (1966) deployed the term "model minority" to characterize Japanese American "success" through hard work, family structure, and cultural values such as perseverance. The story lauded this "success" despite their "evacuation" during World War II. In other words, Japanese Americans were docile minorities whose memories of injustice did not embitter them or prevent them from presumably flourishing within the capitalist state.

As scholars of race have long argued, the model minority stereotype pits people of color against each other. The presumably quiet, family-oriented, hard-working (i.e., unthreatening, nonrioting) Japanese Americans—indeed, all Asian Americans—were used as weapons, in invidious comparisons with other people of color. In particular, this image was used as a wedge against African Americans in the wake of the Watts rebellion of 1965 and the appearance that same year of *The Negro Family: A Case for National Action*, known as the Moynihan Report, that blamed matriarchal family structure—not systemic inequality—for the socioeconomic position of African Americans.[10] Asian Americans thus become beneficiaries of antiblack, antibrown racism, even as anti-Asian racism is occluded. *Seamless* addresses the enduring effects of racism, "even" among model minorities. Diane Kubota's anxious performance of success falters in the face of a past that haunts the present.[11] If the model minority is far from postracial, surely other people of color continue to experience even more searing and life-determining effects of structural racism.

Seamless: Thematics, Politics, Theory

Seamless foregrounds the (im)possibility of knowing, the fallibility of memory. This move toward epistemological indeterminacy destabilizes political claims based on the recovery of lost histories. Organizations such as the Civil Education Defense Fund assume the solidity and truth of such knowledge. It seems commonsensical that the incarceration not be forgotten, yet *Seamless* makes a further move by contesting the epistemological solidity of that history. For strategic purposes, we may have to engage in objectivist political practices at certain moments, but that is different from belief in epistemological certitude, the confidence that we are uncovering unbiased truths, as though such a thing were possible. Whose narratives are preserved, and from what point of view? All narratives are selective, designed for certain audiences, and riven by the unconscious. If conflicts of memory and narrative point of view in everyday life are a constant, what is the epistemological status of truth in history? And what ironies animate our claims of the discovery of hidden truths to ground our politics? In *Seamless*, Diane Kubota faces the affective and epistemological slipperiness of buried truths.

Seamless complicates commonsense ideologies of resistance. Often affiliated with the terpsichorean and following familiar tropes of protest as overt, organized social movement, the concept of resistance tends to reinscribe a whole (always already masculine) subject, who consciously fights the power. Though this can be an effective, exhilarating mode of action—I myself have led protests (Kondo 1997)—I have throughout my career argued for the complexities of "resistance" (Kondo 1990). Organized political protest may be contestatory at one level, even as it may reinscribe power (the Master Subject; Manichean splitting) at others. Conversely, what appears at first glance to be compliance or submission may produce unexpectedly subversive effects.

Recent scholarship highlights the resistance mounted by draft dodgers, the no-no boys,[12] and others who refused to become ur-patriots in the face of incarceration. Chambers-Letson (2013) analyzes the Fair Play Committee in Heart Mountain, Wyoming (the camp where my mother's family was sent), who contested the impossible discursive terms positioning Japanese Americans as either enemy aliens with an assumed allegiance to Japan or as loyal Americans who would fight for the United States. Yet this history of discursive contestation, like most histories of resistance, tends to be masculinist, both providing a necessary complication to stories of heroic combat and reinforcing the terpsichorean view of resistance as direct, conscious challenge. We need to hear those inspirational stories, though I prefer the term "protest," "challenge," or "contestation" to "resistance" (Kondo 1990, 1997). But what about those who just tried to survive? To stay sane? To put one foot in front of the other? Or those who did "go crazy"? Might that be a predictable response to a situation that, structurally, was "crazy-making"?

Conventional valorization of resistance elides the multiple, layered complexities of affect and of the workings of power, in which even resistant acts may have unforeseen consequences that consolidate power, while assumed passivity, even "mental illness"—that racialized diagnostic for what we might otherwise call coping—might have unexpectedly "resistant" effects.[13] We might see the endurance, resistance, and vitality in what Gerald Vizenor (2008) calls "survivance." I focus accordingly on quiet, family stories, in which the forces of race, gender, and historical political economy can shape lives. What does it take simply to get through the day? That more mundane realm (dare I invoke "domestic" for a situation like the camps?) can be the province of women. In *Seamless*, this everyday labor of getting through emerges in oblique invocations of women's agricultural labor and the more dramatic example of childbirth as labor, where the stakes could be mortal.

Gender is crucially significant throughout *Seamless*. At the most basic level of production, it is still all too rare to find a play with an Asian American female protagonist. What difference do women's perspectives offer? Life-altering intersections of gender and race shape Diane's family history and her conflict between work and family. A crucial scene upends Diane's view of her mother:

> MASAKO: I sacrificed for your Daddy. And for you. So you wouldn't have to be like me. I sacrificed so you could be independent. You have all the chances I never had. I didn't have a choice. You do. You know, if I had to do it over, I wouldn't marry your Daddy.
>
> DIANE: What are you saying!
>
> MASAKO: Your Daddy and I had a good life together. But the truth is, if I had all your choices. . . . I wouldn't get married at all. . . . So you don't have to sacrifice. You should stand up for yourself. If you don't want to have a baby, don't. If he can't accept it, then kick him out.
>
> (MASAKO exits, as DIANE watches her leave.)

The audience always gasps at this scene, perhaps because it so startling coming from a seemingly archetypal Nisei woman. The scene is inspired by something my mother actually told me. Masako's no-nonsense attitude toward marriage and children flies in the face of stereotypes of women as nurturers and child bearers generally; it especially subverts stereotypes of Asian American women as submissive and traditional. Masako fosters a meditation on gendered histories in generations who had little choice but to marry and have children. How many women longed for a different kind of life? How much anger, resentment, and depression did those enforced roles engender? Must we perpetuate those roles in a different historical era, when reproductive technologies and "families we choose" (Weston 1991) allow for different kinds of kinship arrangements?

Near the end of the play, we find out a secret about Grandma, based on a family story. Race as "vulnerability to premature death" (Gilmore 2007) and the intersection of gender, race, and class in that traumatic experience deposit traces in subsequent generations, even if the stories remain unspoken. Yet the legacy of Grandma's death in childbirth exceeds a reading as trauma that thwarts "natural" heterosexual reproductivity. Rather, Diane's decision not to have children can point toward expanded possibilities for women.

If Masako challenges stereotypes of the typical Nisei housewife, Ken embodies both Nisei emotional taciturnity and an opinionated liveliness.

I emphasized those qualities in the character descriptions, for in early readings actors tended to play the parents as frail, even doddering, when my parents in their seventies and eighties were lively, fully present, distinctively strong personalities. I layered Ken's character by allowing his ghost to reveal vulnerabilities to Diane that he could not express in life. The tragedy here is that Diane will never know these humanizing admissions. If Ken were alive, the likelihood is slim that he would have explicitly verbalized such feelings. That he is not simply a stereotype but "typical" of many Nisei fathers—whose care more often took the form of action and providing for the family, not mere words—can be seen in other works by Sansei. For example, *Innocent When You Dream*, by Sansei playwright Ken Narasaki, stages a fantasy sequence in which a Nisei father effusively tells his daughter that he loves her unconditionally. The audience bursts out in laughter, so absurd would such a scenario be for a Nisei man.

While Ken may seem archetypal, he performs an alternative martial masculinity. Despite overt racial harassment, he attended medical school when internees could go inland to pursue education or employment, and he dodged the draft after the war, until he could enter the army on his terms—as an officer, not as a buck private. One wonders about other subterranean modes of disobeying state power that receive little attention in academic literatures. I do not disparage the contributions of the highly decorated Nisei who demonstrated bravery on the fields of battle in Europe and who suffered dramatically disproportionate numbers of casualties. I simply want to explore multifarious forms of disobedience that might otherwise remain invisible.

"Inappropriate" affect that might be labeled "crazy"—or its opposite, active forgetting—could be other registers of protest. In *History and Memory*, Tajiri shows that her mother actively repressed memories of incarceration, ultimately confiding that to remember would make one "go crazy," a chilling fate that befell a woman in her camp. This both differs from and resonates with my experience of "feeling crazy" during *Clybourne Park*. If race can be a diagnostic for mental illness, racism can make, then label you, crazy. Racism creates conditions that cause the minoritized subject to feel alone and aberrant for her feelings, then labels her "irrational" for experiencing those very feelings. *Racial affect* thus becomes a crucial node critical race theorists must continue to explore more deeply. "Craziness" as rational response to structural inequality can be politically agentic.[14]

Production, Marketing, Race

Now that *Seamless* is provisionally "finished" until it is on its feet in a rehearsal room, I am sending it out to theaters/literary managers across the country. Race remains a crucial concern during this phase. In the minds of many interlocutors in both theater and academe, the internment theme and largely Asian American cast immediately limit the production possibilities to ethnic-specific theaters. While staging the play at an Asian American theater would indeed be wonderful, these colleagues never mention mainstream theaters, where the prestige is of course greater. This racial hierarchy and racialized notions of universality must be interrogated. Why does a play with Asian American actors, about the afterlife of historical trauma, not count as universal? The overarching themes of the play—the weight of history in the present, the (im)possibility of knowing the past, oneself, one's parents—should translate across races, cultures, and ethnicities, but that is not the common presumption.

Even within Asian American theaters, my play arrives at a time when theaters such as East West Players are seeking to diversify audiences in terms of age and ethnicity. Japanese American themes—incarceration evokes the camp plays of former generations—can seem well worn. Established artists such as George Takei can stage a play about the incarceration on Broadway; this success can open doors, and/or discourage further productions with similar themes, since theaters already have their "internment play." Jeanne Sakata's *Hold These Truths*, now produced widely, centers on Gordon Hirabayashi, whose landmark internment case challenged curfew laws. We laud his activism and this play/production. We need even more plays, views of incarceration and its afterlife through multilayered, gendered, generational experiences, with and without recognizable heroes.

If *Seamless* is indeed produced, marketing and attracting audiences will be a challenge: how to underline historical, ethnic specificity, the deeply political/emotional stakes, *and* the play's lively comedy and theatricality? For example, posters for readings of the play featured images of shattered glass or ripped fabric, to underscore the irony of the title *Seamless*. Ralph Peña of Ma-Yi Theater directed a reading of the play at the Lark Play Development Center and suggested that the poster should reflect its tone. He conjured an image of Diane as Madeline in Paris, to capture the comic aspects of Diane's naive romanticizing of France. Peña's thought-provoking proposal could change the play's reception. Ilani Umel animated one of the scenes from *Seamless,* using dialogue balloons and superimposed text to illustrate Diane's encounter with a barrage of racial epithets in Paris. This cartoonish quality both adds distance and physicalizes Diane's feeling of being bombarded. In Umel's creative image, the taunt "Tu manges beaucoup de riz?" (You eat a lot of rice?) transforms Diane's features into a bag of rice. Individual distinctiveness is literally effaced by racial stereotype (see plates 7 and 8).

Genre is also a matter of labels and marketing, both in theater and in publishing. How do I signal that *Seamless* is about more than the camps? How do I encapsulate the tone of the play? Do I call it a "dramedy?" A "comic drama?" Can I use the synopsis to appeal to broad audiences? Must I invoke the problematic discourse of the universal, which I have already roundly criticized in my scholarly work?

As a playwright trying to break through to production, I have too often come up against the frustrating reality that nonwhiteness marks a work as inherently less universal, as my entr'acte about theater companies illustrates. Recent dramaturgical notes from a white male dramaturg urged me to center Diane's conflict with Ben, because the "personal" is most "universal," and Diane was facing too many conflicts for audiences to follow. For me the marriage is the least interesting plot line, and contemporary women are often negotiating multiple conflicts (as I am during this writing!). The pivotal theme is Diane's relationship to her past and to her parents. Surely, parents and family history are more "universal" than marriage? Apparently, *Seamless* does not sufficiently mirror white men, making it less universal.

Universality—I prefer "translation across difference"—is itself fraught with contradiction, for I simultaneously want to acknowledge the critically significant legacy of Asian American theater. *Seamless* builds on this history. My work is part of a generational shift, distinct from the earlier "camp plays" that, along with the Chinese immigration plays, defined a pioneering generation of Asian American theater.[15] Rather than focusing on the camp experience itself, newer work highlights the phantom memories and indelible traces of the trauma of the incarceration on generations born *after* the camps. We see parallels between this art and what Marianne Hirsch, in her analysis of the children of Holocaust survivors, calls postmemory (Hirsch 2008, 103–28). Even more eloquent are Toni Morrison's "rememory" (Morrison 1987), the continuing presence of traumatic racialized histories in the United States,[16] and Christina Sharpe's concept of living "in the wake" of historical trauma (Sharpe 2016).

Japanese North American Sansei playwrights address the living past: Japanese Canadian playwright Ric Shiomi's *Uncle Tadao*, in which Tadao emerges as the uncanny, haunting the lives of his niece and nephew; Philip Kan Gotanda's *Fish Head Soup*, portraying a dysfunctional Japanese American family scarred by the internment experience; and performance artist Denise Uyehara's *Big Head*, based on her grandfather's letters from camp, which draws explicit parallels with the treatment of Muslims in the United States after 9/11. Japanese Canadian Sansei playwright/actors Julie Tamiko Manning and Matt Miwa use verbatim interviews in their documentary performance *The Tashme Project: The Living Archives* to illuminate life in a Japanese Canadian camp.

Sansei poet and scholar Traise Yamamoto writes lyrically of the transmission of memories of the camps through her own childhood experiences. Her parents left her every day at a babysitter's home, where she was locked in for the day in a shed, released only for a lunch break: "Nine hours, five days a week, for two years . . . that rectangular wooden structure with its single step was so familiar to my parents as to be invisible. They had spent their early childhoods in the Tule Lake and Heart Mountain internment camps, whose long wooden barracks resembled larger . . . versions of the storage shed they saw each morning they dropped me off" (Yamamoto 2014, 5–7). For Yamamoto's parents, enclosure became naturalized, unremarkable. For her, these poignant affective resonances affirm the enduring poetics of memory and forgetting.

Sansei filmmaker Rea Tajiri's *History and Memory* (1991) attempts to make sense of Tajiri's history and of memories for which she has no referent. The documentary begins with a spectacular scene from a Hollywood movie, of the bombing of Pearl Harbor. We then see black screen: the absence of images of Japanese Americans in cinematic histories of World War II. David Eng, channeling Faulkner, argues that a history of affect is at work: "Tajiri's affective predicaments highlight the fact that history is not linear, progressive, or resolute: indeed, it is not even past" (Eng 2010, 172). Tajiri makes the film to give her mother the history that could not be experienced as it unfolded, in an act of reparative creativity.

Thus, indeterminacy and the affective residues of the past do not spell despair. Taking inspiration from other Sansei artists, and despite the epistemological vertigo and elegiac tone that animate the final scene of *Seamless*, I end the play with a gesture toward provisional reintegration and the "and yet?" of political hope (Clifford 2013, 319).

Ethnographer as Artist

What does it mean to participate actively in the realm one is studying as an anthropologist? What can we say about the position of scholar-artist?

First, the stakes are different for observers and for participants. I argued in *About Face* (1997) that participation as a partner in struggle and now, as a creative partner, differs dramatically from the spectator's perspective. Involvement in a production compels the commitment to a common goal, heightening the awareness of finitude and provisionality: the pressure of deadlines, funding, time, talent, expertise. Under these constraints, we must nonetheless mount a production for the public to see. Like other modes of fieldwork, participation in a production fosters humility and the awareness of limits. It demands accountabilities to the creative team and to the audience. It raises particular ethical dilemmas. What accountabilities are at stake when you know that, going forward, you will continue as professional colleagues with people toward whom you feel solidarity and commitment (Wong 2004)? Like fieldwork, creation and production place one's entire being on the line, and writing becomes another register in which to advance one's political, artistic, and scholarly commitments. Full participation enables reparative creativity.

Theater fosters my feminist view of academic writing as a collective political project, a vision the academy generally disavows. Though the arts, like the academy, can fetishize the auratic—the singular genius, fount of creativity and uniqueness—in theater one cannot entirely repress the collective nature of making art. Theater, like many of the performing arts, depends on collaboration and dialogue. The many artists who interact to produce a play render the dialogic, collective process obvious. Foregrounding collaboration subverts the omniscient, singular Master Subject voice.

Indeed, as I was finishing the final revision for this chapter, a productive, twenty-minute conversation with my director/dramaturg Aaron Henne and consultations with dramaturg Yael Prizant led me to some last-minute play revisions. The stage directions now gesture toward the reparative. In the final scene, Diane initially stood with the other characters in separate pools of light, physicalizing the fragmentation of the play's first image of the perfect family portrait. I left the audience with fragmentation that could lead to repair. On further thought, I wanted a more active image of reparation, and Aaron suggested that Diane move among the fragments in the final stage directions. I took his advice. I also tweaked the dialogue between Diane and Kathleen, to clarify the difference between the "real" Kathleen in act 1, scene 2, and her incarnation as Diane's paranoid fantasy in the rest of the play. Diane more clearly rejects Kathleen at the end of the play, to make the quest for the past her own. To appraise these changes, I held a last-minute reading of a few key scenes in my loft. My down-to-the-wire experience further enacts theories of writing as intersubjective exchange.

Participation in theater as dramaturg and playwright, confronting hierarchies and barriers in the flesh, have made me a more generous critic. Active engagement fosters my appreciation of the significant interventions artists such as Anna Deavere Smith and David Henry Hwang have achieved. Theater is a hierarchical, extraordinarily Eurocentric site; to attain their degree of success requires talent, perseverance, and inventive strategies in negotiating with power. For example, becoming a playwright heightened my awareness of how stereotypes work. Participation in theater spotlights the fallaciousness of the intentional fallacy: authorial intention never guarantees meaning. As playwright, one can try to avoid problematic stereotypes, but one cannot preempt them altogether, given the unpredictable assumptions audiences bring to their spectatorship. Serving as a playwright and dramaturg means that one is accountable for the politics of representation, even when one cannot completely control production or reception.

Invoking a stereotype in order to deconstruct it both reinscribes and subverts, as I first argued vis-à-vis Hwang's *M. Butterfly* (1997). Even a subversive performance of the Orientalist fantasy of Madame Butterfly replays the trope; we cannot escape the trope altogether. Unlike others who might suppose that we could create completely problem-free, realistic representations of minoritarian subjects, I am skeptical. Even without invoking racial stereotypes, other idées fixes—the whole subject, gender, class, and sexuality, among others—could be reinscribed. Even works that do not thematize race explicitly exist in a world and on a stage haunted by racial clichés and structural inequality. The stereotype is never excised; at best, it is always *sous rature*.

In a related discovery, I found that truth is sometimes stranger than fiction. I wanted to incorporate a Sansei character like my brother, who was unaware that my father had been interned, but other people in my playwriting group told me that no one would believe it. Further, in early iterations of the play I incorporated my own inexplicable, powerful reaction to questions about internment, but almost all my playwriting colleagues told me it was too far-fetched. A gradual unfolding of Diane's uptight character seemed more realistic to them. Perhaps Diane's curiosity would be piqued, but since she had just met Kathleen, surely Diane—who always performs a seamlessly perfect surface, and who is most emphatically *not* simply "me"—would have reacted differently than I, they argued. The lone dissenter was the leader of the group, Lee Wochner, who said, "No one's asked her before." I still basically agree with Lee, but so many others have vehemently protested otherwise that I bowed to their assessment. Dramaturg Aaron Henne convincingly argued much later that a breakdown in the first scene would tip off the audience to the message of the play too early and that building the narrative made more sense. Consequently, the demands of narrative—that I am engaging the form of the well-made play—overrode a desire for verisimilitude.

The demands of being a *scholar*-artist emerged clearly in my dilemmas in terms of representing Kathleen Goto, the Japanese American psychologist whose specialty is Asian American studies. One colleague criticized this character as "self-serving," if her point of view—that it is better to know your own history—turns out to be right. To some degree, I cannot abandon that position, given that I think it is better to know or try to know than to repress or to remain in ignorance. I realize that my choice of words is telling. However, the play now thematizes the *(im)possibility* of knowing. Asian American studies, cultural studies, ethnography, or any other form of academic knowledge production will not lead us to a singular truth, and political movements premised on the uncovering of these truths operate from epistemologically problematic grounds. However, I keep open the possibility of hope, of the significance of the quest (for lost time, for knowledge), even if our answers are partial, fragmentary, even inarticulable. I both base Kathleen on a "real life" incident and hyperbolize her. Now, Diane appropriates the quest for knowledge through her own "search for lost time" that rejects Kathleen's scholarly protocols and Proust's novelistic worlds.

Playwriting taught me a new mode of writing, of being-in-the-world. Though here I write with the declarative voice, spelling out my intentions and theoretical/political investments, the play deploys the more allusive, evocative techniques of drama to conjure mood, tone, and emotion as well as intellectual reflection. The powers of suggestion, accessing deep emotion, are the hallmarks of dramatic and performative writing. In order to become a playwright, I had to learn these new skills. Interestingly, now that I have advised a number of PhD students who were first trained in the arts, I find that their challenge is precisely the opposite: how to make everything explicit, to footnote properly, to tell exhaustively, to be rigorous and exact, not allusive and suggestive. I should loosen up and trust the nonverbal; they need to *préciser*.

This move in turn intervenes in an academy that marginalizes emotions and the sensorium, registers of experience indispensable for vibrant life. Further, the play's thematics challenge a Eurocentric, male-dominated theater industry, rewriting narrative and protagonism through an Asian American woman's imagination. I claim both interventions as forms of activism, creating work that aims to remake hegemonic worlds.

Finally, including *Seamless* in this book represents the integration of a life. I refuse the splits among art, theory, politics, and affect. Questioning foundations and imagining and performing alternatives to convention are forms of cultural labor with an activist purpose. Writing in multiple registers recognizes the multidimensionality of social life. Within a Western categorical frame, we "are" bodies, emotions, and intellects. Rather than splitting off the Master Subject voice and privileging only the most canonical disciplinary conventions and rules of genre, we should be bold, pushing against genre and the persistence of foundational categories—even as those conventions enable our interventions and render impossible any fantasy of liberation from power. Integrating the creative and the scholarly in the service of an argument against the postracial enacts reparative creativity, opening spaces for remaking the worlds we inhabit in the now. Consequently, I end the book with *Seamless* as culmination, not afterthought or appendix. I leave the reader with one exploration of how the artistic and scholarly can intertwine, meld into and strain against each other, in order to *move* people—intellectually, politically, *and* affectively.

Finally, in future projects life and work may intertwine in scholarship and in playwriting. My encounters with open-heart surgery, slow and uncertain recovery, violent fatigue, people's reactions (both supportive and problematic), hospitals, health care workers, and ongoing battles with insurance have been heart-warming, sobering, surprising, maddening and—too often—terrifying. "Sick woman theory" (Hedva 2016), disability studies, and a play about sick women may be next. In the face of fragmented temporalities, the desperate need to ration energy, a carved and ravaged body, perhaps the metaphor of "repair" resonates powerfully because it acknowledges a savage tearing asunder, after which nothing is ever fully restored. Yet there is life. And hope. Both theater and scholarship offer forms of reparative creativity: a working through of life, death, power, connection, humor, joy, and, in the face of so much that would kill bodies and spirits, the political hope of "and yet?"

SEAMLESS

A Full-Length Play

Characters

DIANE KUBOTA—Japanese American, 40-something corporate lawyer. Tightly wound, attractive, polished, a Francophile. Vulnerable, behind the crisp exterior

BENJAMIN ROTH—Jewish, 45, DIANE's husband. Politically progressive, immigration lawyer

KEN KUBOTA—Japanese American, late 70s, DIANE's father. Retired physician, jaunty, energetic, opinionated

MASAKO KUBOTA—Japanese American, late 70s, DIANE's mother. Seemingly a typical Nisei mother, she ultimately demonstrates surprising strength and feistiness

KATHLEEN GOTO—Japanese American, late 30s, assistant professor of psychology at Harvard. Initially a real character, then the devil on DIANE's shoulder

GRANDMA—Japanese American, 37, MASAKO's mother. Played by the actress who plays KATHLEEN

Other Characters

VOICE OF ANDREW—DIANE's boss, managing partner at her legal firm

WHITE DOCTOR—played by the actor who plays BEN

WAITER—played by the actor who plays BEN

DOCTOR—played by the actor who plays KEN

NURSE—played by the actor who plays MASAKO

CD

DATABASE

MUSEUM WEBSITE

ARCHIVIST, JAPANESE AMERICAN NATIONAL MUSEUM

TIME—Early 21st century

PLACE—DIANE's office in downtown Los Angeles; DIANE's and BEN's home in the affluent West Los Angeles neighborhood of Brentwood; KEN and MASAKO's garage in Gardena, a Japanese American community; MASAKO and GRANDMA's home in Hood River, Oregon, in 1940.

ACT ONE, SCENE ONE

(At rise DIANE, BEN, KEN, and MASAKO stand together center stage, in a formal family portrait. DIANE is perfectly soignée, impeccable in every detail: Armani suit, tasteful makeup, expensive pumps. BEN is rumpled, tweedy. MASAKO wears polyester pants, vest, and a sweater. KEN has a jaunty, "tennis anyone?" air. He wears a golf sweater and a wool cap. They smile a little too broadly. Their positivity is manic.)

DIANE, BEN, MASAKO, KEN: We're a very happy family.

DIANE: We live a comfortable life.

KEN: I was a good provider.

MASAKO: He's a doctor.

KEN: Retired.

MASAKO: I was a pharmacist.

DIANE: Until she got married.

KEN: Married women didn't work in those—

DIANE, MASAKO: Dad!

DIANE: *(Turns toward MASAKO.)* She's a very giving mother. To a fault.

MASAKO: If I didn't look after you and your daddy, where would you be?

KEN: Our daughter is—

KEN, MASAKO:
    Our pride and joy.

DIANE: I'm—

MASAKO: A lawyer.

KEN: Ivy League.

MASAKO: Harvard.

KEN: A.B.

MASAKO: Yale.

KEN: J.D.

KEN, MASAKO:
    Only the best.

DIANE: Stop, you're embarrassing me. (*DIANE, KEN, and MASAKO all turn toward BEN.*)

KEN, MASAKO:
    This is our son-in-law.

DIANE: My husband. (*BEN grins and waves.*)

KEN: Harvard.

MASAKO: Yale.

BEN: A lawyer.

DIANE: Like me.

BEN: We're a very happy family.

BEN, DIANE: The perfect multicultural couple.

DIANE: A symbol of democracy.

BEN: East and West.

DIANE: Interwoven.

BEN, DIANE: In a seamless whole.

DIANE, BEN, MASAKO, KEN:
    We're just average Americans.

KEN: Middle-class.

MASAKO: Close family.

DIANE: Well-educated.

BEN: Nice house.

KEN: Nice yard.

MASAKO: Ever so respectable.

DIANE: This is a wonderful country.

KEN: You work hard, you get ahead.

MASAKO: You can be anything you want to be.

DIANE, BEN, MASAKO, KEN:
We're living the American dream.

KEN: If it didn't sound.

MASAKO: So immodest.

DIANE: Or so ingenuous.

BEN: You could say.

DIANE, BEN, MASAKO, KEN:
Our lives are seamlessly perfect.

MASAKO: Or at least.

DIANE, BEN, MASAKO KEN:
Pretty darned close.

KEN: Because you see.

MASAKO: We're a very.

BEN: Happy.

DIANE: Family.
(Blinding camera flash. Blackout.)

ACT ONE, SCENE TWO

(Lights rise on DIANE's downtown office. She sits with her feet on the desk, gesturing expansively as she talks on the phone.)

DIANE: They're calling me the rainmaker!

(DR. KATHLEEN GOTO enters tentatively. DIANE waves her in.) Someone's here. I'll call you later. *(DIANE hangs up.)*

KATHLEEN: Kathleen Goto. Hope I'm not interrupting. It sounded important.

DIANE: Just won a big case.

KATHLEEN: Congratulations.

DIANE: Thanks. Listen, I have an important call at four thirty. Could we just dive in?

KATHLEEN: Of course. *(Takes out her tape recorder.)*

DIANE: You're going to tape this?

KATHLEEN: For accuracy. Is that a problem?

DIANE: I retain final rights of approval. I assume you'll send me the transcript.

KATHLEEN: Oh. OK. Not everyone makes that request, / but

DIANE: Good. Remind me, what is this for? *(KATHLEEN looks quizzical.)* A book? An article?

KATHLEEN: A book. Just got an NIH grant to finish it.

DIANE: Congratulations.

KATHLEEN: Up for tenure in a couple of years.

DIANE: Good luck. Harvard's tough on junior faculty.

KATHLEEN: I'm doing fine. When were you there?

DIANE: In the '80s. Loved it.

KATHLEEN: Which house were you in?

DIANE: Adams.

KATHLEEN: Really?

DIANE: Surprised? I majored in romance languages and lit.

KATHLEEN: A Euro? Wearing black, smoking clove cigarettes?

DIANE: That was me.

KATHLEEN: Hanging out at Café Pamplona?

DIANE: Exactly. And you were there—

KATHLEEN: Ten years after you. Winthrop House.

DIANE: A serious student. *(KATHLEEN shrugs, smiles.)*

KATHLEEN: We both did foreign languages. I studied Japanese. I felt guilty that none of us Sansei knows how to talk to / our grandparents.

DIANE: Just like all Americans.

KATHLEEN: But I'm glad I did the roots thing. Tokyo was amazing. *(DIANE points to her watch.)* Sorry. I can get carried away. *(KATHLEEN turns on the tape recorder.)* Here we go. For starters, where were you born?

DIANE: Oregon. Portland.

KATHLEEN: And your parents?

DIANE: Close to Portland. Mom's from Hood River. Dad's from Gresham.

KATHLEEN: And were they interned?

DIANE: Yeah.

KATHLEEN: Where?

DIANE: Was there a place called . . . Tule Lake? *(KATHLEEN nods.)* I think Dad was there. And Mom was in Wyoming. Or maybe Colorado?

KATHLEEN: Heart Mountain?

DIANE: Maybe. I can't say for sure.

KATHLEEN: When did you first hear about the camps?

DIANE: I don't remember. My parents never talked about it.

KATHLEEN: Did you learn about it in school?

DIANE: Are you kidding? Our textbooks never mentioned it. *(Pause.)* Wait. I do remember sitting around the dinner table and hearing the word "camp." I thought it meant summer camp.

KATHLEEN: So did I! I imagined my parents canoeing or making s'mores. Lots of my respondents have the same story. You're right in the median range.

DIANE: Good to know. I guess.

KATHLEEN: And what impact do you think the camp experience had on your family?

DIANE: I grew up like any normal American.

KATHLEEN: No family stories? *(DIANE shakes her head no.)* Economic impact? Lots of folks lost their land and possessions. They had to sell everything almost overnight.

DIANE: It never came up.

KATHLEEN: When you were in school, did you ever join Asian American organizations?

DIANE: No. *(Looks skeptical.)*

KATHLEEN: We're just exploring possible correlations. OK. Last question. Do you think internment affected your career choices?

DIANE: What do you mean?

KATHLEEN: You're a labor lawyer. Did your attitude toward justice have anything to do with—

DIANE: Good God, no. I wanted to study French, but there's no money in academe.

KATHLEEN: Touché. *(Pause.)* Well. Thank you for your time.

DIANE: That was fast.

KATHLEEN: Was there more you wanted to say?

DIANE: No, no. Sorry I couldn't be more helpful.

KATHLEEN: Don't apologize. Sometimes people have a lot to say. Sometimes they don't. Findings are findings.

DIANE: Well, good luck. And please give Dean Elliott my regards. He was a great mentor of mine.

KATHLEEN: He'll be delighted I saw you. Here's my card, in case. *(The women shake hands.* KATHLEEN *exits.* DIANE *stares at the doorway for a pensive moment. She shakes it off and picks up the phone.)*

DIANE: Andrew, it's me. Don't worry. A motion for summary judgment is tough, but I can keep it out of court. A trial would be a total disaster for our clients. *(Pause.)* Yeah. The associates are on it. And thanks for your support. "Managing partner" does have a nice ring to it. Not that I could ever really fill your shoes. *(Pause.)* You're right. Today was a big win. This next one should clinch the deal. *(Spotlight suddenly illuminates* KEN *and* MASAKO. *We hear the music from Walter Cronkite's news program,* The Twentieth Century. *Blackout on* MASAKO *and* KEN. *Music cuts off abruptly. Lights return to normal.* DIANE *is disoriented.)* Yes, I'm here. No worries. I have this under control. Enjoy your evening. *(*DIANE *hangs up, gazes pensively at the spot where her parents stood. She gathers her composure, collects her things, and strides out the door. We hear her stilettos clicking down the hall, as lights fade.)*

ACT ONE, SCENE THREE

(Spotlight on DIANE, *who stands center stage.)*

DIANE: Am I paranoid? Or did that Goto woman imply I should be getting in touch with my roots? *(Beat.)* People are always surprised I'm such a Francophile. *(Pause.)* Why is that so shocking? I love France. In college I studied abroad in

Tours, the gateway to chateau country. People know the grands chateaux. Chinon. Chenonceaux. But my favorite? One nobody's ever heard of. Azay-le-Rideau. Cinderella's castle. Small. Exquisite. Jewel-like. The kind of castle you dream about when you're a little girl. And France taught this little girl Culture. Capital C. My God, even the food. I didn't know what quiche was. I'd never had a sip of alcohol. France taught me to eat and drink the best of the best. Before France I'd read literature. Voraciously. But the required reading from my high school seemed so provincial next to the avant-garde shock of surrealism and the nouveau roman. *(Pause.)* Then we read Proust. Most of the people in my class hated it. "Incomprehensible." But one girl in my class understood. For her, reading Proust was like "taking a warm bath." Another friend compared it to "eating a rich dessert." For me, Proust's sentences are like tendrils that slowly envelop you, gently weaving you into their world. The syntax twists and curves, yet each phrase renders the world in delicate, lapidarian detail. It's perfect. Like Azay-le-Rideau. I made the pilgrimage to Illiers, the model for Marcel's village in *Remembrance of Things Past*. It was kind of a letdown. The houses seemed as ordinary and somber as the weather. The museum? Unimposing. But a pâtisserie sold Proust's madeleines. Fluted, buttery scallop shells of pastry. I bought half a dozen from the plump, bespectacled pâtissière. She smiled knowingly. "Pour boire avec du thé?" To drink with your tea? Well, duh. Helloooo. And I did. Drink them with tea, that is. Dipping them into my herbal tisane. Hoping to find the portal to lost time, like Marcel did in *Swann's Way*. It didn't happen. Maybe someday. *(Pause.)* You know, I still love madeleines. Even the ones in those plastic packages at Starbucks. I buy them at least once a week. They remind me of a moment when the world was . . . opening. Ripe with possibility. Discovery. Optimism. When I was a jeune fille en fleurs. *(Lights fade on* DIANE.*)*

ACT ONE, SCENE FOUR

(Lights rise on the Kubota/Roth residence. BEN ROTH, DIANE's *husband, cooks as he consults a* Larousse Gastronomique *propped up on a bookstand. We hear Debussy's opera* Pelléas et Mélisande. DIANE *enters.)*

DIANE: Cooking? We have reservations at Bastide.

BEN: Cancelled 'em. I thought we could celebrate here.

DIANE: Honey, you shouldn't be cooking on your birthday. *(Beat.)* You know, I worked really hard to get that reservation.

BEN: Cooking relaxes me.

DIANE: Well, you still could've / told me.

BEN: Besides, it's your celebration, too! *(He brandishes a bottle of red wine, opens it as they talk.)* You just made the firm millions! *(Hands her a glass of wine.)*

DIANE: The Margaux? I guess we are celebrating. *(Pause.)* Happy birthday.

BEN: To us.

DIANE: To us. *(*BEN *and* DIANE *quaff their Bordeaux.)* Hey. Don't you have closing arguments tomorrow? Weren't you in court all day? What are you doing slaving over a hot stove?

BEN: We got out early. Continuance on the other cases. I wrote closing arguments in my head as I was cooking.

DIANE: I could never be that relaxed / about—

BEN: I'm just defending the indigent, not making it rain. Besides, it's when I do my best thinking.

DIANE: You always amaze me. And for my amazing husband . . . *(She takes out an envelope from her briefcase and hands it to* ben. *He opens it.)*

BEN: Paris!

DIANE:	Just like our honeymoon. Happy Birthday. *(He embraces her, lifts her in the air.)*
BEN:	You spoil me. *(They kiss; he puts her down.)*
DIANE:	I booked the Ritz.
BEN:	Five-star hotels. Sumptuous food. Great sex. It might even make up for turning 45.
DIANE:	Oh silly. You don't look a day over—
BEN:	Hey, it's OK. You don't have to stroke my ego. *(They kiss, then snuggle. BEN slides his hands down DIANE's shoulders, realizes she's tense. He turns her around, sits her down, and starts to give her a shoulder rub. He continues his massage throughout the following conversation.)* So tell Daddy what happened. All that stress, bringing in the millions.
DIANE:	Mmm, right there. *(Pause.)* Would've been a perfect day . . .
BEN:	But?
DIANE:	This Harvard psychologist came to interview me.
BEN:	For what?
DIANE:	Some academic . . . whatever.
BEN:	On labor law? What's a psychologist / doing—
DIANE:	About the camps, of all things.
BEN:	What camps?
DIANE:	Internment. Relocation. Whatever you call it.
BEN:	But that was your parents.
DIANE:	She thinks camp affected Sanseis. It's crazy.
BEN:	So why did you do it? You never have a problem saying no.
DIANE:	She's Elliott's protégé, so I thought I should at least go through the motions. Should've known better. Something about her reminded me of all those P.C. Asian American

	activist types. I could just imagine what she thought of me. (*Lights rise on* KATHLEEN.)
KATHLEEN:	God, that Kubota woman. What an uptight bitch. Banana. Ms. Model Minority. Euro-identified. Clueless. All that talk about France this, France that. It's what I hate about Harvard sometimes, that sense of Eurocentric superiority. You're not European, stupid. They'll never let you in. Yeah, Diane Kubota Esquire has her head up her ass. France isn't all that. New England sucks. I, on the other hand, love Japan. (*Blackout on* KATHLEEN.)
BEN:	Did she actually say that?
DIANE:	No, but—
BEN:	So it's your paranoid fantasy. What's that about? Why do you even care what she thinks? (DIANE *shrugs.*) You know, she may have a point. If the camps affected your folks, there could be some carryover . . .
DIANE:	That's silly. I'm totally fine. (BEN *pushes another tender spot on* DIANE's *shoulders.*) Ow!
BEN:	So I see.
DIANE:	That's not fair.
BEN:	It must've been tough. Losing your home. Being displaced.
DIANE:	But it was so long ago. It's not like it was slavery or the Holocaust or something.
BEN:	It wasn't exactly a picnic. I mean, don't you want to know more about your parents?
DIANE:	Just because your family can't stop talking / about—
BEN:	It's the "never forget" thing.
DIANE:	Let's not get into the Misery Olympics.
BEN:	But it's our baby's history.

DIANE: Aha. *(She turns to him.)* So that's what this means. The best wine. French cooking. *Pelléas et Mélisande.*

BEN: Are you accusing me of something, counselor? Why, I find that highly inappropriate. *(He takes her in his arms, dips her, twirls her around.)*

DIANE: Stop, silly, you'll make me dizzy. *(They kiss. The phone in her suit pocket buzzes. She looks at the display, releases herself from the embrace, and picks up.)* Andrew? *(Pause.)* I'll calm them down. I told you. I can get the case dismissed. I'll get on it right away. Have a lovely evening. *(She hangs up.)*

BEN: I hope you didn't mean that.

DIANE: What?

BEN: That you'll get on it right away.

DIANE: It would just take / a minute.

BEN: God, do you have to kill yourself to be managing partner?

DIANE: Hey! It's not a done deal. Andrew's on board, but we're not sure about Bennett.

BEN: But MPs do all that administrative shit. It's like glorified housekeeping.

DIANE: You get to control the direction of the firm! Why are you dumping on my dream all of a sudden?

BEN: What about *our* dream?

DIANE: You mean—

BEN: A family! You should be ovulating now.

DIANE: Gee, that's hot.

BEN: Hey! You were totally into it. Until Andrew called.

DIANE: Are you jealous?

BEN: No. I'm just—

DIANE: It's not about Andrew.

BEN: I know. It's the MP bullshit.

DIANE: Bullshit?

BEN: (*Pause.*) I'm sorry. I didn't mean it. It just came out the wrong way. You know. Freud. Frustration-aggression. (*DIANE turns away.*) Sometimes I just wonder if you really do want a kid, or—

DIANE: Or what?

BEN: Or whether it's just your career that you care about. (*DIANE shoots him an outraged look, but we see a flicker of doubt beneath the bravado. She walks away. BEN follows.*)

BEN: Hey, don't do that freeze-out thing you do. It's my birthday. (*He tries to take her in his arms. She resists.*)

DIANE: That was quite a buzzkill.

BEN: Aw, c'mon, honey. (*DIANE continues to resist.*) A little kiss for your birthday boy? (*DIANE turns her head away.*) Please? (*She softens a little. He kisses her. She's unresponsive at first, then gradually returns his embrace. He lifts her up and starts to carry her offstage. BEN freezes. GRANDMA appears, carrying a bouquet of gladiolas. She is visible only to DIANE and to us. DIANE stares at GRANDMA in fascination and fear. Images of barracks, a WHITE DOCTOR, GRANDMA. Lights up on DIANE and BEN. DIANE continues to stare at GRANDMA.*)

DIANE: Wait.

BEN: What?

DIANE: Put me down.

BEN: But sweetie—

DIANE: Put me down. (*He puts her down.*) I'm sorry. I just can't. (*Blackout.*)

ACT ONE, SCENE FIVE

(The next day. DIANE enters the kitchen carrying a grocery bag. She picks up her phone, makes a call. BEN appears in spotlight.)

DIANE: How'd it go, honey?

BEN: Good. Jury came back right away. Not guilty.

DIANE: So the extra work paid off. *(Pause.)* You know, I don't even know what time you got to bed.

BEN: A lot later than I'd planned.

DIANE: Hey, you're not mad, are you?

BEN: *(Coolly.)* No.

DIANE: Listen. I hope you'll be home soon. I picked up some treats. Sushi, Dom Pérignon, chocolate cake . . . your favorites. We could re-do your birthday. *(DIANE starts taking food from the grocery bag.)*

BEN: Sure, let's celebrate. Tomorrow. I'm going to the meeting tonight.

DIANE: *(Suggestively.)* Can't you ditch it? I'll make it worth your while.

BEN: We're wrapping up tonight.

DIANE: Oh God. For once, you could say no to all that goody goody pro bono shit. *(Awkward pause.)*

BEN: So it's OK for you to kill yourself trying to make MP, but I can't donate one night a week to a cause I believe in.

DIANE: It's not the same thing.

BEN: Really? If the shoe were on the other foot, would you cancel your meeting?

DIANE: Right now I am under enormous pressure. And if this is about last night—

BEN: This is not about last night.

DIANE: Oh yeah? Coulda fooled me.

BEN: It's about principles.

DIANE: Oh, don't go all highfalutin' on me.

BEN: Whatever. I'll be home late.

DIANE: Honey! Aren't we more important than your Justice for Janitors / or—

BEN: You could at least get it straight. It's the detention case.

DIANE: But it's already six. Don't you want to—

BEN: I'll grab something on the way. Don't wait up. (*He hangs up.* DIANE *absorbs the shock, then takes the bottle of champagne from the grocery bag, pops the cork, pours the champagne into a coffee cup and lifts her glass.*)

DIANE: To us. (*She drains the glass, pours herself more, and continues to quaff the champagne. Suddenly,* GRANDMA *appears, bearing her bouquet of gladiolas.* DIANE *does a double take.*)

GRANDMA: Gonna take a sentimental journey, gonna set my heart at ease.

(*Blackout on* GRANDMA. DIANE *looks around, puzzled, checks out her champagne and the drained glass. She shrugs her shoulders, unpacks her briefcase, and sets up her work as lights fade.*)

ACT ONE, SCENE SIX

(*An hour later.* DIANE *is close to polishing off the champagne. She glances at the time.*)

DIANE: Seven? He's probably at his meeting. (*She drains the glass, pours herself more, and continues to quaff the bubbly as she scrolls through her email. The files appear on the upstage screen. She clicks on a message.*) Well, well, well. (*Spotlight on* KATHLEEN.)

KATHLEEN: Thank you for agreeing to participate in Part Two of the Project on the Effects of Internment on the Children of Internees. Please take the time to fill out this objective questionnaire about your knowledge of the camps.

DIANE: In your dreams, honey.

KATHLEEN: Your responses will be invaluable for our scientific understanding of this traumatic historical event.

DIANE: "Traumatic historical event?" Fuck that! Delete! *(DIANE lifts her hand dramatically, poised to hit the delete button. Lights shift as KATHLEEN steps into DIANE's reality.)*

KATHLEEN: Wait! *(DIANE does a double take.)* A little trouble in paradise?

DIANE: What do you mean?

KATHLEEN: Pressure at work? Abandoned by hubby? Drinking alone?

DIANE: None of your business. Work's fine. Ben's fine. We're . . . fine.

KATHLEEN: Seamlessly perfect. *(Pause.)* Maybe getting in touch with your roots would do you some good.

DIANE: This is insane. Delete. *(DIANE prepares to hit the delete button.)*

KATHLEEN: What about your husband? *(DIANE stops short.)*

DIANE: What about him?

KATHLEEN: You could show him. That you have a sense of history. That family is important to you.

DIANE: Right. By taking your silly test.

KATHLEEN: To know where you're going you have to know where you come from.

DIANE: You sound like a fortune cookie.

KATHLEEN: Sticks and stones. Of course, it won't look good when you fail.

DIANE: I've aced every test I've ever taken. I love tests.

KATHLEEN: You said you didn't know anything about the camps.

DIANE: So?

KATHLEEN: Ms. Straight A's might be less than perfect.

DIANE: Ha! You wish.

KATHLEEN: Unless you're embarrassed about revealing your appalling ignorance.

DIANE: Who cares? It's all in the past.

KATHLEEN: Don't you care about your parents?

DIANE: Of course I do!

KATHLEEN: Then don't you want to know about the most dramatic turning point / in their lives?

DIANE: But maybe the camps were for their own protection. With all the anti-Japanese feeling—

KATHLEEN: Asian American Studies 101. If relocation was for their protection, why were the guns pointed inward? *(DIANE ponders.)* Guns, searchlights, barbed wire. Think about it. Like I tell my students. Learn and grow.

DIANE: God. OK, OK. If it means you'll leave me alone. *(DIANE downs another glass of champagne.)* You're lucky you caught me when I'm feeling mellow.

KATHLEEN: You're a trouper. OK, here we go. Question One. How many camps were there?

DIANE: Oh. Jeez. Five? *(KATHLEEN frowns.)* Twenty? *(KATHLEEN's frown deepens.)* Forty? *(Deeper yet.)* OK, OK, I don't know.

KATHLEEN: Obviously.

DIANE: Hey! How am I supposed to know? They didn't have Asian American Studies at Harvard.

KATHLEEN: That's no excuse. You can read.

DIANE: It's not like it's common knowledge. *(Pause.)* Well? Aren't you going to tell me the answer?

KATHLEEN: Later. The answers will appear in the appendix.

DIANE: Bitch.

KATHLEEN: Flattery will get you everywhere. Next question. What were the names of the camps?

DIANE: I don't even know how many there were!

KATHLEEN: Just do your best.

DIANE: OK. Tule Lake. Where Dad was. And . . . Heart Mountain, right? Where you said Mom was. And Santa Anita—

KATHLEEN: Sorry. That was an assembly center. Where they were "assembled" prior to camp. Sleeping in horse stalls, with straw and manure.

DIANE: Well that's all I've heard of.

KATHLEEN: *(Sotto voce.)* Pathetic.

DIANE: Excuse me?

KATHLEEN: Nothing.

DIANE: Hey, cut the editorializing. It's unprofessional.

KATHLEEN: You were hearing things.

DIANE: No, I wasn't! Who cares if I don't know all this . . . arcane historical minutiae? I can look it up on the Internet any day of the week.

KATHLEEN: True. Although your level of ignorance *is* high: 90th percentile.

DIANE: This questionnaire is stupid.

KATHLEEN: That's right. When you do poorly, blame the test, not yourself. Lucky for you that we finished Section A. Let's move on to Section B.

DIANE: I've had enough.

KATHLEEN: Really? Do you want Ben to know that you were a miserable failure? *(DIANE stops short.)* Just one question. No right or wrong.

DIANE: Shit. If it's just one question.

KATHLEEN: Brilliant! How many times have you talked to your parents about their experiences in camp? A. 0–5. B. 6–10. C. More than 10.

DIANE: This one is easy. Zero to five.

KATHLEEN: Why the low numbers, counselor?

DIANE: It just seemed like something you weren't supposed to bring up.

KATHLEEN: Because?

DIANE: It must've been terrible. Too terrible to talk about.

KATHLEEN: How do you know unless you try? *(KATHLEEN gestures toward a tableau: MASAKO and KEN watching TV.)*

DIANE: But look at them. They're always watching TV. Or gardening. Or visiting the relatives. Even if I wanted to, the right moment—

KATHLEEN: There's no time like the present. *(Blackout on KATHLEEN. DIANE stares at MASAKO and KEN, turns back to her desk and picks up the phone. Lights fade.)*

ACT ONE, SCENE SEVEN

(Lights rise on KEN, MASAKO, and DIANE seated in a restaurant.)

MASAKO and KEN: Thank you for inviting us out.

DIANE: I'm glad you hadn't had dinner.

MASAKO: We haven't seen you in so long.

DIANE: Well, you know how it is.

MASAKO: Always busy.

KEN: Too busy to see us. *(MASAKO shoots KEN a look of warning.)*

MASAKO: Daddy. *(She looks around the restaurant.)* This is very nice.

KEN: Yeah, nice place. *(DIANE scopes out the room.)*

DIANE: You know what? These are lousy seats. It's right by the bathroom. Waiter! Waiter!

KEN: Don't bother. It's OK.

MASAKO: It's OK.

DIANE: We're allowed to ask for a better seat. Waiter! *(She scans the room, searching for a WAITER.)* God, what do you have to do to get served around here?

KEN: Ah, it's too much trouble.

MASAKO: Too much trouble.

KEN: Don't bother them.

MASAKO: It's OK.

DIANE: *(Flags down a WAITER.)* Could we have the seats over there, near the window? We've got all the bathroom traffic here.

WAITER: Actually, we're pretty full today.

KEN: It's OK for us here.

WAITER: All right then, if you're—

DIANE: It's *not* OK. If you can't find us another table, I'd like to speak to the manager.

WAITER: Oh. Well, perhaps I can give you Table 5. Right by the window.

DIANE: Great. Terrific. *(They walk to the new table. The parents address WAITER.)*

KEN: Thank you very much.

MASAKO: Thank you very much.

KEN: We really appreciate it.

MASAKO: We really appreciate it.

KEN: We hate to bother you.

MASAKO: You didn't have to.

WAITER: *(Shows them a seat.)* My pleasure. *(WAITER exits.)*

DIANE: God. You don't have to be so damn grateful.

KEN: But he was nice to us.

MASAKO: He made a special effort.

DIANE: We deserve a decent seat that's not by the kitchen, not by the bathroom—

KEN and MASAKO: We had to thank him.

DIANE: A simple "thank you" is one thing. But I repeat. You don't have to be so grateful just to be treated with respect.

KEN and MASAKO: But we *are* grateful.

DIANE: Fuck it. I give up. *(She grabs her menu.)* Let's order. *(She examines the menu.)* They say the salmon is good here. *(MASAKO and KEN freeze. KATHLEEN appears upstage.)*

KATHLEEN: Pssst. *(DIANE does a double take.)*

DIANE: What are you doing here?

KATHLEEN: Checking up on you.

DIANE: Leave me alone. I'm trying to order.

KATHLEEN: Your parents are a little humble.

DIANE: A little? They drive me nuts!

KATHLEEN: And why do you think they're that way?

DIANE:	Personality. Or maybe it's cultural.
KATHLEEN:	Cop out.
DIANE:	Well, how else—
KATHLEEN:	They're so used to being treated badly, they're grateful for any little crumb of courtesy.
DIANE:	Oh please. Cut the melodrama.
KATHLEEN:	Our study shows that the effects of the internment reverberate far beyond the actual experience. Many trauma victims can't articulate their pain.
DIANE:	There you go again with the victim bullshit! *(Lights up on MASAKO and KEN.)*
KATHLEEN:	Well, if you're so convinced that this is bullshit, why not prove it? Just ask them some questions. *(Pause.)* Or are you too afraid?
DIANE:	Heck no! I'm—*(Blackout on KATHLEEN. DIANE rejoins her parents at the table.)* Mom? Dad?
MASAKO:	What is it?
DIANE:	This researcher from Harvard was interviewing me.
KEN:	Oh, that's good!
DIANE:	No, it wasn't about me, it was about the camps.
MASAKO:	The camps?
DIANE:	For a book or something.
MASAKO:	But you weren't even there.
DIANE:	I know. It's about the impact of the camps on Sansei.
KEN:	You weren't born yet!
DIANE:	Well, obviously I didn't know anything. So I was wondering . . .
MASAKO:	What?
DIANE:	What was it like?

KEN: It wasn't a vacation.

MASAKO: It wasn't summer camp. *(KEN and MASAKO laugh.)*

DIANE: Well . . . what about the physical conditions?

MASAKO: Hot in the summer.

KEN: Cold in the winter.

DIANE: Right, it was a desert. I'd expect that, but . . . was it . . . awful?

KEN and MASAKO: What?

DIANE: The barracks or whatever.

KEN: Wasn't the Hilton.

MASAKO: Tarpaper and wood.

DIANE: And? For God's sake, is that all you have to say?

MASAKO: Omaesan. We were there.

KEN: We don't need to remember. Maybe you do, but.

KEN and MASAKO: We don't.

MASAKO: And besides.

KEN: We're hungry.

MASAKO: Can we order?

DIANE: OK, OK.

KEN: I think I'll have the halibut.

MASAKO: I want the Caesar salad, but they use that awful rich dressing.

DIANE: You can ask for vinaigrette on the side.

MASAKO: Oh, but they have to go through all that trouble.

DIANE: Mom. It's a restaurant. You can ask for whatever you want.

MASAKO: No, I think I'll have a hamburger.

KEN: Not again. With your high blood pressure—

DIANE: Mom, are you sure you don't want the Caesar salad?

MASAKO: It's OK. I like hamburger. *(DIANE looks at them both, sighs.)*

DIANE: OK. If that's what you want. *(She turns around.)* Waiter! *(Blackout.)*

ACT ONE, SCENE EIGHT

(DIANE resumes her work at home. She glances at her watch.)

DIANE: Only ten? Two more good hours. *(She madly types on the keyboard. Suddenly she stops. She rifles through the stack of legal tomes, throwing each to the ground. She stands up and stomps on a book.)* Shit, shit, shit! We're gonna have to go to trial! *(KATHLEEN flies in, wearing samurai garb. She perches on DIANE's desk.)*

KATHLEEN: How's it going, counselor?

DIANE: Not you again! *(KATHLEEN peers at DIANE's computer screen.)*

KATHLEEN: Looks dire.

DIANE: I can handle it!

KATHLEEN: Yeah. That's why you're throwing a tantrum. *(DIANE points toward the door.)* Not so fast, missy. I have the key to all your problems. *(She dangles a book in front of DIANE. DIANE tries to grab it. KATHLEEN jerks it away. KATHLEEN lounges on the desk, continuing to tempt DIANE with the book.)* Con Law 101.

DIANE: That arcane shit isn't gonna help me. *(KATHLEEN unsheathes a sword with her free hand and executes dazzling swordplay.)*

KATHLEEN: A little . . . coram nobis?

DIANE: Oh jeez. That's criminal law. I have a civil case.

KATHLEEN: You still need to think about justice. Constitutional rights. I'll just have to give this to Simpson. *(DIANE tries to grab the book, as KATHLEEN spins out of her reach.)*

DIANE: Let me have that!

KATHLEEN: No way, missy! *(They struggle over the book. DIANE grabs a sword from underneath her desk, and the two spar. The women thrust their swords with each line of dialogue.)*

DIANE: *Dukes vs. Walmart.* The Supreme Court disallowed class action.

KATHLEEN: What about justice?

DIANE: Irrelevant. Individuals only. Case by case.

KATHLEEN: Look at the glass ceilings!

DIANE: The plaintiff was incompetent.

KATHLEEN: Not a single minority in management!

DIANE: Statistical accident.

KATHLEEN: But the smoking guns! The hard drives!

DIANE: That's why they hired us. Everyone deserves the best representation—

KATHLEEN: That money can buy.

DIANE: And we're gonna make a chunk of change.

KATHLEEN: Everybody hates Wall Street now. You'll never get a sympathetic jury. *(A telling blow.)*

DIANE: The case will never get to a jury. Our clients have the judge in their pocket. *(DIANE strikes back.)*

KATHLEEN: Wishful thinking!

DIANE: The plaintiffs have no evidence!

KATHLEEN: Your clients are heinous. The judge will deny your pathetic motion for summary judgment! You'll have to go to trial!

DIANE: Over my dead body!

KATHLEEN: Then prepare to perish! The jury will sympathize with the plaintiff. You'll lose, big time. *(KATHLEEN strikes down DIANE's sword.)* You know what'll happen then. *(DIANE reaches for her sword; KATHLEEN bars her way.)* Simpson. He'll be managing partner.

DIANE: God, that insufferable prick. *(KATHLEEN chases DIANE around the desk.)*

KATHLEEN: It's gonna be fun. He'll give you all the unwinnable cases.

DIANE: But Andrew's been grooming me. For years.

KATHLEEN: He's been playing you two against each other. Simpson fits in. You've tried to master the football stats. But you can't do it like a "real" man.

DIANE: But my record is stellar!

KATHLEEN: After all this time, you still think it's about good work? It's all politics. After you screw up this case, no one will call you the rainmaker again.

DIANE: Stop this mindfuck! *(DIANE grabs the book and her sword from KATHLEEN.)* All mine!

KATHLEEN: Yeah? Let's see how much you really know. Pop quiz.

DIANE: Bring it. *(The two resume their swordplay.)*

KATHLEEN: What law authorized internment?

DIANE: It wasn't a law. Executive Order 9066.

KATHLEEN: What about the Supreme Court decisions?

DIANE: *Hirabayashi v. US* upheld curfew. *Korematsu v. US* upheld internment. National security trumps individual rights.

KATHLEEN: Lucky guess. Extra credit. What was the vote on *Korematsu*?

DIANE: Six to three. Supporters included William O. Douglas. *(DIANE strikes a telling blow.)* Felix Frankfurter. *(Another blow.)* Hugo Black. *(DIANE is now chasing KATHLEEN.)*

	All civil rights pioneers. Supporters of *Brown v. Board of Education*, that ordered desegregation. For all the good it did my mom and dad.
KATHLEEN:	You said you didn't know anything about the camps.
DIANE:	I know about the law, stupid. Just not about my family.
KATHLEEN:	You looked it up on Wikipedia!
DIANE:	*(Triumphantly.)* Hell no! I aced Con Law, baby. So get out! *(DIANE chases KATHLEEN to the edge of the stage.)*
KATHLEEN:	But what about justice?
DIANE:	I'm giving them the best representation that money can buy! That's justice!
KATHLEEN:	How can you defend those assholes?
DIANE:	My whole career is at stake! My dreams! My whole life!
KATHLEEN:	Maybe your whole life is meaningless!
DIANE:	Oh yeah? We'll see about that. *(They spar for their lives. DIANE strikes a mortal blow. KATHLEEN falls to the floor. A golden light illuminates DIANE, who points her sword to the sky.)* Sweet victory! *(Suddenly, lights shift. Spot on KEN and MASAKO, who wear overcoats from the 1940s. Tags bearing numbers hang from their necks.)*
KEN:	15513.
MASAKO:	16321. *(Lights intensify on KEN and MASAKO. DIANE stares at them, transfixed. KATHLEEN has vanished. Lights fade, as DIANE crosses to . . .)*

ACT ONE, SCENE NINE

	(. . . her bedroom and gets ready for bed. BEN is conspicuously absent. She picks up her phone.)
DIANE:	Ben? Where are you? It's almost midnight. Give me a call, OK? Love you. *(She gets into bed, tossing and turning as lights fade. Suddenly, lights rise on a courtroom.*

(*KATHLEEN wears a judicial robe and a white wig, in the style of a British barrister. She sits at the judge's bench. BEN, dressed in barrister's wig and a suit, stands behind a table. MASAKO and KEN wear kimono and sit together in the witness stand. DIANE, still clad in her nightgown, stands in the middle of the courtroom. Everyone stares at her.*)

KATHLEEN: Counselor?

DIANE: I thought I got rid of you.

KATHLEEN: In your dreams. Your witness.

DIANE: But . . . who's on trial?

MASAKO and KEN: We are.

DIANE: For what?

KEN: Hell if we know.

MASAKO: It was your idea.

DIANE: No it isn't! (*To KATHLEEN.*) I can't interrogate them! They're my parents!

KATHLEEN: You must.

DIANE: What happens if I don't?

KATHLEEN: Then off with your head!

DIANE: But isn't that a little drastic? (*KATHLEEN brandishes a samurai sword.*) OK, OK. I get the picture. (*DIANE turns to MASAKO and KEN.*) First of all, would you please tell the court . . . what on earth are you doing in those silly costumes?

MASAKO: That was your idea, too.

DIANE: No way!

KEN: This is your dream, isn't it?

MASAKO: We were born here.

KEN: We've never been to Japan.

MASAKO: We've never worn kimono in our lives!

KEN: They're too damn tight.

MASAKO: You can't breathe.

KEN: They look stupid.

MASAKO: But this is what happened during the war.

KEN: People couldn't tell the difference between Japanese.

MASAKO and KEN: And Japanese Americans.

DIANE: Ah ha. That's the connection. The mind works in mysterious ways.

BEN: Objection!

DIANE: To what?

BEN: Leading the witness.

KATHLEEN: Sustained.

DIANE: Your Honor, I move to dismiss the case.

KATHLEEN: On what grounds, counselor?

DIANE: Faulty presuppositions. Counsel assumes that with just the right question, they'll tell me everything. *(Lights rise on MASAKO and KEN, who don Victorian hats. They speak with British accents, in the mode of high melodrama.)*

MASAKO: Why, what a brilliant question. Just turn on your tape recorder. I'll sing you a dirge replete with pain and suffering. I'll launch into a jeremiad, rageful and bitter. Prepare yourself for the torrent of words, the cascade of injustices, the outpouring of truth. The dam has broken.

KEN: By Jove, they took everything. Those chaps were cads, egregiously unfair, to state it mildly. Here. I have a manuscript I've just completed. It measures the psychological

268   CHAPTER 7

	toll down to the last nightmare. The economic costs down to the last penny. It will clarify any mystery. Dispel the slightest doubt. Exhaustive. Comprehensive. Definitive.
MASAKO and KEN:	
	After this, you'll know everything. *(MASAKO and KEN faint, in a Victorian fit of the vapors. Blackout on MASAKO and KEN.)*
KATHLEEN:	Nice try.
BEN:	You're the one who doesn't want to know.
KATHLEEN:	You're protecting yourself, not your parents.
DIANE:	God. I'm surrounded by psychobabble.
KATHLEEN:	It's up to you, counselor. Cross-examine or forever hold your peace. *(DIANE turns to her parents.)*
MASAKO:	It's OK.
KEN:	Go ahead.
DIANE:	Are you sure?
MASAKO and KEN:	
	We're sure.
DIANE:	So. Mom. Dad. If you could please tell the court. Why didn't you ever talk about camp?
MASAKO:	It's over.
KEN:	We don't want to remember.
MASAKO:	It was shameful.
KEN:	It was hard.
MASAKO and KEN:	
	We're past that now.
DIANE:	*(A little too quickly.)* Yes. I agree. It's in the past. No further questions.
BEN:	Objection.

KATHLEEN: Sustained.

BEN and KATHLEEN:
Proceed, counselor.

DIANE: But it'll kill them to talk about it.

BEN: Objection. Conjecture.

DIANE: Just watch. *(She turns to her parents.)* Mom? Dad? What happened to Grandma? *(Her parents collapse.)* You see? You've killed them! They're bleeding!

BEN and KATHLEEN:
We don't see any bleeding.

DIANE: You fools! It's all on the inside! *(She holds up her parents' hands. A moment. They leap up.)*

KEN and MASAKO:
We're fine!

BEN: It was all your projection.

KATHLEEN: And we say.

BEN and KATHLEEN:
You should know your history. *(KATHLEEN turns to KEN and MASAKO.)*

KATHLEEN: You know you really want to share your stories.

BEN: For your grandchildren.

KATHLEEN: For your daughter.

BEN: For yourselves.

KATHLEEN: For history.

DIANE: Mom, Dad, that's a lotta bunk. Don't listen to them.

KATHLEEN: *(Points to DIANE.)* Her job is to elicit your testimony.

BEN: Otherwise the court will never hear your case.

KATHLEEN: If she doesn't do her job, we say.

KATHLEEN and BEN:
: Off with her head! *(They gesture for MASAKO and KEN to join in.)*

DIANE: But that's ridiculous.

KATHLEEN: All together now!

KEN: Do you really want to hear—

KATHLEEN and BEN:
: Of course!

MASAKO: Well, then.

MASAKO and KEN:
: *(Sotto voce.)* Off with her head.

DIANE: Mom! Dad!

KATHLEEN and BEN:
: All together now.

KATHLEEN, BEN, MASAKO, and KEN:
: Off with her head!

DIANE: Objection! Leading the witness!

KATHLEEN: Overruled.

KATHLEEN, BEN, MASAKO, and KEN:
: Off with her head!

DIANE: How could you—

KATHLEEN, BEN, MASAKO, and KEN:
: Off with her head! Off with her head! Off with her head!

DIANE: *(Simultaneously.)* No! Leave me alone! Leave me alone! *(They create a phalanx, advancing toward DIANE.)* Stop! I can't! I can't! I can't! *(They close in on DIANE and chase her back to her bed. She dives under the covers. Blackout on KATHLEEN, BEN, MASAKO, and KEN. DIANE peeks out, glances around the room, then sinks back into bed, tossing and turning as lights fade. Suddenly, lights slam up on DIANE, who sits bolt upright, terrified. We see GRANDMA, writhing, screaming.*

Fragmented images of a dilapidated farm, gladiolas, barracks. Lights crash down.)

ACT ONE, SCENE TEN

(The alarm rings. Lights rise. DIANE *bolts out of bed.)*

DIANE: Shit. *(*BEN *is still sleeping.* DIANE *tiptoes to the bathroom and returns, brushing her teeth. Her cell phone buzzes. She grabs it.* BEN *stirs.)*

BEN: Morning.

DIANE: Sorry. I was trying not to wake you. *(Toothbrush still in her mouth,* DIANE *answers the phone.)* Mom, I can't talk now. I have to go to work. *(Spot up on* MASAKO.*)*

MASAKO: Diane. It's your daddy. *(Blackout.)*

ACT ONE, SCENE ELEVEN

*(*DIANE *sits at her desk. It's a mess. She breaks down, recomposes herself. She turns to the computer with a vengeance and starts pounding on the keyboard. The phone rings.)*

DIANE: Andrew. *(Pause.)* I know. But we still have a few days to prepare. The judge will dismiss the case, I promise. *(Pause.)* Yeah, I'm sorry I couldn't talk to them yesterday. My dad and all that. *(Pause.)* No, I'm OK. I just need to take care of some estate stuff later today. At my parents' house. *(Pause.)* No, no, no need to ask Simpson. Thanks. Bye.

(She hangs up, goes back to her computer, bangs on the keyboard, then throws up her hands in frustration.) Aaaagh!

(Spot on KEN, *who stands upstage.)*

KEN: Wassamatta?

DIANE: Dad!

KEN: Shikkari shinasai!

DIANE:	Dad. You know I don't understand that Japanese-y stuff.
KEN:	Get your act together. You can't be a crybaby because of me.
DIANE:	But I miss you. You tried so hard. I wish you could've had it easier. We were so pathetic. We should've called 9-1-1 right away.
KEN:	I was in bad shape, all right. Wish you guys knew CPR.
DIANE:	Me too.
KEN:	I wanted to feel better.
DIANE:	I know. *(She breaks down.)* I never knew the death rattle was real. I can't even do it. Bbbbbrrrrrr. Like you were expelling every last ounce of breath from your body.
KEN:	You know what they say. Dying is a verb.
DIANE:	That's an understatement. And that obituary was ridiculous. "He died of natural causes." If that's natural, let me die of blunt force trauma. And how about, "He died surrounded by family?" Yeah. Like that did you any good.
KEN:	Aw, don't say that. Shiyō ga nai.
DIANE:	Translation!
KEN:	Can't be helped. What's done is done. I can't be here anymore.
DIANE:	To give me grief.
KEN:	To help you! *(He gestures toward her work space and picks up some of the documents.)* Look at the people you're defending. Nihonjin haiseki.
DIANE:	Dad. Cut the Japanese.
KEN:	I know what it's like. For people to beat you up. Keep you out. Like the hakujin who sent us to camp.
DIANE:	Oh, come on. This isn't a hundredth as bad.
KEN:	Still. They're trying to keep us out. Nihonjin haiseki.

DIANE: What do you mean? Did people beat you up physically? Did they discriminate against you in your job? *(KEN seems poised to speak. Lights dim on KEN)* Dad? Dad! *(KEN is silent.)* I just wish I knew you better. Not as Dad. But as Ken. *(Lights intensify on KEN.)* What was your life like as a little boy? What did you dream about as a young man? How did you survive everything you went through? What *did* you go through? You never told me. *(KEN gazes at her.)* And I never asked. *(Lights fade.)*

END OF ACT ONE

ACT TWO, SCENE ONE

(Spot illuminates DIANE.)

DIANE: OK. Coulda woulda shoulda. Dad's death left a huge hole in my heart. You never know how precious they are till they're gone. But Mom is still here. She can tell me about Dad. About both of them. *(Beat.)* You know, when I was in France, people would ask me about Japan, like I was supposed to know. My parents were born here. But I don't know much about that, either. *(Beat.)* Maybe this is my own quest for lost time. Remember when Marcel dipped his madeleine into the tea? *(She picks up* Swann's Way.*)* And from that cup, the village of his childhood "rose up like a stage set . . . and with the house the town . . . the Square . . . the country roads we took when it was fine." I want to know my mom and dad and their world. Like Proust knew his. I want every detail. After all, I'm a great lawyer. Managing-partner-to-be lawyer. I know how to do research, how to cross-examine witnesses. I have the skills. All I have to do is ask. *(Lights fade as DIANE crosses to her parents' basement.)*

ACT TWO, SCENE TWO

(KEN and MASAKO's garage. DIANE and MASAKO rummage through boxes. DIANE finds a photograph of her father and holds it aloft. Lights rise on KEN in an army uniform,

decorated with a captain's stripes. He salutes. Camera flash. DIANE and MASAKO cannot see or hear KEN, except as he is represented in the photograph. When DIANE and MASAKO speak, KEN freezes in salute. DIANE lifts out an army uniform, holds it in front of her.)

DIANE: Wow. Dad saved this?

MASAKO: It meant a lot to him. He was in the army medical corps.

DIANE: When was that?

MASAKO: I'm not sure. It was before I met your daddy. *(KEN turns toward DIANE.)*

KEN: At camp, they let us go inland if we had school or a job outside the West Coast. So I finished medical school in Kansas City in 1945. *(He turns to MASAKO.)* Our daughter finally wants to know something about us. So tell her!

MASAKO: Your daddy was a draft dodger.

DIANE: You're kidding!

KEN: Hey! That makes it sound bad, like I was un-American. *(He turns to DIANE.)* The Gresham Draft Board wanted to draft me as a buck private. Here I was, with a medical degree! No hakujin with that kind of education would have to go into the army as a private. So I said, screw them!

DIANE: So what did he do to dodge the draft?

MASAKO: He had to keep moving around. I . . . think he went to Chicago.

KEN: No! I went to Chicago after New York.

DIANE: Didn't Dad go to New York or something?

MASAKO: Oh. That's right. I guess New York was after Chicago.

KEN: Before! Before! How many times did I tell you the story about landing at Penn Station, fresh out of camp, hauling my big old ugly trunk on the bus. God, I must've seemed like a hick. But I made it to the clinic. Found a place to

	live. I had gumption in those days. *(He turns to* DIANE.*)* You would've been proud of your daddy.
MASAKO:	He talked about how poor he was then. Even had to darn his own socks.
KEN:	Aw, I did OK. I found a cheap Chinese restaurant where you could get a meal for ten cents. You had to walk up three flights of stairs, but it was worth it. The subway was just a nickel then. I know how to save a penny. *(Beat.)* I should've given you a few pointers. Make sure you're putting enough away for retirement. Add a month's payment to your mortgage every year. You'll pay it down before you know it.
DIANE:	So he probably didn't have much fun.
MASAKO:	Probably not.
KEN:	Aw, I got out once in awhile. Sometimes I went to see ball games at Ebbets Field. Or took the ferry to Staten Island to see one of my friends. You don't have to feel sorry for me.
MASAKO:	He said it was tough when he went off to school. Lots of prejudice.
DIANE:	What did he mean, "lots of prejudice?" Did they say awful things? Did they beat him up? What?
MASAKO:	I don't know.
DIANE:	Gosh, Mom. You're no help. *(MASAKO shrugs.)*
KEN:	Things like that, I never wanted to tell our daughter. Hazukashii. Shameful. I had a hard time, even finding a place to live. "We don't rent to Japs." Prejudice was bad then. Sometimes people would sic their dogs on me. *(Pause.)* In medical school, everybody wore uniforms. The medical corps. But a couple of us who got out of camp didn't have uniforms. A lot of guys didn't like it. And they let you know. *(He turns to* DIANE.*)* Maybe if you knew what we went through, it could help you. Like that case you're working on. You'd see it from a different angle. Maybe you

wouldn't think of your mama and me as . . . you know, those twins from the nursery rhyme. Tweedledum and Tweedledee. Silly old gooses. Maybe . . . I wasn't a good father to you. *(DIANE picks up another photo.)*

DIANE: Who's this with Dad?

MASAKO: That was his friend George Iwataki.

KEN: Hey. That's not George Iwataki. That's Tosh Kaneko. *(DIANE and MASAKO continue to rummage through the boxes.)*

DIANE: Mom, here's that guy again. What did you say his name was?

MASAKO: Gene. . . . Oh, I don't know. I never knew him.

DIANE: I thought you said it was George something.

MASAKO: No . . . it was . . .

KEN: It was Tosh *Kaneko*. We visited him in Portland once. *(MASAKO looks confused.)*

DIANE: Are you OK, Mom?

MASAKO: Funny. I can't remember.

DIANE: Now it'll bother you all day. *(Pause.)* I wish Dad were here. We could ask him.

MASAKO: I don't know about that. Your daddy didn't always remember so well.

DIANE: What, like you?

MASAKO: What are you talking about? My memory is fine. Just too much information up here. *(She points to her head.)* Just takes a little time to shake it loose.

DIANE: But what do you mean about Dad? He was still watching the news, reading the *New England Journal* . . .

MASAKO: Most of the time he was OK. But sometimes he'd ask something. Then ask the same question a few minutes later.

KEN:	Aw, I was just trying to make conversation.
DIANE:	Are you sure? I never noticed.
MASAKO:	I'm the one who lived with him every day. You hardly ever saw us.
DIANE:	OK! Enough with the guilt trip.
MASAKO:	His memory was starting to go.
KEN:	Urusai! There was nothing wrong with my memory!
MASAKO:	So even if he was here. If you wanted the whole story . . . (MASAKO and DIANE turn to gaze at KEN's photo. He is frozen in salute. Camera flash. Blackout.)

ACT TWO, SCENE THREE

(Lights rise on BEN and DIANE in their bedroom.)

BEN:	Nice outfit.
DIANE:	Thanks. *(He tries to kiss her.)*
DIANE:	I have to get up early tomorrow. Only two days before we meet with the judge.
BEN:	Yeah. How could I forget. *(He turns away.)*
DIANE:	Good night.
BEN:	*(Coolly.)* Good night. *(DIANE turns to BEN.)*
DIANE:	What's wrong?
BEN:	Nothing.
DIANE:	Oh God. I know that tone.
BEN:	I'm tired.
DIANE:	Yeah, right. You were hot to trot a minute ago. *(A moment.)* OK. 'Fess up. *(Silence.)* Now I'm really worried. *(More silence.)* What is it? You're not mad because I didn't want to—
BEN:	It's not just that.

DIANE: Then what?

BEN: It's true, isn't it? You don't really want to have a kid.

DIANE: I want to, but with the case, MP, my dad . . . I can't. Not now.

BEN: But you won't. Ever. I can't believe I missed all the signs. *(Lights shift. BEN and DIANE stand; BEN throws a coat over DIANE's La Perla chemise.)*

DIANE: Remember what they told us. All kinds of things could go wrong. *(We are in a memory. DOCTOR and NURSE appear, each in a pool of light. BEN and DIANE face DOCTOR and NURSE, who offer rapid-fire, parodically dire pronouncements.)*

DOCTOR: You're an elderly primigravida.

BEN: What?

NURSE: A little long in the tooth to be a first-time mother.

DOCTOR: And you're at greater risk for.

NURSE: Birth defects.

DOCTOR: Diabetes.

NURSE: Preeclampsia.

BEN: What's that?

DOCTOR: Pregnancy-induced hypertension.

NURSE: It can cause kidney problems.

DOCTOR: In the worst cases, the mother may have seizures.

NURSE: Or even die.

DIANE: And remember the other complications.

DOCTOR: Harder labor.

NURSE: More C-sections.

DOCTOR: More forceps deliveries.

NURSE: Placental problems.

DOCTOR: Miscarriages.

NURSE: Stillbirths.

DOCTOR: Frankly speaking.

DOCTOR and NURSE:
It's a mess. *(Back to the present.)*

BEN: You're completely exaggerating.

DIANE: But it sounded so dire.

BEN: Wait a minute. They said. *(Lights up on a memory of DOCTOR and NURSE.)*

DOCTOR: Keeping track of schedules and giving shots can be tedious. But if you keep to it religiously.

DOCTOR and NURSE:
Your chances are excellent. *(Blackout on DOCTOR and NURSE. Back to the bedroom.)*

DIANE: That's not what I remember.

BEN: Selective memory. You *made* it dire. And then there was . . . *(Lights shift to the past.)*

DIANE: I barely had time to go to the gynecologist for the one appointment, much less do all the turkey basting or whatever.

BEN: I know it'll be hard, but if anyone can find a way to do both, it would be you.

DIANE: Are you kidding? You know how it is. How could I give them 200 percent? They'd never say it was because you're a woman, but pregnancy? Swollen belly. Morning sickness. Exhaustion. My whole body would be like a neon sign: "Divided loyalty. Divided loyalty." *(Back to reality.)* I think you're the one suffering from selective memory. You seem to have conveniently forgotten my mantra. *(Lights shift to the past.)* Our baby will be brilliant. Devastatingly good-looking. Olympic athlete. Brain surgeon *and* artist.

	A Supreme Court justice. In fact, chief justice. President. Nobel Prize winner. The most fabulous child ever. And of course she.
BEN:	Or he.
DIANE:	Will go to Harvard. Adams House.
BEN:	I'd go for Dunster, myself. Or one of the Radcliffe houses. Less pretentious.
DIANE:	But Radcliffe is so far from the Square. *(BEN glares.)*
DIANE:	OK, OK. Whatever she—or he—wants. But one thing's for sure. With us as her parents, how can she.
BEN:	Or he.
BEN and DIANE:	Go wrong? *(Back to reality.)*
BEN:	You said it only once. And it was so long ago! We were still undergrads! Having dinner at Grendel's.
DIANE:	I've said it a bunch of times. But it wasn't at Grendel's. It was Café Pamplona.
BEN:	It was Grendel's. I remember the dark. You ordered something with tofu.
DIANE:	You and I never went to Grendel's.
BEN:	Hell yeah, we did. How can you avoid it? There are only so many places in the Square.
DIANE:	I think you're confusing me with some other Asian woman. Becky Chan? Your big love?
BEN:	I'll never hear the end of that one. Yes, until I met you. And no, I'm positive it was you at Grendel's. You were wearing that red sweater / I like so much.
DIANE:	You're completely delusional. It was Café Pamplona. And I was dressed in black. It was the only color I wore then!
BEN:	I could swear—

DIANE: And you've conveniently forgotten that I used to talk about it in law school. Remember the time when we were studying together at Sterling?

BEN: We studied at Sterling every day of the week! You never said anything about kids. Wait. Maybe once. At Atticus. You found a book on motherhood or something.

DIANE: Whatever. It doesn't matter.

BEN: Hell yeah, it does.

DIANE: You're completely wrong about Atticus. But at least concede the point.

BEN: Which point?

DIANE: That I talked about—

BEN: That's ancient history! It's not like you've been gushing about having a kid in—oh, the last fifteen years.

DIANE: That's so unfair. What about this year? *(Lights shift to the past.)* I'm taking the afternoon off, so I can see the fertility specialist. *(Back to the bedroom.)*

DIANE: What more do I have to do? I've taken off from work. I've done all this research. We've spent a year trying. My God, all I do is work and go to the doctor! I never even have time to see friends! After I make managing partner—

BEN: Look, I know you need some space. Your dad. The case.

DIANE: Thank God you understand! I was worried for a minute.

BEN: But the clock is ticking.

DIANE: It's just a little while longer. Whatever happens, we'll make it through.

BEN: I'm not so sure.

DIANE: What are you saying? We're soulmates. Together forever. I'll keep trying. But no matter what, aren't we more important than . . . progeny?

BEN: But having a family is everything to me. I thought you understood that. Maybe it's atavistic, but this . . . drive to keep our people going. It's in the blood. I can't just excise it like a tumor. We had a pact. *(She reaches out to him. BEN turns away. DIANE tries to soothe him as she speaks.)*

DIANE: Sweetie, we're going to France this summer. Our second honeymoon. Maybe we'll get pregnant. But if not, not. It might take you a little time to get used to it but—

BEN: If not, not? *(BEN pushes her away and starts to walk out of the bedroom. DIANE follows him, grabs his arm.)*

DIANE: But, sweetie—

BEN: I'm never gonna "get used to it." You can't make this better. *(He wrests his arm from her grasp, exits. Lights rise on GRANDMA. GRANDMA and DIANE stare at the bedroom door, then lock gazes, as lights fade.)*

ACT TWO, SCENE FOUR

(Morning. The lights are especially bright. DIANE is in her kitchen, with a mug of coffee and a pile of papers. She looks exhausted. As she reads, something catches her eye. She grabs the document, rifles through papers. The doorbell rings. MASAKO enters, carrying a grocery bag brimming over with containers of prepared food.)

DIANE: You're a little early.

MASAKO: I'll do this. You're busy. *(She takes a good look at DIANE.)* You don't look so good.

DIANE: I was up all night.

MASAKO: You shouldn't be doing that anymore. You're not in college.

DIANE: Don't remind me.

MASAKO: Go ahead. Finish your work. *(DIANE returns to her laptop, as MASAKO puts away the food.)*

DIANE: I'm having a hard time with this case.

MASAKO: Looks important. I probably wouldn't understand.

DIANE: Maybe not the details, but it's a discrimination case. One person is suing, but it's worse than I'd realized. Minorities and women aren't getting the same salaries or getting promoted as often.

MASAKO: Reminds me of nihonjin haiseki.

DIANE: What?

MASAKO: Nihonjin haiseki. Before the war. Even after the war. People wouldn't serve us. Or help us at the store. Or even cut our hair. *(DIANE stops short.)*

DIANE: Mom, you've never talked about that before!

MASAKO: You never asked.

DIANE: I didn't think I was supposed to. Why didn't you ever say anything?

MASAKO: We didn't want to burden you with all those depressing things. But I guess you have to see haiseki anyway.

DIANE: Well, people are being kept out of upper management. *(Beat.)* And my job is to explain it away.

MASAKO: So you're helping the company, not the people?

DIANE: Yup.

MASAKO: Seems like you'd want to help the people getting passed over. They should get reparations.

DIANE: Mom, I need to get the case dismissed if I want to make managing partner.

MASAKO: Sō ka ne.

DIANE: Oh, don't pull that Japanese-y shit on me.

MASAKO: I'm not pulling anything.

DIANE: I have to do some thinking.

MASAKO:	At least now you won't have to cook. I got up extra early so I could get Mrs. Hasegawa's sushi.
DIANE:	Thanks, Mom. Mrs. Hasegawa's sushi is pretty good. Maybe not as good as Grandma Kubota's, but—
MASAKO:	Aw, Grandma Kubota's wasn't that good.
DIANE:	What do you mean?
MASAKO:	All those years I had to listen to her monku.
DIANE:	What?
MASAKO:	Never good enough for her son. I was just a poor farm girl. She wanted somebody more "high tone,"' cause her son was a doctor.
DIANE:	But I thought you two got along.
MASAKO:	You were always playing with your cousins. You never came into the kitchen.
DIANE:	I had no idea.
MASAKO:	Now that she's gone, it's easier. *(Pause.)* Besides, those Buddhist ladies make good makizushi.
DIANE:	Yeah, they do all right.
MASAKO:	You're so busy now, I know you can't take time to go. *(Pause.)* Looks like you still got a lot to do. *(MASAKO gathers herself to leave.)* Say hi to Ben.
DIANE:	I'm not sure where he is.
MASAKO:	What do you mean?
DIANE:	He spent the night at Larry's. *(Pause.)* He and I have been having some issues lately.
MASAKO:	Like what?
DIANE:	I . . . decided I don't want kids. After all these years.
MASAKO:	Huh.

DIANE: It's been kind of a shock to Ben. *(Pause.)* Did you have your heart set on grandchildren?

MASAKO: Grandchildren are OK as long as I don't have to babysit. I'm too old for that. *(Pause.)* Childbirth is scary, you know. The women in our family . . .

DIANE: So what *did* happen to your mom?

MASAKO: Aw, someday I'll tell you, but not now. *(Lights shift. GRANDMA appears in spotlight, writhing in childbirth. MASAKO and DIANE watch, transfixed. Blackout on childbirth scene.)* Things have changed. Doctors are better now.

DIANE: So you don't care if I have kids?

MASAKO: Whatever makes you happy. Kids are a lot of work. You can't be like you are now.

DIANE: I know. Unless Ben and I can compromise, I'm afraid we won't make it. *(MASAKO stands stiffly upright, as though uttering a weighty proclamation.)*

MASAKO: Omaesan. Marriage is about sacrifice.

DIANE: That's where you and I are different, Mom. *(Pause.)* I can't be like you. *(They stare at each other.)*

MASAKO: I sacrificed for your daddy. And for you. So you wouldn't have to be like me. I sacrificed so you could be independent. You have all the chances I never had. I didn't have a choice. You do.

DIANE: And I'm trying to make the most of—

MASAKO: If I had to do it over, I wouldn't marry your daddy.

DIANE: What are you saying!

MASAKO: Your daddy and I had a good life together. But the truth is, if I had all your choices—I wouldn't get married at all. *(They stare at each other from separate pools of light. MASAKO breaks the gaze and starts to walk away, then faces DIANE once again.)* So you don't have to sacrifice. You should stand up for yourself. If you don't want to have a baby, don't. If he can't accept it, kick him out. *(MASAKO exits. Lights fade to black.)*

ACT TWO, SCENE FIVE

(DIANE stands center stage.)

DIANE: After Mom left, this incident from college keeps popping up in my head. Something I'd totally forgotten. *(Pause.)* You know, France wasn't completely perfect. In everyday life you always have a few hassles. Like the unwanted attention young girls get from men. You know how the French are. Walking down the streets of Paris was like running the gauntlet. "La jolie chinoise." "La petite vietnamienne." Never just "la jolie jeune fille." Once I was strolling down the rue de Rivoli. On my way to the designer boutiques, where I used to linger, staring through the windows at the mannequins. I wanted to be *that* woman. Impossibly chic. Impossibly elegant. *(Beat.)* A group of young guys—they looked about junior high age—shouted at me, "Tu manges beaucoup de riz?" "You eat a lot of rice?" I breezed past them, strode down the street, pretending I didn't hear. I lifted my head even higher. If I didn't acknowledge it, it wasn't there. *(Pause.)* But that feeling. Like they'd torn off my disguise. Revealed the difference I could never erase. *(DIANE lights up.)* Like Proust, right? A Jewish man and an "invert," as it was so charmingly called. The years of the Dreyfus Affair, when France was riven by anti-Semitism. Proust gained entrée to the beau monde. But he was always an observer. Always apart. Never completely safe. *(Beat.)* Huh. I never thought of that before. *(Blackout.)*

ACT TWO, SCENE SIX

(The next day. DIANE stares at a mirror, getting ready for work. She examines her reflection critically, checking for the slightest hint of imperfection. She breaks down for a moment.

Conflicting voices—over-the-top, needling, funny—assail her, in rapid-fire exchanges. KATHLEEN *enters, bearing a briefcase, and thrusts it into* DIANE's *hands.*)

KATHLEEN: Don't forget this. (DIANE *rifles through it.*)

KATHLEEN: A little distraught?

DIANE: I'm fine. (KATHLEEN *approaches* DIANE, *peers at her closely.*)

KATHLEEN: Mascara's a little smudgy.

DIANE: Shit. (DIANE *madly wipes off the smudges.* KATHLEEN *whips out a tube of Great Lash and gives it to* DIANE, *who reapplies her mascara and fixes her makeup as they exchange barbs.*)

KATHLEEN: I saw the trouble with hubby.

DIANE: He's going to leave me.

KATHLEEN: Bad timing, eh?

DIANE: Never a good time for that sort of thing.

KATHLEEN: But you still have to soldier on.

DIANE: This is my day of glory.

KATHLEEN: Or ignominious defeat.

DIANE: I love the vote of confidence.

KATHLEEN: The judge will never throw out the case.

DIANE: I'm gonna do my best to / convince him.

KATHLEEN: Too bad there were so many lawyers like you when your parents were carted off to the camps.

DIANE: That is totally unfair.

KATHLEEN: You could have been a hero. Like one of the Sansei lawyers who led the redress movement. Brilliant strategy. Used the doctrine of coram nobis to win reparations.

DIANE: Oh my God! Enough of your guilt trips!

KATHLEEN: In fact, you could even be more like Ben. Do more pro bono work for the downtrodden.

DIANE: Go back to Cambridge and prep for your stupid tenure.

KATHLEEN: Just remember. Coram nobis. Pro bono. Coram nobis. Pro bono. *(DIANE throws the tube of mascara at KATHLEEN. Blackout on KATHLEEN. Lights up on MASAKO and KEN.)*

DIANE: Dad! I thought you were dead.

KEN: I thought I should come back. Looks like you need some help.

MASAKO: You should listen to that lady.

KEN: She know's what she's talking about.

DIANE: She's full of shit.

KEN: We sent you to Harvard to learn that dirty language?

MASAKO: Uchi no ojōsan wa totemo ogyōgi ga warui desu.

DIANE: OK, so I used a curse word. She's still full of it.

MASAKO: It seems like you'd be for the people who suffered—like us.

KEN: Nihonjin haiseki.

DIANE: But you never told me that you suffered.

MASAKO and KEN: You never asked.

DIANE: I did too! And you didn't say anything.

MASAKO: Well, we wanted you to ask again.

KEN: But we just couldn't say it.

MASAKO: Unless you ask again.

KEN: And again.

MASAKO: We'll die.

KEN: And you'll never know us.

MASAKO: Our history.

KEN: What we went through.

MASAKO and KEN:
Gone forever.

DIANE: Nothing like an unbearable burden of guilt.

MASAKO and KEN:
What are parents for? *(Blackout on MASAKO and KEN. ANDREW is represented by a booming voice.)*

ANDREW: Don't listen to them. You'd better win. Get that case thrown out.

DIANE: But what if I don't?

ANDREW: Then managing partner is down the tubes. We'll give it to Simpson.

DIANE: But he's such a prick!

ANDREW: He's one of the boys. Not like you.

DIANE: But I can't be one of the boys.

ANDREW: Then you have to be better than the boys. Win big, baby. *(Spotlight on BEN, who holds a "baby.")*

DIANE: What are you doing here? You were going to chill out at Larry's.

BEN: I came to remind you. What we could have had. What we can still have. *(He grabs her, puts one arm around her and gives DIANE the baby. A family portrait. Camera flash. DIANE tries to bolt, but BEN pushes a script into her hands.)* Here. Read this. With feeling. *(DIANE glares and at first participates reluctantly. By the end, she's smiling like a Stepford Wife.)*

BEN and DIANE:
We're a very happy family.

DIANE: We met in college.

BEN: She had this energy.

DIANE: He had this confidence.

BEN: She seemed so—mysterious.

DIANE: Really? What a weird thing to think! *(BEN glowers and points again to the script.)*

DIANE: OK, OK. He seemed so—worldly.

BEN: A woman of depth.

DIANE: A man of substance.

BEN: Her smile.

DIANE: His eyes.

BEN and DIANE:
We fell in love.

BEN: And now, at last.

DIANE: Our family is complete.

BEN: A child.

DIANE: The perfect blend.

BEN: Of East and West.

DIANE: A symbol of democracy.

BEN: People have called us.

BEN and DIANE:
The perfect multicultural family.

DIANE: All of us interwoven—

BEN and DIANE:
In a seamless whole. *(They gaze at each other rapturously, then DIANE looks down quizzically at the baby, at BEN, at herself.)*

DIANE: Wait a minute. Are you nuts? *(She grabs the "baby" and throws it at BEN.)*

BEN: Hey! Stop that!

DIANE: This is ridiculous.

BEN: If you won't have my baby, I'll have one with someone else. Someone better.

DIANE: Oh yeah? Who?

BEN: Blair Winthrop.

DIANE: That WASPY bitch?

BEN: She's hot. And she wants kids.

DIANE: I *knew* you had a shiksa goddess fetish!

BEN: She's blonde. A blueblood.

DIANE: Gee. Sorry my grandparents were poor Japanese farmers.

BEN: Blair's rich. Fertile. We'll be blissfully happy. And you'll be a lonely, miserable workaholic. *(Lights up on KATHLEEN, MASAKO, KEN, and BEN, who grab DIANE and pull her in different directions. ANDREW is a booming voice.)*

KATHLEEN: Give up.

BEN: Give birth.

MASAKO and KEN:
Remember.

ANDREW: Win.

KATHLEEN: Give up.

BEN: Give birth.

MASAKO and KEN:
Remember.

ANDREW: Win.

KATHLEEN: Give up.

BEN: Give birth.

MASAKO and KEN:
Remember.

ANDREW: Win.

KATHLEEN: Give up.

BEN: Give birth.

MASAKO and KEN: Remember.

ANDREW: Win. *(DIANE frees herself from the tug of war and turns to face them.)*

DIANE: Stop it, all of you! *(Blackout on MASAKO, KEN, KATHLEEN, and BEN. DIANE takes one last look in the mirror, grabs the briefcase, and walks out briskly.)*

ACT TWO, SCENE SEVEN

(DIANE stands center stage, phone to her ear.)

DIANE: Andrew. It's me. Great. Listen, I need to talk to you. *(Pause.)* The motion didn't work. We have to go to trial. *(Pause.)* I tried my best. Our top associates. . . . Yes, I know our clients aren't happy. I'm sorry. But they have to think long-term. If they don't clean up their business practices, they set themselves up for another lawsuit down the road. *(Pause.)* I'm sorry you feel that way. I did my best for the firm. *(Beat.)* Andrew. I need to tell you something. I can't continue with this case. I know everyone deserves the best representation. But I just can't ethically justify— *(Pause.)* Sure. I understand. I figured as much. Well . . . I guess Simpson is your man. *(She lowers the phone. Fadeout.)*

ACT TWO, SCENE EIGHT

(DIANE walks into the kitchen. BEN is going through the cupboards and drawers, selecting kitchenware to pack into a cardboard box.)

DIANE: What are you doing?

BEN: Hello to you too. Just packing a few things I might need.

DIANE: But it looks so . . . final.

BEN: Well, what did you expect?

DIANE: I guess I hadn't thought about . . . *(She gestures toward the boxes.)*

BEN: This is what moving out looks like.

DIANE: Guess so.

BEN: What are you doing home so early? How did it go?

DIANE: The judge ruled against us.

BEN: That sucks!

DIANE: It's going to trial. Without me.

BEN: After all the work you've done?

DIANE: I just couldn't go through with it. Andrew's giving the trial to Simpson. So much for MP.

BEN: Assholes. Both of 'em.

DIANE: Am I crazy? What have I done to myself?

BEN: I'm proud of you. You did the right thing. *(DIANE's face crumples. BEN embraces her.)*

DIANE: You can be so incredibly sweet. *(Beat.)* I just wish you weren't so rigid about the kid thing. *(They separate.)*

BEN: We've been through this a million times. Let's just get this over with. *(He picks up a Cuisinart food processor and puts it in a box.)*

DIANE: Hey! You can't take that! *(DIANE grabs the Cuisinart.)* You can't just take everything that was ours.

BEN: I'm the one who cooks. You won't miss it a bit.

DIANE: Yes I will! It was our wedding present.

BEN: Along with everything else in the kitchen. Don't worry. I'm not taking everything. Just a few things I use and you

	don't. If you really miss 'em, I'll bring 'em back, but I know you. You won't.
DIANE:	Don't be so sure about that! *(They struggle over the food processor for a minute.)*
BEN:	Diane, don't be ridiculous. Are you going to start pureeing stuff all of a sudden? *(He wrestles the Cuisinart away from her and gently places it into the box.)*
DIANE:	We were supposed to be together forever. We didn't even get a chance to go to Paris. *(BEN stops short, glares.)* I know. The case. *(BEN takes a long look at her. Beat.)*
BEN:	Hey. The case is over now. Fresh start. *(Pause.)* You've had a tough day. Let me make you dinner. I'm really good at pureeing. *(DIANE touches BEN's face.)*
DIANE:	I've got a lot to figure out.
BEN:	Look, I know the MP thing is disappointing. But maybe it's an opportunity in disguise. You could rethink your life. Whether you'll stay at the firm. Whether the corporate dream is really what you want. *(He tentatively gives it one last try.)* Maybe you'll even think about having a family? *(DIANE speaks through tears.)*
DIANE:	Never. *("Soave sia il vento" from Mozart's Così fan Tutte plays softly. BEN turns away, finishes packing the box, closes it. DIANE approaches him. They hold each other tightly for a moment. BEN picks up the box and exits. Lights rise on KATHLEEN, who sits on the counter, taking notes furiously. DIANE and KATHLEEN exchange a look, as lights fade to black.)*

ACT TWO, SCENE NINE

	(DIANE enters her parents' garage carrying a cardboard box.)
DIANE:	*(Shouting.)* Mom? I'm just gonna put this in the garage for now, OK? Just some more stuff for the estate sale.

MASAKO (O.S.): Leave it out in the middle. *(DIANE puts down the box, opens it, and takes out a volume of Proust.)*

DIANE: Proust. Ben and I never made it to his village. *(She breaks down. MASAKO enters.)*

MASAKO: What's the matter?

DIANE: Oh, nothing.

MASAKO: Omaesan. It's OK. *(Pause.)* I know it's hard right now. But you'll figure out what to do.

DIANE: Doesn't really feel that way.

MASAKO: Just give it some time. *(Pause.)* So . . . you're not going back to Ben?

DIANE: As long as he wants kids, I don't see how.

MASAKO: Sō, ne. But what about your job?

DIANE: I don't know. Can I stay in a firm where I'm just window dressing? Working under Simpson? I just don't know how much better it would be anywhere else.

MASAKO: You could go on a vacation.

DIANE: Maybe I should. *(Wryly.)* To France, maybe.

MASAKO: Wherever you want.

DIANE: Right. *(Pause.)* Well, shall we get down to work? *(MASAKO nods. DIANE opens a box and rummages through its contents. She finds an old forties-style sweater and holds it up.)* Look at this sweater. It must be ancient. *(She takes out a skirt patterned in houndstooth checks.)* And this.

MASAKO: We were so poor I used to have only two sweaters and two skirts. Wore one one day, washed it the other. I was so sick of houndstooth.

DIANE: Why don't you just throw it away?

MASAKO: I want to remember that we survived those hard times. The Depression. Just leave it. *(DIANE continues to dig. She*

	finds an old music box. We hear the tune "Shina no yoru.") "Shina no yoru." Remember it from when you were little?
DIANE:	I always thought it was so Japanese-y. (*DIANE drops the music box on top of the clothes.*)
MASAKO:	Don't throw it around! You'll break it!
DIANE:	Sorry. (*DIANE places it more carefully on top of the clothes.*) There.
MASAKO:	I had that when I was a teenager.
DIANE:	Ah. (*She stops short.*) Wait. Does that mean . . . when you were in camp?
MASAKO:	Uh huh.
DIANE:	I thought you wanted to forget all about that.
MASAKO:	We could take only what we could carry. It was something I just had to bring. (*MASAKO picks up the music box.*) "Shina no yoru" was my favorite song. Maybe it's because of that part that goes, "Ah AH. Ah AH."
DIANE:	Pretty juicy, all right.
MASAKO:	They played it so much in camp, I could have left it home. But my mother gave it to me.
DIANE:	Grandma?
MASAKO:	It was for my birthday. We didn't have much in those days. I wanted to have something to remember her by.
DIANE:	How old were you when she died?
MASAKO:	I was . . . eleven.
DIANE:	You just said you were a teenager in camp.
MASAKO:	Maybe I was thirteen or fourteen. Who remembers exactly?
DIANE:	So what happened to Grandma?
MASAKO:	Aw, I'll tell you someday.

DIANE: You always say that. But I need to know.

MASAKO: It's not important.

DIANE: Are you kidding? It's this deep, dark, icky secret. So terrible no one could ever talk about it.

MASAKO: I don't want to tell you terrible things.

DIANE: But what I imagine might be even more terrible. Tell me, Mom. Please.

MASAKO: Aw, I don't know.

DIANE: Please.

MASAKO: Some other time.

DIANE: Mom! *(Harsh lights reveal a scene of childbirth.* GRANDMA *lies screaming on a table. A* WHITE DOCTOR, *played by the actor who plays* BEN, *attends her.* MASAKO *becomes her childhood self. The screaming is intolerable.* MASAKO *runs up to the* DOCTOR.*)*

MASAKO: Can't you do something?

WHITE DOCTOR: Don't worry, little girl. I'm doing the best I can.

MASAKO: But my mommy's hurting.

WHITE DOCTOR: It hurts to have a baby. Go away. I have a job to do. *(He continues his ministrations.* MASAKO *reenters the present.)*

MASAKO: We heard her scream. All night. *(The screams gradually subside. Silence. The* DOCTOR *pulls a sheet over* GRANDMA's *body. The table is bloody.)*

WHITE DOCTOR: I'm sorry.

MASAKO: The nurse told me, "It was the most terrible death I've ever seen." *(*WHITE DOCTOR *picks up a cigar.)*

WHITE DOCTOR: Mind if I smoke this? It'd be a shame for it to go to waste.

        (He lights up, smoking the cigar with gusto. MASAKO goes to the childbirth table, removes a sheet.)

MASAKO: I had to wash the bloody sheets. *(MASAKO takes a sheet and spreads it out so we see the blood. Blackout on the childbirth tableau.)*

DIANE: That's horrible!

MASAKO: What can you do? It can't be helped.

DIANE: So what went wrong?

MASAKO: It was placenta previa.

DIANE: What's that?

MASAKO: The placenta lies too low in the uterus. The baby is sideways or upside down. The placenta can tear easily. You can bleed to death. Grandma and the baby both died. She was only thirty-seven.

DIANE: Younger than I am.

MASAKO: I became the mother. For years after, I used to dream of her. Every night. Rising from the coffin. *(GRANDMA appears, picking gladiolas.)* Coming into the house. Carrying gladiolas from the garden.

GRANDMA: I was a moga, a modan gaaru. I spoke English.

MASAKO: Most of the Issei women didn't speak English.

GRANDMA: I acted in plays.

MASAKO: She was outgoing. She sang shigin, Japanese poetry.

GRANDMA: I even drove.

MASAKO: Most Issei women didn't drive.

GRANDMA: I had all kinds of friends. Even hakujin.

MASAKO: Most of the Issei kept to themselves. Not your grandma. *(To us.)* My mother. So gracious.

DIANE: My grandma. So happy.

MASAKO and DIANE: It was the most terrible death I've ever seen. *(Lights fade.)*

ACT TWO, SCENE TEN

(DIANE is in bed, tossing and turning. GRANDMA watches. DIANE wakes up, wild-eyed. Blackout on GRANDMA.)

DIANE: Fuck. *(She grabs her laptop. A screen upstage represents her computer monitor. She types on the keyboard.)* Chisao Tamura. She has to be in the database. *(The screen is blank.)* This can't be right. Mom said their family was at Heart Mountain. *(DATABASE speaks in spotlight.)*

DATABASE: The name you requested could not be found.

DIANE: What the . . . ? *(She pounds the keyboard, presses return. The museum's website speaks.)*

MUSEUM WEBSITE: Please consult the archives at the Japanese American National Museum. Due to budget cuts, we are open from 11 to 2 on the weekends only.

DIANE: Are you kidding me?

MUSEUM WEBSITE: If you want to donate a few hundred thousand to keep us open all week, we'll gladly take it. *(Lights shift. DIANE is at the Museum. ARCHIVIST appears.)*

ARCHIVIST: The records you requested. *(ARCHIVIST hands a sheaf of papers to DIANE, who frantically leafs through them.)*

DIANE: Grandma isn't here. It doesn't make sense. There's my grandfather. And look who's listed as head of household!

ARCHIVIST: Masako Tamura.

DIANE: My mom. Where's Grandma?

ARCHIVIST: Are you sure she was in camp?

DIANE: My mom's family was in Heart Mountain. Isn't there any other way to find records?

ARCHIVIST: The National Archives. It takes several weeks. You request the form, send it back by snail mail, then they have to find the files and Xerox everything. Or scan it onto CD.

DIANE: You mean they can't just pdf it?

ARCHIVIST: Nope. Maybe they can computerize everything one day, but—

DIANE: The budget cuts.

ARCHIVIST: Precisely.

DIANE: What about medical records? Hospital records?

ARCHIVIST: National Archives.

DIANE: Shit. What's a girl to do? *(Lights change. Weeks later. DIANE bears a CD, puts it in the computer.)*

DIANE: Finally! *(We see page after page of data. CD speaks.)*

CD: Chisao Tamura, maiden name Shima, died in Hood River.

DIANE: But that can't be! She was in camp!

CD: She died seven years before camp.

DIANE: But it's impossible. My mom said—*(MASAKO appears.)*

MASAKO: I never said your grandma died in camp. She died at home. All six of us kids heard her screaming all night. I was only . . . eleven. I had to become the mother. That's why I was head of household.

DIANE: But why didn't you tell me?

MASAKO: You never asked. *(Lights up on GRANDMA, who bears a bouquet of gladiolas.)*

GRANDMA: Gonna take a sentimental journey. Gonna set my heart at ease.

DIANE: So what's this about? *(DIANE gestures toward GRANDMA.)*

MASAKO: Your grandma never sang "Sentimental Journey." She sang shigin.

DIANE: What's that?

MASAKO: Japanese poetry. She could speak English, but she usually sang in Japanese.

(*Blackout on* GRANDMA.)

DIANE: So am I nuts? Where did that song come from?

MASAKO: Your Uncle Shōji. That was his favorite song.

DIANE: He died before I was born?

MASAKO: He was only twenty.

DIANE: How did he die?

MASAKO: TB. They sent him to Japan in the Occupation, but he was already sick. They shipped him back here. I visited him in the hospital every day.

DIANE: Sounds awful.

MASAKO: He was a soft-hearted kid. Oshii koto, ne.

DIANE: Mom. Translation, please.

MASAKO: What a waste. He was special. Too bad you never knew him.

DIANE: Guess there's a lot I don't know. So if I ask you, maybe you'll tell me?

MASAKO: Oh, I don't know.

DIANE: But Mom, you're always saying, "You never asked." I'm asking.

MASAKO: I'll be in the kitchen. (*Does she mean she will talk someday? Now? Never?* MASAKO *exits. Blackout.*)

ACT TWO, SCENE ELEVEN

(DIANE *is at her desk, checking her email.*)

DIANE: Well, LeBoeuf and Harrison don't want me. Great. (*She scrolls down.*) Oh, no. Not you again. (*Spotlight on* KATHLEEN.)

KATHLEEN: The study on the intergenerational impact of Japanese American internment thanks you for your participation in our study.

DIANE: So what do you want now?

KATHLEEN: You have been selected for a second round of in-depth interviews. Your participation will contribute to our knowledge of the effects of internment—

DIANE: Knowledge? It's just mystery after mystery. *(KATHLEEN steps into DIANE's reality.)*

KATHLEEN: What mystery? You've already discovered so much! That your grandmother died in childbirth, thanks to a racist doctor. That—

DIANE: But I'm just more confused. My grandma died before camp.

KATHLEEN: So? The camps wouldn't have happened if not for racism.

DIANE: Who knows how much race was involved? Medicine was terrible back then. Lots of women died.

KATHLEEN: But you decided you didn't want to have children and your marriage broke up because you're haunted by your grandma. Look at the weight of history!

DIANE: I don't know! Is that the reason? Maybe I never really wanted kids in the first place. Why does everyone have to have kids anyway?

KATHLEEN: You're ignoring the evidence! Clearly—

DIANE: But nothing is clear. Internment isn't the cause of *everything*.

KATHLEEN: We're gathering knowledge.

DIANE: A smidgen of this. A shred of that.

KATHLEEN: Little by little.

DIANE: I used to think I knew what I wanted. But now? Nothing is certain.

KATHLEEN: Uncertainty opens possibilities.

DIANE: But I've lost everything. My husband.

KATHLEEN: You discovered you weren't compatible anyway.

DIANE: Yeah? What about my job?

KATHLEEN: You actually care about ethics and justice more than money and status.

DIANE: Well, Miss Smarty Pants, what about my dad? Come up with a sound bite for that one!

KATHLEEN: You tried to learn about your dad as a person. You discovered how precious your parents are.

DIANE: Too little too late.

KATHLEEN: You have some inkling now of the depth of your loss. If we didn't care about each other, we wouldn't feel the pain.

DIANE: You sound like Kahlil Gibran.

KATHLEEN: Loss is part of human life. Get used to it.

DIANE: But I can't! I even lost my dream!

KATHLEEN: Face it, honey. It was a fucked-up dream.

DIANE: Hey, isn't that unprofessional language?

KATHLEEN: I'm in your head, babe. I can say anything I want.

DIANE: Go away! It's getting way too noisy in here!

KATHLEEN: Dear me. Uncertainty, unraveling the fine fabric of your seamlessly perfect life. *(She perches on DIANE's desk.)*

DIANE: Who knows what'll happen? It's scary.

KATHLEEN: And exciting.

DIANE: You can't put a positive / spin on—

KATHLEEN: You've gotta tear down in order to rebuild. You watch HGTV. You should know that.

DIANE: Enough with the platitudes.

KATHLEEN: So give us the interview.

DIANE: For all the good it'll do.

KATHLEEN: No one can know everything. But we still have to try. Come on.
(KATHLEEN *gestures for* DIANE *to join her. Beat.*)

DIANE: No. I've had enough.

KATHLEEN: But my "N" isn't big enough! I need more respondents!

DIANE: The size of your N is not my problem.

KATHLEEN: Pretty please. You won't / regret it.

DIANE: Out! I want my own search for lost time. (*Blackout on* KATHLEEN. DIANE *no longer needs her.*)

ACT TWO, SCENE TWELVE

(*Lights shift.* DIANE *moves to center stage.*)

DIANE: On a different note. A few months later, Ben and I divorced. (*Lights up on* BEN, *sitting at his desk. He continues to work on his legal documents throughout the scene, remaining faintly visible.*) It was amicable. We sold the house, split everything fifty-fifty. He took the Cuisinart. I quit my job. Couldn't bear the thought of working under Simpson. I'm at a new firm. Really landed on my feet. I'm an equity partner, and I have a chance to become managing partner. There are women in upper management. They do labor law—for workers, not employers. And they encourage social responsibility. It's fulfilling. (*She and* BEN *exchange looks.*) I hear he's dating now. I'm . . . almost ready. But I miss him. (*Lights up on* KATHLEEN.) I'm spending more time with Mom these days. Sometimes I ask her questions. She told me a story about how Dad never really asked her to marry him. He asked her to "go to St. Louis." (*Lights rise on* MASAKO.)

MASAKO: Back in those days, people didn't hop into bed like they do now. If we went to St. Louis, we'd have to stay overnight someplace. So of course we'd have to get married.

DIANE: Not very romantic. *(Lights rise on KEN.)*

KEN: Not "mushy." But you don't have to be like hakujin and say, "I love you. Marry me." And get divorced a year later. She knew what I meant.

DIANE: Guess Dad wasn't direct, even with Mom. *(Pause.)* And now and again, I try really hard to remember things I might have heard about camp. *(DIANE turns toward MASAKO.)* I think we were watching Walter Cronkite and something came on about the camps. I thought I heard Dad say . . . *(Lights shift to the past. We hear music from Walter Cronkite's program, The Twentieth Century. KEN steps into the light with MASAKO. Both wear forties-style overcoats. Tags bearing numbers hang from their necks.)*

KEN: Hey, you remember your number? *(KEN and MASAKO laugh wryly.)*

DIANE: I didn't know you had numbers.

MASAKO: Family 16321.

KEN: Family 15513.

DIANE: Like little Oriental packages. Trundled off to the desert.

MASAKO: Block 29-14-B. Heart Mountain.

KEN: Block 65-2-A. Tule Lake.

MASAKO: Middle of the desert.

KEN: Barren.

MASAKO: Desolate.

DIANE: My parents. So harmless.

MASAKO: One suitcase only.

KEN: Losing our land.

MASAKO:	It was . . . hard.
KEN:	Good thing we were young. (*MASAKO and KEN take off their coats. The tags remain suspended from their necks. Blackout on KEN.*)
DIANE:	So what were those numbers about? Did you need them in camp? Were they just for the trip to camp?
MASAKO:	They were like luggage tags. Some people wore them around their necks.
DIANE:	Like you were the luggage. (*MASAKO shrugs.*)
DIANE:	What else did you need the number for? (*Silence.*) Mom? (*Silence.*) I gave up on that topic. And tried something else. (*She turns to MASAKO.*) When you got out of camp, did you go back to the house you'd left?
MASAKO:	When we got back to our old house in Hood River, everything was gone. Even the piano. Everything was filthy. I just sat down and bawled. (*Pause.*) When I went to our neighbors' place to use the phone, I saw *our* linoleum on *their* floor. Boy, that really got to me.
DIANE:	So was that when people wouldn't cut your hair? When you were treated like second-class citizens? Or was there a lot of prejudice before the war? / Were you—
MASAKO:	Too many questions. I don't remember. I don't need to remember. (*Pause.*) I don't want to remember. (*DIANE turns to the audience.*)
DIANE:	I guess she has a point. Then, the other day, a wake-up call.
MASAKO:	Look! I just got a letter from Itty. You know, from Block 34?
DIANE:	Mom, I don't know who you're talking about. I wasn't there.
MASAKO:	Oh that's right. You weren't born yet. (*Lights dim on MASAKO. Spotlight on DIANE standing alone, in the spot she occupied in the family portrait.*)

DIANE: I still ask her questions every so often. She tells me little bits here and there. She never says much. And what she does say . . . who knows what's true and what isn't? It's like trying to piece together a handful of shreds and tatters. Stitch two together and the rest fall through your fingers. I, on the other hand, want a seamless story. Like Proust. *(DIANE picks up* Swann's Way *and reads aloud.)* A whole world, "taking shape and solidity, sprang into being, towns and gardens alike, from my cup of tea." I want Proust's village, whole and vibrant, memories so lush they refuse to be contained in a simple, declarative sentence or a single book. I want Proustian memories, luxuriant tendrils of words that spill over each other, tracing arabesques over thousands of pages and six entire volumes. Memories so exquisitely observed, they seem etched in filigree. *(She puts down the Proust. Beat.)* But Mom and Dad aren't French aristocrats. They weren't surrounded by writers who observed their every peccadillo, every turn of phrase, turning their lives into stories that live on as great art. *(Pause.)* I wish I could give them a story. One that's happy and heroic. A story of resistance. Resilience. The definitive answer. Incontrovertible history. *(Pause.)* But all I have are questions. *(Lights up on MASAKO and KEN. DIANE turns toward her parents.)* How did it feel to lose everything? What was camp really like? How did you manage to recover and go on? *(She turns to her father.)* And you, Dad. Do you have any regrets? Mom said you told her.

KEN: I wasn't a good father to her.

MASAKO: He sprang it on me. I never knew what he meant.

DIANE: Did you mean the Nisei thing? That you weren't emotionally "mushy"? It's OK. I didn't expect it. I thought you were a wonderful father. You died, not knowing.

KEN: There's so much I never told you. *(DIANE turns away from them, finds the music box.)*

DIANE: I have this. *(DIANE picks up the music box, returns it to its place.)* These. *(She picks up the old clothes, returns them to the box.)* Shards of memory. Or are they memories? *(Pause.)* Was my mom eleven? Or fourteen? Does it matter that my grandma died before camp? What stories could Dad have told me? *(DIANE picks up the music box, then the clothes.)* How do these fragments go with all the other fragments?

(We see fractured images: gladiolas, GRANDMA in childbirth, the old farm, the camp barracks, the WHITE DOCTOR with the cigar. KATHLEEN watches with DIANE, then moves upstage. Images fade. DIANE puts down the clothes and winds the music box. "Shina no yoru" plays for a few bars, then cuts off abruptly, as though the music box has broken. And yet . . . a moment, perhaps, of hope? Lights intensify on DIANE, BEN, MASAKO, and KEN, each standing in the same positions they assumed during the family portrait. This time they freeze in separate, fractured pools of light. KATHLEEN exits. Lights fade as DIANE searches among the fragments).

END OF PLAY

notes

Overture

1. As I explain more fully in chapter 2, Los Angeles has hundreds of small theaters with ninety-nine seats or fewer. These theaters do not have to pay Actors' Equity wages.

2. Thanks to Ken Wissoker for this term.

3. Jafari Allen locates "interstitial analysis" in "close attention to lived experience. . . . We must push beyond a few influential . . . scholarly works and political positions. My work . . . privileges the up-close ethnography of everyday practice, which demonstrates . . . that race is (still) lived— . . . inextricable from gender, sexuality, and class" (Allen 2011, 9).

4. See Ramón Rivera-Servera's "theories in practice" (2012).

5. My work on artisanal identities argues that the crafting of objects (or ephemeral objects, like performance) are ways of crafting selves (Kondo 1990).

6. See McAuley (2012); Atkinson (2004). Atkinson attributes the lack of ethnographic attention to opera, symphony, ballet, and theater to the "reverse snobbism" that deems popular culture the proper object of ethnographic analysis.

7. Among anthropology's "participatory observers" is Robert Desjarlais (2012), a competitive chess player who wrote about chess.

8. In preview performances, the playwright may continue to revise; on opening night, writing and production elements are presumably finalized.

9. See Fred Moten (2003) and Uri McMillan (2015) on agency, pleasure, and danger in minoritarian objecthood.

10. See Christen Smith (2016) on the intersections of performance and premature death in Brazil.

11. Jodi Byrd (2011) offers a trenchant critique of both Butler and Berlant as occluding the continuing colonizing dispossession of indigenous peoples.

12. See Giorgio Agamben (1998) and, in particular, Hortense Spillers's (2003) pathbreaking work, including her distinction between body and flesh.

13. As I later elaborate, my use of "affect" takes inspiration from work in psychoanalytic theory in critical race studies and queer of color critique. My approach allies to some degree with the "public feelings" literature (Berlant 2011; Stewart 2007; Cvetkovich 2012) but accords central importance to issues of race that tend to be elided in the work on public feelings. I remain skeptical about strands of affect theory inflected through Brian Massumi's appropriations of Deleuze and neuroscience. The Eurocentricity of these literatures is never interrogated, and "the body" as "real-material-but incorporeal" (Massumi 2002, 5) still depends on an unproblematized, foundational "body" that Maurice Leenhardt (1947) long ago problematized. Sara Ahmed dissects the marginalization of pathbreaking feminist work as mere precursor, among those who herald "affect" as new paradigm (Ahmed 2014, 208–89). "Affect" represents the sensory, potentiality, and abstract energy, while "emotion" seems mired in intentionality and the individual subject. We thus confront yet another transposition of (gendered) mind/body dualisms. "Affect" appears in this scheme to represent the ineffable, that which escapes the specificity of emotion and signification (the two are seen as binding, constraining prior "freedom" figured as potentiality) and inscribes universality: "the virtual co-presence of potentials" (Massumi 2015, 5). Emotion can seem too messy and "stuck" in specificity. As an advocate of fleshy messiness—which is not necessarily antithetical to "rigor" but may not yield to easy classification, closure, or abstraction—I am skeptical about pitting affect *against* emotion. Massumi's version of affect marginalizes both feminism and anthropological studies of emotion. For other critiques, see Wolff (2016), Brinkema (2014), and, importantly, Leys (2011).

Entr'acte 1

1. *Superior Donuts* is now a weekly sitcom on CBS.

Chapter 1. Theoretical Scaffolding, Formal Architecture

1. Writings on multimodality and multisensory ethnography in visual anthropology are expanding literatures on the senses in anthropology and other disciplines. Among notable works are Chio (2017); Classen (1993, 2005); Howes (1991, 2004, 2013); Cox, Irving, and Wright (2016); Pink (2015); Stoller (1997); and Vidali (2015, 2016).

2. For Austin (1962), performatives "say" *and* "do," essaying a socially meaningful action in the world. For Butler (1990), performativity theorizes agency within fields of power, as the (re)iteration of norms that consolidate/subvert normative power. Norms must be continuously enacted, thus introducing possibilities for subversion, consolidation, unfaithful citation. Performativity refigures race not as fixed identity but as fabricated essence and historically, culturally specific citational practice, mining both the coercive and creative potentialities of Foucaultian notions of power (Butler 1987).

3. Rofel (2007) insightfully deconstructs a reified "neoliberalism." She shows how neoliberalism is *made*, in "its" temporal, cultural, geopolitical specificity.

4. Performativity and precarity (Butler 2004a) transpose the subject-structure binary into a different key. Judith Butler argues that gender performativity has everything to do with precarity: who lives a legible life, who is allowed to die. Though race is not her primary concern, precarity clearly shows the imbrications of the subject and the structural, opening ways to think multiple fields of power, including race/racism. An ethics/politics based on our primary vulnerability to each other (Butler 2004a) opens out performativity to this multiplicity, including political action. The next move would turn performativity, precarity, and vulnerability even more explicitly toward race and colonialism: the dispossession of people of color and indigenous peoples, as Nguyen (2016) and Byrd (2011) eloquently argue.

5. New contests over meaning arise: can a formation that was conceived as a leftist/progressive coalition now account for "Asian Americans" who are politically conservative (Nguyen 2002)?

6. Scholars of affect, particularly of the Deleuzian/Massumian persuasions, eschew psychoanalysis in favor of "affect" as physiological, sensory, and as relational—the capacity to affect and be affected. From a different perspective, I am in print as a passionate critic of psychoanalysis, uninterested in subjective "interiority" except as a Foucaultian fabrication of essence (Molino and Ware, 2001).

7. See, e.g., Spillers (2003); Sedgwick (2006); Eng (2010); Muñoz (2006); Cheng (2001); Viego (2007); Stephens (2014); and Chambers-Letson (2006).

8. Here, the subject/world binary, even if fluid, still acts as an epistemological foundation.

9. On reparation, see the special issue of *Women and Performance* 16, no. 2 (2006).

10. Pandian's textually innovative analysis of "creation" in Tamil cinema mobilizes Deleuzian/Massumian/Bergsonian concerns animating affect theory and the new materialisms. He foregrounds "an ecology of creative processes, less an exercise of human agency on an inert . . . world than a way of working resourcefully with the active potential of diverse forces, feelings, beings, and things" (Pandian 2015, 272). "Impersonal forces" seem particularly resonant in the case of cinema, where technologies reign. Performance spotlights "live" embodiment in collaborative interaction with a lively world. Lines between the impersonal and the animate can be differently drawn across space, culture, and time, as my work with Japanese artisans attests. For them, machines and tools are collaborators imbued with spirit (Kondo 1990).

11. Theories of cultural politics, conventional notions of political action, and theater artists themselves recycle these Platonian assumptions. Rancière deconstructs the assumptions of distance and hierarchy between artist and audience that underlie both Brecht's political theater of estrangement and Artaud's theater of cruelty. Further, from Rancière's point of view, those like myself, Kushner, and

Román, who might see a communitarian function in the very notion of theater as a gathering of people in the same space/time, would be problematic, linked to assumptions present in German Romanticism.

12. In this sense, Rancière echoes Lévi-Strauss in *La pensée sauvage* (1962), who argued that all people, including "primitives," utilize equally sophisticated conceptual strategies. This position does not necessarily erase the hierarchy between artist/audience or "savage"/"civilized." "Their" mental operations are as sophisticated as "ours," yet "we" remain the standard for comparison.

13. Nic Ramos (2017) argues that race is a diagnostic for mental illness. Jolie Chea (2015) details the ways Cambodian American coping behavior is read as mental illness by the state. Claudia Rankine (2014) details the ways minoritarian subjects can be perceived as and made to feel "crazy."

14. See S. Williams (2016) for an insightful analysis of what I call reparative mirroring/narcissism.

15. Corporeal epistemologies and dramaturgical critique highlight our locations as embodied participants with inevitably partial knowledge. When staging a play, artistic labor is divided. Few people see the entire process; the director and the stage manager enjoy the most panoramic overviews. Professional duties limit one's ability to have a deep sense of all aspects of the production, but engagement in one's area of expertise in service of a common goal is a rewarding form of participatory knowledge.

16. Sex-positive feminism might see nothing particularly heinous in the logic of pornography. What about Foucault's proliferation of pleasures? Further, as in Sedgwick's case, a hermeneutics of suspicion and the logic of revelation paradoxically structure Chow's argument.

17. See Catherine Belsey (1980) and the Frankfurt School—Adorno, Horkheimer, and Benjamin, among others—and their disputes with Marxist critics such as Lukács.

18. One way to address issues of racial diversity involves nontraditional casting "even" in the classics. For example, Stephen Wadsworth's production of *Agamemnon* at the Getty in 2008 featured Delroy Lindo as Agamemnon and Tyne Daley as Clytemnestra. On nontraditional casting, see chapter 2 of this book; Pao (2010); J. Lee (2003); and Banks (2013).

19. This will never completely preempt a (mis)reading as multicultural multiplicity. I simply underscore the paradoxes of any political intervention; one can simultaneously contest and reinscribe audience readings of individualist, pluralist multiculturalism.

20. Anthropologists and performance studies scholars, among others, have experimented with integrating creative forms with academic writing. These include fiction/short story (Visweswaran 1994; K. M. Brown 1991), memoir (Phelan 1993; Hartman 2007; Behar 2013), episodic writing that enacts intensities and potentialities (Stewart 2007; Pandian 2015), music (Feld 2012), assemblage and rhizomatics (Tsing 2015), and poetry (R. Rosaldo 2013; Pandian and McLean 2017). Textual layout offers opportunities for performative experimentation.

J. Taylor (1998); D. Taylor (2016); and Pandian (2015) visually stage arguments through design, font, spacing, and for Julie Taylor, a flip book.

Drama has occasioned textual innovation, including a full-length play (Savigliano 2003), epigraphs (Chatterjee 2001), a short play (Brody 2008), theater as inspiration for ethnographic writing (Narayan 2012), and solo performance (Ulysse 2017). Johnson and Rivera-Servera (2016) combine performance scripts, interviews, and scholarly articles in their edited volume.

21. See Taussig (1993, 2011); Crapanzano (2004); Stewart (2007); Pandian (2015).

22. See Jakobson and Halle's (1956) analysis of metaphor/metonym and Crapanzano on montage (2004).

23. Thanks to Sophia Li for this insight.

Chapter 2. Racialized Economies

1. These terms reflect different theoretical stances. "Art worlds" (Becker 2008) arises from American empiricist sociology. Howard Becker argues that to understand the arts, we must investigate institutions and staff: "creatives," crew, box office, marketing, audience, suppliers. Aesthetics become a socially produced body of assumptions. "Art industry" evokes the work of the Frankfurt School's Marxist-inflected analysis of the culture industries. Bourdieu's (post)structuralist, neo-Durkheimian "field of cultural production" demarcates domains of academe, fashion, and art, among others, linking "taste" with social structures.

2. A lively discussion on Facebook noted the exclusion of Asian American arts organizations from the article and the DeVos report.

3. The rate runs from seven dollars per performance and free parking in theaters with one to fifty-nine seats and a ticket price of eighteen dollars or less. The wage rises to nine dollars per performance if the run extends for more than four weeks; at nine to twelve weeks, the wages rise to twelve dollars. The highest wage paid according to these regulations is sixteen dollars per performance, in theaters with sixty to ninety-nine seats and a nine- to twelve-week run (Actors' Equity 2013).

4. The membership vote was advisory to the Equity Council. National Equity overrode the vote, still allowing exemptions: (1) theaters with forty-nine seats or fewer (down from the ninety-nine-seat agreement); (2) self-produced work; and (3) membership companies in which members pay dues and donate time in exchange for the chance to be creatively involved in the company.

5. "After adjusting for inflation, average federal funding fell sharply in 2011 from high levels in 2008 to 2010" (Voss and Voss 2012). "In 2010, 2% fewer staged readings and workshop performances were offered than in 2006" (Voss and Voss 2011). Between 2001 and 2006 the number of performances increased by 10 percent; between 2005 and 2006 performances decreased by 7 percent (Voss and Voss 2007).

6. "In 2007, 2% of all federal funding was earmarked for support of touring, dwindling over the years to 0% in 2011" (Voss and Voss 2012).

7. "The average number of people served by outreach and education activity declined slightly over time, from a high of 17,200 in 2007 to a low of 15,400 in 2011" (Voss and Voss 2012, 8).

8. Among playwrights writing for television are Warren Leight (whose salary for one or two episodes for television equaled his earnings for the entire run of his Broadway play *Side Man*), David Mamet, Marsha Norman, David Rambo, Julia Cho, and Itamar Moses.

9. Producers are willing to pay high salaries to stars that could attract an audience. As for the union rank and file, Equity spokesperson Maria Somma stated, "It is Actors' Equity Association policy to keep confidential our members' information, including their earnings. However, Actors' Equity Association negotiates a minimum weekly salary (currently at $1,605). This is the minimum for any Actor—whether the person is making his or her debut, working in the chorus or is the leading Actor. An Actor (or the actor's agent) can negotiate higher than the weekly minimum, but never accept a salary less than the negotiated minimum" (Simonson 2010).

10. Winkler (2017) writes vividly of theater artists' financial struggles to survive in New York.

11. Even within a single institution, significant structural differences can exist. At USC playwrights could hold positions in either the School of Dramatic Arts (structural equal to the College of Letters and Sciences, Cinema, Business) or the Masters in Professional Writing Program in the college. Therefore, SDA (formerly the School of Theater) holds far greater structural power. It can offer tenure, and its dean is equal to the deans of the other schools. Instructors in the Masters of Professional Writing Program held non-tenure-track appointments that were evaluated yearly. The program was dissolved in 2016.

12. Due to open-heart surgery and a lengthy recovery.

13. See Catanese (2011); Pao (2010); Kondo (1997); Gallela (2015); and J. Lee (1998).

14. Thanks to Yael Prizant for this insight.

15. Better known are casting controversies over "whitewashing" in cinema: e.g., Scarlett Johansson in *Ghost in the Shell* (a Japanese girl in the original anime) or Matt Damon in *The Great Wall*. The assumption is that protagonists of color cannot attract large audiences. We will see whether *Black Panther*, *A Wrinkle in Time*, and *Coco* open more possibilities for actors of color, including Asian Americans.

Chapter 3. (En)Acting Theory

1. There were three major versions of *Twilight*; the world premiere at the Mark Taper Forum, where I served as dramaturg, ran for ninety minutes without intermission.

2. For analyses of the evolution of Stanislavski's thought, see Carnicke (2008). For an insightful analysis of acting theory, see Pang (1991).

3. Jay (2007, 125) argues that "performative empathy . . . helps us see the gaps between our own understanding and the perceptions of the subject whom we reenact."

4. Many have challenged the Method and its assumptions: the avant-garde and non-Western theater generally, as well as artists such as Jerzy Grotowski, Antonin Artaud, Eugenio Barba, Tadashi Suzuki, and SITI Company. Smith's challenges to conventional acting theory address race and power in ways these other forms do not. Feminist critics have mounted critiques of hegemonic theatrical representation, the Method, and Stanislavski, including Case (1995); Dolan (1988); and Phelan and Hart (1993).

5. See Gregory Jay (2007) for an insightful analysis of *Fires in the Mirror* and the way the invocation of holocausts can preempt opportunities for understanding the specificities of historical trauma.

6. Judith Butler argues that drag performances problematize the notion of gender as authentic or original by showing gender to be a cultural norm (Butler 1987, 137).

7. Hoch contrasts his own work with Smith's: "She approaches the work anthropologically and journalistically. . . . I'm . . . writing about my own experience." With Smith's plays, "because of the lack of opinion, the audience is allowed to detach themselves from any responsibility. . . . So people walk out of her shows saying, '. . . now I don't have to do anything about racism, because I came and saw this show'" (K. Taylor 2008, 6, 36). While some audience members may embrace such an attitude, Smith holds strong opinions despite her performance of multiple perspectives. The open-endedness of her plays is politically progressive, in a Brechtian sense. For a cogent critique of Hoch's work, see Hodges-Persley (2009).

8. Interviewees display a wide range of investments in their portrayals. Twilight Bey, the eponymous character who ends the play, never came to the theater. In contrast, Denise Harlins, the aunt of Latasha Harlins (the young African American woman shot by a Korean American storekeeper soon after the beatings of Rodney King) voiced unhappiness at being cut from the world premiere version. The Latasha Harlins case appeared in the film of *Twilight*, as searing precursor to the verdict that fanned the 1992 uprisings.

9. A classic deconstructive move (Derrida 1976).

10. Debby Thompson (2003) notes that Smith's portrayals often begin with this (gently) humorous critique.

11. My book *About Face* (1997) analyzes Japanese fashion, and I knew the costume designer, Candace Donnelly, from our work on *Twilight*.

12. One day during rehearsal for *Let Me Down Easy*, director Stephen Wadsworth asked Smith to view the gallery of photos of interviewees to select key costume elements and props for the designers. For bull rider Brett Thompson, she chose boots and, at the suggestion of costume designer Ann Hould-Ward, who is originally from Montana, a belt buckle worn by rodeo champions. Boxer Michael Bentt needed wrist wraps and a cup of Starbucks coffee.

13. One exception seems to be Smith's early work *The Piano*, a well-made play about the Cuban Revolution (1989). Still, though we could say that the Afro-Cuban woman was a protagonist, protagonism is proliferated to the level of the

collective. *The Piano* thematizes solidarity among people of color who rise in revolt against the colonizer.

14. Smith may occasionally spend more time with a particular character. For example, in *Twilight*, Maria narrates a hilarious segment about the small group dynamics and racialized guilt that unfolded in the jury room during the Federal Trial of the police officers accused of the Rodney King beating.

15. For example, Alisa made sure the surtitles were correct; Stephen asked Alisa and me to come up with a list of objects to be displayed onstage, to evoke associations with the characters. Running shoes, a small medical model of a human body, and a stuffed animal, among other objects, ultimately made the cut.

Chapter 4. The Drama behind the Drama

1. Duong (2012) theorizes the dual valences of "collaboration." In the arts, it is a generative process; politically, it denotes treason and betrayal.

2. A florescence of literature on dramaturgy is notable among theater scholars. See Manning (2015).

3. The choice of terminology is both controversial and politically revealing. "Riot" connotes social chaos and often indexes identification with the dominant group. "Rebellion" or "revolution" tropes events as political critique. "Civil unrest" is perhaps the most neutral, with its air of social scientific objectivity. Among Korean Americans, *Sa-I-Gu*, "April 29," is the most common term.

4. Cambodian American businesses were among those burned during these events in Long Beach. "More than 17,000 Cambodians live in this city of 440,000, and much of the destruction affected their small businesses, including restaurants, grocery stores and other small shops in the neighborhoods along Anaheim Street" (Mydans 1992).

5. Perhaps it felt especially satisfying to immerse ourselves in a process that seemed to present productive alternatives to the violence outside the theater. Of course, theater is an upper-middle-class, protected site far from "the streets," and putting up a theater production assumes a common goal: mounting the best possible production, even if opinions differ dramatically on how to achieve that end. Still, the theater is itself a significant cultural institution shot through with power relations, and interventions in theater matter, as I have argued throughout.

6. Many feedback techniques in the arts try to protect the vulnerability of the artist (e.g., Liz Lerman's postshow discussion techniques). Unlike the academy, which is based on debate and the performance of impenetrability, the performing arts require openness and vulnerability. Consequently, I am all the more impressed that Smith was able to listen to notes, no matter how bluntly stated, and to incorporate what she found useful.

7. See Chang (2014) and Gordon and Newfield (1996) for overviews on multiculturalism in the arts and on multiculturalism more generally during this period.

8. Wendy Brown's critique (1995) suggests that Mouffe and other "radical social democrats" court idealism, through their emphasis on "postindividualist concepts" of freedom shorn of specific social, historical, or political-economic

"contexts." Brown further argues that these theorists presume the relative autonomy of the sociopolitical from the economic, a "liberal" stance. All these writers, including Brown, take Western democracy as their model.

9. See Cheng (2001); J. Y. Kim (2015); Song (2005); Cherise Smith (2011).

10. Thanks to Sharon Luk for this insight.

11. Nontheater specialists may not realize that the specification of the particular production of "the same" play is pivotal, indeed, definitive of its significance, perhaps never more so than in *Twilight*. First, different versions had different directors: Emily Mann for the world premiere at the Taper and its slight revision at Princeton's McCarter Theater, where Mann is artistic director; George C. Wolfe for the versions at the Public in New York and on Broadway; Sharon Ott for the touring version; Mark Levin for the film of *Twilight* for PBS. Smith collected interviews in a book entitled *Twilight: Los Angeles 1992* that does not reproduce any particular script of the play. Each version featured a different running order and included different characters in different sequences: the Taper play was one act with twenty-six characters; the Broadway version comprised two acts with over forty characters; the touring version comprised two acts, but the characters and sequencing differed substantially from the New York production. Smith made the film of *Twilight* for PBS ten years after its theatrical world premiere; it differs substantially from the various theatrical versions. Filmmakers had to explain the historical context of the "riots," using period footage in order to reacquaint audiences with the events of 1992. As in all versions of *Twilight*, the sequencing and list of characters differed from all other versions. (See plates 3 and 4.)

Different directors brought different aesthetic visions. The Taper version, directed by Emily Mann, was aesthetically spare, featuring a white backdrop and a window / video screen, Lucia Hwong's abstract music, and Allen Lee Hughes's painterly lighting. Robert Brill's scaffolding on each side of the stage projected supertitles that resembled urban billboards, casting angular shadows onto the cityscape. The New York versions unfolded at a sprightly clip, with many characters occurring in trios, rather than the Park family as the sole triptych as in the LA version. George C. Wolfe placed his distinctive imprint on the production through brisk, engaging pacing and his signature visuals: Jules Fisher and Peggy Eisenhauer's hot, white light on a pitch-black stage; mobile sets gliding in and out. Sharon Ott's touring production opened onto a scene of mismatched chairs, as Smith entered and hung her bag on a coatrack. This version included a roundtable discussion not present in the other versions of the play.

While all these versions are called *Twilight*, the productions differ dramatically. The Taper premiere was a first attempt to construct order and significance from the chaos of events and multiplicity of perspectives. The Public/Broadway version's epic embrace and crisp pacing imparted a vivid sense of the dangers and utopian possibilities of Los Angeles. The touring version, more distant temporally from the actual uprisings, focused less on events and more on general discussions of race. The film, on which I also served as dramaturg, was a different incarnation in a different medium.

12. Héctor and I attended several times a week, not daily, since we both had demanding schedules. I was teaching a full load at Pomona College, serving as coordinator of women's studies, and had to find a new apartment and move; Héctor was a full-time reporter at the *Los Angeles Times*. Elizabeth flew in from the University of Chicago several times. Eustis, the only dramaturg on the full-time staff at the Taper, was most available to attend regularly.

13. A play can change through previews, but the production is considered fixed on opening night. In theory no changes can occur after that moment.

14. Sparks (2012) offers a production studies analysis of the writers' room during the making of a television series. Time in television is a precious commodity that drives production and contributes to the recirculation of conventional racial representation. Stereotypes take less time and thought, especially when writers have to turn out weekly episodes. Wadsworth (2008) commented in our interview on the toll the time pressures have on Smith, especially as deadlines approach: "Everyone wants to crack down on her and say, 'Oh come on, lady, it's time.' So she . . . needs protection in that time so that she can . . . function and . . . not have to worry about all the people who want something from her. . . . They just say, 'Pull the plug,' . . . and you're expected to turn out product. You can't be result-oriented with Anna."

15. The unwieldiness of Asian/American racial formation recurs in David Henry Hwang's work (chapter 5).

16. See also Zia (2000); *Los Angeles Times* (1992); Ong and Hee (1993).

17. These concerns point to shifts in Asian American studies and critical race studies that I address in chapter 5.

18. Cheng (2001) is disturbed by the fact that Parker is motivated by revenge that reproduces hegemonic logics of violence. Yet revenge is both entirely predictable and problematic; minoritized subjects can identify with the aggressor. Parker presents a crucial, power-sensitive view of race that counters Denny's power-evasive perspective.

19. Theaters have supported Smith's processual method. Gordon Davidson, artistic director of the Mark Taper Forum, delayed opening night of *Twilight* for ten days, until the play could incorporate late-breaking interviews. The same was true for Smith's *House Arrest: An Introgression*, which at points featured Smith coming onstage as herself to clarify her intentions with the still unfinished play. A second production of *Let Me Down Easy*, differing slightly from its world premiere at the Long Wharf (the version for which I was a dramaturg), opened at the American Repertory Theatre in Cambridge, Massachusetts. The play was not "finished"; at one point, Smith talked to the audience about her intentions. The touring production became the "final" version.

Chapter 5. Revising Race

1. Rajiv Joseph's *Bengal Tiger at the Baghdad Zoo*, starring Robin Williams, was on Broadway from March to July 2011. *Allegiance*, a musical based on actor George Takei's childhood experiences in Japanese American internment camps,

premiered on Broadway in November 2015. Ayad Akhtar's *Disgraced*, first produced at Lincoln Center, was revived on Broadway in 2014.

2. Brantley's review is ambivalent. First, he reduces the play to "one man's personal and social identity crisis," then opines that the play suffers from its own identity crisis. Brantley finds the two acts to be disparate in tone, but I view this disjuncture as necessary politically, to underline the impossibility of easy racial crossings, as long as structural racism persists. Brantley acknowledges that a scene with a journalist for the *New York Times* made him uncomfortable as a fellow *Times* writer. Ultimately, Brantley dismisses the play as "a scattershot, personal venting of painful emotions, still waiting to assume a polished form." I counter that *Yellow Face*'s innovations include formal experimentation and its sophisticated theoretical/political stance. The free play of farce cannot hold in the face of the confrontation with race as vulnerability to premature death. Hwang's interventions are illegible to Brantley, who reads the work in terms of highly conventional protocols: public/private, the well-made play genre, and race as always and only power-evasive.

3. For example, Justin Lin directed several installments in the *Fast and Furious* franchise in part to finance edgier projects that speak to him as a minoritarian subject. The *Fast and Furious* series is the only major Hollywood franchise that actually mirrors the racial diversity of the United States, and of California in particular.

4. Actors' Equity first cancelled the production in solidarity with Asian Americans, then capitulated to the producer's demands: hire Pryce or he would withdraw the production, resulting in the loss of millions in revenue and wages.

5. The Wen Ho Lee case became a political cause célèbre for Asian Americans.

6. A YouTube version of *Yellow Face*, directed by Jeff Liu and starring Ryun Yu, is a different genre; I analyze the stage version.

7. See J. Jackson (2005) on racial "authenticity" and racial "sincerity."

8. *Rich Relations* (1986) was Hwang's first and only play with an all-white cast. Thematizing family dysfunction at the intersections of wealth and evangelical Christianity, the play centers on Keith, a prep school debate coach, who returns to his Los Angeles home with his underage girlfriend. Hinson, Keith's father, emerges as a comic if problematic figure: larger than life, fascinated with technology, a man who left the ministry to become a real estate entrepreneur. Critically and commercially, the play was a disappointment. Hwang later commented that one often learns more from failures than from successes.

9. The accusations against Asian Americans were ultimately disproved.

10. Successive versions amplified Hwang's self-deprecating humor. DHH acts as a "cultural consultant" for the ill-fated Margaret Cho sitcom *All American Girl*, the first prime-time television show about Asian Americans. In the first draft, Cho complains about DHH's attempts to make her more "Asian": use chopsticks, use an abacus. In later versions, DHH himself utters these humiliating and stereotypical suggestions, heightening the humor.

11. In *Yellow Face*, Frank Chin says, "David Henry Hwang is a white racist asshole" (Hwang 2007d, 2).

Chapter 6. Playwriting as Reparative Creativity

1. See Yoneyama (1999); Sturken (1997); LaCapra (1994); Benjamin and Arendt (2007); J. Taylor (1998); Taussig (1993); Nguyen (2016); Cho (2008); Gordon (1997).

2. See Eng (2011); Chambers-Letson (2006).

3. It is difficult to confirm the number of living Nisei; I consulted the Japanese American National Museum, the Japanese American Citizens' League, and the census, but clear answers are elusive. While 73 percent of the 2011 Japanese American population was US-born (Pew Research Center 2013), the statistics do not differentiate among generations. By this point, there could be fifth-generation Japanese Americans.

4. I am a fledgling playwright; my dramaturg/director said it wasn't till his seventh play that he learned about his own distinctive style.

5. Sarita See (2009) and Jacobs-Huey (2006) discuss comedy and humor as minoritarian strategies of subversion. Ochoa (2014) discusses the significance of "frivolity" and denigrated popular genres such as melodrama.

6. Certain characters are highly theatrical for a reason. Some theater colleagues offered the note that Kathleen was "a device." A white man powerful in the theater world objected to the depiction of white men, especially Diane's boss Andrew (then an actual character) as insufficiently complex. I ultimately stylized Andrew as a disembodied voice of authority—literally just a booming voice—because he occupies that position within Diane's psyche. He is precisely *not* a complex character. Andrew represents for Diane the voice of paternal authority, the key to her promotion to managing partner. I discuss Kathleen extensively in this chapter.

7. See Inouye (2016); Adachi (1976); Kobayashi (1989, 69–82); Sunahara (1981); Robinson (2009); and Miki and Kobayashi (1991). An extensive literature documents the similar, but not identical, incarceration of Japanese Canadians. Two key differences from the US case: first, the Canadian government sought explicitly to break up the concentration of Japanese Canadians in Western Canada, primarily British Columbia, and embraced policies to move Japanese Canadians inland during the war. Second, the state seized and sold Japanese Canadian property, using profits from the sales to fund the incarceration.

8. Thanks to Karen Shimakawa for discussing these legal points with me, after a reading of *Seamless* at the Lark.

9. Day (2016) theorizes racial triangulation among white settler colonists, First Nations peoples, and Asian Canadians.

10. Takaki (1979) shows the interarticulation of the histories of peoples of color, women, and the working class, as Others against which hegemonic white male subjectivity took shape.

11. Writing an unsympathetic minority character presented challenges. The first scene stages a picture-perfect portrait of an all-American family: mother, father, daughter, son-in-law. Three are Japanese American; Diane's husband, Ben, is white. Diane is white-identified, high-achieving, uptight; such a minoritarian subject would surely be heterosexual, with a white spouse. As Carbado and Gulati

argue (2013), choice of residence, spouse, and dress can reproduce hegemonic standards. That Ben is Jewish, not WASP, implicitly invokes affinity/difference between two historical injustices. Some audience members find Diane's identification with the dominant off-putting.

12. In 1943, during the incarceration, the War Relocation Authority circulated the "loyalty questionnaire." Question 27 was "Are you willing to serve in the armed forces of the United States on combat duty, wherever ordered?" Question 28 asked, "Will you swear unqualified allegiances to the United States of America and faithfully defend the United States from any or all attack by foreign or domestic forces, and forswear any form of allegiance or obedience to the Japanese emperor, or other foreign government, power or organization?" Those who answered "yes" to both were drafted into the US Army, some to what became the highly decorated 442nd Regimental Combat Team. The families of these men remained in camp, a savage irony.

The "no" responses could be nuanced. If a Japanese American born in the United States had no allegiance to the Japanese emperor in the first place, how could he forswear that allegiance? A "no" could also represent principled protest of the injustice of internment. The "no-no boys" were shipped from various camps to Tule Lake. John Okada's classic novel *No-No Boy* (1977) writes the story of one such Japanese American man after resettlement. Ken Narasaki's play based on the novel premiered in 2010.

13. Ramos (2017); Chea (2015). Inouye (2016) analyzes the afterlife of internment through its transformation into legible political action: e.g., scholarship, pilgrimages, the redress movement.

14. A burgeoning literature investigates minoritarian subjects and diagnoses of "madness." See *American Quarterly* 69, no. 2 (2017): 291–345.

15. The landmark anthology *Aiiieeeee!* (1974) includes canonical Asian American dramas: Frank Chin's *Chickencoop Chinaman*, important though problematically masculinist; Momoko Iko's *The Gold Watch*; and Hisaye Yamamoto's "And the Soul Shall Dance," a short story that eventually became a play.

16. Thanks to Paulla Ebron for this suggestion. See Ebron (2011, 147–68).

works cited

Abraham, Nicolas, and Maria Torok. 1994. *The Shell and the Kernel: Renewals of Psychoanalysis*. Edited by Nicholas T. Rand. Chicago, IL: University of Chicago Press.
Actors' Equity Association. 2008. "Agreement and Rules Governing Employment in Resident Theatres." http://www.actorsequity.org/docs/rulebooks/lort_Rulebook_09-12.pdf.
Actors' Equity Association. 2011a. "Minimum Salaries—LORT Agreement." https://www.actorsequity.org/agreements/agreement_info.asp?inc=031.
Actors' Equity Association. 2011b. "Minimum Salaries—Off Broadway Agreement." https://www.actorsequity.org/agreements/agreement_info.asp?inc=520.
Actors' Equity Association. 2012. "Minimum Salaries—Production Agreement (Broadway and National Tours)." http://www.actorsequity.org/agreements/agreement_info.asp?inc=001.
Actors' Equity Association. 2013. "Minimum Salaries—Small Professional Theatre Agreement." https://www.actorsequity.org/agreements/agreement_info.asp?inc=060.
Adachi, Ken. 1976. *The Enemy That Never Was: An Account of the Deplorable Treatment Inflicted on Japanese Canadians during World War Two*. Toronto, Canada: McCleland and Stewart.
Adorno, Theodor W. 2010. *Aesthetics and Politics*. London: Verso.
Agamben, Giorgio. 1998. *Homo Sacer: Sovereign Power and Bare Life*. Translated by Daniel Heller-Roazen. Palo Alto, CA: Stanford University Press.
Ahmed, Sara. 2004. *The Cultural Politics of Emotion*. New York: Routledge.
Ahmed, Sara. 2006. *Queer Phenomenology*. Durham, NC: Duke University Press.

Ahmed, Sara. 2010. *The Promise of Happiness*. Durham, NC: Duke University Press.

Ahmed, Sara. 2014. *Willful Subjects*. Durham, NC: Duke University Press.

Allen, Jafari S. 2011. *¡Venceremos?: The Erotics of Black Self-making in Cuba*. Durham, NC: Duke University Press.

Anzaldúa, Gloria. 1990. *Making Face, Making Soul, Haciendo Caras: Creative and Critical Perspectives by Feminists of Color*. San Francisco, CA: Aunt Lute Foundation Books.

Arnott, Christopher. 2008. "Woman of a Thousand Faces—No One Builds Characters Like Playwright Anna Deavere Smith. Find Out Why in Her New World Premiere at Long Wharf Theatre." *New Haven Advocate,* January 3. NewsBank Access World News.

Arzumanova, Inna. 2013. "Traveling Kaleidoscope: Racial Performance and Transformation in Global Cultural Industries." PhD diss., University of Southern California.

Asian Americans / Pacific Islanders in Philanthropy (AAPIP). 2015. "Who We Are." Accessed May 15, 2015. http://aapip.org/who-we-are.

Association of Black Foundation Executives (ABFE). 2013. "Black Economics." Accessed August 14, 2016. http://blackeconomics.co.uk/wp/association-of-black-foundation-executives-abfe/.

Atkinson, Paul. 2004. "Performance and Rehearsal: The Ethnographer at the Opera." In *Qualitative Research Practice*, edited by C. Seale, G. Gobo et al., 94–105. London: Sage.

Auslander, Philip. 1999. *Liveness: Performance in a Mediatized Culture*. New York: Routledge.

Austin, J. L. 1962. *How to Do Things with Words*. Cambridge, MA: Harvard University Press.

Banet-Weiser, Sarah. 2012. *Authentic [Tm]: The Politics of Ambivalence in a Brand Culture*. New York: NYU Press.

Banks, Daniel. 2013. "The Welcome Table: Casting for an Integrated Society." *Theatre Topics* 23 (1): 1–18.

Baraka, Amiri. 1967. "The Changing Same (R&B and New Black Music)." In *Black Music*, 180–212. New York: William Morrow.

Barnwell, Ashley. 2015. "Entanglements of Evidence in the Turn against Critique." *Cultural Studies* 30 (6): 906–25.

Barthes, Roland, and Stephen Heath. 1977. "The Death of the Author." In *Image, Music, Text*, 142–48. New York: Hill and Wang.

Batiste, Stephanie Leigh. 2011. *Darkening Mirrors: Imperial Representation in Depression-Era African American Performance*. Durham, NC: Duke University Press.

Becker, Howard S. 2008. *Art Worlds*. Berkeley: University of California Press.

Behar, Ruth. 2013. *Traveling Heavy: A Memoir in between Journeys*. Durham, NC: Duke University Press.

Belsey, Catherine. 1980. *Critical Practice*. London: Routledge.

Benjamin, Walter. 2007. *Illuminations: Essays and Reflections*. Edited by Hannah Arendt. New York: Schocken Books.

Benveniste, Émile. 1971. *Problems in General Linguistics*. Translated by Mary Elizabeth Meek. Coral Gables, Florida: University of Miami Press.

Berlant, Lauren. 2011. *Cruel Optimism*. Durham, NC: Duke University Press.

Best, Stephen, and Sharon Marcus. 2009. "Surface Reading: An Introduction." *Representations* 108 (1): 1–21.

Boehm, Mike. 2015. "Study Sends 'Wake-Up Call' about Black and Latino Arts Groups' Meager Funding." *Los Angeles Times*, October 12. Accessed July 28, 2017. http://www.latimes.com/entertainment/arts/culture/la-et-cm-diversity-arts-study-devos-black-latino-groups-funding-20151009-story.html.

Boehm, Mike, and David Ng. 2015. "Music Center Cuts Back Its Art Education at Schools." *Los Angeles Times*, June 24. Accessed June 25, 2015. http://www.latimes.com/entertainment/arts/la-et-cm-music-center-education-20150624-story.html.

Bonacich, Edna. 1973. "A Theory of Middleman Minorities." *American Sociological Review* 38 (5): 583–94.

Bourdieu, Pierre. 1993. *The Field of Cultural Production: Essays on Art and Literature*. Translated by Randal Johnson. New York: Columbia University Press.

Bourdieu, Pierre, and Yvette Delsaut. 1975. "Le couturier et sa griffe: contribution à une thèorie de la magie."*Actes de la recherche en sciences sociales* 1 (1): 7–36.

Brantley, Ben. 2007. "A Satirical Spin on Stereotypes, at Home, Abroad and on Broadway." *New York Times*, December 11.

Brater, Jessica, and Jessica Del Vecchio et al. 2010. "'Let Our Freak Flags Fly': *Shrek the Musical* and the Branding of Diversity." *Theatre Journal* 62 (2): 151–72.

Brecht, Bertolt, and John Willett. 1964. *Brecht on Theatre: The Development of an Aesthetic*. New York: Hill and Wang.

Breslauer, Jan. 2006. "It Cuts Both Ways." *Los Angeles Times*, September 17. http://articles.latimes.com/2006/sep/17/entertainment/ca-plays17.

Breyer, Christopher. 2007. "The People of the 'Big Song.'" Program notes for *Yellow Face* at the Mark Taper Forum. Los Angeles, CA, 10.

Brinkema, Eugenie. 2014. *The Forms of the Affects*. Durham, NC: Duke University Press.

Brodkin, Karen. 1998. *How Jews Became White Folks and What That Says about Race in America*. New Brunswick, NJ: Rutgers University Press.

Brody, Jennifer DeVere. 2008. *Punctuation: Art, Politics, and Play*. Durham, NC: Duke University Press.

Brooks, Daphne. 2006. *Bodies in Dissent: Spectacular Performances of Race and Freedom, 1850–1910*. Durham, NC: Duke University Press.

Brown, Jayna. 2008. *Babylon Girls: Black Women Performers and the Shaping of the Modern*. Durham, NC: Duke University Press.

Brown, Karen McCarthy. 1991. *Mama Lola: A Vodou Priestess in Brooklyn*. Berkeley: University of California.

Brown, Wendy. 1995. *States of Injury: Power and Freedom in Late Modernity*. Princeton, NJ: Princeton University Press.

Brown, Wendy. 2015. *Undoing the Demos: Neoliberalism's Stealth Revolution*. Brooklyn: Zone Books.
Bruner, Edward. 1993. "Epilogue: Creative Persona and the Problem of Authenticity." In *Creativity/Anthropology*, edited by Smadar Lavie, Kirin Narayan, and Renato Rosaldo, 321–23. Ithaca, NY: Cornell University Press.
Butler, Judith. 1987. *Subjects of Desire: Hegelian Reflections in Twentieth-Century France*. New York: Columbia University Press.
Butler, Judith. 1990. *Gender Trouble: Feminism and the Subversion of Identity*. New York: Routledge.
Butler, Judith. 1997. *The Psychic Life of Power: Theories in Subjection*. Stanford, CA: Stanford University Press.
Butler, Judith. 2004a. *Precarious Life: The Powers of Mourning and Violence*. London: Verso.
Butler, Judith. 2004b. *Undoing Gender*. New York: Routledge.
Butler, Judith. 2015. *Senses of the Subject*. New York: Fordham University Press.
Byrd, Jodi. 2011. *The Transit of Empire: Indigenous Critiques of Colonialism*. Minneapolis: University of Minnesota Press.
Caldwell, John Thornton. 2008. *Production Culture: Industrial Reflexivity and Critical Practice in Film and Television*. Durham, NC: Duke University Press.
Carbado, Devon, and Mitu Gulati. 2013. *Acting White? Rethinking Race in "Post-Racial" America*. New York: Oxford University Press.
Carlson, Marvin. 2001. *The Haunted Stage: The Theatre as Memory Machine*. Ann Arbor: University of Michigan Press.
Carnicke, Sharon Marie. 2008. *Stanislavsky in Focus: An Acting Master for the Twenty-First Century*. London: Routledge.
Case, Sue-Ellen. 1995. "Performing Lesbian in the Space of Technology: Part I." *Theatre Journal* 47.1: 1–18.
Catanese, Brandi Wilkins. 2011. *The Problem of the Color(Blind): Racial Transgression and the Politics of Black Performance*. Ann Arbor: University of Michigan.
Cervenak, Sarah Jane. 2014. *Wandering: Philosophical Performances of Racial and Sexual Freedom*. Durham, NC: Duke University Press.
Chambers-Letson, Joshua Takano. 2006. "Reparative Feminisms, Repairing Feminism—Reparation, Postcolonial Violence, and Feminism." *Women and Performance: A Journal of Feminist Theory* 16 (2): 169–89.
Chambers-Letson, Joshua Takano. 2013. *A Race So Different: Performance and Law in Asian America*. New York: NYU Press.
Chang, Jeff. 2014. *Who We Be: The Colorization of America*. New York: St. Martin's Press.
Chatterjee, Piya. 2001. *A Time for Tea: Women, Labor, and Post/Colonial Politics on an Indian Plantation*. Durham, NC: Duke University Press.
Chea, Jolie. 2015. "University of California President's Postdoctoral Fellowship Program Research Proposal." Unpublished ms.
Chen, Anna. 2012. "Memo to the RSC: East Asians Can Be More Than Just Dogs and Maids." *Guardian*, October 22.

Cheng, Anne Anlin. 2001. *The Melancholy of Race*. Oxford: Oxford University Press.

Chin, Frank. 1974. *Aiiieeeee! An Anthology of Asian-American Writers*. Washington, DC: Howard University Press.

Chio, Jenny. 2017. "Guiding Lines." *Cultural Anthropology*. Accessed June 16. https://culanth.org/fieldsights/1118-guiding-lines.

Cho, Grace. 2008. *Haunting the Korean Diaspora: Shame, Secrecy, and the Forgotten War*. Minneapolis: University of Minnesota Press.

Chow, Rey. 2012. *Entanglements, or Transmedial Thinking about Capture*. Durham, NC: Duke University Press.

Chuh, Kandice. 2003. *Imagine Otherwise: On Asian Americanist Critique*. Durham, NC: Duke University Press.

Chuh, Kandice, and Karen Shimakawa, eds. 2001. *Orientations: Mapping Studies in the Asian Diaspora*. Durham, NC: Duke University Press.

Classen, Constance. 1993. *Worlds of Sense*. New York: Routledge.

Classen, Constance. 2005. *The Book of Touch*. Oxford: Berg.

Clément, Catherine. 1988. *Opera, Or, The Undoing of Women*. Translated by Betsy Wing and Susan McClary. Minneapolis: University of Minnesota Press.

Clifford, James. 1997. *Routes: Travel and Translation in the Late 20th Century*. Cambridge, MA: Harvard University Press.

Clifford, James. 2013. *Returns: Becoming Indigenous in the Twenty-First Century*. Cambridge, MA: Harvard University Press.

Columbia University School of the Arts. 2016. "David Henry Hwang." Accessed August 5, 2016. https://arts.columbia.edu/profiles/david-henry-hwang.

Commission on Wartime Relocation and Internment of Civilians (CWRIC). 1997. *Personal Justice Denied*. Seattle: University of Washington Press.

Cox, Aimee. 2015. *Shapeshifters: Black Girls and the Choreography of Citizenship*. Durham, NC: Duke University Press.

Cox, Gordon. 2015a. "Noah Wylie Urges 'No' Vote on Actors' Equity's 99-Seat Theater Proposal." *Variety*, March 25.

Cox, Gordon. 2015b. "Charlayne Woodard Urges 'Yes' Vote on Actors' Equity's 99-Seat Theater Proposal." *Variety*, April 6.

Cox, Rupert, Andrew Irving, and Christopher Wright, eds. 2016. *Beyond Text? Critical Practices and Sensory Anthropology*. Manchester, UK: Manchester University Press.

Crapanzano, Vincent. 1980. *Tuhami: Portrait of a Moroccan*. Chicago, IL: University of Chicago Press.

Crapanzano, Vincent. 2004. *Imaginative Horizons: An Essay in Literary-Philosophical Anthropology*. Chicago, IL: University of Chicago Press.

Cvetkovich, Ann. 2012. *Depression: A Public Feeling*. Durham, NC: Duke University Press.

Davé, Shilpa, Pawan Dhingra, et al. 2000. "De-Privileging Positions: Indian Americans, South Asian Americans, and the Politics of Asian American Studies." *Journal of Asian American Studies* 3 (1): 67–100.

Davis, Angela and Elizabeth Martinez. 1998. "Coalition Building Among People of Color: A Discussion with Angela Davis and Elizabeth Martinez." *Angela Davis Reader*, edited by Joy James. Boston: Blackwell.

Day, Iyko. 2016. *Alien Capital: Asian Racialization and the Logic of Settler Colonial Capitalism*. Durham, NC: Duke University Press.

De León, Jason. 2015. *The Land of Open Graves: Living and Dying on the Migrant Trail*. Berkeley: University of California Press.

Deggans, Eric. 2011. "Latest TV Trend? The Black Best Friend." *Washington Post*. Last modified October 28. https://www.washingtonpost.com/lifestyle/style/latest-tv-trend-the-black-best-friend/2011/10/25/gIQAwYw4OM_story.html.

Deleuze, Gilles, and Félix Guattari. 1987. *A Thousand Plateaus: Capitalism and Schizophrenia*. Translated by Brian Massumi. Minnesota: University of Minnesota Press.

Derrida, Jacques. 1988. "Signature, Event, Context." In *Limited Inc.*, edited by Gerald Graff, translated by Samuel Weber and Jeffrey Mehlman, 1–25. Evanston, IL: Northwestern University Press.

Desjarlais, Robert. 2012. *Counterplay: An Anthropologist at the Chessboard*. Berkeley: University of California Press.

Diamond, Elin. 1992. "The Violence of 'We.'" In *Critical Theory and Performance*, edited by Janelle G. Reinelt and Joseph R. Roach, 390–98. Ann Arbor: University of Michigan Press.

Dolan, Jill. 1988. *The Feminist Spectator as Critic*. Ann Arbor: University of Michigan Press.

Dolan, Jill. 2005. *Utopia in Performance: Finding Hope at the Theater*. Ann Arbor: University of Michigan Press.

Dornfeld, Barry. 1998. *Producing Public Television, Producing Public Culture*. Princeton, NJ: Princeton University Press.

Duong, Lan P. 2012. *Treacherous Subjects: Gender, Culture, and Trans-Vietnamese Feminism*. Philadelphia, PA: Temple University Press.

Duranti, Alessandro, and Donald Brenneis. 1986. "The Audience as Co-Author." *Text—Interdisciplinary Journal for the Study of Discourse* 6 (3): 239–47.

Dwyer, Kevin. 1987. *Moroccan Dialogues: Anthropology in Question*. Long Grove, IL: Waveland Press.

East West Players. 2015. "51% Preparedness Plan for the American Theatre." http://www.eastwestplayers.org/wp-content/uploads/2015/01/012015_51-Percent-Preparedness-Plan_a.pdf.

Ebron, Paulla. 2011. "Slavery and Transnational Memory: The Making of New Publics." In *Transnational Memory: Circulation, Articulation, Scales*, edited by Chiara De Cesari and Ann Rigney, 147–68. Berlin: Walter de Gruyter.

Edwards, Brent Hayes. 2003. *The Practice of Diaspora: Literature, Translation, and the Rise of Black Internationalism*. Cambridge, MA: Harvard University Press.

Eng, David L. 2010. *The Feeling of Kinship: Queer Liberalism and the Racialization of Intimacy*. Durham, NC: Duke University Press.

Eng, David L. 2011. "Reparations and the Human." *Columbia Journal of Gender and the Law* 21 (2): 561–83.

Eng, David L., and David Kazanjian. 2003. *Loss: The Politics of Mourning*. Berkeley: University of California Press.

Eustis, Oskar. November 2007. In discussion with the author.

Fabian, Johannes. 1983. *Time and the Other: How Anthropology Makes Its Object*. New York: Columbia University Press.

Fabian, Johannes. 1990. *Power and Performance: Ethnography through Proverbial Wisdom and Theater in Shaba, Zaire*. Madison: University of Wisconsin Press.

Facing History and Ourselves. 2016. "About Us." Accessed July 22, 2016. https://www.facinghistory.org/about-us.

Fanon, Frantz. 1967. *Black Skin, White Masks*. London: Pluto.

Fassin, Didier. 2014. "True Life, Real Lives: Revisiting the Boundaries between Ethnography and Fiction." *American Ethnologist* 41 (1): 40–55.

Feld, Steven. 2012. *Jazz Cosmopolitanism in Accra: Five Musical Years in Ghana*. Durham, NC: Duke University Press.

Ferguson, Roderick. 2012. *The Reorder of Things: The University and Its Pedagogy of Minority Difference*. Minneapolis: University of Minnesota Press.

Fortun, Kim. 2001. *Advocacy after Bhopal: Environmentalism, Disaster, New Global Orders*. Chicago, IL: University of Chicago Press.

Foucault, Michel. 1976. *An Introduction*. Vol. 1 of *The History of Sexuality*. New York: Pantheon.

Foucault, Michel. 1984. *The Foucault Reader*. New York: Pantheon.

Foucault, Michel. 1995. *Discipline and Punish: The Birth of the Prison*. Translated by Alan Sheridan. New York: Random House.

Foucault, Michel. 2003. *Society Must Be Defended: Lectures at the Collège De France, 1975–76*. Edited by Mauro Bertani, François Ewald, and Alessandro Fontana. New York: Picador.

Fox, Ashley. 2015. "How the Rooney Rule Succeeds . . . And Where It Falls Short." *ESPN*, May 14.

Fraser, Nancy. 1989. *Unruly Practices: Power, Discourse, and Gender in Contemporary Social Theory*. Minneapolis: University of Minnesota Press.

Freud, Sigmund. 1989. *The Freud Reader*. Edited by Peter Gay. New York: W. W. Norton.

Freud, Sigmund. 1997. *Writings on Art and Literature*. Stanford, CA: Stanford University Press.

Fujii, James A. 1993. *Complicit Fictions: The Subject in the Modern Japanese Prose Narrative*. Berkeley: University of California Press.

Fuss, Diana. 1995. *Identification Papers*. New York: Routledge.

Gallela, Donatella. 2015. "Racializing the American Revolution, Review of the Broadway Musical *Hamilton*." *Advocate*. November 16. http://gcadvocate.com/2015/11/16/racializing-the-american-revolution-review-of-the-broadway-musical-hamilton/.

Geertz, Clifford. 1973. *The Interpretation of Cultures*. New York: Basic Books.

Gener, Randy. 2013. "REPRESENT-ASIAN CONTROVERSY | Asian American Actors Accuse Roundabout's Broadway Hit MYSTERY OF EDWIN DROOD of 'Brownface' Casting." *Culture of One World*, February 1. Accessed May 29, 2015. http://cultureofoneworld.org/2013/02/01/representasian-controversy-asian-american-actors-accuse-roundabouts-broadway-hit-mystery-of-edwin-drood-of-brownface-casting/.

Gilmore, Ruth Wilson. 2007. *Golden Gulag: Prisons, Surplus, Crisis, and Opposition in Globalizing California*. Berkeley: University of California Press.

Gilroy, Paul. 2000. *Against Race: Imagining Political Culture beyond the Color Line*. Cambridge, MA: Belknap Press of Harvard University Press.

Ginsburg, Faye D., Lila Abu-Lughod, and Brian Larkin. 2002. *Media Worlds: Anthropology on New Terrain*. Berkeley: University of California Press.

Gopinath, Gayatri. 2005. *Impossible Desires: Queer Diasporas and South Asian Public Cultures*. Durham, NC: Duke University Press.

Gordon, Avery. 1997. *Ghostly Matters: Haunting and the Sociological Imagination*. Minneapolis: University of Minnesota Press.

Gordon, Avery and Christopher Newfield. 1996. *Mapping Multiculturalism*. Minneapolis: University of Minnesota Press.

Gould, Deborah. 2009. *Moving Politics: Emotion and ACT UP's Fight against AIDS*. Chicago, IL: University of Chicago Press.

Gutting, Gary. 2016. "The Real Humanities Crisis." *New York Times*, November 30, 2013. Accessed February 29. http://opinionator.blogs.nytimes.com/2013/11/30/the-real-humanities-crisis/.

Habermas, Jürgen. 1970. "On Systematically Distorted Communication," *Inquiry* 13 (1–4): 205–18.

Halberstam, Judith. 2011. *The Queer Art of Failure*. Durham, NC: Duke University Press.

Hansberry, Lorraine. 1959. *A Raisin in the Sun*. New York: Vintage.

Haraway, Donna. 1988. "Situated Knowledges: The Science Question in Feminism and the Privilege of Partial Perspective." *Feminist Studies* 14 (3): 575–99.

Haraway, Donna. 1991. *Simians, Cyborgs and Women: The Reinvention of Nature*. New York: Routledge.

Harney, Stefano, and Fred Moten. 2013. *The Undercommons: Fugitive Planning and Black Study*. Wivenhoe, UK: Minor Compositions.

Harris, Lyle Ashton. 1996. Interview by Michael Cohen. *Flash Art* (May–June): 107.

Harper, Phillip Brian. 2015. *Abstractionist Aesthetics: Artistic Form and Social Critique in American Culture*. New York: NYU Press.

Hart, Lynda and Peggy Phelan, eds. 1993. *Acting Out: Feminist Performances*. Ann Arbor: University of Michigan Press.

Hartman, Saidiya V. 1997. *Scenes of Subjection: Terror, Slavery, and Self-Making in Nineteenth-Century America*. New York: Oxford University Press.

Hartman, Saidiya V. 2007. *Lose Your Mother: A Journey along the Atlantic Slave Route*. New York: Farrar, Straus and Giroux.

Harvey, David. 2005. *A Brief History of Neoliberalism*. New York: Oxford University Press.
Harvie, Jen. 2013. *Fair Play: Art, Performance, and Neoliberalism*. Basingstoke, UK: Palgrave Macmillan.
Hastrup, Kirsten. 1990. "The Ethnographic Present: A Reinvention." *Cultural Anthropology* 5 (1): 45–61.
Hastrup, Kirsten. 2004. *Action: Anthropology in the Company of Shakespeare*. Copenhagen: Museum Tusculanum.
Hauser, Arnold. 1968. *The Social History of Art*. London: Routledge.
Healy, Patrick. 2012. "New York Stagecraft Plies the High Seas." *New York Times*, March 13. Accessed February 29, 2016. http://www.nytimes.com/2012/03/14/theater/disney-taps-new-york-stage-talent-for cruise-line-theater.html.
Hedva, Joanna. 2016. "Sick Woman Theory." *Mask Magazine*, January. http://www.maskmagazine.com/not-again/struggle/sick-woman-theory.
Hesmondhalgh, David. 2013. *The Cultural Industries*. London: Sage.
Hirsch, Marianne. 2008. "The Generation of Postmemory." *Poetics Today* 29 (1): 103–28.
History and Memory (for Akiko and Takashige). 1991. Directed by R. Tajiri. New York: Electronic Arts Intermix.
Ho, Karen. 2009. *Liquidated: An Ethnography of Wall Street*. Durham, NC: Duke University Press.
Hodges-Persley, Nicole. 2009. "Sampling Blackness: Performing African-Americanness in Hip-Hop Theater and Performance." PhD diss., University of Southern California.
Holtham, J. 2015. "Money Talks, but Are We Listening?" *American Theatre* 32 (8): 112–18.
Hong, Grace Kyungwon. 2015. *Death beyond Disavowal: The Impossible Politics of Difference*. Minneapolis: University of Minnesota Press.
Hopkins, D. J. 2013. "Research, Counter-Text, Performance: Keywords for Reconsidering the (Textual) Authority of the Dramaturg." In *The Routledge Companion to Dramaturgy*, edited by Magda Romanska, 420–25. New York: Routledge.
Hoskins, Janet, and Viet Thanh Nguyen. 2014. *Transpacific Studies: Framing an Emerging Field*. Honolulu: University of Hawai'i Press.
Howes, David, ed. 1991. *Varieties of Sensory Experience: A Sourcebook in the Anthropology of the Senses*. Toronto, Canada: University of Toronto Press.
Howes, David, ed. 2004. *Empire of the Senses*. Oxford: Berg.
Howes, David. 2013. *Ways of Sensing: Understanding the Senses in Society*. London: Routledge.
Hughes, Langston. 1951. *Montage of a Dream Deferred*. New York: Henry Holt.
Hutcheon, Linda. 1992. *A Poetics of Postmodernism: History, Theory, and Fiction*. New York: Routledge.
Hwang, David Henry. 1988. *M. Butterfly*. New York: Penguin.
Hwang, David Henry. 2001. "An Afternoon with David Henry Hwang." Lecture. East West Players, Los Angeles California.

Hwang, David Henry. 2005. *Yellow Face.* MS 1. New York. Unpublished ms.
Hwang, David Henry. 2007a. Lecture, April 18. Alliance of Los Angeles Playwrights, Los Angeles, California.
Hwang, David Henry. 2007b. Discussion with the author, June 20.
Hwang, David Henry. 2007c. "Stanford Alumni Talks." Lecture, June. Center Theatre Group, Los Angeles, California.
Hwang, David Henry. 2007d. *Yellow Face.* Final draft of MS. Center Theatre Group, Los Angeles.
Hwang, David Henry. 2009. *Yellow Face.* New York: Theatre Communications Group.
Hwang, David Henry. 2012. *Chinglish.* New York: Theatre Communications Group.
Hwang, David Henry. 2014. *Kung Fu.* Directed by Leigh Silverman. New York: Signature Theatre.
Hwang, David Henry. 2015a. *Chinglish.* Directed by Jeff Liu. Los Angeles: East West Players.
Hwang, David Henry. 2015b. E-mail message to author, October 31.
Ingold, Tim. 2013. *Making: Anthropology, Art, Archaeology, and Architecture.* New York: Routledge.
Inouye, Karen M. 2016. *The Long Afterlife of Nikkei Wartime Incarceration.* Stanford, CA: Stanford University Press.
Ivey, William J. 2008. *Arts, Inc.: How Greed and Neglect Have Destroyed Our Cultural Rights.* Berkeley: University of California Press.
Jackson, John L. 2005. *Real Black: Adventures in Racial Sincerity.* Chicago, IL: University of Chicago Press.
Jackson, John L. 2013. *Thin Description: Ethnography and the African Hebrew Israelites of Jerusalem.* Cambridge, MA: Harvard University Press.
Jackson, Shannon. 2011. *Social Works: Performing Art, Supporting Publics.* New York: Routledge.
Jacobs-Huey, Lanita. 2006. "The Arab Is the New Nigger." *Transforming Anthropology* 14 (1): 60–64.
Jakobson, Roman, and Morris Halle. 1956. *Fundamentals of Language.* The Hague: Mouton.
Janiak, Lily. 2013. "A Whole New Ballgame in Arts Hiring." *Theater Bay Area*, November 3.
Jay, Gregory. 2007. "Other People's Holocausts: Trauma, Empathy, and Justice in Anna Deavere Smith's *Fires in the Mirror.*" *Contemporary Literature* 48 (1): 119–50.
Johnson, E. Patrick. 2003. *Appropriating Blackness: Performance and the Politics of Authenticity.* Durham, NC: Duke University Press.
Johnson, E. Patrick, and Ramón Rivera-Servera, eds. 2016. *Blacktino Queer Performance.* Durham, NC: Duke University Press Books.
Joseph, May. 2012. "Aquatopia: Harmattan Theater, Neoliberal Provisionality, and the Future of Water." In *Neoliberalism and Global Theatres*, edited by Lara Nielsen and Patricia Ybarra, 253–65. Basingstoke, UK: Palgrave Macmillan.

Joseph, Miranda. 2002. *Against the Romance of Community*. Minneapolis: University of Minnesota Press.

Keeling, Kara. 2007. *The Witch's Flight: The Cinematic, the Black Femme, and the Image of Common Sense*. Durham, NC: Duke University Press.

Kelley, Robin D. G. 2002. *Freedom Dreams: The Black Radical Imagination*. Boston: Beacon Press.

Kelley, Robin D. G. 2013. E-mail message to the author, May 23.

Khanna, Neetu. Forthcoming. *The Visceral Logics of Decolonization*. Durham, NC: Duke University Press.

Kim, E. Tammy. 2006. "Performing Social Reparation: 'Comfort Women' and the Path to Political Forgiveness." *Women and Performance: A Journal of Feminist Theory* 16 (2): 221–49.

Kim, Elaine. 1982. *Asian American Literature: An Introduction to the Writings and Their Social Context*. Philadelphia, PA: Temple University Press.

Kim, Ju Yon. 2015. *The Racial Mundane: Asian American Performance and the Embodied Everyday*. New York: NYU Press.

Klein, Melanie. [1929] 1975. "Infantile Anxiety Situations Reflected in a Work of Art and in the Creative Impulse." In *Love, Guilt, and Reparation: And Other Works, 1921–1945*, 210–18. New York: The Free Press.

Klein, Melanie. 1984. *Love, Guilt, and Reparation: And Other Works, 1921–1945*. New York: The Free Press.

Klein, Melanie, and Joan Rivière. 1964. *Love, Hate, and Reparation*. New York: Norton.

Kobayashi, Audrey. 1989. "This Historical Context of Japanese-Canadian Uprooting." In *Social Change and Space: Indigenous Nations and Ethnic Communities*, edited by L. Müller-Wille, 69–82. Montreal, CA: McGill University.

Kondo, Dorinne. 1985. "The Way of Tea: A Symbolic Analysis." *Man (N.S)*. 20:287–306.

Kondo, Dorinne. 1986. "Dissolution and Reconstitution of the Self: Implications for Anthropological Epistemology." *Cultural Anthropology* 1:74–96.

Kondo, Dorinne. 1990. *Crafting Selves: Power, Gender, and Discourses of Identity in a Japanese Workplace*. Chicago, IL: University of Chicago Press.

Kondo, Dorinne. 1993a. Field Notes. Unpublished.

Kondo, Dorinne. 1993b. "Los Angeles, City of Angels." Program Notes for Twilight: Los Angeles 1992. *Performing Arts*. The Music Center of Los Angeles County, Los Angeles, CA, June, 7.

Kondo, Dorinne. 1996. "Shades of Twilight: Anna Deavere Smith and *Twilight: Los Angeles 1992*." In *Connected: Engagements with Media*, edited by George E. Marcus, 313–46. Vol. 3. Chicago, IL: University of Chicago Press.

Kondo, Dorinne. 1997. *About Face: Performing Race in Fashion and Theater*. New York: Routledge.

Kroll, Jack. 1993. "Fire in the City of Angels." *Newsweek*, June 28.

Kushner, Tony. 2014. "Carl Weber Lecture." Lecture, April 16. Stanford Department of Theatre and Performance Studies, Palo Alto, California.

Kwei-Armah, Kwame. 2010. *Beneatha's Place*. MS. Center Stage version, Baltimore.
"L.A. Is Burning: 5 Reports from a Divided City." 1993. Directed by Elena Mannes. Frontline: Public Broadcasting Service.
Lacan, Jacques. 2002. "The Mirror Stage as Formative of the Function of the I as Revealed in Psychoanalytic Experience." In *Écrits: A Selection*, translated by Bruce Fink, 3–9. New York: W. W. Norton.
Lacan, Jacques. 2004. "The Subversion of the Subject and the Dialectic of Desire in the Freudian Unconscious." In *Écrits*, translated by Bruce Fink, 281–312. New York: W. W. Norton.
LaCapra, Dominick. 1994. *Representing the Holocaust: History, Theory, Trauma*. Ithaca, NY: Cornell University Press.
Lacoue-Labarthe, Philippe. 1989. *Typography: Mimesis, Philosophy, Politics*. Cambridge, MA: Harvard University Press.
Lahr, John. 1993. "Under the Skin." Review of *Twilight: Los Angeles 1992*, by Anna D. Smith. *New Yorker*, June 28. http://www.newyorker.com/culture/culture-desk/the-best-theatre-of-the-year.
Latour, Bruno. 2004. "Why Has Critique Run Out of Steam? From Matters of Fact to Matters of Concern." *Critical Inquiry* 30 (2): 225–48.
Lavie, Smadar, Kirin Narayan, and Renato Rosaldo, eds. 1993. *Creativity/Anthropology*. Ithaca, NY: Cornell University Press.
Le, C. N. 2015. "Interracial Dating and Marriage." *Asian-Nation: The Landscape of Asian America*. Accessed August 10. http://www.asiannation.org/interracial.shtml.
Lee, Hoon. 2007. Discussion with the author, June 30.
Lee, Josephine. 1998. *Performing Asian America: Race and Ethnicity on the Contemporary Stage*. Philadelphia, PA: Temple University Press.
Lee, Josephine. 2003. "Racial Actors, Liberal Myths." *XCP: Cross Cultural Poetics* 13, 88–110.
Lee, Josephine. 2010. *The Japan of Pure Invention: Gilbert and Sullivan's 'The Mikado.'* Minnesota: University of Minnesota Press.
Lee, Rachel. 2014. *The Exquisite Corpse of Asian America: Biopolitics, Biosociality, and Posthuman Ecologies*. New York: NYU Press.
Leenhardt, Maurice. 1947. *Do Kamo: La personne et le mythe dans le monde mélanésien*. Paris: Gallimard.
Lehman, Daniel. 2012. "La Jolla Playhouse's Casting Controversy over 'The Nightingale.'" *Backstage*, July 18. https://www.backstage.com/news/la-jolla-playhouses-casting-controversy-over-the-nightingale/.
Lepecki, André, and Cindy Brizzell. 2003. "On Dramaturgy: The Labor of the Question is the (Feminist) Question of Dramaturgy." *Women and Performance*. 13 (2): 15–16.
Letts, Tracy. 2008. *August: Osage County*. New York: Theatre Communications Group.
Lévi-Strauss, Claude. 1962. *La pensée sauvage*. Paris: Plon.

Leys, Ruth. 2011. "The Turn to Affect: A Critique." *Critical Inquiry* 37:434–72.
Lipsitz, George. 1998. *The Possessive Investment in Whiteness: How White People Profit from Identity Politics*. Philadelphia, PA: Temple University Press.
Locsin, Aurelio. "Theater Director Starting Salary." *Houston Chronicle*. http://work.chron.com/theater-director-starting-salary-2447.html.
Loffreda, Beth, Claudia Rankine, and Max King Cap. 2015. *The Racial Imaginary: Writers on Race in the Life of the Mind*. Albany: Fence Books.
London, Todd, Ben Pesner, and Zannie Giraud Voss. 2009. *Outrageous Fortune: The Life and Times of the New American Play*. New York: Theatre Development Fund.
Los Angeles Times. 1992. *Understanding the Riots: Los Angeles before and after the Rodney King Case*. Los Angeles, CA: Los Angeles Times.
Lott, Eric. 1993. *Love and Theft: Blackface Minstrelsy and the American Working Class*. New York: Oxford University Press.
Love, Heather. 2010. "Truth and Consequences: On Paranoid Reading and Reparative Reading." *Criticism* 52 (2): 235–41.
Lowe, Lisa. 1996. *Immigrant Acts: On Asian American Cultural Politics*. Durham, NC: Duke University Press.
Lowe, Lisa. 2015. *The Intimacies of Four Continents*. Durham, NC: Duke University Press.
Lucas, Ashley. 2006. "Performing the (Un)imagined Nation: The Emergence of Ethnographic Theatre in the Late-Twentieth Century." PhD diss., University of California, San Diego and University of California, Irvine.
Luckhurst, Mary. 2008. *Dramaturgy: A Revolution in Theatre*. Cambridge: Cambridge University Press.
Macpherson, C. B. 1962. *The Political Theory of Possessive Individualism: Hobbes to Locke*. Oxford: Oxford University Press.
Mahmood, Saba. 2005. *Politics of Piety: The Islamic Renewal and the Feminist Subject*. Princeton, NJ: Princeton University Press.
Manalansan, Martin. 2003. *Global Divas: Filipino Gay Men in the Diaspora*. Durham, NC: Duke University Press.
Mankekar, Purnima. 2015. *Unsettling India: Affect, Temporality, Transnationality*. Durham, NC: Duke University Press.
Manning, Susan. 2015. "On the Making of Moses(es): Notes from a Dramaturg's Journal." *TDR: The Drama Review* 59 (1): 34–54.
Marcus, George. 1998. *Ethnography through Thick and Thin*. Princeton, NJ: Princeton University Press.
Marcus, George, and Michael M. J. Fischer. 1986. *Anthropology as Cultural Critique: An Experimental Moment in the Human Sciences*. Chicago, IL: University of Chicago Press.
Marcus, George, Paul Rabinow, James Faubion, and Tobias Rees, eds. 2008. *Designs for an Anthropology of the Contemporary*. Durham, NC: Duke University Press.
Marks, Laura. 2000. *The Skin of the Film: Intercultural Cinema, Embodiment, and the Senses*. Durham, NC: Duke University Press.

Martin, Carol. 1993. "Anna Deavere Smith: The Word Becomes You." *TDR: The Drama Review* 37 (4): 45–62.

Martin, Emily. 1994. *Flexible Bodies: Tracking Immunity in American Culture from the Days of Polio to the Age of Aids*. Boston: Beacon Press.

Martin, Randy. 1998. *Critical Moves: Dance Studies in Theory and Politics*. Durham, NC: Duke University Press.

Marx, Karl, and Friedrich Engels. 1959. "The Eighteenth Brumaire of Louis Bonaparte." In *Marx and Engels: Basic Writings on Politics and Philosophy*, edited by Lewis Feuer, 320–48. Garden City, NY: Doubleday.

Massumi, Brian. 2002. *Parables for the Virtual: Movement, Affect, Sensation*. Durham, NC: Duke University Press.

Massumi, Brian. 2015. *The Politics of Affect*. Cambridge: Cambridge University Press.

Mauss, Marcel. 1938. "Une catégorie de l'esprit humain: La notion de personne, celle de 'moi.'" *Journal of the Royal Anthropological Institute of Great Britain and Ireland* 68:263–81.

Mbembe, Achille. 2003. "Necropolitics." Translated by Libby Meintjes. *Public Culture* 15 (1): 11–40.

McAuley, Gay. 2012. *Not Magic but Work: An Ethnographic Account of a Rehearsal Process*. Manchester, UK: Manchester University Press.

McCray, Nancy. 1993. "Video: *Fires in the Mirror* Starring Anna Deavere Smith." *Booklist*, October 15.

McGurl, Mark. 2009. *The Program Era: Postwar Fiction and the Rise of Creative Writing*. Cambridge, MA: Harvard University Press.

Mcleod, Maurice. 2015. "Why the Black Best Friend Had Its Day." *Guardian*, June 2. https://www.theguardian.com/global/commentisfree/2015/jun/02/why-black-best-friend-had-its-day-david-oyelowo.

McMillan, Uri. 2015. *Embodied Avatars: Genealogies of Black Feminist Art and Performance*. New York: NYU Press.

McNulty, Charles. 2012a. "Critic's Notebook: Real World Concerns about a Fantasy 'Nightingale.'" *Los Angeles Times*, July 24. Last Modified 2015.

McNulty, Charles. 2012b. "Regional Theater's Art Moving off Center Stage." *Los Angeles Times*, February 19.

McNulty, Charles. 2013. "Difficult Truths to Face as Theater Leaders Talk Diversity, Economics." *Los Angeles Times*, December 21.

Meads, Joy. 2015. "What Lies Beneath: The Truth about Unconscious Bias." *American Theatre* 32 (8): 48–50.

Melamed, Jodi. 2006. "The Spirit of Neoliberalism: From Racial Liberalism to Neoliberal Multiculturalism." *Social Text* 89:1–24.

Menon, Jisha. 2012. "Palimpsestic City: Nostalgia in Neoliberal Bangalore." In *Neoliberalism and Global Theatres: Performance Permutations*, edited by Lara Nielsen and Patricia Ybarra, 237–52. Basingstoke, UK: Palgrave Macmillan.

Michaelis, Karen. 1929. *Flammende Tage: Gestalten und Fragen zur Gemeinschaft der Geschlechter*. Dresden, Germany: Blackwell.

Miki, Roy, and Cassandra Kobayashi. 1991. *Justice in Our Time: The Japanese Canadian Redress Settlement*. Vancouver, BC: Talonbooks.

Miller, Monica. 2009. *Slaves to Fashion: Black Dandyism and the Styling of Black Diasporic Identity*. Durham, NC: Duke University Press.

Mitchell, Sean. 1994. "The Tangle over 'Twilight': Anna Deavere Smith, Journalist? Anna Deavere Smith, Playwright? Her 'Twilight Los Angeles, 1992' Has Been Both Hailed as a Sensation and Beset by Debate over Whether the Piece Is a Play or Just Reportage. Who's Right, Tony or Pulitzer?" *Los Angeles Times*, June 12.

Modleski, Tania. 1997. "Doing Justice to the Subjects: Mimetic Art in a Multicultural Society: The Work of Anna Deavere Smith." In *Female Subjects in Black and White: Race, Psychoanalysis, Feminism*, edited by Elizabeth Abel, Barbara Christian, and Helene Moglen, 57–76. Berkeley: University of California Press.

Molino, Anthony, and Christine Ware. 2001. *Where Id Was: Challenging Normalization in Psychoanalysis*. Middletown, CT: Wesleyan University Press.

Morgan, Marcyliena. 2009. *The Real Hip-Hop: Battling for Power, Knowledge, and Respect in the L.A. Underground*. Durham, NC: Duke University Press.

Morrison, Toni. 1987. *Beloved: A Novel*. New York: Alfred A. Knopf.

Moten, Fred. 2003. *In the Break: The Aesthetics of the Black Radical Tradition*. Minneapolis: University of Minnesota Press.

Mouffe, Chantal. 2013. *Agonistics: Thinking the World Politically*. London: Verso.

Moynihan, Daniel P. 1965. "The Negro Family: The Case for National Action." Washington, DC: United States Department of Labor.

Muñoz, José Esteban. 1999. *Disidentifications: Queers of Color and the Performance of Politics*. Minneapolis: University of Minnesota Press.

Muñoz, José Esteban. 2006. "Feeling Brown, Feeling Down: Latina Affect, the Performativity of Race, and the Depressive Position." *Signs* 31 (3): 675–88.

Muñoz, José Esteban. 2009. *Cruising Utopia: The Then and There of Queer Futurity*. New York: NYU Press.

Murphy, Sherry L., Jiaquan Xu, and Kenneth Kochanek. 2013. "Deaths: Final Data for 2010." *National Vital Statistics Reports* 61 (4): 1–17.

Mydans, Seth. 1992. "AFTER THE RIOTS: Tumult of Los Angeles Echoed in Long Beach." *New York Times*, May 20. Accessed February 29, 2016. http://www.nytimes.com/1992/05/20/us/after-the-riots-tumult-of-los-angeles-echoed-in-long-beach.html.

Nagata, Donna K. 1993. *Legacy of Injustice: Exploring the Cross-Generational Impact of the Japanese American Internment*. New York: Plenum Press.

Narayan, Kirin. 2012. *Alive in the Writing: Crafting Ethnography in the Company of Chekhov*. Chicago, IL: University of Chicago Press.

National Theatre. 2017. "Facts and Figures." Accessed May 22. https://www.nationaltheatre.org.uk/about-the-national/key-facts-and-figures.

Ngai, Sianne. 2005. *Ugly Feelings*. Cambridge, MA: Harvard University Press.

Nguyen, Viet Thanh. 2002. *Race and Resistance: Literature and Politics in Asian America*. New York: Oxford University Press.

Nguyen, Viet Thanh. 2016. *Nothing Ever Dies*. Cambridge, MA: Harvard University Press.

Nielsen, Lara, and Patricia Ybarra, eds. 2012. *Neoliberalism and Global Theatres: Performance Permutations*. Basingstoke, UK: Palgrave Macmillan.

Norris, Bruce. 2011. *Clybourne Park*. New York: Faber and Faber.

Norris, Bruce. 2012. "The Freedom to Provoke." Interview by Beatrice Basso. Program notes for *Clybourne Park* at the Mark Taper Forum, Los Angeles, CA.

Nyong'o, Tavia. 2009. *The Amalgamation Waltz: Race, Performance, and the Ruses of Memory*. Minneapolis: University of Minnesota Press.

Ochoa, Marcia. 2014. *Queen for a Day: Transformistas, Beauty Queens, and the Performance of Femininity in Venezuela*. Durham, NC: Duke University Press.

Okada, John. 1977. *No-No Boy*. Seattle: University of Washington.

Omi, Michael, and Howard Winant. 1986. *Racial Formation in the United States: From the 1960s to the 1980s*. New York: Routledge.

Ong, Paul, and Suzanne Hee. 1993. *Losses in the Los Angeles Civil Unrest, April 29–May 1, 1992: Lists of the Damaged Properties and the L.A. Riot/Rebellion and Korean Merchants*. Los Angeles: Center for Pacific Rim Studies, University of California, Los Angeles.

"'The Orphan of Zhao' Controversy: East Asian Actors Demand Apology from Royal Shakespeare Company." 2015. *Huffington Post*. Last modified May 29. http://www.huffingtonpost.com/2012/10/31/east-asian-actors-adress-_n_2050353.html.

Orr, Shelley. 2014. "Critical Proximity: A Case for Using the First Person as a Production Dramaturg." *Theatre Topics* 24 (3): 239–45.

Ortner, Sherry. 2013. *Not Hollywood: Independent Film at the Twilight of the American Dream*. Durham, NC: Duke University Press.

Ossman, Susan. 2010. "Making Art Ethnography: Painting, War and Ethnographic Practice." In *Between Art and Anthropology: Contemporary Ethnographic Practice*, edited by Arnd Schneider and Christopher Wright, 127–34. New York: Berg Publishing.

Palumbo-Liu, David. 1994. "Los Angeles, Asians, and Perverse Ventriloquisms: On the Functions of Asian America in the Recent American Imaginary." *Public Culture* 6 (2): 365.

Palumbo-Liu, David. 1999. *Asian/American: Historical Crossings of a Racial Frontier*. Stanford, CA: Stanford University Press.

Pandian, Anand. 2015. *Reel World: An Anthropology of Creation*. Durham, NC: Duke University Press.

Pandian, Anand, and Stuart McLean, editors. 2017. *Crumpled Paper Boat*. Durham, NC: Duke University Press.

Pang, Cecilia. 1991. "The Angst of American Acting: An Assessment of Acting Texts." PhD diss., University of California, Berkeley.

Pao, Angela. 2010. *No Safe Spaces: Re-Casting Race, Ethnicity, and Nationality in American Theater*. Ann Arbor: University of Michigan Press.

Parker, Andrew and Eve Kosofsky Sedgwick. 1995. *Performativity and Performance*. London: Routledge.

Pellegrini, Anne. 1997. *Performance Anxieties: Staging Psychoanalysis, Staging Race*. New York: Routledge.

Petersen, William. 1966. "Success Story, Japanese-American Style." *New York Times*, January 9.

Peterson, Lisa. 2002. "Twenty Questions." *American Theatre* 19 (2): 104.

Pew Research Center. 2013. "The Rise of Asian Americans." Accessed June 28, 2016. http://www.pewsocialtrends.org/files/2013/04/Asian-Americans-new-full-report-04-2013.pdf.

Phelan, Peggy. 1993. *Unmarked: The Politics of Performance*. London: Routledge.

Phelan, Peggy, and Lynda Hart, eds. 1993. *Acting Out: Feminist Performances*. Ann Arbor: University of Michigan Press.

Phillips, Adam. 2013. *Missing Out: In Praise of the Unlived Life*. New York: Farrar, Straus and Giroux.

Pierce, Chester M., and Jean Carew et al. 1977. "An Experiment in Racism: TV Commercials." *Education and Urban Society* 10 (1): 61–87.

Pincus-Roth, Zachary. 2008. "ASK PLAYBILL.COM: Broadway or Off-Broadway—Part I." Accessed February 7, 2015. http://www.playbill.com/features/article/ask-playbill.com-broadway-or-off-broadwaypart-i-147549.

Pink, Sarah. 2015. *Doing Sensory Ethnography*. London: Sage.

Playbill. 2014. "Raisin in the Sun—Tickets and Discounts." Accessed May 14, 2014. http://www.playbill.com/production/a-raisin-in-the-sun-2016–2017.

Powdermaker, Hortense. 1950. *Hollywood, the Dream Factory: An Anthropologist Looks at the Movie-Makers*. Eastford, CT: Martino Fine Books.

Public Culture: Bulletin of the Project for Transnational Studies 1988. Vol. 1 (1).

Rabinow, Paul. 1977. *Reflections on Fieldwork in Morocco*. Berkeley: University of California Press.

Ramos, Nic. 2017. "Worthy of Care: Comprehensive Healthcare and King-Drew Medical Center." PhD diss., University of Southern California.

Rancière, Jacques. 2004. *The Politics of Aesthetics: The Distribution of the Sensible*. London: Continuum.

Rancière, Jacques. 2011. *The Emancipated Spectator*. London: Verso.

Rankine, Claudia. 2014. *Citizen: An American Lyric*. Minneapolis: Graywolf.

Rawls, John. 1999. *A Theory of Justice*. Cambridge, MA: Belknap of Harvard University Press.

Reagon, Bernice Johnson. 1983. "Coalition Politics: Turning the Century." In *Home Girls: A Black Feminist Anthology*, edited by Barbara Smith, 356–67. New York: Kitchen Table-Women of Color Press.

Redmond, Shana. 2013. *Anthem: Social Movements and the Sound of Solidarity in the African Diaspora*. New York: NYU Press.

Richards, David. 1994. "Review/Theater: Twilight—Los Angeles, 1992; A One-Woman Riot Conjures Character amid the Chaos." *New York Times*, March 24.

Rivera-Servera, Ramón. 2012. *Performing Queer Latinidad: Dance, Sexuality, Politics*. Ann Arbor: University of Michigan Press.

Robinson, Greg. 2009. *A Tragedy of Democracy: Japanese Confinement in North America*. New York: Columbia University Press.

Rofel, Lisa. 2007. *Desiring China: Experiments in Neoliberalism, Sexuality, and Public Culture*. Durham, NC: Duke University Press.

Román, David. 2005. *Performance in America: Contemporary U.S. Culture and the Performing Arts*. Durham, NC: Duke University Press.

Romanska, Magda. 2014. *The Routledge Companion to Dramaturgy*. London: Routledge.

Rooney, Ellen. 1989. *Seductive Reasoning: Pluralism as the Problem of Contemporary Literary Theory*. New York: Cornell University Press.

Rosaldo, Michelle Zimbalist. 1980. *Knowledge and Passion: Ilongot Notions of Self and Social Life*. Cambridge: Cambridge University Press.

Rosaldo, Renato. 1989. *Culture and Truth: The Remaking of Social Analysis*. Boston: Beacon Press.

Rosaldo, Renato. 2013. *The Day of Shelly's Death: The Poetry and Ethnography of Grief*. Durham, NC: Duke University Press.

Rose, Jacqueline. 1993. *Why War? Psychoanalysis, Politics, and the Return to Melanie Klein*. Oxford: Blackwell Publishers.

Rose, Nikolas. 1999. *Powers of Freedom: Reframing Political Thought*. Cambridge: Cambridge University Press.

Rowe, John Carlos. 2000. *Post-Nationalist American Studies*. Berkeley: University of California Press.

Sabel, Charles F., and Michael J. Piore. 1986. *The Second Industrial Divide: Possibilities for Prosperity*. New York: Basic Books.

Said, Edward W. 1979. *Orientalism*. New York: Vintage.

Saldanha, Arun. 2007. *Psychedelic White: Goa Trance and the Viscosity of Race*. Minneapolis: University of Minnesota Press.

Salinas, Ric. 2007. "Culture Clash Lecture and Performance." Lecture, USC School of Theatre, Los Angeles, California, January 31.

Savigliano, Marta. 1995. *Tango and the Political Economy of Passion*. Boulder, CO: Westview Press.

Savigliano, Marta. 2003. *Angora Matta: Actos fatales de traduccion Norte-Sur / Fatal Acts of North-South Translation*. Middletown, CT: Wesleyan University Press.

Schechner, Richard. 1985. *Between Theater and Anthropology*. Philadelphia: University of Pennsylvania Press.

Schechner, Richard. 1993. "Anna Deavere Smith: Acting as Incorporation." *TDR: The Drama Review* 37 (4): 63–64.

Schenkkan, Robert. 2014. *All the Way*. New York: Grove.

Schneider, Rebecca. 2011. *Performing Remains: Art and War in Times of Theatrical Reenactment*. London: Routledge.

Scott, Joan W. 1988. "Deconstructing Equality-versus-Difference: Or, the Uses of Poststructuralist Theory for Feminism." *Feminist Studies* 14 (1): 32–50.

Sedgwick, Eve Kosofsky. 2003. *Touching Feeling: Affect, Pedagogy, Performativity*. Durham, NC: Duke University Press.

Sedgwick, Eve Kosofsky. 2006. "Three Poems." *Women and Performance: A Journal of Feminist Theory* 16 (2): 327–28.
See, Sarita Echavez. 2009. *The Decolonized Eye: Filipino American Art and Performance*. Minneapolis: University of Minnesota Press.
Segal, Hanna. 1991. *Dream, Phantasy, and Art*. London: Routledge.
Seizer, Susan. 2005. *Stigmas of the Tamil Stage: An Ethnography of Special Drama Artists in South India*. Durham, NC: Duke University Press.
Sharpe, Christina. 2016. *In the Wake: On Blackness and Being*. Durham, NC: Duke University Press.
Shimakawa, Karen. 2012. "Staging a Moving Map in Byron Au Yong's and Aaron Jafferis's Stuck Elevator." In *Neoliberalism and Global Theatres: Performance Permutations*, edited by Lara Nielsen and Patricia Ybarra, 97–112. Basingstoke, UK: Palgrave Macmillan.
Shteir, Rachel, and Celise Kalke. 2003. "My Dinner with Celise: A Mischievous Meal Starring Dramaturgy and Desire." *Women and Performance: A Journal of Feminist Theory* 13 (2): 133–40.
Silverman, Kaja. 1988. *The Acoustic Mirror: The Female Voice in Psychoanalysis and Cinema*. Bloomington: Indiana University Press.
Silverman, Leigh. 2007. Discussion with the author, May.
Simonson, Robert. 2010. "ASK PLAYBILL.COM: Actors' Salaries and The Levels of Stage Management—Playbill.com." Playbill.com, August 1. Accessed 2015. http://www.playbill.com/features/article/ask-playbill.com-actors-salaries-the-levels-of-stage-management-170516.
Smith, Anna Deavere. 1989. *Piano*. New York: Theatre Communications Group.
Smith, Anna Deavere. 1993a. Letter to Dorinne Kondo, Héctor Tobar, Emily Mann, Elizabeth Alexander, Oskar Eustis, Natsuko Ohama, April 22.
Smith, Anna Deavere. 1993b. Letter to Oskar Eustis, April 28.
Smith, Anna Deavere. 1993c. *Twilight—Los Angeles, 1992 on the Road: A Search for American Character*. MS, Taper World Premiere version, Los Angeles. Unpublished ms.
Smith, Anna Deavere. 1994. *Twilight—Los Angeles, 1992 on the Road: A Search for American Character*. New York: Anchor.
Smith, Anna Deavere. 1995. "Not So Special Vehicles." *Performing Arts Journal* 17 (2): 77–90.
Smith, Anna Deavere. 1997. *Fires in the Mirror: Crown Heights Brooklyn and Other Identities*. New York: Dramatists Play Service.
Smith, Anna Deavere. 1998. E-mail message to author, March 10.
Smith, Anna Deavere. 1999. E-mail message to author, October 5.
Smith, Anna Deavere. 2000. *Talk to Me: Listening between the Lines*. New York: Random House.
Smith, Anna Deavere. 2002. *Twilight: Los Angeles, 1992*. New York: Dramatists Play Service.
Smith, Anna Deavere. 2007. "Address." Commencement Address, Bates College Graduation. Coram Library Quadrangle, Lewiston, May 27.

Smith, Anna Deavere. 2008. *Let Me Down Easy*. MS. Long Wharf World Premiere version, Los Angeles.
Smith, Anna Deavere. 2011. *Let Me Down Easy*. MS. A.R.T. version, Los Angeles.
Smith, Anna Deavere. 2012a. "Let Me Down Easy," Television, *Great Performances*, VA: Public Broadcasting Services.
Smith, Anna Deavere. 2012b. Discussion with the author, April 26.
Smith, Anna Deavere. 2013a. E-mail message to author, April 7.
Smith, Anna Deavere. 2013b. E-mail message to author, November 16.
Smith, Anna Deavere. 2014a. E-mail message to author, March 2.
Smith, Anna Deavere. 2014b. *Anna Deavere Smith: A YoungArts Master Class*. Episode no. 1–1, first broadcast February 17 by HBO. Directed by Karen Goodman and Kirk Simon.
Smith, Anna Deavere. 2015. *Morning Edition*. By Michelle Norris. National Public Radio, December 7.
Smith, Anna Deavere. 2016. *Let Me Down Easy*. New York: Dramatists Play Service.
Smith, Anna Deavere. 2018. "A Conversation with Anna Deveare Smith." Lecture presented USC Annenberg School of Communications. Los Angeles, CA, February 15.
Smith, Anna Deavere, Anne Epperson, and Robert McDuffie. 2015. *"Never Givin' Up."* Broad Stage, April 15–26, Los Angeles, California.
Smith, Cherise. 2011. *Enacting Others: Politics of Identity in Eleanor Antin, Nikki S. Lee, Adrian Piper, and Anna Deavere Smith*. Durham, NC: Duke University Press.
Smith, Christen. 2016. *Afro Paradise: Blackness, Violence, and Performance in Brazil*. Springfield: University of Illinois.
Soloski, Alexis. 2015. "She'll Play the Jewish Mother, and Wants Other Asian-Americans to Get the Best Parts, Too." *New York Times*, June 25. https://www.nytimes.com/2015/06/28/theater/an-asian-american-theater-company-cuts-a-fresh-casting-trail.html.
Song, Min. 2005. *Strange Future: Pessimism and the 1992 Los Angeles Riots*. Durham, NC: Duke University Press.
Sparks, Anthony. 2012. "Image Breakers, Image Makers: Producing Race, America, and Television." PhD diss., University of Southern California.
Spillers, Hortense. 2003. *Black, White, and in Color*. Chicago, IL: University of Chicago Press.
Spivak, Gayatri Chakravorty. 2003. *Death of a Discipline*. New York: Columbia University Press.
Stanislavski, Konstantin. 1936. *An Actor Prepares*. Translated by Elizabeth Hapgood. New York: Theatre Arts.
State Health Facts. 2013. "Number of Deaths per 100,000 Population by Race/Ethnicity." Accessed November 21. http://kff.org/other/state-indicator/death-rate-by-raceethnicity/.
Steedman, Carolyn. 1986. *Landscape for a Good Woman: A Story of Two Lives*. New Brunswick, NJ: Rutgers University Press.

Stephens, Michelle. 2014. *Skin Acts: Race, Psychoanalysis, and the Black Male Performer*. Durham, NC: Duke University Press.
Stewart, Kathleen. 2007. *Ordinary Affects*. Durham, NC: Duke University Press.
Stoller, Paul. 1997. *Sensuous Scholarship*. Philadelphia: University Press of Pennsylvania.
Sturken, Marita. 1997. *Tangled Memories: The Vietnam War, the AIDS Epidemic, and the Politics of Remembering*. Berkeley: University of California Press.
Sunahara, Ann. 1981. *The Politics of Racism: The Uprooting of Japanese Canadians during the Second World War*. Toronto, Canada: Lorimer.
Takaki, Ronald. 1979. *Iron Cages: Race and Culture in the 19th Century*. New York: Oxford University Press.
Takezawa, Yasuko I. 1995. *Breaking the Silence: Redress and Japanese American Ethnicity*. Ithaca, NY: Cornell University Press.
Tambiah, Stanley J. 1981. *A Performative Approach to Ritual*. London: British Academy.
Taussig, Michael. 1993. *Mimesis and Alterity: A Particular History of Senses*. New York: Routledge.
Taussig, Michael. 2011. *I Swear I Saw This: Drawings in Fieldwork Notebooks, Namely My Own*. Chicago, IL: University of Chicago Press.
Taylor, Diana. 2003. *The Archive and the Repertoire: Performing Cultural Memory in the Americas*. Durham, NC: Duke University Press.
Taylor, Diana. 2016. *Performance*. Durham: Duke University Press.
Taylor, Julie. 1998. *Paper Tangos*. Durham, NC: Duke University Press.
Taylor, Kate. 2008. "Assault on the Gentrifiers, and the Audience." *New York Times*, November 16.
Taylor, Lucien. 1996. "Iconophobia." *Transition* 69:64–88.
Thompson, Debby. 2003. "'Is Race a Trope?': Anna Deavere Smith and the Question of Racial Performativity." *African American Review* 37:127–38.
Thompson, James. 2009. *Performance Affects: Applied Theatre and the End of Effect*. Basingstoke, UK: Palgrave Macmillan.
Torres, F. Javier, Ralph Peña, Roche Schulfer, Adam Thurman, and Suzanne Wilkins. "Ensuring the Sustainability of Our Field." Proc. of TCG National Conference, Boston. Theater Communications Group, June 23, 2012.
Tran, Diep. 2017. "The Most-Produced Plays and Playwrights of 2017–18." *American Theatre* 34 (8): 42.
Tsing, Anna Lowenhaupt. 2005. *Friction: An Ethnography of Global Connection*. Princeton, NJ: Princeton University Press.
Tsing, Anna Lowenhaupt. 2015. *The Mushroom at the End of the World: On the Possibility of Life in Capitalistic Ruins*. Princeton, NJ: Princeton University Press.
Ulysse, Gina. 2017. *Because When God Is Too Busy: Haiti, Me, and THE WORLD*. Middletown, CT: Wesleyan University Press.
Vidali, Debra. 2015. "A Language for Re-Generation: Boundary Crossing and Re-Formation at the Intersection of Media Ethnography and Theatre." In *Media,*

Anthropology, and Public Engagement, edited by Sarah Pink and Simone Abram, 92–107. New York: Berghahn.

Vidali, Debra. 2016. "Multisensorial Anthropology: A Retrofit Cracking Open of the Field." *American Anthropologist* 118:395–400.

Viego, Antonio. 2007. *Dead Subjects: Toward a Politics of Loss in Latino Studies*. Durham, NC: Duke University Press.

Visweswaran, Kamala. 1994. *Fictions of Feminist Ethnography*. Minneapolis: University of Minnesota Press.

Vizenor, Gerald. 2008. *Survivance: Narratives of Native Presence*. Lincoln, NB: University of Nebraska Press.

Voss, Zannie G., and Glenn B. Voss. 2007. "Theatre Facts 2006: A Report on Practices and Performance in the American Not-for-Profit Theatre Based on the Annual TCG Fiscal Survey." *Theatre Communications Group*. http://www.tcg.org/Default.aspx?TabID=1576.

Voss, Zannie G., and Glenn B. Voss. 2011. "Theatre Facts 2010: A Report on the Fiscal State of the Professional Not-for-Profit American Theatre." *Theatre Communications Group*, 11.

Voss, Zannie G., and Glenn B. Voss. 2012. "Theatre Facts 2011: A Report on the Fiscal State of the Professional Not-for-Profit American Theatre." *Theatre Communications Group*, 8.

Wadsworth, Stephen. 2008. Discussion with author, September 1.

Watt, Ian. 1957. *The Rise of the Novel: Studies in Defoe, Richardson, and Fielding*. Berkeley: University of California Press.

Weber, Anne Nicholson. 2006. *Upstaged: Making Theatre in the Media Age*. New York: Routledge.

Weber, Carl. 1995. "Brecht's Street 'Scene'—On Broadway of All Places? A Conversation with Anna Deavere Smith." In *Brecht Then and Now*, edited by John Willett, 50–65. Vol. 20. Madison, WI: International Brecht Society.

Werry, Margaret. 2012. "Nintendo Museum: Intercultural Pedagogy, Neoliberal Citizenship, and a Theatre without Actors." In *Neoliberalism and Global Theatres: Performance Permutations*, edited by Lara Nielsen and Patricia Ybarra, 25–41. Basingstoke, UK: Palgrave Macmillan.

Weston, Kath. 1991. *Families We Choose: Lesbians, Gays, Kinship*. New York: Columbia University Press.

Wetherbe, Jamie. 2012. "Tony Winner David Henry Hwang Wins $200,000 Playwriting Prize." *Los Angeles Times*, August 23.

Whitty, Jeff, Robert Lopez, and Jeff Marx. 2006. "The Script of Avenue Q!" In *Avenue Q: The Book*, edited by Zachary Pincus-Roth, 96–156. New York: Hyperion.

Williams, Raymond. 1981. *Culture*. London: Chatto and Windus.

Williams, Stephanie Sparling. 2016. "Speaking Out of Turn: Race, Gender, and Direct Address in American Art Museums." PhD diss., University of Southern California.

Win, Thet Shein. 2014. "Marketing the Entrepreneurial Artist in the Innovation Age: Aesthetic Labor, Artistic Subjectivity, and Creative Industries." *Anthropology of Work Review* 35 (1): 2–13.

Winkler, Leah Nanako. 2017. "How to Make It as a Poor Theatre Artist in New York City." *American Theatre*, January. www.americantheatre.org/2017/01/24/how-to-make-it-as-a-poor-theatre-artist-in-new-york-city/.

Winnicott, Donald. 1953. "Transitional Objects and Transitional Phenomena." *International Journal of Psychoanalysis* 34:89–97.

Winnicott, Donald. 2005. *Playing and Reality*. New York: Routledge.

Wolff, Janet. 1993. *The Social Production of Art*. New York: NYU Press.

Wolff, Janet. 2016. "After Cultural Theory: The Power of Images, the Lure of Immediacy." In *Beyond Text? Critical Practices and Sensory Anthropology*, edited by Rupert Cox, Andrew Irving, and Christopher Wright, 189–201. Manchester, UK: Manchester University Press.

Wong, Deborah. 2004. *Speak It Louder: Asian Americans Making Music*. New York: Routledge.

Woods, Alan. 1993. "Consuming the Past: Commercial American Theatre in the Reagan Era." In *The American Stage: Social and Economic Issues from the Colonial Period to the Present*, edited by Ron Engle and Tice L. Miller, 252–66. Cambridge: Cambridge University Press.

Worthen, Hana. 2014. "For a Skeptical Dramaturgy." *Theatre Topics* 24 (3): 175–86.

Worthen, William. 2005. *Print and the Poetics of Modern Drama*. Cambridge: Cambridge University Press.

Yamamoto, Traise. 2014. "Remembering and Forgetting." April 19, 2014. Association for Asian American Studies, San Francisco, California.

Yoneyama, Lisa. 1999. *Hiroshima Traces: Time, Space, and the Dialectics of Memory*. Berkeley: University of California Press.

Zia, Helen. 2000. *Asian American Dreams: The Emergence of an American People*. New York: Farrar, Straus, and Giroux.

index

AAPIP. *See* Asian Americans / Pacific Islanders in Philanthropy
ABFE. *See* Association of Black Foundation Executives
About Face (Kondo), 10, 172, 173
Abraham, Nicolas, 215
Academy of Motion Pictures Arts and Sciences, 83
acting theory: everyday practice and, 99; genre-bending in, 114, 119–22; innovations in, 100–101, 105; performative production of subject in, 101–13; self-other in, 104; speech rhythms in, 113; stylized naturalism in, 114–18; theoretical/political insights in, 99–101; 105, 120
Actor's Equity, 69–70
affect: vs. emotion, 312n13; history of, 232; in labor, 35–36; in performance, 15–16, 25–26, 31; studies, 49–50, 201; use of term, 15, 312n13. *See also* racial affect
affective violence, 16, 18; copresence in theater and, 26; microaggression and, 21; public existence and, 37; as race-making, 11, 20, 21, 40, 51; reparative creativity and, 5, 40, 55, 209, 212; spectatorship and, 16, 18, 35–40

Afro-alienation, 50
Ahmed, Sara, 37, 38, 312n13
Aida (musical), 169, 170
Alexander, Elizabeth, 133, 144
Alfaro, Luis, 81
alienation effect, 48, 50, 113, 114, 116; *Verfremdung*, 50, 116, 117
Alien Land Law, 222
Allen, Jafari, 311n3
All the Way (Schenkkan), 20–21
Angels in America (Kushner), 76
arts as cultural work, 58–59
Arzumanova, Inna, 90
Ashley, Christopher, 84
Asian American Repertory Theater, 3
Asian Americans: model minority stereotype of, 157, 171, 225–26; public existence of, 172; racial formation, 169, 198, 201–2, 204; representation of, 84–85, 147, 149, 151, 157; roles in theater/television/film, 38, 45–46, 67, 71, 73, 82, 84, 174, 202–3, 219; stereotypes of women, 228; tensions among, 169, 202–3; theater, 1–3, 68, 77, 82, 205–6, 221, 230. *See also* Chinese Americans; Japanese Americans; *Seamless* (Kondo); works by Hwang

Asian Americans / Pacific Islanders in Philanthropy (AAPIP), 165
Asian American studies, 197, 198–99, 201, 213–14, 222, 235
Association of Black Foundation Executives (ABFE), 165–66
audiences and race, 86–88. *See also* spectatorship
August: Osage County (Letts), 20, 74, 172–73
authorship: death of the author, 123, 127, 128; theories of, 51, 123–29
autodramaturgy, 53, 222–29
avant-garde, 46, 72, 105, 128, 219–20, 317n4
Avenue Q (musical), 21

backstage practice. *See under* practice
Banks, Daniel, 85
Baraka, Amiri, 18, 88
Barnwell, Ashley, 43
Barthes, Roland, 49, 127
Batten, Susan, 165–66
Becker, Howard, 83, 315n1
Belsey, Catherine, 58
Beneatha's Place (Kwei-Armah), 20
Bengal Tiger at the Baghdad Zoo, A (Joseph), 320–21n1
Benjamin, Walter, 19, 49
Bergson, Henri, 35
Berlant, Lauren, 13, 185, 311n11, 312n13
Big Head (Uyehara), 232
biopolitics, 13–14, 185
Black Skin, White Masks (Fanon), 215
Blancs, Les (Hansberry), 82
Blu's Hanging (Yamanaka), 202
Book of Mormon, The (musical), 21, 68, 172–73, 217
Boston Court, 81
Brantley, Ben, 171, 321n2
Brater, Jessica, 72
Breaking the Silence (Nagata), 223
Brecht, Bertolt: alienation effect, use of, 48, 50, 113, 114, 116; on hermeneutics of suspicion and the logic of pornography, 43; critical reflection of, 27; on lack of closure, 161; on hermeneutics of suspicion, 43; on naturalism, 50, 116; political practice of, 6, 116, 122, 317n7; theory/practice, 50, 116, 121, 175, 216
Brizzell, Cindy, 40
Broadway theaters, 71–74
Broderick, Matthew, 77
Brooks, Daphne, 50
Brown v. Board of Education, 216
Bruner, Edward, 33
But Can He Dance? (Kondo), 3, 7, 66, 216
Butler, Judith, 3, 27–28, 313n4

Carradine, David, 202
Chambers-Letson, Joshua Takano, 223, 227
Cheng, Anne, 109–10, 201, 214
Chinese Americans, 199, 201, 203
Chinglish (Hwang), 21, 73, 75, 197, 198, 199–201, 204
Chuh, Kandice, 201
Civil Education Defense Fund, 226
Civil Liberties Act (1988), 225
Civil Liberties Fund, 223, 225
Clifford, James: on law of genre, 3; "and yet" phrase, 232, 236, 309
Clybourne Park (Norris), 17–20, 21, 217
Coffey, Shelby, 111–12, 154
collaboration: artistic, 8; as betrayal, 318n1; in fieldwork, 7; grant makers on, 67; as political intervention, 8–11; in theater, 6, 27, 82, 233
colorblind ideology, 13, 63, 108, 175, 178, 179, 190, 225
Commission on Wartime Relocation and Internment of Civilians (CWRIC), 224
Connerly, Ward, 135
corporeal epistemologies, 4–8, 26, 27, 139, 162–63, 218, 314n15
Cox, Aimee, 8
crafting. *See* making, use of term
Crafting Selves (Kondo), 55
Crapanzano, Vincent, 34, 47, 315nn21–22

creative process, 11; authorship and, 119, 124, 137; backstage, 4, 8, 29, 139; collaboration in, 132; corporeal epistemologies in, 139, 218; dramaturgical critique in, 43–44, 132; institutional inertia and, 146; multiple perspectives in, 160; politics of affiliation/agonistics in, 4–5, 128–29, 136, 163; racial discourse in, 168; racial representation in, 140, 144; revision in, 5, 52–53, 183–86, 216, 233; theory/practice of, 4–5, 33–34, 51, 136–37, 163, 210, 213–22, 313n10; work of creativity, 6, 8, 29, 40, 54–55, 105, 132. *See also* reparative creativity

critical race studies, 20, 26, 176, 183, 197, 201, 204, 312n13

critique: laughter as, 11; queer of color, 139, 198, 225, 312n13; reparative, 43; turn against, 43. *See also* dramaturgical critique

cross-racial performance, 30, 107–8, 110, 175, 179, 202–3

Culture Clash (performance troupe), 87

Cvetkovich, Ann, 18, 49–50

CWRIC. *See* Commission on Wartime Relocation and Internment of Civilians

Dang, Tim, 82, 173
David Henry Hwang Playwriting Institute, 1–2
Davidson, Gordon, 140
Davis, Mike, 164
Deleuze, Gilles, 3, 35, 312n13. *See also* affect
Del Vecchio, Jessica, 72
Denny, Reginald, 162
depressive position, 32–33
Derrida, Jacques, 27, 94
Desai, Snehal, 82
DeVos Institute of Arts Management, 67
DeWitt, John, 222
Diamond, Lydia, 22
disability studies, 236
(Dis)graceful(l) Conduct (Kondo), 3, 216

Disney Corporation, 71–72, 170, 171–72
documentary theater, 47–48, 97, 124. *See also Twilight* (Smith)
Dolan, Jill, 36, 109
Dong people, 175, 177–78, 186–87, 192–97
drama. *See* genre
Dramatists' Guild, 78, 79
dramaturgical critique: embodied participation and, 42, 163, 314n15; purpose of, 41–42, 52; as reparative, 42–44, 52, 168, 172–74, 191–98; in reparative creativity, 131–32, 168–69, 172–74, 191–95
dramaturgy, 7–8; autodramaturgy, 53, 222–29; genre and, 4–5; for Hwang plays, 191–95; polite consensus in, 51, 131; power-evasive modes of, 52; for Smith plays, 9, 30–31, 40, 41, 52, 103, 124–26, 133–40, 144–64. *See also* reparative creativity
"Dream Deferred, A" (Hughes), 17
Dreamworks, 71–72
Duong, Lan, 318n1

East West Players, 1, 67–69, 82, 168, 173, 200, 201, 206, 230
Edelstein, Gordon, 74
emotions, 94, 149–50, 312n13. *See also* affect
Eng, David, 201, 225, 232
entrepreneurialism. *See* neoliberalism
Equity Waiver, 69–70
estrangement. *See* alienation effect
ethnography: affect as relationality in, 25; of backstage practice, 7, 99; corporeal epistemologies in, 4–8, 26, 27, 139, 162–63, 218, 314n15; participatory observation and, 4, 6, 7–8, 233–36; performative, 26, 47, 235–36. *See also* genre
Eurocentricity, 37, 44, 46, 48, 63, 136, 158, 234, 236, 312n13
Eustis, Oskar, 4, 7, 56–57, 79, 133, 144, 149–50, 168, 173–74, 178, 184
Executive Order 9066 (Roosevelt), 222

Face Value (Hwang), 167
Facing History and Ourselves, 165
Fair Play Committee (Heart Mountain, WY), 227
Fanon, Frantz, 38, 215
fantastic, the, 53, 217
Fassin, Didier, 47
feminist film theory, 35, 39
Finley, Karen, 61–62
Fires in the Mirror (Smith), 117, 140, 144
Fires in the Mirror (Smith film), 106–7, 111, 117
First Nations peoples, 224, 322n9
Fish Head Soup (Gotanda), 232
Fleck, John, 61–62
Flynn, Kimberly, 97
For Colored Girls Who Have Considered Suicide / When the Rainbow Is Enuf (Shange), 121
Fortun, Kim, 8
Foucault, Michel, 13, 27, 28, 36, 127
Freud, Sigmund, 32, 38
Friction (Tsing), 3
Full Circle Theater, 1–2
fusion: acceptance and, 192–93, 195; with the object, 32; paranoia and, 43; with pre-Oedipal mother, 192–93

Gallela, Donatella, 73
Garcés, Michael John, 81
Geertz, Clifford, 3, 12
genre: color and gender of, 45–46; genre-bending works, 8, 47–48, 114, 119–22, 176, 181, 213; marketing and, 231; montage model of experimental writing, 49; nonfiction, 44, 47–48, 114, 124, 176, 180; textual innovation in ethnography, 49–50, 313n10, 314–15n20; as worldmaking, 44–55. *See also* writing
Gilbert, W. S. (of Gilbert and Sullivan), 84–85
Gilmore, Ruth Wilson, 13
Gordon, Avery, 135
Gotanda, Philip Kan, 232

Guattari, Félix. *See* affect
Guernica (Picasso), 33–34

Habermas, Jürgen, 109
Hall, Katori, 22
Hall, Stuart, 29–30
Hamilton (Miranda), 21–22, 68, 73, 202
Hansberry, Lorraine, 17, 78, 82
Harper, Phillip Brian, 50
Harris, Ed, 94
Harris, Lyle Ashton, 39
Hart-Celler Act (1965), 201
Harvie, Jen, 61
hate crimes, 13
Head of Passes (McCraney), 82
Heisenberg (play), 82
Hello, Dolly! (musical), 77
Henne, Aaron, 221, 233, 235
hermeneutics of suspicion, 27–28, 43, 314n16
Hermosillo, Xavier, 148–49
Hesmondhalgh, David, 59
Highways, 68–69
Hillman, Melissa, 84–85
Hirabayashi, Gordon, 224, 230
Hiroshima (band), 133, 151
Hirsch, Marianne, 231
Hispanic Playwrights' Project, 74–75
History and Memory (Tajiri film), 223, 229, 232
Hoch, Danny, 108–9
Hold These Truths (Sakata), 230
Holocaust and postmemory, 231
Hong, Grace, 88
Honky (Kalleres), 82
hope, politics of, 90–91, 139, 166, 235, 236, 309
Hopkins, D. J., 41
Horibe, Cole, 202, 203
House Arrest (Smith), 9, 74, 102–3, 109, 320n19
Hudes, Quiara Alegría, 78, 82
Hughes, Holly, 61–62
Hughes, Langston, 17
humor, 53, 187–88, 199–200, 217, 321n10

Hwang, David Henry, 1–2, 4, 8–11, 21, 51, 167; as artrepreneur, 63, 65–67; creative process of, 168; genre bending by, 47, 176; interviews with, 65–66, 173, 181–83, 184–85, 187–90, 199; juxtaposition, use of, 161; on liberal subject, 13; mainstream acceptance of, 169–71; on performativity, 30; on public existence, 37; race in works of, 73–74; reparative creativity of, 40; style and issues in works, 8–9; as subject-in-process, 101; works, awards, 10, 65, 169–70, 173. *See also* specific works

identity politics, 12, 29–30, 37, 39, 196
Imaginary, 34
imagination, theory of, 34–35
individualism, 13, 32, 58, 117, 151; liberal, 12–13, 39, 99, neoliberal, 65
Innocent When You Dream (Narasaki), 229
internment camps for Japanese Americans, 53, 206, 210, 214–15, 222–23
interview-based writing. *See under* writing
In the Heights (Miranda), 73
invisibility, 18, 20, 37, 133–34
Ito, Lance, 214

Jackson, Shannon, 83
Janiak, Lily, 80–81
Japanese American Citizens' League, 224
Japanese Americans, 147, 201; historical context, U.S., 222–26; incarceration of, 53, 206, 210, 214–15, 222–23; masculinity, 203, 211, 229; model minority stereotype, 225–26; redress movement, 215, 223–25; resistance by, 211, 226–27. *See also Seamless* (Kondo)
Jewishness, 177
John, Elton, 169, 170
Joseph, Rajiv, 81, 82, 320–21n1
Jujamcyn, 71

Kalleres, Greg, 82
Katigbak, Mia, 77
Kaufman, Moisés, 84
Keeling, Kara, 35
Kelley, Robin, 18
Khanna, Neetu, 215
Kim, Jacqueline, 82
King, Martin Luther, 20–21
King, Rodney, beating, 97–98, 133, 143, 158, 317n8, 318n14
Kjär, Ruth, 34–35
Klein, Melanie, 5, 12, 31–35, 43, 50, 210, 211–12. *See also* paranoid reading; psychoanalysis; reparative (concept)
Kung Fu (Hwang), 73, 198, 202–4
Kung Fu (television series), 202
Kuramoto, Dan, 133–34, 151, 160
Kushner, Tony, 76, 79, 97, 313n11
Kwei-Armah, Kwame, 20

Lacan, Jacques, 12, 31, 34, 38, 112, 114, 118
"L.A. Is Burning" (television program), 135
Landscape for a Good Woman (Steedman), 49
Lane, Nathan, 77
LA riots. *See* Los Angeles uprisings (1992)
Lark Development Center, 3
Lee, Bruce, 73, 197–98, 202–3
Lee, Chung, 148–49
Lee, Hoon, 173, 181
Lee, Young Jean, 219
Lepecki, André, 40
Let Me Down Easy (Smith), 9, 14–15, 64, 74, 76, 109, 121–22, 123, 125, 320n19
Letts, Tracy, 20–21, 74
Lewis, Jim, 21, 103
liberal humanism, 13, 52, 100–101, 131–32, 160, 163, 165, 166, 191. *See also* individualism; subject, the
Lloyd, Charles, 111–12
London, Todd, 77–78
LORT theater, 70–71, 80, 84, 86, 87
Los Angeles Times (newspaper), 86, 164

Los Angeles uprisings (1992), 40, 52, 97, 128–29, 130, 133, 141. *See also Twilight* (Smith)
Love, Heather, 43
Lowe, Lisa, 60, 88
Luckhurst, Mary, 40

Magwili, Dom, 94
Mahmood, Saba, 3
making, use of term, 6–7, 28–29. *See also* race-making; worldmaking
Man from Nebraska, The (Letts), 20
Mann, Emily, 133, 144–45, 148, 319n11
Manning, Julie Tamiko, 232
Mapplethorpe, Robert, 61
marginalization: aesthetic assumptions and, 58; alienation and, 50; of artists of color, 10, 205–6; of emotions, 236, 312n13; of feminism, 312n13; of Filipino Americans, 202; of MLK, 20–21; new languages and, 99; public existence and, 37, 39; representation and, 131; in theater, 4, 18, 21
Mark Taper Forum, 17, 68, 82, 125, 140
Martin, Emily, 62
Massumi, Brian, 312n13
Master Subject, 12–13, 93–94, 122, 161, 233, 236
Mauss, Marcel, 12
M. Butterfly (Hwang), 10, 73–74, 89, 171, 172–73, 233
McCraney, Tarell, 82
McNulty, Charles, 84, 86
Meads, Joy, 78
me-ism, 39–40. *See also* narcissism
Melamed, Jodi, 63
melancholia, 201, 210, 214
memory and trauma: Holocaust and postmemory, 231; phantom, 215; rememory, 231. *See also Seamless* (Kondo); *History and Memory* (Taijiri film)
Method acting, 51, 102, 103–4, 120, 317n4
microaggression, use of term, 21
Midler, Bette, 77

Mikado, The (Gilbert/Sullivan), 84–85
Miller, Tim, 61–62
mimesis, 59
minstrelsy, 30, 107–8, 110
Miranda, Lin-Manuel, 21–22
Miss Saigon (musical), 85
Mitchell, Sean, 124
Miwa, Matt, 232
Mixed Blood Theater, 3
model minority stereotype, 157, 171, 225–26
Moonlight (film), 83
Mountaintop (Hall), 21–22
Moving Arts Company, 68
Moynihan Report, 226
multiculturalism, 63, 90, 135, 158
Muñoz, José Esteban. *See* hope, politics of; performance, ephemerality of; queer of color critique
Murphy, Donna, 82
Mystery of Edwin Drood, The (musical), 85

Nagata, Donna, 213–14, 220, 223
Nájera, Marcos, 86–87
Narasaki, Ken, 87, 229
narcissism: pathological, 38, 151; primary, 38–39, 151; public existence and, 37; redemptive, 39–40; reparative, 39, 118; self-confirmation as, 19; subject formation and, 12. *See also* Ahmed, Sara; Freud, Sigmund; Lacan, Jacques
National Asian American Theater Company, 77
National Coalition for Redress and Reparations, 224
National Council for Japanese American Redress, 224
National Endowment for the Arts (NEA), 61–62
National Program Committee for the American Studies Association, 9
NEA Four, 61–62
Nederlander Organization, 71
Nelson, Brian, 1–2

neoliberalism: arts and, 51, 57, 58, 59–63, 74, 88–89; entrepreneurialism in, 57, 62, 63–67; flexibility in, 61, 62, 65; multiculturalism in, 63, 90, 135, 158; multitasking in, 62–63; privatization in, 57, 60, 62
Newfield, Chris, 135
New Play Festival (Lark Development Center), 3
New Yorker (magazine), 125, 160
New York Times (newspaper), 170–71, 225
Ngai, Sianne, 201
Nguyen, Viet Thanh, 201
Nightingale, The (musical), 84, 85–86
Nisei generation, 213, 223, 224, 228–29
Norman, Jessye, 115
Norris, Bruce, 17, 19
nostalgia, 154, 192, 194

Oedipus El Rey (Alfaro), 81
Off-off Broadway, 69
On the Road (Smith), 101, 103–4, 106, 142
Orphan of Zhao, The (play), 85
Orr, Shelley, 41
Otherness, 31–32, 45, 114, 118, 193–94

Pandian, Anand, 7, 313n10
paranoid reading, 27, 43
Park, Steve, 144
participatory observation, 4, 6, 7–8, 233–36
Passion (Sondheim musical), 82
Paulus, Diane, 73
Pearl Harbor, bombing of, 216, 222, 232
Peña, Ralph, 85, 86, 221, 230
performativity: contrast to cinema, 26–27; making and, 27–29; precarity and, 313n4; race-making and, 27, 29–31, 118; theoretical work on, 27, 312n2
performance: affect in, 15–16, 25–26, 31; ephemerality of, 26, 90; identity and, 118; neoliberalism and, 58; practices of, 88–89; race-making and, 27, 29–31; theoretical work on, 25–27, 28, 312n2. *See also* cross-racial performance

Personal Justice Denied (CWRIC), 224
Pesner, Ben, 77–78
Petersen, William, 225
Piano, The (Smith), 317–18n13
Picasso, Pablo, 33–34
Pierce, Chester, 21
Pixar, 170
Platt, Ben, 21
play vs. production, 27–29, 41, 44, 54, 163, 174–83, 197, 210, 230
political depression, use of term, 18
political economies, 74–91
politics of affiliation, 4–5, 39–40, 42, 52, 99–101, 129, 132, 136–39
politics of agonistics, 4–5, 52–53, 137
Politics of Piety (Mahmood), 3
politics of pleasure, 11, 15
politics of racial representation, 148–52
postmemory, use of term, 231
practice: backstage, 5, 7, 40, 51, 83–86, 99; of acting, 101–13; Brechtian, 116, 121, 175, 216; creative process theory, 4–5, 33–34, 136–37; of performance, 88–89; in theater studies, 51; theory vs. 110–11; of *Twilight*, 52, 132–40, 151, 163
precarity, 29, 57, 60, 67, 70, 313n4
privatization, 57, 60, 62
Prizant, Yael, 233
Producers, The (musical), 77
psychoanalysis: vs. affect, 313n6; depressive position in, 32–33; on fusion/acceptance, 192–93; on identification, 118; imagination in, 34–35; as insufficiently cross-cultural, 31–32; on negative emotions, 32, 34; openness to history, 31–32; on melancholia, 201, 210, 214; on narrative, 115–16; object relations theory in, 12; paranoia, 43; premises of, 31–32; pre-Oedipal mother, 192–93; race and, 31, 184, 214, 312n13; on "real," 51, 184; reparative and, 5, 31–35, 211–12; stage theory in, 32. *See also* specific individuals (e.g. Eng, Freud, Klein, Lacan, Segal); specific topics (e.g. narcissism, paranoid reading, the subject)

public existence, 12, 37, 39, 172. *See also* me-ism; narcissism

Public Theater, 7, 56, 73, 97

Pulitzer Price controversy, 124, 127, 148

queer of color critique, 90, 312n13. *See also* Chambers-Letson, Joshua Takano; Eng, David

Quinn, Alice, 125

race-making: backstage, 5, 40, 83–86; concept of, 4; performativity and, 27, 30–31, 118; reparative creativity in, 40; structure/the subject in, 13; theater and, 11–16, 25, 83–86

racial affect, 10, 15; creativity and, 54; in internment camps, 211; microaggression and, 21; need for exploration of, 229; racialization through, 11, 35; in redress movement, 215; spectatorship and, 35–40; in theater, 15–16, 18, 25, 31, 35–40

racialization: performativity and, 29–31, 88–91; through racial affect, 11, 35

racial melancholia, 201, 210, 214

racism: anti-Asian, 179, 226; biopolitics and, 185; hierarchies of, 202–3; hipster, 21; in hiring/workplace, 80; in immigration policies, 37, 38; nationalism and, 38; persistence of, 52, 176, 179–80, 190, 225–26; prejudice as inadequate definition of, 86, 165; premature death and, 14–15, 185–86; reverse, 13; structural, 13–15, 63, 67, 165–66, 184, 210–11, 223, 226, 229; in theater, 51, 84–86, 87; white guilt and, 19. *See also* cross-racial performance

Raisin in the Sun, A (Hansberry), 17, 20

Rancière, Jacques, 35–36, 313–14nn11–12

Rashōmon (film), 106, 111

Reagon, Bernice Johnson, 138

real vs. true, 47

redress movement, 215, 223–25

re-membering, 4, 5, 28

reparative (concept), 5, 31–32, 49–50, 54

reparative creativity: affective violence and, 55, 209, 212; artistic production as, 32–33, 211–13; 236; dramaturgical critique as, 131–32, 168–69; for minoritarian subjects, 39; participatory observation and, 233; playwriting as, 21–22, 44, 51, 53, 209–12, 236; politics of affiliation and, 129; in race-making, 40; as remaking worlds, 211–13; systematic inequalities and, 33, 51; as theory and politics, 210–13; use of term, 5, 32, 212

reparative critique, 42–44, 50, 51, 52, 164, 169, 172–73, 191–98

reparative mirroring, 12, 16, 21, 37–40, 52, 118, 132, 172

resistance, 80–81, 210, 211, 226–27

revision process. *See under* writing

Rich Relations (Hwang), 320n8

Road Theatre Company, 81–82

Roberts, Julia, 77

Rogue Machine Theater, 81–82

Román, David, 87–88

Romanska, Magda, 41

Romanticism, 58–59, 314n11

Rooney, Ellen, 161–62

Roosevelt, Franklin Delano, 222, 223

Rosaldo, Michelle, 50

Rosaldo, Renato, 7, 50

Roth, Maya, 209

Roundabout Theatre, 85

Roxas, Elizabeth, 125

Sakata, Jeanne, 230

Salas, Rudy, 133–34, 148–49

Sansei generation, 213, 221, 224, 229, 232, 234

Savigliano, Marta, 49

Schenkkan, Robert, 20–21, 124

Seamless (Kondo), 3, 45–46, 53, 66–67; characters, 239; creative process of, 213–22; full-length play, 239–309; gender in, 227–28; historical context for, 222–26; production, marketing, and race, 230–32; reparative creativ-

ity of, 210–13; structure of, 46, 121; synopsis, 209; thematics, politics, theory in, 226–29
Sedgwick, Eve Kosofsky, 28, 43, 313n7, 314n16
Segal, Hanna, 32–34, 35, 211–12
self-confirmation, 19
Serrano, Andres, 61
Shange, Ntozake, 121
Sharpe, Christina, 231
Sheik, Duncan, 84
Shiomi, Ric, 1–2, 93, 232
Showcase Code, 69
Shrek (musical), 72
Shubert Organization, 71
Sibrian, Gladys, 121, 134
sick woman theory, 236
Silverman, Leigh, 173, 188–89
slow death, use of term, 13–14
Smith, Anna Deavere, 4, 7–11, 21, 51; acting theory/practice, 98–101, 102–5, 113, 120, 123–29; artistic practices of, 51–52, 98–99; as artpreneur, 63–65; on audiences of color, 86–87; Brechtian practices, use of, 116, 121, 317n7; de-essentializing of race by, 108; dramaturgy for, 9, 30–31, 40, 41, 52, 103, 124–26, 133–40, 144; genre bending by, 47–48, 119–22, 124; on identity, 104–5, 109–10, 117–18; interview theater writing by, 8, 9, 47–48, 51–52, 97, 102–3, 109–10, 111–12, 113, 115, 119, 123–28, 130, 144; interviews with, 64–65, 76, 83–84, 103–6, 119–20, 125–26; on liberal subject, 13, 101; on listening, 124; master class by, 105–6, 112; one-person shows, 74, 99; on performativity, 30, 118; on public existence, 37; Pulitzer Price controversy, 124, 127; reparative creativity of, 40; on speech as poetry, 126–27; style and issues in works, 8–9; stylized naturalism, use of, 114–18; as subject-in-process, 101; theoretical interventions of, 100; works, acting, awards, 9, 64. *See also* specific works

Smith, Cherise, 111, 112
Soft Power (Hwang), 82
Solomon, Alisa, 103, 123, 125–26
Son, Diana, 75
Sondheim, Stephen, 82
South Coast Repertory, 74–75
spectatorship: audiences of color, 86–88; cinematic, 35–36; racial affect and, 35–40; racialized, 36–37
Stage Directors and Choreographers Society, 85–86
Steedman, Carolyn, 49
stereotypes: of artists, 59, 212; of Asian Americans, 157, 171, 199, 226, 228–29; of Asians, 185; authenticity and, 110–13; gendered, 132; inequality and, 113; as oppressive, 15; racial, 30, 107, 156, 231, 234, 320n14; vs. realistic portrayals, 219; signifiers of, 117; in theater, 89, 107, 234; urban, 140–41; of women, 100, 228–29
Stick Fly (Diamond), 21
Stoller, Amy, 103, 125
stylized naturalism, use of, 114–18
subject, the: de-essentializing of, 107; of *énoncé/énonciation*, 113; foreign body within, 215, 223; the "I" and, 13, 101; individualism of, 13, 32, 39, 58, 99, 117, 151; -in-process, 101, 102; liberal individualist, 12–13, 39, 99; mirroring and, 112; narcissism and, 12, 38–40; as human capital, 62; Master Subject, 12–13, 93–94, 122, 161, 233, 236; neoliberal individualist, 65; Other and, 118; performative production of, 101–13; postracial and, 210–11; power and, 15; racialization of, 105; structural and, 12, 29, 313n4; substance-attribute metaphysics of, 12, 102, 161; whiteness and, 18, 54–55, 63, 131–32, 152, 169, 202
"Success Story: Japanese American Style" (Petersen), 225
Sullivan, Arthur (of Gilbert and Sullivan), 84–85

Superior Donuts (Letts), 20, 312n1
survivance, use of term, 227

Taft Hartley Act (1954), 222
Tajiri, Rea, 223, 229, 232
Takei, George, 230, 320–21n1
Tango and the Political Economy of Passion (Savigliano), 49
Tarzan (musical), 73, 169, 170
Tashme Project, The (Manning/Miwa documentary performance), 232
Teatro Campesino, El, 68, 82
theater: affective violence in, 5, 16, 18, 20, 21, 26, 51; as art industry, 51, 56–58; Asian American, 1–3, 68, 77, 82, 205–6, 221, 230; classifications, 69–74; collaboration in, 6, 27, 82, 233; diversification in, 77–83, 87–88; vs. film and television, 26, 116–17; institutional landscapes of, 68–69; making a living in, 75–83; marginalization in, 4, 18, 21; national, 60–61; race-making and, 11–16, 25, 83–86; racial affect in, 15–16, 18, 25, 31; regional, 70–71, 84; relationality in, 25; small, 60–70; suspension of belief in, 27; underfunding of, 57–58, 61, 74–75; whiteness of, 44, 128, 136, 152
Theater Mu, 1–2
Theatre Communications Group, 85
theory vs. practice. *See under* practice
Three Days of Rain (play), 77
Tobar, Héctor, 133–34, 144–45, 148
Torok, Maria, 215
transnationalism, 44, 169, 177, 198–204
Tsing, Anna, 3
Twilight (Smith), 17, 73, 83, 131; backstage drama, 52, 132–49, 151, 163; back story of, 140–41; dramaturgical process, 9, 40, 41, 52, 103, 124–26, 133–40, 144–64; first workshop, 145–48; incommensurability of interpretations to, 156–57, 160–62; lack of closure in, 161; making whiteness in, 152–56; narrative dilemmas in, 142–44; opening, 157–64, 320n19; preproduction, 144; preview of, 97–98, 157–58; Pulitzer Price controversy, 124, 127; race/ethnicity in, 109; racial representation in, 148–56; rehearsal, 148–53; versions, 319n11; view from 20 years after, 164–66
Twilight (Smith film), 9, 115, 117

Uncle Tadao (Shiomi), 232
universality, 18, 54–55, 63, 131–32, 152, 169, 202, 230–31
university employment, 77
Uyehara, Denise, 232

Verfremdung. *See* alienation effect
visions of possibility, use of term, 19
Vizenor, Gerald, 227
Voss, Zannie Giraud, 77–78

Wadsworth, Stephen, 61, 121–22, 123, 125, 314n18
Warren, Earl, 216
Wasow, Omar, 124
Water by the Spoonful (Hudes), 82
"We Don't Need No Stinking Dramas" (Mixed Blood Theater award), 3
Werry, Margaret, 89
whiteness: critical studies, 20; Jewishness and, 177; of mainstream theater, 44, 128, 136; marking, 152–56; privilege of, 30, 109, 152; reinforcement of, 31; subversion of, 73; as universal, 18, 54–55, 63, 131–32, 152, 169, 202
white supremacy, 37
Williams, Raymond, 59
Winnicott, Donald, 33
Wolfe, George C., 97, 155
Woods, Alan, 89
worldmaking: as collaborative, 54; culture and, 14, 28; genre as, 44–55; reparative, 33, 50, 164; sociopolitical transformation in, 29
Worthen, William, 126–27
writing: authorship, nature of, 51, 123–29; death of the author, 123, 127, 128; interview as, 8, 9, 47–48, 51–52, 97,

105, 109–10, 111–12, 113, 115, 123–24, 127–28, 130, 144–46, 232; interview theater, 8, 9, 47–48, 52, 53, 97, 102–3, 111, 119, 124, 130, 232; montage model of experimental writing, 49; revision process, 5, 26, 52–53, 168–69, 183–86, 197, 200–201, 216, 233. *See also* genre

Yamamoto, Traise, 232
Yamanaka, Lois-Ann, 202
Yellow Face (Hwang), 4, 8–9, 73–74; acceptance/belonging in, 175, 177–78, 187, 192–95, 197; color/gender in, 45; Dong people in, 175, 177–78, 186–87, 192–97; endings, 184–91; final version, 168, 172, 186–88, 196; first draft, 168, 185–90; free play of identity in, 179–83; genre-bending in, 47, 176; multiple perspectives on, 167; plot, 48, 174–75, 177–78, 182–83, 185–86; race as mobile fiction in, 175–78; reparative critique of, 168, 169, 172–73, 191–98; revision process of, 52–53, 168–69, 183–86, 197, 200–201; style and issues in, 8–9, 10, 168; world premier version, 4, 168, 172, 183, 184–85, 187, 190, 195

Yellow Fever (Shiomi), 1–2
Yew, Chay, 218

Zimmerman, Martin, 81
Zoot Suit (musical), 93